The Global Gamble

The Global Gamble

*Washington's Faustian Bid for
World Dominance*

PETER GOWAN

VERSO

London • New York

TO MY SONS

First published by Verso 1999
© Peter Gowan 1999
All rights reserved

The moral rights of the author have been asserted

Verso
UK: 6 Meard Street, London W1V 3HR
USA: 180 Varick Street, New York, NY 10014–4606

Verso is the imprint of New Left Books

ISBN 1–85984–874–5
ISBN 1–85984–271–2 (pbk)

British Library Cataloguing in Publication Data
A catalogue record for this book is available from the British Library

Library of Congress Cataloging-in-Publication Data
A catalog record for this book is available from the Library of Congress

Typeset by M Rules
Printed by Biddles Ltd, Guildford and King's Lynn

Contents

Preface

During the 1990s, American government and business elites have attempted to 'go global': in other words, to entrench the United States as the power that will control the major economic and political outcomes across the globe in the twenty-first century. This is a commonplace amongst those who follow such matters; but the distinctive methods employed in this project are less widely recognised. This book is an attempt to investigate some of these methods, many of them innovative, and some of their effects.

In historical perspective, the distinctive feature of American expansion, in contrast to the west European juridical empires of the first half of the twentieth century, has been the attempt to use the international system of *sovereign states* as a mechanism of American global dominance. During the postwar decades, the internal environment of many states was determined by threats from Communism and other leftist movements, while their external environment was determined by the American–Soviet contest. Both these contexts encouraged the dominant social groups in such states to accept American 'leadership'. But the decline and collapse of both Communism and the Soviet Union has prompted a search for new ways of brigading states under American leadership and of anchoring American economic ascendancy.

The American post-Cold War global project, as practised by the Clinton administration, has involved two new ways of altering the internal and external environments of states in directions which will induce them to continue to accept US political and economic dominance. The transformation of the domestic environments of states goes under the name of neo-liberalism: this involves a shift in the internal social relationships within states in favour of creditor and rentier interests, with the subordination of productive sectors to financial sectors and with a drive to shift wealth and power and security away from the bulk of the working population.

The transformation of the external environment of states goes under the name of globalisation: this involves the opening of a state's political economy to the entry of products, companies, financial flows and financial operators from the core countries, making state policy dependent upon developments and decisions taken in Washington, New York and other main capitalist centres.

The two changes feed each other: the shift in domestic social power relationships, known as neo-liberalism, strengthens the constituencies favouring globalisation. And the forces favouring globalisation will favour these same domestic transformations. Those states and social systems that try to resist these transformations will find themselves increasingly shut out from the US market and from its allied EU market, and subjected to hostile economic statecraft. The most internationally competitive of their productive sectors, fearing such exclusion, can thus also be turned into supporters of globalisation and neo-liberalism. Both types of change favour the transnational expansion of US economic and political influence, since both provide openings for US financial operators and the US financial markets, as well as for US transnational corporations.

Both globalisation and neo-liberalism were spreading across the Western world before the collapse of the Soviet Bloc but it has been during the 1990s that American administrations have actively sought to radicalise and generalise these trends, articulating them in ways which would anchor other political economies to American political and economic interests. This anchoring process has been pursued both bilaterally and through reorganising the programmes of multilateral organisations so that they, too, become instruments of the campaign.

These changes in the internal and transnational linkages of states are consolidated into a new regime, which in turn tends to make state leaderships want what American state and business elites want. On the other side, the project involves ensuring that it is the states themselves that retain complete responsibility for everything that befalls their populations. Thus the benefits of the global transnational order will accrue to the United States, while the risks and costs can be distributed abroad. This is the main distinctive form of the US's global project. This is the global gamble.

After an uneasy start at the beginning of the decade, the main West European powers have become junior partners in this project, in a relationship which combines subaltern co-operation with some elements of friction and competition. The relationship between the United States and Japan, on the other hand, has been much more conflictual, since the national and regional dynamics of Japanese capitalism have been far less in tune with Washington's global project than have those of Western Europe.

The processes usually associated with globalisation are often thought to be driven by technological and/or economic forces rather than by the political capacities and capitalist interests of the American state and business elites.

But in the first part of this book I argue that the process of globalisation has been driven most crucially by the enormous political power placed in the hands of the American state and of US business through the particular type of international monetary system and associated international financial regime that was constructed – largely by the US government – in the ashes of the Bretton Woods system. Once we appreciate the nature of the current monetary and financial regime, we can appreciate how it can be used as a formidable instrument of economic statecraft in the hands of successive US administrations, and how they have used it to drive forward both the globalisation process and the associated neo-liberal domestic transformations.

The second part of this book consists of studies of various aspects of international politics in this era of the global gamble. The US capacity to exclude and target states which resist its sway takes a paradigmatic form in the long siege of Iraq following Desert Storm. The chapter on this topic is devoted above all to the ideological justifications for such sieges through appeals to supposedly liberal values. Other chapters in this part of the book examine the political economy and ideology of the Atlantic states' drive to impose regimes favourable to their interests upon the states of East Central and Eastern Europe. The concluding chapter argues that Washington's determination to maintain its political leadership over Western Europe through NATO expansion is bound to generate new threats to European security.

A central irony of the global gamble lies in the fact that, although it is presented as driven by organic economic and technological change rather than by politics, it is in fact economically destabilising – and probably economically unviable. It brings in its wake chronic financial instability and systematically generates economic blow-outs in the most vulnerable and sensitive economies. At the same time, it tends to produce extreme forms of boom–bust cycles in those advanced capitalist economies which follow the American neo-liberal path of locking the economy's fate into the performance of securities markets. This economic weakness has hitherto been combined with extraordinary political success: the United States has, so far in the 1990s, faced no significant threat or challenger.

Yet this political success has been the product of two absences during the last decade: firstly, the disarray on the international left and the consequent retreat by international labour; and secondly, the long habits of subordination to US leadership bred within its 'allied' states during the Cold War. Neither of these absences is likely to last for ever. And because of this, we should bear in mind the opportunity costs of the global gamble, the potential costs of the path not taken: the nonchalant rejection on the part of the American government and its Atlantic junior partners of any attempt to construct a more inclusive and more institutionalised system of global government for the twenty-first century, both at a transnational and at a domestic social level.

The collapse of the Soviet Bloc presented American elites with a temptation reminiscent of Faust's. A door seemed to swing open on to a vista of
hitherto unimaginable cosmopolitan power. Yet within a little decade, the
signature of Mephistopheles is already visible. The economic formula of the
'Washington Consensus' is structurally flawed but is simultaneously vital for
the dynamism of the American economy. States have been restructured
with great political success but in ways that will make them, in the future, far
less capable of containing and managing their own domestic revolt;
American military ascendancy over the globe is greater than that of any state
in world history, but its panoply of power is of little use in the face of state
breakdowns and popular revolt.

This book is not an attempt to produce a comprehensive treatment of
these transnational developments in the 1990s. It simply attempts to analyse
some important aspects of the story. The studies contained here are not
guided by any coherent, self-conscious grand theory. But they are guided by
what could be called two rules of thumb.

The first is that the external policies of the Atlantic powers are not transparent, and that their operational goals are rarely captured by their public
presentation. The culture of the Foreign Offices of the Western powers is
that of realist power politics: media presentation is never couched in those
terms. And since the foreign policy-making process both in state executives
and in many of the multilateral organisations is largely closed to public
scrutiny, understanding Western strategies is never straightforward. If a
democratic public opinion is to be able to exercise its responsibility to try to
influence the behaviour of the states in which we are living, then we must try
to understand how the powers of those states are being wielded and for what
purposes: and this requires that we don't take policy on trust. It also, I have
found, usually requires delving into the detail and engaging in 'backward
mapping': reading back from actual policy outputs to hypotheses about
policy goals.

The second rule of thumb is that the statecraft of the great powers in the
modern world, though often blundering and inept when viewed within a
longer historical perspective, is sophisticated, arcane and complex in its
tactics and detail. Of special importance here is the fact that contemporary
statecraft encompasses policy instruments that go well beyond the traditional coercive coinage of diplomacy, and include at their centre a range of
tools of *economic* statecraft, market management and information management.

The integration of this repertoire of instruments within state executives is
often not matched by an equivalent integration of social scientific disciplines for the study of state policy. Many of the real dynamics seem to work
in zones which fall *between* the territories covered by professional academic
social science disciplines, whether economics or political science. The

studies in this book, therefore, have required that I stray across disciplinary boundaries even where I have felt ill-equipped to do so.

The material in Part II has either been published already in the form of articles or has drawn upon earlier published essays. Chapter 8 first appeared as 'The Gulf War, Iraq and Western Liberalism' in *New Left Review* 187 (May–June 1991). Chapter 9 was previously published as 'Neo-Liberal Theory and Practice for Eastern Europe' in *New Left Review* 213 (September–October 1995). Chapter 10 previously appeared as 'Liberalism, Neo-Liberalism and Civil Society' in *Labour Focus on Eastern Europe* 53 (Summer 1996). An earlier version of chapter 11 was published as 'The Post-Communist Parties in the East' in Donald Sassoon, ed., *Looking Left* (IB Tauris, 1997). An earlier version of chapter 12 appeared as 'The Dynamics of "European Enlargement"', *Labour Focus on Eastern Europe* 56 (Spring 1997). I am grateful to these publishers for permission to reproduce this material here.

I would like to thank a number of people for very helpful criticisms of various parts of this book, notably the following: Perry Anderson, Robin Blackburn and other colleagues on *New Left Review*; Leo Panitch, Gus Fagan and my other colleagues on *Labour Focus on Eastern Europe*; Laszlo Andor; and Donald Sassoon. I would like to thank my colleagues in the Humanities Faculty in the University of North London and in the School of European and Language Studies in particular for the way in which, despite the difficulties facing higher education, they have managed to preserve an extremely congenial context for both teaching and research. I owe a special debt in this context to Mike Newman. And I would also like to thank my students at UNL for being a constant stimulus and challenge for my thinking.

I would like to thank Verso, and in particular Sebastian Budgen, the copy-editor Jon Haynes, and Susan Watkins, who made a final comprehensive (and extremely thorough) check on the manuscript, for being so efficient and accommodating.

Finally, I would like to thank two people very close to me. One is my friend Patrick Camiller, with whom I have been talking for a quarter of a century and from whom I have learned so much. And the other is my wife, Halya, whose integrity, sensitivity and generosity have been an inspiration as well as a great support.

List of Acronyms and Terms

AFL-CIO   American Federation of Labour–Congress of Industrial Organisations, the main American trade union federation
AMF   Asian Monetary Fund, a Japanese proposal in autumn 1997 that was not implemented
APEC   Asia-Pacific Economic Co-operation. It includes the USA, Canada and the main Asian economies
ASEAN   The Association of South-East Asian Nations
Ba'ath   The Arab Socialist Renaissance Party – the ruling party in Iraq and Syria
BEMs   The Big Emerging Markets, as defined by the Clinton administration
BIS   Bank for International Settlements – the 'central bank' of central banks
BSP   Bulgarian Socialist Party
CAP   The EU's Common Agricultural Policy
CEE   Central and Eastern Europe
CEECs   Central and Eastern European Countries
CFE   The Treaty on Conventional Forces in Europe
CIA   Central Intelligence Agency
CIS   Commonwealth of Independent States
CMEA   The Council for Mutual Economic Assistance – the Soviet Bloc's economic association
CPSU   Communist Party of the Soviet Union
Comecon   Another name for the CMEA
CSCE   Conference on Security and Co-operation in Europe, now transformed into the organisation for Security and Co-operation in Europe
CSFR   Czech and Slovak Federal Republic

DGB	German trade union federation
DWSR	Dollar–Wall Street Regime
EBRD	European Bank for Reconstruction and Development
EC	European Community, now called the European Union (EU)
ECB	European Central Bank, formed to manage the euro, the EU's single currency
EU	European Union
Ex-Im Bank	The US government's trade credit and credit guarantee agency
FDI	Foreign direct investment
FRG	Federal Republic of Germany
FSU	Former Soviet Union
G3	Group of 3: USA, Germany, and Japan
G7	Group of 7: USA, Germany, Japan, France, Britain, Canada, Italy
GATT	General Agreement on Tariffs and Trade
GDP	Gross Domestic Product
HSP	Hungarian Socialist Party
HSWP	Hungarian Socialist Workers' Party, the name of the Hungarian Communist Party
ICP	Iraqi Communist Party
IFIs	International financial institutions (the IMF and WB)
IFT	Intra-firm trade
IGC	EU Inter-governmental Conference for amending the EU's basic treaties
IMF	International Monetary Fund
ISI	Import Substituting Industrialisation
LDCs	Less Developed Countries
LSE	London School of Economics and Political Science
LTCM	Long-Term Capital Management
MAI	The Multilateral Agreement on Investment
MDF	Hungarian Democratic Forum
MERCOSUR	A free trade area in Latin America involving Brazil, Uruguay, Paraguay and Argentina
MIT	Massachussets Institute of Technology
MNCs	Multi-national corporations
NACC	North Atlantic Co-operation Council
NAFTA	The North American Free Trade Association, involving the USA, Canada and Mexico
NATO	North Atlantic Treaty Organisation
NEC	National Economic Council, set up by the Clinton administration

NPT	Non-Proliferation Treaty
NSC	American National Security Council
NSF	National Salvation Front of Romania
NTBs	Non-tariff barriers
OECD	Organisation for Economic Co-operation and Development – an association of the richest capitalist states
OPEC	Organisation of Petroleum Exporting Countries
OPIC	Overseas Private Investment Corporation
OSCE	Organisation for Security and Co-operation in Europe, formerly the CSCE
OTC	Over-the-counter financial deals, as opposed to trades through exchanges
P4P	Partnership for Peace
PCA	Partnership and Co-operation Agreement, treatise between the EU and the former Soviet republics
PDS (Italy)	Party of the Democratic Left, successor to the Italian Communist Party
PDS (Germany)	Party of Democratic Socialism, successor to the East German Communist Party
PHARE	The EU aid programme for East Central Europe
PLO	Palestine Liberation Organisation
PSDR	Party of Social Democrats of Romania
PSL	Polish Peasant Party
PWP	Polish United Workers' Party, the name of the Polish Communist Party
SDPR	Social Democrats of the Polish Republic
SED	Socialist Unity Party, the name of the East German Communist Party
SLD	Democratic Left Alliance
SPD	German Socialist Party
ST	Shock Therapy
START	Strategic Arms Reduction Treaty
Super 301	An American trade law obliging the President to act against states using unfair trade practices
TABD	The Transatlantic Business Dialogue
TNCs	Trans-national corporations
TPCC	Trade Promotion Co-ordinating Committee – a US government inter-agency body
UAR	United Arab Republic, formed by Syria and Egypt in the 1950s
UL	Union of Labour
UNCTAD	United Nations Conference on Trade and Development
UN ECE	United Nations Economic Commission for Europe
UNICEF	Now officially the 'United Nations Children's Fund'; (previous title UN International Children's Emergency Fund)
USTR	US Trade Representative

VER	Voluntary Export Restraint
VIE	Voluntary Import Expansion
Visegrad	Poland, Czech Republic, Slovakia, Hungary
WB	World Bank
WEU	West European Union
WTO	World Trade Organisation, successor to the GATT

PART I

The Globalisation Gamble

Introduction

The 1990s have been the decade of globalisation. We see its effects everywhere: in economic, social and political life, around the world. Yet the more all-pervasive are these effects, the more elusive is the animal itself. An enormous outpouring of academic literature has failed to provide an agreed view of its physionomy or its location and some reputable academics of Right and Left even question its very existence. Others, notably Anglo-American journalists and politicians, insist it is a mighty beast which savages all who fail to respect its needs. They assure us that its gaze, 'blank and pitiless as the sun',[1] has turned upon the Soviet Bloc, the European Social Model, the East Asian Development Model, bringing them all to their knees. For these pundits, globalisation is the bearer of a new planetary civilisation, a single marketplace, a risk society, a world beyond the security of states, an unstoppable, quasi-natural force of global transformation.

Yet, as the East Asian crisis turned into a global international financial scare, some who might be thought to be deep inside the belly of this beast, the big operators on the 'global financial markets', wondered whether globalisation might be in its death agony. At the start of 1998, Joe Quinlan, senior analyst for the American investment bank Morgan Stanley, raised the possibility that globalisation may be coming to an end. He noted that 'globalisation has been the decisive economic event of this decade' and stressed that 'no one has reaped more benefits from globalisation than the United States and Corporate America . . . The greater the velocity and mobility of global capital, the more capital available to plug the nation's low level of savings and boost the liquidity of financial markets. In short, globalisation has been bullish for the world economy in general and for the United States in particular.' But Quinlan worried that governments in various parts of the world might be turning against globalisation and might decide to bring it to an end in 1998. As he put it: '. . . the biggest risk to the world economy next year is not slower growth, but rather an unravelling of global interdependence – and therefore the end of globalisation.'[2] For Quinlan, then, globalisation is a rather fragile, vulnerable creature, dependent upon the nurturing care of states.

Thus, we are left with an awareness that there have indeed been powerful new forces in the international political economy of the 1990s, which we label globalisation, but their contours, dynamics and causes remain obscure: as elusive to our grasp as a black cat in a dark room.[3]

This is yet another attempt to catch this cat called globalisation, or rather to catch one of its main organs: its central nervous system. We will argue that this lies in the way in which international monetary and financial relations have been redesigned and managed over the last quarter of a century. This new monetary and financial regime has been one of the central motors of the interlocking mechanisms of the whole dynamic known as globalisation. And it has been not in the least a spontaneous outcome of organic economic or technological processes, but a deeply political result of political choices made by successive governments of one state: the United States. In this sense we are closer to the Morgan Stanley view of globalisation as a state-policy-dependent phenomenon than to the notion of globalisation as a deep structure favoured by Anglo-American media pundits. To indicate its location in international reality we call it a 'regime', although, as we will explain, it is not a regime in the quasi-juridical sense in which that term has been used in American international relations literature.

International monetary and financial relations are always the product of both economic and above all political choices by leading states. Studies of globalisation which fail to explore the political dimensions of the international monetary regime that has existed since 1973 will miss central features of the dynamics of globalisation. This international monetary regime has operated both as an international 'economic regime' and as a potential instrument of economic statecraft and power politics. The name given to it here is the 'Dollar–Wall Street Regime' (DWSR). We will try to trace its evolution from origins in the 1970s through the international economics and politics of the 1980s and 1990s up to the Asian crisis and the panic of '98.

We are not going to claim that the history of international monetary and financial relations of the last quarter of a century gives us the key to understanding the contemporary problems in the advanced capitalist economies. As Robert Brenner has demonstrated, these problems of long stagnation have their origins in a deep-seated crisis of the productive system of advanced capitalist societies.[4] The onset of this stagnation crisis formed the *background* to the changes initiated by the Nixon administration in international monetary and financial affairs: but the production crisis did not determine the *form of the response*. There were a range of options for the leading capitalist powers to choose from and the one chosen, which has led to what we call globalisation, was the outcome of international political conflicts won by the American government. Since the 1970s, the arrangements set in motion by the Nixon administration have developed into a patterned international regime which has constantly reproduced itself, has had very far-reaching effects on transnational economic, political and social life and which has been available for use by successive American administrations as an enormously potent instrument of their economic statecraft. One of the most extraordinary features of the whole story is the way in which these great levers of American power have simply been ignored in most of the literatures on globalisation, on international regimes and on general developments in the international political economy.[5]

In exploring this Dollar–Wall Street Regime we need no algebra or geometry and almost no arithmetic or even statistics. The basic relationships and concepts can be understood without the slightest familiarity with neo-classical economics. Indeed, for understanding international monetary and financial relations, lack of familiarity with the beauties and ingenuities of neo-classical economics is a positive advantage.

Part I of this book, The Globalisation Gamble, examines workings of the DWSR. We begin with a brief discussion of terms, concerning the meaning of 'capital markets' and the roles and forms of financial systems. In chapter 3 we look at the new mechanisms established for international monetary relations by the Nixon administration in the 1970s. The resulting regime gave leverage both to the US government and to Anglo-American financial markets and operators. One of the fascinating features of the regime is the way in which it established a dynamic, dialectical relationship between private international financial actors in financial markets and US government dollar policy. Most of the literature on globalisation tends to take as a governing assumption the idea that the relationship between the power of markets (and market forces) and the power of states is one mainly marked by antagonism – an idea deeply embedded in much liberal thought.[6] Yet, in a seminal article written at the time of the Nixon changes, Samuel Huntington noted how false that idea is: 'Predictions of the death of the nation-state are premature . . . They seem to be based on a zero-sum assumption . . . that a growth in the power of transnational organisations must be accompanied by a decrease in the power of states. This, however, need not be the case.'[7] We try to show how the DWSR, steered by the US government, worked in and on the international political economy and how it latched on to and changed the internal economics, politics and sociology of states and their international linkages.

Chapter 4 looks at the operations of the Dollar–Wall Street Regime over the last quarter of a century. We look at how US administrations have sought to use the regime, and the responses of the European Community states, Japan, the countries of the South and of the former Soviet Bloc to the regime. We also look at how the regime contributed towards changing the US domestic financial, economic and political systems.

In chapter 5, we try to place the DWSR and its effects into the framework of the dynamics of international politics as a whole in the early 1990s. We look at these issues, so to speak, from the angle of the lead state: the United States. And we try to build in the effects of the Soviet Bloc collapse on how American leaders formulated their strategic goals and recombined their tactics. I argue that they rationally had to, and did, recognise that their key challenge lay in East and South-East Asia. To tackle that challenge and to frustrate future challenges to US global leadership, they had to radicalise the DWSR and may perhaps have used it as an instrument of economic statecraft in East Asia: the evidence is circumstantial but significant.

In chapter 6 we argue that the conventional view of the unfolding of the central drama of the East Asian crisis in the autumn of 1997 – the events in South Korea – is mistaken insofar as it assumes the central actors to have been exclusively market forces. A critical role was played by the US Treasury, which acted in quite new ways during the Korean crisis. It was this Treasury intervention in South Korea which was responsible for the subsequent Indonesian collapse and which indirectly and unintentionally set in motion the triggers which turned the East Asian crisis into a global financial crisis during 1998. At the same time, the reason why the US Treasury's action could play this triggering role lay in the effects of twenty years of US exploitation of the Dollar–Wall Street Regime on the world economy. We conclude by considering whether there is a possible social-democratic capitalist alternative strategy which could reverse the dynamics of globalisation.

Notes

1. W. B. Yeats: 'The Second Coming'.
2. Joe Quinlan, 'Devaluations, Deficits and the End of Globalisation?', Morgan Stanley Global Economic Forum, The Global Economics Team, Special Year-End Issue, 22 December 1997 (Morgan Stanley & Co., 1997).
3. I must acknowledge the source of this metaphor in an excellent joke by Professor Wagener at a recent conference in Berlin. The joke goes as follows: economic history is chasing a black cat in a dark room; economics is chasing a black cat in a dark room when the cat isn't there. Econometrics is chasing a black cat in a dark room when the cat isn't there and you claim that you have caught it!
4. See the superb analysis in Robert Brenner, 'The Economics of Global Turbulence', *New Left Review* 229 (1998).
5. A major exception to this blindness has been the work of Susan Strange, who constantly sought to educate us on the politics of international monetary and financial affairs especially in her classic, *Sterling and British Policy* (Oxford University Press, 1971). A path-breaking article on the role of states in globalisation is Leo Panitch, 'The Role of States in Globalisation', *Socialist Register* (1995).

6. I do not wish to suggest that tensions between the goals of governments and the dynamics of markets are not an important object of investigation. See Robert Boyer and Daniel Drache (eds.), *States Against Markets: The Limits of Globalization* (Routledge, 1996).

7. Samuel Huntington: 'Transnational Organisations in World Politics', *World Politics*, 25 (April 1973).

2

'Capital Markets', Financial Systems and the Postwar International Monetary System

Most of the various notions of what globalisation is about focus on the growing mobility of capital across the globe in the 'global capital market' and upon the impact of this mobility on national economies. But the term 'capital market' is analytically incoherent, because it embraces radically different phenomena in the field of finance, most of which have nothing directly to do with capital in the usual common sense meaning of the term, while at the same time it excludes a great deal of the operations of what capital actually does. So we need to clarify our notions about 'capital markets', global or otherwise, in order to understand this international phenomenon known as globalisation.

The So-called Capital Markets

In common sense language we associate the word capital with the idea of funds for productive investment, for putting together machines, raw materials and employees to produce sellable items. This is a useful starting point for using the word capital because it stresses its socially beneficial role within a capitalist system.

One of the central confusions concerning globalisation lies in the widespread belief that the so-called 'global capital markets', in which trillions of dollars are bouncing back and forth across the globe, are in some way assisting the development of the productive sector of capitalism. It is because we imagine that the 'global markets' are integral to production that we imagine that we have no choice but to accept them. Yet in reality the great bulk of what goes on in the so-called 'global capital markets' should be viewed more as a charge upon the productive system than as a source of funds for new production. The idea that the current forms of 'capital markets' are functionally indispensable investment mechanisms is a serious error. The 'capital market' is both much more and much less than the funnel for productive investment. It is much more because it includes all forms of credit, savings and insurance as well as large, diversified markets in titles to future income and not just credits for productive investment. And it is much less because very large flows of funds into productive investment do not pass through the so-called 'capital markets' at all.

This confusion about the role of capital markets is linked to another, concerning mergers and acquisitions. Thus, it is often assumed that when one company buys control of another company, some kind of capital investment is taking place. Yet frequently such acquisitions of assets may have nothing to do with new real investment at all, indeed, the reverse may be occurring: the acquisition may be concerned with running down the activities of the acquired asset, in order that the buyer of the asset can eliminate competition and gain greater market power. During the last quarter of a century this process of 'centralisation of capital' has been proceeding apace internationally. It is called 'Foreign Direct Investment' but in most cases it simply means changing the ownership of companies and may have to do with disinvestment in production rather than the commitment of new resources to expansion of production.

The notion that a great expansion of the size of 'capital markets' is a symptom of positive trends in capitalist production is as false as imagining that a vast expansion of the insurance industry is a sign that the world is becoming a safer place. Insurance can operate in the opposite way: the more crime the bigger the property insurance market. Similarly, when great fortunes are being made overnight on 'capital markets', the most useful rule of thumb for interpreting such trends is one which says that something in capitalism is functioning very badly from a social point of view.

We will explore some of these terms, starting with the most obvious feature of financial systems, their role in supplying credit.

Credit involves lending money to people on the understanding that they will pay the money back later along with a bonus or 'royalty', usually in the form of a rate of interest.[1] There is nothing necessarily capitalist about credit and large parts of national credit systems are not related to production at all. Workers can put their savings into a credit co-operative and draw loans from it in hard times in the hope of paying the money back in better times. They pay a royalty for the service but this can be small because the co-operative is non-profit-making. Such co-operatives serve consumption needs, not production and they are not capitalist. Building societies confined to the housing market play a similar role in supplying credit for people to purchase housing. A common feature of these kinds of organisations is that the credit-money that they issue is directly derived from savings deposited within them. In other words, their resources come from the past production of value in the economy: employees' savings come from wages that they have already earned in production.[2]

Banks are different because they are able to *create new money* in their credit operations. We can see this when we realise that at any one time, the banks as a whole could be giving overdrafts to everybody in the entire economy. Thus, far more money is circulating in the economy than the money derived from savings generated by past value creation. Part of the money is actually what we can call fictitious money – money derived not from the past but from expectations that it will be validated by future productive activity.[3] Within capitalism, banks also do not have to be operated as private capitalist companies. At the beginning of the 1990s, for example, more than half of the 100 biggest banks in Europe were publicly owned and their financial criteria for operating were, in principle, matters of public choice. And even if they are private, the banks play such an essential and powerful role in the public economy because of their capacity to issue credit-money that any sensible capitalist class will ensure that the state is constantly interfering in their operations (even though, for ideological reasons, one wants to keep these state functions 'low profile'). As Kapstein puts it: 'Banks are told how much capital they must hold, where they can operate, what products they can sell, and how much they can lend to any one firm.'[4]

The existence of this fictitious credit-money is very beneficial for the whole economy because of its role in facilitating the circulation of commodities. Without it, economic development would be far slower. It is especially important to employers, enabling them to raise large amounts of money for equipment which will yield up its full value in production only over many future years. If employers could invest only real savings – the money derived from past value-creation – investing in fixed capital would be far more costly – too costly for a lot of investment. And credit has also become a very important means of expanding the sales of goods to consumers. This is another way of saying that modern economies run on large amounts of debt. So the banks do play an important role in both channelling savings and creating new funds (fictitious money) for productive investment. An entire capitalist economy could be run with a financial system consisting entirely of such banks.

But historically, other forms of financial institutions have grown up, especially in the Anglo-Saxon world which has played such a central role in the historical development of capitalism. First there has been the development of shares and bonds as means of raising funds. A company can offer shares for sale and use the funds from the sale to invest in the business. The shares are pieces of paper giving legal titles to a claim on future profits from the company's activities. Companies or governments can also sell bonds and use the funds from the sale for an infinite variety of purposes. These bonds are similarly pieces of paper giving legal titles to a fixed stream of future income to the holder for a fixed period of time. A special feature of shares and bonds (known collectively in England since the eighteenth century as 'stocks') is that secondary markets have grown up enabling people to buy and sell these pieces of paper entitling the holder to future royalties. Today there are all kinds of pieces of paper that can be bought and sold and that entitle the holder to some kind of future royalty or right. I can buy and sell paper giving me the right to buy or sell a currency at a certain rate at a certain time in the future. There has been a huge growth in markets for such paper claims. The generic term for all such tradable pieces of paper is 'securities'.

It is important to recognise that while the initial issuing of a set of shares or bonds *is* a means of raising funds that may (or may not) be used for productive capital investment, the secondary markets in these securities are not contributing directly at all to productive investment.[5] Instead the people on these markets (such as the Stock Market) are buying and selling *claims on future value created in future productive activity.* They are not handing over funds for that productive activity; they are claiming future royalties from it. These claims on future royalties from future production are either direct or indirect claims. A share in Ford Motors is a direct claim on future value created in Fords. A Russian government bond which I hold is an indirect claim on future Russian production of value. I hold the bond not because I think the Russian government will produce the value but because I imagine that it will pay me my royalty by extracting taxes from the productive activity of others in Russia: no production, no royalty on my bond.

Against this background, we can now return to the phrase 'capital market'. What is mainly (although not only) referred to by this phrase is actually *securities markets.* And we thus discover that 'capital market' in the sense of a securities market may have nothing directly to do with supplying funds for capital investment. It may have to do with the opposite process: trading in claims to draw profits *from future productive value-creation.* At the same time, both bank credits and bonds may be used for capital raising functions but they may equally be used for other purposes. And neither foreign exchange markets nor the so-called derivatives markets have anything directly to do with capital investment – we will examine later what their functions are.

How could such an apparent abuse of language, whereby various kinds of financial markets are all described as capital markets, occur? The answer is that it is not an abuse of language for one group of the population: rentiers and speculators. Rentiers are those who derive their income from extracting royalties from future production. The speculators are those who derive their income from trading in securities or currencies by trying to sell them at higher prices than they bought them for.

As has been implied by our analysis, rentiers are not, in principle, an integral element in capitalism. Those parts of the system's reproduction which necessarily involve the channelling of funds of money from past value-creation and from credits in the form of fictitious money could be handled entirely by commercial banks (which could themselves be publicly owned).

Thus, when we examine the growth of the so-called 'global capital markets', we will find that much of their activity is not about the supply of capital for productive activity. It is about trading in royalties on future production in different parts of the world or about businesses engaging in various kinds of insurance against risks. And the trend in the organisation of the flows of finance has been increasingly one which privileges the interests of rentiers and speculators over the functional requirements of productive investment. This fact is revealed through an examination of the tensions between what we may call the two poles of capitalism, that of money-dealing capital and that of the employers of capital in the productive sector.

The Two Poles of Capitalism and Their Regulation

Whether the financial system is organised predominantly in the form of commercial banks or in the form of securities markets, we notice a division which is inherent in capitalism: the division between money-dealing capital on the one side and productive capital on the other. These two entities have different kinds of concerns because of the different circuits of their capitals. For the employer of capital in the productive sector the circuit runs as follows: capital starts as money (some of which is borrowed from the money-capitalist), which is then turned into plant, raw materials and employees in the production process. The capital then emerges from production as a mass of commodities for sale; when the sale is completed capital reappears in the form of money with the extra-surplus extracted from the production process. Out of this extra-surplus, the employer of capital pays back the money-capitalist the sum initially advanced, along with royalties.

But from the angle of the money-capitalist, the circuit looks different. It starts with a fund of money. This money is then locked into a project for a certain time. At the end of that time, the money-capitalist hopes to get the money back with a royalty. For the money-capitalist absolutely any project which will offer a future royalty is what capitalism is all about. If buying a share in Fords gives a royalty of 6 per cent in a year, while a Ukrainian government bond will give a royalty of 34 per cent and buying a case of Château Lafitte to sell it in a year will yield 150 per cent, the problematic is the same for the money-capitalist in each case: in an uncertain future, which of these different 'capital markets' will give me the best mix of safety and high yield?

Property that can be used as capital thus appears simultaneously in two polarised embodiments: on the one side stand the *money-capitalists* controlling enormous accumulations of funds; and on the other side stand the *employers of capital* managing the enterprises. These are two forms of the same thing, analogous to God the Father and God the Son. But their polar-isation is very important because it enables money-capital as the controller of funds to play a planning role in capitalist development. By being dis-tanced and relatively autonomous from the employers of capital in the productive sector, the money-capitalists can pick and choose what sectors they advance money capital to. If a branch has reached 'maturity', barely achieving the average rate of profit, then resources of value from that sector as well as fictitious money can be advanced to other sectors which seem likely to produce higher rates of return. Through such redeployments, the financial system in the hands of the money-capitalists is supposed to spur growth.

For supporters of capitalism this development co-ordination role of the money-capitalists is considered to be one of the most ingenious and beauti-ful aspects of the entire system. One might say that the relationship between the productive sector and the financial sector is one where the productive sector is determinant but the financial sector is dominant. The productive sector is determinant because it produces the stream of value out of which the money-capitalists in the financial sector ultimately gain their royalties, directly or indirectly. On the other hand the financial sector is dominant because it decides *where it will* channel the savings from the past and the new fictitious credit-money – who will get the streams of finance and who will not. The actual power balances between the two sectors are partly governed by the business cycle. In the boom productive capital is flush with cash and can, so to speak, dictate terms to the money-capitalists; but in the recession the money-capitalists become ruthless, bullying tyrants as the employers of productive capital beg for credit to tide them over. But power relations between the two are also crucially affected by institutional design – by the social relations of production. The state, through a highly charged and politicised process, can and does tilt the balance between the money-capital pole and the productive-capital pole and between the money-capital pole and all parts of the credit system, keeping, for example, money-capital out of whole sectors of the credit system, if it wants to. The state also makes cru-cial decisions about the internal structure and interactions within the money-capital pole itself. What will banks be allowed to do, and what will they be kept out of? Will we have a private securities market or not? And so on. And we must also remember that the state is not just designing relations between the two poles of capital; it is also designing its own relation with the financial pole because it too will wish to use the credit system.

From our analysis of these two poles of capital, another very important distinction emerges, between the tempos and rhythms of two kinds of finan-cial flows linked to the two different kinds of circuits. For the money-capitalist there is a tendency to seek quick returns and to keep cap-ital in as liquid a state as possible, for reasons of safety. The employer of capital seeks to set up much longer-term circuits, particularly concerning funds for fixed capital investment, which yield their full value only over many years. The tendency for the first group is thus to generate 'hot money' flows, extremely sensitive to even very small changes in their environment; while the second group tends to generate cold, long flows which have to be robust to significant changes in their environment. The hot flows are linked to royalty seeking from either securities trading or from very short-term loans. This difference is extremely important when we seek to analyse international movements of funds. Insofar as all kinds of money can flow freely internationally, we would expect to see very radical differences between these two kinds of flows: a small change in the exchange rate of one country or in the short-term, government-fixed interest rates in another can produce sudden, major shifts in flows of hot money, but exert no significant influence on flows of funds concerned with real, long-term investment in production.[6]

The relationship between capital and labour within the productive sector is, of course, an absolutely fundamental social relationship in the functioning of any actual capitalist system. But the relationship between money-capital and the productive sector is another absolutely central social relationship. Some of the sharpest conflicts within capitalist societies have occurred around these social relationships between the financial sector and the rest of society.

At the end of the war, politics in the Atlantic world was governed by forces who favoured what the neo-liberals call 'financial repression' and what Keynes approvingly referred to as 'euthanasia for the rentiers'. The story of the last quarter of a century has been that of the resurrection of the rentiers in a liberation struggle against 'financial repression'. This has gone hand in hand with the idea that the approach to the design of financial systems championed by people like Keynes and the US occupation regimes in Germany and Japan after the war – 'financial repression' – is an approach alien to genuine capitalism, apparently of Far Eastern origin! These debates concern not only the institutional-power relations between money-capital and the employers of capital but also the role of the state and the forms of class relationships across the entire society.

But to understand this whole story we must appreciate that these social and institutional design issues are not necessarily resolvable at a purely national level. It is actually an activity *also of the interstate system, insofar as funds can flow more or less freely from one national currency zone to another*. For the money-capital pole plays its role only through acting as money. And insofar as the currencies of states are more or less freely convertible by private economic actors into the currencies of other states, financial relations in one capitalist society can be subjected to powerful influences from the financial sectors of other capitalist states.

The transformation of the relations between the money-capital pole and the productive sector of national capitalisms has been a central feature of what has come to be known as 'neo-liberalism' over the last quarter of a century. But this transformation has been achieved in close connection with profound changes in the field of international monetary and financial relations. Against this background, we will examine the international monetary system and how it relates to international and national financial systems.

The International Monetary System

The need for an international monetary system is not, in itself, something derived from capitalism. It arises from the political as well as economic fact that the world is divided into separate states with separate currencies and from the fact that groups within one state wish to do business with (and inside) other states. Historically, most of that international business has been concerned with trade in goods. The problem of international monetary relations arises in the first place over how two groups in different currency zones can buy and sell goods. One obvious way of handling this problem is to use neither of the currencies of each state but instead to use a third form of money, say gold, which has an exchange price with each of the two currencies. Alternatively, there may be an established exchange rate directly between the two currencies and the seller of the goods may be prepared to accept payment in either of the two currencies, etc. The important point, for the moment, is simply that some sort of international monetary system is necessary for the functioning of an international economy.

These exchanges in the international monetary system are monitored closely at an interstate level to answer one important question: are the economic operators of a state buying more from other states than they are selling to other states? In other words, what is a state's so-called balance of payments in current transactions? Is the account in surplus or in deficit? These questions are important because if a state is heavily in deficit people start to wonder whether it will be able, in the future, to find the internationally acceptable money that it will need to pay all its international obligations. Does a deficit state have enough reserves of international money to keep paying off its deficit? Can it borrow internationally acceptable money from somewhere to keep meeting its obligations? The more such doubts grow, the more the economic operators within the state concerned can face difficulties of one kind or another.

But this system is not a 'natural' or a purely economic one. It is both economic and political. The whole concept of the balance of payments rests on the political division of the world into different states with different moneys. The arrangements for establishing acceptable forms of international money are also established by political agreement among states. And the treatment of countries with current account deficits or surpluses is also politically established. Should there be an arrangement whereby states with current account deficits cut back on their purchases from abroad to get rid of their deficits? Or should the surplus states be pressurised to buy more from the deficit countries? Arrangements of either sort can be put in place. If the deficit countries must adjust, that will have a depressive effect internationally, because they will cut back on their international purchases. If the opposite approach is used, it will have a stimulative effect on international economic activity. Which approach is adopted will depend upon international political agreement between states over the nature of the international monetary regime that is to operate. And this agreement will not be one between equals. The biggest powers, or perhaps even one single big power, can lay down what the regime will be. All the other states will be 'regime takers', rather than 'regime makers'.[7]

The Bretton Woods Regime for International Monetary and Financial Relations

The concerns of Keynes and Dexter White in their efforts to construct a new international monetary system for the postwar world were to construct arrangements which would privilege international economic development. This required a predictable and stable international monetary regime that would be rule-based and would not be manipulable by powerful states for mercantilist advantage.

They therefore retained gold as the anchor of the system – a money separate from the currency of any nation-state. And they laid down that the dollar would have its price fixed against gold. Other states then fixed their currency prices against the dollar and were not allowed to unilaterally change that price as they pleased. Changes in currency prices would be settled co-operatively between states through a supranational body, the International Monetary Fund, which would be obliged to accept the change in a currency's par value only if it was needed to correct 'fundamental disequilibrium' in the state's current account (mainly concerned with trade). The aim of these arrangements was to ensure that economic operators enjoyed stability in the prices of the main currencies against each other since all were fixed at a given price against gold. In practice, the dollar was the main international currency in use for trade, but its exchange price was fixed like that of any other currency, against gold, which remained the numeraire of the system as a whole.

The second major feature of the Keynes–White system was that it largely banned private financial operators from moving funds around the world freely, giving states authority to control and prevent such financial movements.

Private finance was allowed to transfer funds for the purposes of financing trade. There was also provision for funds to be moved across frontiers for foreign productive investment. But other movements of private finance were to be banned: 'financial repression' on an international scale. Such repression then meant that investment resources would be 'home-grown' within states. And it also meant that money-capital had to confine its royalty-seeking operations to those activities which its nation-state would allow. In other words, states were given the right to dominate and shape the activities of their financial sectors in ways that would suit the state's economic development goals.

The Bretton Woods regime had a rather short and turbulent life for the simple reason that the two powers which designed it, the US and the UK, became hostile to various central aspects of the rules they had themselves designed. The regime was designed during the war and approved in 1944, long before the United States had established its global political-military strategy in the Cold War which would in turn become the international underpinning of the expansion of American capitalism. The Roosevelt administration, therefore, could not imagine a situation in which the US would face a structural deficit in its external payments. But the US's military power projection was to produce just such a structural deficit and this was to take an acute form with the Vietnam war. And the deficit was exacerbated by the US's export of capital into the EC in the 1960s as it sought to ensure its continued dominance in key West European markets within the EC.

But under the rules of the Bretton Woods system, the states in surplus – the other side of the coin of the US deficit – could demand that their surplus dollars be exchanged for gold and by the late 1960s, US gold reserves were becoming insufficient to honour the Bretton Woods requirement of the dollar's free convertibility into gold. There were, of course, obvious solutions to this problem within the Bretton Woods rules: either the US could undertake the necessary economic adjustments to bring its deficit under control – cutting back on external military expenditure and reducing imports, perhaps through domestic deflation – or it could devalue the dollar against gold, thus ensuring that the surplus countries could buy less gold with their surplus dollars. But the Nixon administration was not prepared to take either of these steps: it preferred to break up the Bretton Woods regime instead.

As far as 'financial repression' was concerned, both Wall Street and the City of London were unhappy with the restrictions imposed upon them by the Bretton Woods frameworks. Already in the 1940s, Wall Street had managed to water down White's original scheme for financial repression. White's own fate symbolised the dramatic shift in political climate between 1943 and the late 1940s: he died from a heart attack while before the House Un-American Affairs Committee in the late 1940s, charged with being or having been a Communist. Financial interests in the City of London also managed to exert sufficient political influence to establish themselves as an off-shore, unregulated international private financial centre and acquired growing significance in the 1960s through the so-called Eurodollar and Euro-bond markets. And the growth of London and of US banks and multinational corporations operating with off-shore funds created growing speculative pressures against the Bretton Woods system of fixed but adjustable exchange rates in the 1960s.

The Nixon administration's refusal to accept the Bretton Woods discipline of requiring the US to remain in surplus was justified by the argument that its deficit was caused by European and Japanese mercantilism, their determination to maintain undervalued currencies in order to seize market share from US companies and challenge American industrial capitalism. With this argument it sought to justify its campaign in the early 1970s to scrap the central institutions of the Bretton Woods regime.[8]

Notes

1. The term 'royalty' covers interest, ground rent, taxes, financial service fees and dividends. I derive the term from Shaikh and Tonak (though they do not include dividends in their definition). See Anwar M. Shaikh and E. Ahmet Tonak, *Measuring the Wealth of Nations: The Political Economy of National Accounts* (Cambridge University Press, 1994).

2. Throughout this chapter, the term 'production' refers to those activities that produce use-values. Not all such production in capitalist societies is controlled by private capital: e.g., cooking or the supply of housing may not be. But the bulk of the productive sector will be. On the definition of this term, see Shaikh and Tonak, ibid.

3. See Bob Rowthorn, *Capitalism, Conflict and Inflation* (Lawrence and Wishart, 1980) and David Harvey, *The Limits of Capital* (Blackwell, 1984). Harvey's very important book provides an excellent survey of the roles of finance within capitalism.

4. Ethan B. Kapstein, *Governing the Global Economy: International Finance and the State* (Harvard University Press, 1994).

5. The economic justification for these 'secondary markets' is that their existence facilitates the search of companies and governments for buyers of their offerings of shares or bonds: the buyers have the safety of knowing that they can sell their bonds or shares easily later on the secondary markets.

6. For further discussion on these differences, see G. Epstein and H. Gintis, 'International Capital Markets and National Economic Policy', *Review of International Political Economy*, 2: 4 (Autumn 1995).

7. On these issues, see David Calleo and Susan Strange, 'Money and World Politics,' in Susan Strange (ed.), *Paths to International Political Economy* (Allen & Unwin, 1984).

8. On the history of the Bretton Woods regime, see M. De Cecco, 'The Origins of the Post-War Payments System', *Cambridge Journal of Economics*, 3 (1979); James Crotty 'On Keynes and Capital Flight', *Journal of Economic Literature*, vol. 21 (1983); Richard N. Gardner, *Sterling–Dollar Diplomacy in Current Perspective* (Columbia University Press, 1980); and Andrew Walter, *World Power and World Money* (Harvester Wheatsheaf, 1993).

3

The Dollar–Wall Street Regime

The New International Monetary System Created in the 1970s

The collapse of central pillars of the Bretton Woods regime in the early 1970s has often been presented, both in the US and in other countries, as some sort of defeat for a weakened American capitalism, involving the breakdown of its favoured international monetary order and a slide into a chaotic 'non-system'. But the reality was very different. The Nixon administration was determined to break out of a set of institutionalised arrangements which limited US dominance in international monetary politics in order to establish a new regime which would give it monocratic power over international monetary affairs. US capital was indeed being challenged by its capitalist rivals in product markets at the time. The break-up of the Bretton Woods system was part of a strategy for restoring the dominance of US capitals through turning the international monetary system into a dollar-standard regime.

We will not survey the details of the international monetary crisis of the late 1960s and early 1970s.[1] There were two decisive moments in the story. The first was Nixon's decision to cut the link between the dollar and gold in August 1971. And the second was the oil price rise in the autumn of 1973 and the way in which the financial consequences of that price rise were handled by the main Western powers.

The Inauguration and Structure of the Dollar–Wall Street Regime

The August 1971 decision to 'close the gold window' meant that the US was no longer subject to the discipline of having to try to maintain a fixed par value of the dollar against gold or anything else: it could let the dollar move as the US Treasury wished and pointed towards the removal of gold from

19

international monetary affairs. It thus moved the world economy on to a pure dollar standard.

Support for such a move towards a pure dollar standard had been growing within the United States during the 1960s. Supporters of this move, such as Paul Volcker, had entered the Nixon administration at the end of the 1960s and the international monetary crisis of 1971 gave them their opportunity. But the problem was that a pure dollar standard was not acceptable to Western Europe or Japan. Williamson, an insider in the negotiations at this time, has expressed what was at stake clearly: 'The central political fact is that a dollar standard places the direction of the world monetary policy in the hands of a single country, which thereby acquires great influence over the economic destiny of others. It is one thing to sacrifice sovereignty in the interests of interdependence; it is quite another when the relationship is one way. The difference is that between the EEC and a colonial empire . . . The fact is that acceptance of a dollar standard necessarily implies a degree of asymmetry in power which, although it actually existed in the early postwar years, had vanished by the time that the world found itself sliding to a reluctant dollar standard.'[2]

In order to manage the rest of the world's hostility to its closing of the gold window, the Nixon administration supported the establishment of a conference on world monetary reform. The conference was initiated within the IMF through the so-called Group of Twenty and it carried on its work between 1972 and 1974. The main idea, which met with broad support at the conference, was to establish a new, reformed system in which Spacial Drawing Rights (SDRs) would play a central role as the international monetary anchor or numeraire to which the dollar would be subordinated. But it is now clear that the Nixon administration had no intention of going along with such a scheme or with respecting the consensus of the conference. It was using the whole exercise as a means of buying time while it imposed its own will on events outside the conference discussions. With the quadrupling of oil prices in the autumn of 1973, as Williamson points out, all the conference participants realised that collective planning of a new consensual international monetary order was dead and the whole negotiation fizzled out.

The Nixon administration thus gained its dollar standard and in the upheavals of the early 1970s increasing numbers of countries were forced to abandon attempts to maintain fixed exchange rates between their currencies and the dollar. This suited the US administration because it wished to force a revaluation on other states and could now do so through its own policy for the dollar. This was an enormously important development, because, for reasons which we will discuss later, the US government could, alone among governments, move the exchange price of the dollar against other currencies by huge amounts without suffering the economic consequences that would face other states which attempted to do the same.

The Nixon administration's second step was to try to ensure that international financial relations should be taken out of the control of state central banks and should be increasingly centred upon private financial operators. It sought to achieve this goal through exploiting US control over international oil supplies. It is still widely believed that the sharp and steep increase in oil prices in 1973 was carried out by the Gulf states as part of an anti-Israel and anti-US policy connected to the Yom Kippur war. Yet as we now know, the oil price rises were the result of US influence on the oil states and they were arranged in part as an exercise in economic statecraft directed against America's 'allies' in Western Europe and Japan. And another dimension of the Nixon administration's policy on oil price rises was to give a new role, through them, to the US private banks in international financial relations.

The Nixon administration was planning to get OPEC to greatly increase its oil prices a full two years before OPEC did so,[3] and as early as 1972 the Nixon administration planned for the US private banks to recycle the petrodollars when OPEC finally did take US advice and jack up oil prices.[4] The Nixon administration understood the way in which the US state could use expanding private financial markets as a political multiplier of the impact of US Treasury moves with the dollar. But according to Nixon's Ambassador in Saudi Arabia at the time, the principal political objective behind Nixon's drive for the OPEC oil price rise was to deal a crippling blow to the Japanese and European economies, both overwhelmingly dependent on Middle East oil, rather than to decisively transform international financial affairs.[5] Nevertheless, Nixon's officials showed far more strategic insight into the consequences of what they were attempting than most political scientists would credit any government with. Its capacity for deception both over the oil price rise and in the way in which it manipulated discussions with its 'allies' in the IMF over so-called 'international monetary reform' was brilliant.

The US government realised that the oil price rises would produce an enormous increase in the dollar earnings of oil states that could not absorb such funds into their own productive sectors. At the same time, the oil price rises would plunge very many states into serious trade deficits as the costs of their oil imports soared. So the so-called petrodollars would have to be recycled from the Gulf through the western banking systems to non-oil-producing states. Other governments had wanted the petrodollars to be recycled through the IMF.[6] But the US rejected this, insisting the Atlantic world's private banks (at that time led by American banks) should be the recycling vehicles. And because the US was politically dominant in the Gulf, it could get its way.

The debate about recycling the petrodollars was part of a wider debate among the main capitalist powers over whether to scrap international 'financial repression' and the system of maintaining control over international financial movements firmly in the hands of the central banks of states. In

these debates, which took place within the IMF, the US was completely isolated, as all other governments as well as the IMF staff wanted to retain
strict controls on private international financial movements.[7] But the US got
its way through unilateral actions, supplementing the petrodollar move with
its own abolition in 1974 of restrictions on the flow of funds into and out of
the US (known, in the jargon, as the abolition of 'capital controls').

It is true that the Nixon administration was able to exploit a breach in the
Bretton Woods system that had already existed since the 1950s: the international role of the City of London in financial transactions. Britain's
government had allowed the City of London to operate as an 'off-shore'
centre for international private financial operations of all sorts almost
entirely unregulated.[8] During the 1960s, the City's international business
grew rapidly through the development of the so-called Eurodollar market:
banks in the City accepting deposits in off-shore dollars and then lending
these off-shore dollars to governments and businesses throughout the world.
But this role of the City as an off-shore centre was itself largely dependent
upon US government policy (which allowed US banks to operate free of
domestic US banking regulation by establishing operations in London).

The new role for private finance in international monetary relations was
qualitatively different from the movement of private capital under the
Bretton Woods system. While it is true that under almost any capitalist international monetary regime private capital will devise ways to move its
monetary property across frontiers, and while it is also true that private
speculative capital movements were growing stronger under Bretton Woods
in the 1960s, the new arrangements brought international private finance
into the very centre of the workings of the new international monetary
system and enabled this force to operate on a scale qualitatively different
from that under the old regime.

It is worth stressing that in 'liberating' the private banks from 'international financial repression' the Nixon administration was not mainly
responding to interest-group lobbying from American banks or allowing
supposedly spontaneous market forces in finance to do as they pleased.
The US banks themselves were initially far from happy about recycling the
petrodollars to countries in the South. The US government had to lean on
them to do so and had to provide incentives for such lending.[9] One such
incentive was to involve the IMF/WB in new, parallel lending to such countries; another was the removal of controls on the US capital account in 1974
to enable domestic US banks to become involved in such lending so that the
operations were not confined to US and other banks operating in London.
A further incentive was the decision to scrap the ceiling on the amount of a
bank's total lending that could go to any single borrower.[10] And finally, the
US government gave its banks to understand that if they got into difficulties
as a result of such lending, their government would bail them out.[11]

The Nixon strategy in 'liberating' international financial markets was based on the idea that doing so would *liberate the American state from succumbing to its economic weaknesses and would strengthen the political power of the American state.* According to Eric Helleiner, US officials understood in the 1970s that a liberalised international financial market would preserve the privileged global financial position of the US and grasped also that this would help preserve the dollar's central international role. Helleiner sums up the fundamental point about the overall political and economic significance of the changes: 'the basis of American hegemony was being shifted from one of direct power over other states to a more market-based or "structural" form of power.'[12]

We shall see below how these processes actually worked to strengthen the political power and economic policy freedom of the US. But first we must point out the significance of the rise of private international finance for international monetary relations between states. This rise altered the basis upon which governments maintained the international stability of their own currencies: under the old Bretton Woods system, the basis for a currency's stability was closely tied both to its trade balance and to the attitude of the IMF and of the governments (central banks) of the main capitalist powers towards the government of the country in trade balance difficulties. States with surpluses on their 'current account' (trade in goods and 'invisible' earnings, e.g. from profits and dividends from its companies overseas or from shares in companies overseas) had stable, strong currencies. If a state developed a current account deficit, it would need to use its foreign exchange reserves to defend its currency or persuade the IMF and other governments to help.

Under the new system states with current account surpluses were still generally in a strong position. But the effective basis of their currency's stability came to depend upon another factor: the state's *creditworthiness in private international financial markets.* Under the previous system, private financial markets had been largely excluded – banned by 'financial repression' – from involvement in the international monetary system. Now they were to play a central role.

At first sight, these new arrangements might appear to be a liberation for governments from earlier rigidities. Even if they got into current account deficits they could borrow in the at first London-centred, later Anglo-American, private financial markets to tide themselves over. And they would be free to allow their currency's exchange rate to move more flexibly rather than having to subordinate all other economic objectives to maintaining a fixed rate against other main currencies. Yet the bulk of the states involved in the international capitalist economy soon discovered that the liberation was, over the longer term, an illusion. It was more like a trap.

The way the system would actually work depended on its two central mechanisms: the dollar and the increasingly American-centred international financial markets. Thus, the new international monetary arrangements gave the United States government far more influence over the international monetary and financial relations of the world than it had enjoyed under the Bretton Woods rules. It could freely decide the price of the dollar. States would become increasingly dependent upon developments in Anglo-American financial markets for managing their international monetary relations. And trends in these financial markets could be shifted by the actions (and words) of the US public authorities, in the Treasury Department and the Federal Reserve Board (the US Central Bank). Thus, Nixon gave Washington more leverage than ever at a time when American relative economic weight in the capitalist world had substantially declined and at a time when the productive systems of the advanced capitalist economies were entering a long period of stagnation.

The Dollar–Wall Street Regime (DWSR for short) was not of course *exclusively* centred on the dollar: other currencies, particularly the mark, did acquire large roles as international currencies. And Wall Street and its large London satellite were not the exclusive sources of finance. But the Dollar–Wall Street nexus has been the dominant one by far throughout the last quarter of a century.

And it is important to note how the two poles of this system – the dollar and Wall Street – have reinforced each other. First we can see how the new centrality of the dollar turned people towards Wall Street for finance. Because the dollar has been the dominant world currency, the great majority of states would want to hold the great bulk of their foreign currency reserves in dollars, placing them within the American financial system (or in London). Similarly, because many central commodities in the world economy were priced in and traded for dollars, those trading in such commodities would wish to raise their trade finance in New York and London. Thus, the dollar's role greatly boosted the size and turnover in the Anglo-American financial markets. At the same time, there was feedback the other way. The strength of Wall Street, as a financial centre, reinforced the dominance of the dollar: for anyone wanting to borrow or lend money, the size and strength of a financial system is a very important factor. The bigger a financial market's resources and reach, the safer it is likely to be, and the more competitive its rates for borrowers. And the same is true of securities markets (for bonds or shares). For those seeking royalties from securities a big market with very high rates of buying and selling is safer because you can easily withdraw at any time by finding a buyer for your bonds or shares. Furthermore, if you are a saver looking for high returns in more risky markets, it is much better to place your funds in the hands of a big, diversified operator which can absorb losses in one area of trading and compensate with gains elsewhere. Thus the size and depth of the US financial markets and the growing strength of US financial operators acts as an attraction for people to place their funds at the centre of the dollar area or to raise funds in that centre. In this way, the strength of Wall Street has reinforced the dominance of the dollar as an international currency.[13]

The Economic and Political Significance of Dollar Seigniorage

The economic and political significance of this new regime can be appreciated only when we understand the role of seigniorage in giving the American government an immensely potent political instrument in the form of the new regime.

As we saw when we initially discussed international money, a state has to acquire funds of internationally acceptable money in order to be able to pay for goods and services from abroad. To take an extreme example, few people would accept payment from Chad in Chad's own currency: it would be useless to all but a handful of people outside Chad. So Chad has to earn (or borrow) an international currency, say the dollar, before it can buy anything from abroad. But this huge constraint is non-existent for the US under the new, post-Bretton Woods international monetary regime, because the international currency is the dollar and the US does not need to earn dollars abroad: it prints them at home!

Seigniorage is the name for the privileges which this position gives: these can be summarised by saying that the US does not face the same balance of payments constraints that other countries face. It can spend far more abroad than it earns there. Thus, it can set up expensive military bases without a foreign exchange constraint; its transnational corporations can buy up other companies abroad or engage in other forms of foreign direct investment without a payments constraint; its money-capitalists can send out large flows of funds into portfolio investments (buying securities) similarly. As we have already seen, dollar seigniorage includes giving the US financial system great advantages as the world's main source of credit. And it is very important to appreciate the significance of seigniorage for trade relations – imports and exports. When many of the key goods bought and sold in international markets have their trade denominated in dollars, American companies importing or exporting are far less affected by changes in the dollar exchange rate than is the case in other countries. Thus, the international grain trade does business in dollars. If the dollar exchange rate rises massively against other currencies, US exporters of grain are far less seriously affected than they would otherwise be. And if the high dollar produces a flood of imports into the United States, generating a very big, long-term deficit on the current account of its balance of payments, the deficit can be funded in dollars. Thus seigniorage gives the US government the ability to swing the price of the dollar internationally this way and

that, having great economic consequences for the rest of the world while
the US remains cushioned from the consequences that would apply to
other states.[14]

The Economic and Political Significance of Wall Street Dominance

The Nixon administration's victory in 'liberating' the Anglo-American private banking systems for international operations had four key effects. First,
it suddenly catapulted private banks into the centre of international finance,
pushing out the earlier dominance of the central banks and led quickly to
the international dominance of the Anglo-American financial systems and
American financial operators. Secondly, it opened up an enormous hole in
the public supervision of international financial operators. Thirdly, it made
the financial systems and exchange rates of other states, especially countries
of the South, increasingly vulnerable to developments in the American
financial markets. And finally, it generated powerful competitive pressures
within the banking systems of the OECD countries and enabled the
American government largely to determine what kinds of competitive pressures and what kinds of international regulation of international financial
markets should exist. It is impossible to exaggerate just how important these
changes were.

The first beneficiaries of the liberation of international private finance
were the City of London and the big, internationally-oriented US money-
centre banks. In 1981 the Reagan administration enacted a law allowing
so-called 'International Banking Facilities' in the US, thus giving Wall Street
the same off-shore status as the City.[15] It might be thought that the role of
the City of London suggests that it should be given at least equal status with
Wall Street. But this is wrong for one simple reason: the City was acting as a
financial marketplace in dollars and its entire pattern of off-shore operations was dependent upon US government policies for international
finance. It thus operated principally as a servicing centre for the dollar currency zone and as a satellite of Wall Street.

Since the early 1980s, the great bulk of the international financial market
activity has thus been centred in Wall Street (and its London satellite). It is
necessary to be precise about what this signifies. Frequently, it is held to sig-
nify that there is a so-called 'global' financial market. This is true if it means
that London and New York do business with people from all over the world.
Funds flow out from and back in to those two centres from most countries of
the world. But this does *not at all* mean that all the financial markets of the
world are unified in a single, integrated financial market. On the contrary,
financial markets remained – and largely still remain – compartmentalised,
not only between countries but even within countries: we can see this if we

realise that even within Euroland after the launch of the euro there will still be substantial barriers to the full integration of financial markets. But what did happen in the 1970s was that London and New York operators did begin to establish linkages between their international financial markets and national financial systems around the world which were far stronger than in the 1960s. The expansion of these international private financial operations can be appreciated by comparing the size of international bank loans and bond lending between 1975 and 1990: bank loans rose from $40 billion in 1975 to well over $300 billion by 1990; during the same period bond lending rose almost tenfold, from $19 billion to over $170 billion.

Talk of a *global* financial market, rather than of the increasing influence of the American financial market over other national financial markets, obscures the power dimension of US financial dominance. Those who believe that the adjective 'American' is trivial or even redundant should ask themselves a simple question: would they, then, be quite happy from an economic and political point of view if the international financial system was dominated by the markets and operators of China or Iraq, just so long as they could offer similar kinds of credit or other financial services on similar terms to those of Wall Street? But to make the point much more directly, we can simply note that because the American financial markets have been dominant within the hierarchical networks of financial markets, access to that market, different kinds of linkages between national economies and that market, and price movements within that market, have had enormous economic *and political* significance.

The story since the 1970s has been one of growing pressure from the Wall Street centre to weaken the barriers to its penetration into domestic financial systems. This pressure has a triple target: first, to remove barriers to the free flow of funds in both directions between Wall Street and private operators within the target state; second, to give full rights to Wall Street operators to do business within the financial systems and economies of the target states; and thirdly, to redesign the financial systems of target states to fit in with the business strategies of Wall Street operators and of their American clients (transnational corporations, money market mutual funds, etc.).

Of course, Wall Street and London have not had a monopoly. Tokyo has grown and some of the biggest financial operators are Japanese. Frankfurt, Zurich, Paris, Hong Kong and Singapore are all important. But none of these other centres as yet comes close to rivalling the size of Wall Street and London, and in financial affairs even more than in any other sector of business, size – both market size and the size of the funds that operators can mobilise – is *competitively decisive*.[16] You can do what smaller players can't, so you can set the pace of most of the innovations in the field.

This competitive advantage was multiplied by the almost entirely unregulated nature of the London and Wall Street operators. Such regulation as existed amounted only to rather vague, non-legal guidelines agreed by central banks in the Bank for International Settlements.[17] This, together with scale advantages, not only maintained Wall Street's dominance but started a corrosive process of undermining the public regulation of financial operators *within* other states, as operators there escaped off-shore themselves to compete, found ways around local rules and exerted pressures on their governments to liberalise in order to enable them to compete against Wall Street.

As we saw above, it is dangerous for banking systems if banks' operations are allowed to go unregulated. Unbridled competition between banks leads them to compete with each other to the point of collapse. But because of the dominance of Wall Street in private international finance, what competition, what regulation and what international arrangements for banks becoming insolvent should be established became questions largely in the hands of the American government, in alliance with the British authorities. If the US government chose not to regulate, it became extremely difficult for the other main capitalist states to maintain their regulatory frameworks. If the US decided to regulate, other banking authorities would follow suit, but the US could still largely dictate the form and scope of regulation. Thus a whole chain reaction of effects and pressures on banking systems around the world was unleashed by the decisions taken in Washington.

Let us mention some of these chain reactions. First, the US Federal Reserve could largely dictate the levels of international interest rates through moving US domestic interest rates. It could thus determine the costs of credit internationally, with enormously powerful effects on other economies. When international private credit is cheap, economic operators with access to cheap international credit start projects which seem viable in the current conditions. But if US decisions suddenly make credit very expensive, fundamentally sound enterprises may find themselves going bankrupt because of a sudden contraction of cheap credit. And an international financial system dominated by the US financial market can swing wildly, oversupplying credit at one moment and dramatically contracting it at another. To make matters worse, the tempo of the US business cycle is impossible to predict with accuracy and the direction of US policy is equally impossible to predict because the US has qualitatively greater freedom of policy choice as a result of its dominant political position in the international economy.

Secondly, through its regulatory interventions or the lack of them, Washington was the manager of what might be called the microeconomics of international finance: it could dictate how much regulation and supervision of bank lending there would be. De facto it managed the international tension between encouraging the banks to take risks and preventing them from acting recklessly and then collapsing. Frequently during the last quarter of a century, Washington has been happy to forget about regulating its international financial operators, whether, as in the 1970s, they are the big US money-centre commercial banks or whether they are the investment banks or hedge funds of the 1990s. When this happens, enormous competitive pressures are placed upon financial operators elsewhere, and they pressurise their governments to relax their regulations, or find ways of evading what regulations exist. The cry is often heard in Washington that for technological or other reasons regulation is impossible. But when it suits Washington to introduce regulation it has been shown to have been able to achieve it, with remarkable ease.

This was shown with the so-called Basle Accord of 1988, laying down guidelines for international banking supervision. The Basle Accord was achieved through the US government forming an alliance with London for a joint Anglo-American regulatory regime. This was enough to ensure that all other OECD governments would come together to establish a common regime. The resulting regulatory regime has been a 'gentlemen's agreement' skewed towards serving US interests since it gives all banks an incentive to privilege the buying of government bonds, a pressing US need, given its government's indebtedness, and a disincentive to lend to industry. This Accord demonstrated just how easy it is for states to regulate international financial markets, on one condition: that the regulation is done with US support.[18]

Thirdly and very importantly, US governments discovered a way of combining unregulated international banking and financial markets with minimal risk of the US banking and financial systems suffering a resulting collapse. Using its control over the IMF/WB and largely with the support of its European partners, Washington discovered that when its international financial operators reached the point of insolvency through their international activities, they could be bailed out by the populations of the borrower countries at almost no significant cost to the US economy. This solution was first hit upon during the Latin American international financial crisis at the start of the 1980s and it was a solution with really major economic and political significance. We will return to this experience later.

At the same time, the US government developed ways of extending the influence of Wall Street over international finance without putting its big commercial banks at risk. It successfully sought to change the form of lending to the more rentier-friendly bond market and towards more short-term lending rather than medium or long-term bank loans.

The final and most important area in which Wall Street dominance over international finance has political significance lies in the fact that financial systems are both enormously important parts of any capitalist system and that they are, at the same time, interwoven with core control functions of capitalist states. It is through control over financial flows that capitalist states exercise much of their political power over society. Insofar as Wall Street could strengthen its linkages with national financial systems, breaking down state barriers to the thickening of linkages with domestic financial systems, these latter would tend to slip out of the control of their domestic states. In a crisis within a national financial system, the American state itself could open the whole capitalist system of the state concerned to being re-engineered in the interests of American capitalism.[19]

The US and Global Management

Just as the state plays a central role in domestic monetary and financial affairs, whether the domestic regime is Keynesian in structure or neo-liberal, so the main states or state play a central role in international monetary and financial affairs. The fact that these continual political interventions in these central aspects of the international economy tend not to register in much of the literature on international economics is the result of ideological blinkers, all the more powerful for being entrenched in the professional academic division of labour between political science and economics. These blinkers are evident in those definitions of globalisation which suggest it is a purely techno-economic force not only separate from state-political controls but inimical to them.

But these blinkers are reinforced also by the fact that state-political influence over the international monetary and financial system is not neatly parcelled out between states. To put it mildly, political influence in these areas is distributed *asymmetrically: during the last quarter of a century it has been distributed overwhelmingly to one single state.* Under the Bretton Woods regime, there was something like a global authority, resting on the co-operative agreements laid down in the 1940s: gold functioned as a supranational monetary anchor, the IMF and central banks sought to manage monetary and financial flows. Of course, the US was overwhelmingly the most influential player within this IMF system. But it too was constrained in what it could do by the supranational rules of the system. The central point about the new, post-Nixon regime was that the US was still overwhelmingly dominant but not it was not constrained by rules. The Dollar–Wall Street Regime has been a bit like the British constitution: the dominant power has been able to make up the rules as it went along. The US could decide the dollar price and it could also have the deciding influence on the evolving dynamics of international financial relations.

So we arrive at a question of absolutely cardinal importance both economically *and politically*: would the US government run the new Dollar–Wall Street Regime in the American national interest? Or would the United States government rise above mere national interest and pretend it was a supranational world government subordinating all national interests including those of the USA to the collective global interest? Or – a third possibility – would the US government steer a middle course, and set up a collegiate board of the main capitalist states in a more or less large (or small) oligarchy in which the US would compromise its national interest to some extent for the collective good of the oligarchy?

The answer is that the United States government has done its constitutional duty. It has put America first. The whole point of the Nixon moves to destroy the Bretton Woods system and set up the Dollar–Wall Street Regime *was to put American first.*

There is a straightforward test that can be applied to detect the direction in which US policy has been applied. Has the US sought to establish rules and instruments for the effective public management of international money and international finance within the DWSR of the kind shown to be necessary in domestic economic management? We can run through the check-list of issues:

1) There is a very strong international interest in international monetary stability. Yet instead, the DWSR has seen the price of the main international currency driven up and down in wild swings without historical precedent, swings that make even the 1930s look like an era of relative monetary calm! This extraordinary volatility has been the product of deliberate US policy and of Washington's refusal to work towards a stable, rule-based system.

2) Public macro-regulation of the supply of credit within the world economy to ensure some measure of stability: instead international flows of credit have swung wildly from over-supply to chaotic contraction in cycle after cycle, again overwhelmingly because Washington has wished matters to be handled in this way.

3) Public micro-regulation of the main private credit suppliers to try to ensure minimally responsible behaviour, to try to restrict dangerous competitive pressures and prevent major collapses in either the financial sector or productive sector: instead of this there has been a free-for-all in this area, except insofar as the American government has wished to impose such regulation.

4) Public management of the interface between finance and the productive sector internationally to provide incentives for channelling funds into productive activity rather than speculation, market rigging and corruption. The record in this area speaks for itself: there has been a systematic drive to make state after state subordinate its management of productive activity to the unregulated dominance of international finance and to make all states increasingly powerless to resist such dominance (again using the IMF and the World Bank as central instruments against the role of public authorities in this area).

A number of authors have suggested that the subsequent history of US international monetary and financial policy has been bound by the rules of co-operative oligarchy with the rest of the G7. But the evidence for this is extremely weak as regards the main strategic lines of US policy. The existence of the G7 proves nothing except that the US has sought to use it to get the other main capitalist powers to do what the US has wanted. The fact that on many occasions other G7 countries have not been prepared to do the US's bidding does not mean the US itself has adopted a collegiate approach. Some authors have pointed to the supposedly great significance of the 1978 Bonn summit as an instance of co-operative policy-making.[20] It was, but in the form of Germany's government agreeing to do most of what the US government wanted. And whatever co-operative spirit there was in the Carter administration vanished under Reagan.[21] The strongest claim for collegiality in high monetary politics concerns the Plaza Accord to lower the dollar price in 1985. It is quite true that this meeting did agree to bring down the dollar and it subsequently was brought down. But as Destler and Randall Henning show, US Treasury Secretary Baker had already decided to bring down the dollar, had already started to bring it down and was interested in using the G7 agreement as a tactical ploy within US domestic politics against those who were opposing his already decided policy for a fall in the dollar.[22]

And in the management of international finance, the America First policy has been equally evident. During the 1970s, the US governments first treated the IMF with contempt (under Nixon), then allowed it to sink towards oblivion (in the late 1970s). What discussions on the regulation of international finance did take place shifted to the Bank for International Settlements and to bilateral discussions. The Reagan administration was at first downright hostile (and vitriolically hostile to the World Bank). It changed its tune towards these organisations not out of any abandonment of America First unilateralism, but because Baker saw, during the Latin American debt crisis, just what extraordinarily valuable tools of American economic statecraft these two institutions could be, once their new, subordinate roles were defined. Oligarchic collegiality had nothing to do with the matter. The record is one of US administrations seeking to be extremely collegial, provided the co-operation is about working together along the lines of action laid down in Washington already.

A whole academic paradigm has been constructed in the United States to justify this American unilateralism. This explains that there can be stability in international monetary affairs only when one single power is overwhelmingly dominant (hegemonic). The theory goes on to explain the turbulence: it is because the US is no longer totally dominant. The theory has been intellectually demolished.[22] But it at least has the merit of trying to explain the extraordinary behaviour of US governments in the management of international monetary affairs over the last quarter of a century.

This, then, brings us to a final question: if US policy over international monetary and financial affairs has governed the US national interest, does this mean the perceived national economic interest or the national political interest or both? To provide a satisfactory answer to this question we need to have a theory of what the economic and political interests of capitalist states at the top of the international hierarchy of capitalist states actually are. This in turn requires a grasp of the dynamic internationalising drives within capitalism itself. We will not address these questions until later. Instead, we will simply restrict ourselves to the propositions which we have sought to demonstrate so far: first, that a new international regime for money and financial relations was created in the 1970s. Secondly, that the dynamics of this regime were inescapably and integrally tied to the behaviour of one state in the inter-state system (the USA) and of one financial market in the networks of international finance ('Wall Street'). And thirdly, that US administrations followed their constitutional duties in approaching their management of this regime from a national interest perspective.

The DWSR as a Self-Sustaining Regime

We are now in a position to notice the pattern of functioning of the DWSR. The dollar is the international money to which all other convertible currencies are linked by exchange rates. The American government chooses not to seek fixed exchange rates with the other main currencies, since that would require the US government to give up its use of the dollar price as an instrument for achieving other goals. Therefore, under the regime, the dollar moves in great gyrations up and down against the other currencies, utterly transforming their trading and other environments. And within these macro-swings there is constant micro-volatility. States and economic operators around the world must structurally adapt their operations to this constant macro- and micro-volatility of the dollar or risk various kinds of domestic economic imbalance or crisis.

At the same time, the American-dominated international financial market and its private financial operators interact to an ever-greater extent with the international monetary relations of the dollar system. The dollar's dominance as the international currency means that states build up foreign exchange reserves mainly in dollars. Exchange rate turbulence means that states wishing to try to maintain the stability of their own currency need larger reserves than before. These reserves are placed in the US financial markets (such as US Treasury bonds) because their liquidity means the funds can easily be withdrawn for exchange rate stabilisation purposes. At the same time, Wall Street offers the most competitive terms for governments wishing to borrow money for various purposes (including defending their currencies) and it offers new instruments so that governments and economic operators can tackle problems of exchange rate turbulence: not only a vastly expanding foreign exchange market but a whole new range of so-called derivative markets such as forward foreign exchange derivatives, swaps of currencies, loans etc. Although many attribute these innovations to 'technology', they are simply a creative response to enormous turbulence in the currency markets: the forward foreign exchange markets and interest rate swaps markets, for example, enable operators to hedge against the risk of future shifts in currency prices.

Much of the globalisation literature which seeks to persuade us of the unstoppable, crushing strength of 'international capital markets' refers us to the huge size of the foreign exchange derivatives markets, the huge volumes of currencies traded in the foreign exchange markets or the extraordinarily rapid turnover in the US Treasury bond markets. Yet these volumes are overwhelmingly the result of politically driven volatility in international monetary relations.

To cope with their volatile environment, governments borrow from the private financial markets, but such borrowings are typically themselves subject to volatile repayment terms (by being linked to movements in US short-term interest rates) and furthermore they are borrowing in dollars and since the dollar swings wildly, the value of their debts (in terms of real domestic resource claims) will vary with their exchange rates with the dollar. Thus the links with Wall Street subject borrowers to further turbulence.

The international dynamics of the regime then interact with domestic economic management on the part of individual governments. Sudden swings in the dollar produce sudden swings in a state's trade balance and terms of trade. The government faces a choice: use Wall Street borrowing as a cushion, or engage in domestic macroeconomic adjustment. Ease of the latter choice depends on the domestic socio-political strength of the government: can it easily balance its budget and right a trade deficit by imposing costs on various domestic social groups or not? If this is difficult, the government may choose to borrow dollars from Wall Street. When Wall Street is flush with inflowing funds, it is eager, if not desperate to lend and offers governments inducements to borrow. But this may only cause a greater adjustment problem down the road, a problem which can strike suddenly through a further shift in the dollar or in US interest rates (or Treasury bond rates).

These dilemmas are faced particularly acutely by economies weakly inserted in international product markets, with weak economies and adjustment problems which the governments are too weak socio-politically to manage. These problems are, of course, especially prevalent in countries of the South. Thus the regime systematically generates payments and financial crises in the South. Every year one country after another suffers financial crises. As the Wall Street economist Henry Kaufman points out, national financial crises have come repeatedly on the international side in 'the last twenty years'.[24] An internationally provoked crisis then provides the role of the IMF/WB in the regime as auxiliary players. If such financial break-downs were not a systematic element in the regime, the IMF's role would have been marginal, if not redundant. Their task is to ensure that the state concerned adjusts domestically so that it can maintain the servicing of its Wall Street debts. At the same time the IMF acts internationally, in the way that a domestic state acts when its central financial operators get into trouble: it bails them out. But there is a crucial difference in the international field. When an American bank gets into trouble in the American domestic economy the US tax-payer bails it out. But when the same American bank gets into trouble abroad, the bail-out is paid for not by the American tax-payer but by the population of the borrowing country. Thus the bank's risk is borne by the people of the borrower country, via the IMF's auspices.

Through IMF/WB intervention the state in crisis is eventually able to re-integrate into the DWSR, but this time with heavy debt-servicing problems and usually with a weakened domestic financial and economic structure. Meanwhile the external environment is as volatile as ever and the state concerned is more likely than not to face a further financial blow-out in the not-too-distant future.

But one of the paradoxes of the DWSR is that such financial crises in the South do not weaken the regime: they actually strengthen it. In the first place, in the crises, funds tend to flee from private wealth-holders in the state concerned into Wall Street, thus deepening and strengthening the Wall Street pole. Thus during the debt crises of the early 1980s in Latin America, the following very large outflows of funds occurred: from Argentina, $15.3 billion; from Mexico, $32.7 billion; from Venezuela, $10.8 billion.[25] Secondly, to pay off its now higher debts the state concerned must export into the dollar area to find the resources for debt servicing. This further strengthens the centrality of the dollar. Thirdly, the risks faced by US financial operators are widely covered by the IMF, enabling them to return to international activity more aggressively than ever. Finally, the weakening of the states of the South strengthens the bargaining power of the Wall Street credit institutions in decisions on the form of future financing. Forms which are safer for the creditor money-capitalist are increasingly adopted: securitised debt and short-term loans rather than long-term loans. And so on and so on.

Through all the gyrations of American policies for the world economy, the DWSR has remained firmly in place, constantly reproducing itself. In 1995 the dollar still remained overwhelmingly the dominant world currency: it comprised 61.5 per cent of all central bank foreign exchange reserves; it was the currency in which 76.8 per cent of all international bank loans were denominated, in which 39.5 per cent of all international bond issues were denominated, and 44.3 per cent of all Eurocurrency deposits; the dollar also served as the invoicing currency for 47.6 per cent of world trade and was one of the two currencies in 83 per cent of all foreign exchange transactions. And if intra-European transactions were eliminated from these figures, the dollar's dominance over all other transactions in the categories listed above becomes overwhelming.[26]

The DWSR and the Conventional Notion of Regimes

The notion that there are regimes in international relations was first put forward in the 1970s by Robert Keohane and Joseph Nye,[27] and was given its classic definition by Stephen Krasner in 1983.[28] Krasner defined regimes as 'principles, norms, rules and decision-making procedures around which actor expectations converge in a given issue area'. This concept has become extremely influential in the analysis of international relations and in the functioning of multi-lateral organisations. The notion of regime which is used here overlaps in some respects with Krasner's notion but differs from it in certain fundamental respects.

The DWSR is a regime in Krasner's sense in three respects. First, it corresponds to the idea that international relations do not consist simply of states interacting with each other in an anarchic void alongside economic operators interacting with each other as atoms in a world market. There are patterned, structured regimes governing these interactions. The DWSR is a regime in this sense of an international mechanism which structures and patterns interactions. Secondly, the DWSR corresponds to the idea implicit in Krasner's notion, that the states participating in these regimes do so because they find it in their interest to co-operate in the regime. This is true also of the DWSR. Thirdly, Krasner is prepared to accept that one state, the dominant state, is often the decisive and even unilateral actor in establishing the regime: it is not to be imagined that it is established consensually or in a collegial fashion. This imposed character of a regime can apply also to the DWSR.

But here the agreement ends. Krasner conceives of his regimes as being quasi-legal in character. States have, in his view, come to adopt a set of rules or norms or principles or a fixed set of collective decision-making procedures. Yet dollar dominance and the governing of international currency prices by the dollar exchange rate is not a quasi-legal norm or rule: it is *a fact* which regularly reproduces itself. All states that maintain any degree of currency convertibility *participate in this fact*: the price of their currency will be fixed, directly or indirectly, in relation to the dollar. States do have the option of exit from the regime: they can make their currency inconvertible. But if they do they will tend to be excluded from significant participation in the world economy. And the fact that states do participate in the regime does not indicate that they find it beneficial: it simply indicates that they lack the power to do anything about it.

The same applies to the other pole of the regime: the American financial market. States and economic operators do not have to participate in this market. They can avoid placing their reserves there, they can avoid borrowing there, but in practice it is almost impossible for them to avoid being drawn in because of their need for finance for their economic activities as a whole. And if they need to borrow from abroad, the most economically rational source of borrowing is from the biggest, most competitive/unregulated and most liquid markets – Wall Street.

There is another problem with the Krasner definition. Its attempts to present regimes as operating within discrete 'issue areas'. The DWSR does not occupy an 'issue area': it occupies a position as the monetary and financial framework facing states in their attempts to come to grips with a vast range of issue areas in international and domestic politics and economics. And the attempt to confine regimes to 'issue areas' chops reality up in trivialising ways: there is no equivalence of kind between an international legal regime for ensuring air safety and a framework regime like the DWSR. A further problem lies in the fact that regime theorists will tend to treat institutions like the IMF/WB as Krasner-type regimes, divorcing them from the patterned regularities of the DWSR in which they operate and which gives meaning to the dynamics of the IMF/WB's activities. And a final problem with the Krasner definition of regimes is that it presupposes a separation between regimes on the one side and both states and markets. Yet the DWSR includes as integral parts of its structures both states and markets.

Notes

1. The crisis of the Bretton Woods system in the late 1960s and early 1970s is well covered in Ernest Mandel, *Decline of the Dollar* (Monad Press, 1993) and, from an orthodox point of view, by John Williamson, *The Failure of World Monetary Reform*, 1971–1974 (Nelson, 1977).

2. See John Williamson, *The Failure of International Monetary Reform, 1971–74* (Nelson, 1977), p. 37.

3. See Terzian, *OPEC: The Inside Story*.

4. See A. A. Kuburi and S. Mansur, 'The Political Economy of Middle Eastern Oil', in G. R. D. Underhill and R. Stubbs, *Political Economy and the Changing Global Order* (Macmillan, 1994).

5. See V. H. Oppenheim, 'Why Oil Prices Go Up? The Past: We Pushed Them', *Foreign Policy*, 25 (Winter 1976–77). Oppenheim draws upon Nixon's Ambassador in Saudi Arabia, Akin, for her insight into the administration's thinking.

6. See Eric Helleiner, 'Explaining the Globalization of Financial Markets: Bringing States Back In', *Review of International Political Economy*, 2:2 (Spring 1995). This article and others by Helleiner are essential reading on the evolution of financial markets during the last quarter of a century.

7. See Margaret De Vries, *The International Monetary Fund 1972–78, Vol. 1* (International Monetary Fund, 1985).

8. This decision, pushed through by Harold Wilson in 1950 when he was President of the Board of Trade in the Attlee government, was undoubtedly Wilson's major contribution to the history of the world and indeed to the subsequent evolution of British capitalism.

9. Paul Volcker later acknowledged that the recycling of petrodollars by the US banks was 'accompanied by a certain amount of cheerleading by the United States government'. See Gordon Smith and Fohn Cuddington (eds), *International Debt and the Developing Countries* (World Bank, 1985). The word 'cheerleading' is a euphemism for Washington's active role.

10. See Kapstein, who points out that this 1979 US government decision went beyond what any of the US banks themselves had asked for. *Governing the Global Economy: International Finance and the State* (Harvard University Press, 1994).

11. See Kapstein, *Governing the Global Economy*.

12. Helleiner, 'Explaining the Globalization of Financial Markets'.

13. This does not mean that the US commercial banks have been the biggest international banks. For much of the period the Japanese banks and some of the European banks have been bigger. But the money markets of other centres outside New York and London have been much smaller and the American investment banks have played an increasingly dominant role in providing clients with access to these pools of finance.

14. These and other advantages deriving from possession of the dominant currency are known, technically, as seigniorage. For a classic discussion, see Susan Strange, *Sterling and British Policy*. On dollar seigniorage after the destruction of Bretton Woods, see Pier Carlo Padoan, *The Political Economy of International Financial Instability* (Croom Helm, 1986).

15. See Jerry Coakley and Laurence Harris, *The City of Capital* (Blackwell, 1983).

16. See Eric Helleiner, 'The Challenge from the East: Japan's Financial Rise and the Changing Global Order' in P. G. Gerny (ed.), *Finance and World Politics: Markets, Regimes and States in the Post-Hegemonic Era* (Edward Elgar, 1993).

17. The so-called Basle Committee of the BIS drew up a 'concordat' among central banks in December 1975 which was revised in 1983 and again in 1991. It was a gentleman's agreement, which failed to establish clearly 'lender-of-last-resort' responsibilities, supervision of banks' overseas subsidiaries and agencies, reserve requirements and measures for combating fraud.

18. For further details of the Basle Accord, see Kapstein, *Governing the Global Economy*.

19. On the centrality of financial systems for state power, see Jeffrey Winters, 'Power and the Control of Capital', *World Politics*, 46 (Winter 1994). See also Sylvia Maxfield, *Governing Capital: International Finance and Mexican Politics* (Cornell University Press, 1990); and Jung-en Woo, *Race to the Swift: State and Finance in Korean Industrialisation* (Columbia University Press, 1991).

20. Richard N. Cooper, Robert Putnam, Barry Eichengreen, C. Randall Henning and Gerald Holtham, *Can Nations Agree? Issues in International Co-operation* (The Brookings Institution, 1989).

21. See Robert D. Putnam and Nicholas Bayne, *Hanging Together: The Seven-Power Summits* (Heinemann, 1984). They argue that the summits were useful, but make no claim for co-operation on international monetary policy.

22. I. M. Destler and C. Randall Henning, *Dollar Politics: Exchange Rate Policy-making in the United States* (Institute for International Economics,1989).

23. See Andrew Walter, *World Power and World Money* (Harvester Wheatsheaf, 1993).

24. Henry Kaufman, 'Fundamental Precepts Guiding Future Financial Regulation', address to the International Organisation of Securities Commissions, London, 27 October 1992, cited in Kapstein, *Governing the Global Economy*.

25. See Mohsin S. Khan and Nadeem Ul Haque, 'Capital Flight from Developing Countries', *Finance and Development*, 24:4 (March 1987).

26. See statement by C. Randall Henning before the US Senate Committee on the Budget, 21 October 1997.

27. See R. Keohane and J. Nye, *Power and Interdependence* (Little, Brown & Co., 1977).

28. S. D. Krasner, *International Regimes* (Cornell University Press, 1983).

The Evolution of the DWSR
from the 1970s to the 1990s

I   The US Policy for the Evolution of the DWSR from Nixon to 1993

After Nixon the story of US administrations and the DWSR is a mixture of two
strands: first, an extraordinary series of gambles both with the dollar and with
international private finance, in both cases exploiting the regime; and second,
a growing belief in the central importance of the DWSR for US international
interests and attempts to deepen the DWSR and radicalise it. These two
themes both involved an approach of 'America first', but there was no consis-
tent master plan until the 1990s and the Clinton administration. Rather, a
strategic view of the regime's role in a US national strategy emerged gradually,
often in the midst of crises caused by earlier gambles going wrong. At every
stage, American administrations managed to expel the costs of these blunders
outwards on to others and throw themselves into new tactics which had the
effect of deepening the regime. Only in the 1990s, and especially under the
Clinton administration, did a consensus seem to emerge within the American
capitalist class that maybe at last they had discovered a master plan, comprehensive in scope and with all the tactical instruments for its ultimate complete
success. But this too, in the form pursued by the Clinton administration, may
also turn out to be another blundering gamble. Each phase of this story does
not end with the world back where it started. Instead it is marked by a constant
evolution of the inner logic of a DWSR exploited in American interests.

The Carter administration was attempting to use a low dollar to maintain
some sort of growth strategy centred on the industrial sector and on traditional quasi-Keynesian techniques. Between 1975 and 1979 the dollar lost
over a quarter of its value against the yen and the mark as the administration
sought to boost output and exports of the US manufacturing sector. At the
same time, apart from its interest in using the flexible dollar-price for industrial policy, the Carter administration was indifferent to the potentialities of
developing or exploiting the DWSR.

Matters changed only with the Reagan administration. The shift in dollar policy had begun before Reagan's election. Worried that the dollar's fall might slip out of control and worried about rising inflation combined with industrial overcapacity, Federal Reserve Chairman Volcker made his famous turn, jacking up interest rates, swinging towards a strong dollar and a drive to restore money's role as a stable standard of value (rather than just as an inflationary means of circulation). These steps were taken much further by the Reagan administration.

The central features of the Reaganite turn in matters of political economy were twofold: first, to put money-capital in the policy saddle for the first time in decades; and secondly to extend and exploit the DWSR in the interests of America First. Putting money-capital in the saddle involved squeezing out inflation (which eroded royalties on money-capital), taking steps to deregulate the banking and financial sector, offering huge tax cuts for the rich which always boost the financial sector and rentier activity and pursuing a high dollar policy. Industrial growth would be driven principally by a great expansion of the defence budget, running an expanding budget deficit and sucking in capital from abroad. This aspect of policy essentially meant that the US state was acting as a surrogate export market for the industrial sector. The new dominance of money-capital and the anti-inflation drive was essentially an incentive to employers of capital to begin an assault on the power, rights and security of their workers to restore profitability.

But Reagan's team also began to seek to deepen the DWSR, initially as a pragmatic set of solutions to discrete problems. Thus, maintaining a very high dollar could have meant chokingly high US domestic interest rates unless the US government could attract very large inward flows of funds into US financial markets. To achieve such flows, it began a drive to get rid of capital controls in other OECD countries, especially Japan and Western Europe. Thus began a long campaign to dismantle capital controls.

The first decision of the Thatcher administration on coming into office in 1979 had been to end British controls over financial movements. Holland followed in 1981 and Chancellor Kohl swiftly did the same in 1982 on coming into office. A major breakthrough for the campaign came with the French government's decision in 1984 to promote the idea of the European Single Market: this was above all a decision to remove controls on financial movements throughout Western Europe. Denmark liberalised in 1988, Italy started a phased liberalisation in the same year and France started phasing out capital controls in 1989.[1] During the 1980s, the US pressured the Japanese government with some success to liberalise its restrictions on the free exit and entry of funds. This was a major step in boosting the size and weight of the Anglo-American financial markets.

At the same time, the turn to the high dollar/high interest rates posture from the Volcker shift in 1979 set the stage for the Latin American and East

Central European debt crises of the early 1980s. Volcker did not raise interest rates and support a high dollar in order to produce this crisis. It nearly produced a collapse in the US banking system, but in the course of managing the crisis, the Reaganites, who were very interested in bringing Third World capitalisms to heel, learned some very powerful lessons. They learned an old truth from the days of European imperialism: the imperial power could take advantage of a country's debt crisis to reorganise its internal social relations of production in such a way as to favour the penetration of its own capitals into that country. Thus started the use of the DWSR to open countries' domestic financial regimes and domestic product markets to American operators. The second lesson, learnt by American financial operators, was that the kinds of long or medium-term syndicated bank loans used for recycling the petrodollars was too rigid since it locked the funds of these banks up in the fates of the borrowing countries. Therefore they sought to shift towards much safer operations with interest-bearing capital: lending through bonds from which they could withdraw by trading them on the securities markets. They also learnt that they could get crisis-ridden target countries to build domestic stock markets and could start to play these as a profitable way to earn royalties. But these kinds of operations would require removing the controls on the capital accounts of such countries. Yet another fundamental lesson from the Latin American crisis was a very important paradox: financial crisis in a country of the South could actually boost Wall Street through capital flight. When a financial crisis hit a country, large funds would flee not only that country but others fearing contagion and the funds would flee to the Anglo-American financial nexus, boosting liquidity, lowering interest rates and having a generally healthy impact.

And the final, and in some ways most important lesson was that the IMF/WB were not, after all, a waste of time for American capitalism. With the establishment of the DWSR, the IMF was elbowed out of the way by the US Treasury and the US financial markets and seemed headed for history's proverbial dustbin. Reagan came in with no intention of reviving it. As for the World Bank, the Reaganites viewed it as a semi-subversive institution, saturated with old-style quasi-Keynesian 1950s US 'development' nonsense. But Reagan's Treasury Secretary, James Baker, learnt in the debt crisis just what a powerful tool these bodies could be as façade-cosmopolitan agencies for advancing the interests of American capitalism. Thus from the unveiling of the so-called Baker Plan for generalised 'Structural Adjustment' in Seoul in 1985 the IMF/WB found themselves with new international roles.

It is important to note how they have served above all US interests: they have not done so mainly through conspiratorial manipulation (which does not mean, of course, that there were no conspiracies – there were no doubt lots – hence the extraordinary veil of secrecy surrounding their decision-making). Instead their role has rested on two mechanisms: first, by defending the integrity of the international financial system, the IMF was defending a system of US exploitation of the DWSR. Second, by restructuring domestic economies to enable them to pay off their debts, the WB was adapting them to the same US-centred international system: the necessities of its structure pushed them towards domestic deflation, currency devaluation and an export drive along with measures to ease budget deficits and earn foreign currency on the capital account by privatising with the help of foreign capital and attracting inward flows of hard-currency funds through liberalising the capital account. Thus did US rentiers get their debts paid, US industry got cheaper imports of the inputs needed for production, US companies could buy up assets including privatised utilities in the country concerned, and the capital account would be liberalised so that local stock markets could be played. And the whole system could be made even more rule-based by the fact that neoclassical economics supplies us with hundreds of rules and norms and almost all of them are never quite operating in any country at any time. So the IMF and WB could simply pick and choose whichever aspect of a domestic economy they wanted to concentrate change upon and could always point to some rule or norm of neoclassical economics that was not being met!

Just as the Nixon–Ford–Carter phase left a hangover for the Reaganites, so the Reagan period left a hangover for Bush: this time the huge double deficits on the balance of payments and the deficit and no money in the kitty for exerting influence over the Soviet Bloc region as it collapsed, especially because of the domestic speculative blow-out in the housing sector of the financial system. But the dialectics of progress through blundering gambles continued to work since the debt crisis had produced a development of the DWSR which could be exploited by the US to overcome its weaknesses in its efforts to dominate developments in Russia and Eastern Europe. The IMF-World Bank Structural Adjustment sub-system could be imposed upon the region with the claim that it was the new global development paradigm and not an ad hoc device for serving US interests in the Latin American crisis. Bush showed great skill in persuading the West Europeans to knuckle under to IMF (US Treasury) leadership over the transition in the East, and the result was to perpetuate and strengthen the reach of the DWSR, giving great scope for US financial operators to link up with the ex-nomenklaturas of the region in orgies of speculative, corrupt and extremely profitable ventures, through privatisations, through using local stock markets as playthings in the hands of US investment banks, through using dollars to buy huge quantities of assets in Russia and elsewhere, through earning extraordinarily high yields on East European government debt in the bond markets, through enormous injections of (largely criminal) East European flight capital into the Anglo-American markets and through, at every turn, taking large, juicy fees for services rendered. It was, all in all, a remarkable success story, especially given the fact that the catastrophic costs of the whole enterprise lie in far-away Eastern Europe as a problem which the West Europeans have to try to contain, no doubt with the help of NATO.

At the time that Clinton became President in 1993 the DWSR had thus sustained itself for a full twenty years. The dollar was still the overwhelmingly dominant international currency and the weight of Wall Street in the international economy was far greater than it had been in the 1970s. The various kinds of boundaries which had existed between national financial and economic systems and the Wall Street-centred international financial markets had been eroded and in some countries almost entirely swept away. And the linkages between countries in the former Eastern Bloc and the South with Wall Street had been greatly strengthened through debt dependence, while the form of that debt dependence was changing from one based upon long or medium-term bank loans to one based upon debt securities or short-term loans – a form of dependence far more vulnerable to short-term movements in the Wall Street securities markets. Alongside these developments the other main feature of the regime's evolution was the increasingly important role of the IMF as a public authority for managing the effects of the regime on countries of the South and former Eastern Bloc. The IMF was not acting as a public authority *above all states* but as a public authority for transmitting the policy of the states controlling it – which meant, above all, the USA – into the states in varying degrees of crisis as a result of the regime's operations.

During the Clinton administration, as we shall see, there would be a drive to radicalise the DWSR, both to sweep away the barriers between the Wall Street-centred international financial markets and states and to impose a new set of restrictions on the domestic actions of states. There would also be a dramatic attempt to radicalise the way the US government used the DWSR for the purposes of national economic statecraft. But before examining the Clinton period we will briefly survey the impact of the DWSR on the rest of the international political economy during the period from the 1970s to the early 1990s.

II   The Responses of Political Economies to the DWSR

Up to now we have concentrated only upon the role of the US in the DWSR. But we must briefly survey the responses of the other main components of the world economy to this system since its launch in the 1970s.

During the post-war period, the core of the world economy was made up of a German-centred Western Europe and Japan, along with North America. The revival of the capitalisms at the two opposite ends of Eurasia had followed very different patterns from the angle of international political economy. Germany's revival was built upon the development of deepening regional links within Western Europe. Japan's revival took place largely in isolation and through deepening links with first the American and then also with the West European markets. Thus the move towards the Dollar–Wall Street system in the 1970s had very different impacts upon these two non-American centres, as we shall see. Neither the leaders of German capitalism nor those of Japan welcomed or approved of either the inauguration or the evolution of the DWSR nor of the various ways in which the US has sought to exploit it. On the other hand, in both regions the DWSR has had its supporters and even enthusiasts, especially, of course, in countries like Britain and Holland with powerful financial sectors and amongst those most closely involved with private international finance.

Germany and Western Europe

Both Western Europe and Japan were, of course, extremely hostile to and worried by the international monetary chaos inaugurated by the DWSR in the early 1970s. The West European responses developed along four axes. First a defensive response to the regime in the monetary field by building a new regional monetary regime in Western Europe: the exchange rate mechanism, leading towards a full monetary union. Secondly, a shift towards a new accumulation strategy which placed money-capital in dominance over employers of capital. Thirdly, an attempt to exploit the DWSR internationally; and fourthly, an intra-European conflict over the role of rentier capitalism within Western European society. We will look at each of these strands in turn.

1) The regional monetary regime

Without a defensive regional response to the DWSR the development of the European Community towards a customs union would have been destroyed by chaotic intra-European currency movements which would have made a mockery of intra-European free trade. So Germany was able to persuade its main West European partners to manage their currencies under deutschmark leadership. In this way, monetary stability could be maintained within Western Europe. The mark would be the point of contact between the West European economy and the wild dollar. And German governments in the 1970s were prepared to claim that their leadership would be just a phase on the road to full monetary union (as the French wanted). Despite a very shaky start in the 1970s and various crises in the 1980s and 1990s, this system has held.

The Soviet Bloc collapse raised uncertainty about this system, through raising uncertainty about the future direction of German capitalism.

Chancellor Kohl responded with the decision to maintain the regional arrangements by deepening them into full monetary union. This decision has held.[2]

2) Free financial flows and the new centrality of money-capital

A number of West European states sought to maintain the Keynesian mode of accumulation in which industrial capital's expansion was the central target of policy. The French socialist government attempted this in the early 1980s. This effort was frustrated not least because of the Reagan administration's economic statecraft. It used the high dollar and high interest rates as a weapon against the French project.[3] The failure of the French project led the Mitterrand government to accept the scrapping of controls on international financial movements as part of a wider strategy (the single market and the achievement of monetary union). With a policy framework consisting of fixed exchange rates and free movement of finance, West European governments except Germany's lost most of their control over monetary policy to the private financial markets of Europe.[4] When European governments declared that 'globalisation' had meant that they had lost the ability to steer their domestic economies as before, they actually meant that their determination to subordinate domestic economic management to fixed European exchange rates and free movement of finance was what was tying their hands domestically. This shift brought about a similarity in domestic macroeconomic priorities between Western Europe and the USA: the priority of low inflation, maintaining money's role as a fixed standard of value in the interests of money-capital and pushing employers of capital to engage in labour-shedding activity and downward pressure on wage costs. This was the real basis for the inauguration of Atlantic neo-liberalism.

3) The attempt to exploit the DWSR internationally

At the same time, Western European capital, faced with domestic long-term stagnation over the last quarter of a century, was able to exploit the possibilities offered by the DWSR to turn outwards beyond the core in search of new fields of accumulation. It was thus able to live with and benefit from the use of this regime to open economies elsewhere, and to live with US leadership of the regime.

4) The conflict over the role of the rentier sector

Although the power of money-capital within the balance of money-capitalists/employers of capital was sharply shifted by the changes described above, most governments in Western Europe did not go along with the idea of dismantling the entire institutional framework for controlling their financial systems and their interfaces with the productive sector. Attempts were made to maintain a financial structure centred on large, regulated banks, relatively small securities markets and very large parts of the financial system in state hands. In doing so they faced growing competitive pressures from deregulated Anglo-American operators and a growing chorus of propaganda to transfer all those parts of the financial system connected to funding health, pensions and welfare programmes into the private sector under rentier control. The propaganda campaign had a strongly anti-workerist edge to appeal to employers of capital to reduce their tax burdens by favouring the privatisation of these parts of the financial system. But the capitalist classes of Western Europe generally maintained resistance to this campaign, partly for political reasons (fear of future domestic political vulnerability to revolts) and partly because such moves would enormously increase the opportunities for Anglo-American financial operators to acquire sway over their productive sectors as well as their financial sectors.[5] The battles over these issues were fought out mainly between the German and British governments over alternative approaches towards the regulation of investment banks (merchant banks, in traditional British parlance). In late 1992 a compromise EU directive on investment services and capital adequacy standards was adopted, one which favours greater liberalisation in this area.

Thus the spontaneous dynamics of the Euroland region will lead to the hollowing-out of the nexus of institutional barriers to the triumph of the rentiers because the regional regime is constructed for a competition between regulatory authorities that ensures that the least regulated operators in the financial sector win. Without a strong political authority in Euroland its euro shield against the dollar will be shielding a financial system and productive sector under the increasing sway of Wall Street and American business.

Japan

Japan found itself in a far more vulnerable position for coping with the new monetary chaos that arose in the 1970s. Because of its dependence upon the US market, it faced one American-induced adjustment crisis after another, has been subjected to great political pressure to establish a managed trade regime with the US and constant attempts by the US to interfere with its internal social relations of production. Attempts to diversify into the West European market met with strong EU opposition, only partially overcome through the British back door. The very dependence of the American state upon Japanese financial flows into New York only fuelled the growth of an aggressive trend in US public opinion towards Japan. By succumbing to US pressures in the late 1980s to loosen Japanese domestic economic policy, the Japanese government found itself unleashing the kind of enormous bubble in its financial system that German governments had always managed to repudiate, and the bursting of the bubble at the start of the 1990s plunged the Japanese domestic economy into a long stagnation from which it has not recovered.

Yet in the second half of the 1980s, Japanese elites did start to develop a new accumulation strategy: the development of a strong regional network in East and South-East Asia and one not based on West European-style neo-mercantilist regional trade policy, but rather on the export of productive capital into the region to boost regional growth – the kind of policy so obviously lacking in West European policy towards Eastern and East Central Europe or for that matter in American policy towards Latin America. Through this strategy, Japanese capital could cope with the wild swings of the dollar: a high dollar gave scope for the Japanese domestic base, while a low dollar gave scope for the regional bases of Japanese and Japanese-linked capital to flourish since these economies had exchange rates largely tied to the dollar. The regional economies in turn were exporting to North America and Europe as well as developing intra-regional trade and financial flows.

This Japanese defensive strategy meshed with the already strong growth in East and South-East Asia and greatly reinforced that growth. The result was to create an entirely new *growth centre* within the world economy and one which has acted like a magnet for capital throughout the rest of the core economies in the 1990s. Thus, the regionalist response of Japanese capitalism to the Dollar–Wall Street system was a stunningly successful one from the point of view of spontaneous economic rationality. Japan was creating a great virtuous circle of dynamic accumulation between its own capitals and East and South-East Asia. In purely regional terms this was a far more dynamic solution than that found by German capitalism within the West European arena. But there was also a dimension of great vulnerability. German governments had been able to construct a strong politico-monetary shield in the form of a Monetary Union and a mass political idea (European unity), both of which the capitalist classes of Germany's European neighbours shared. But Japan's regional strategy had no such politico-monetary counterpart. If Germany had, in this field, something like the shield of Achilles, Japan was left with his heel: most of the region in the dollar zone and thus a split in the political-monetary centre of the regional strategy; and no political bloc in the region at either the level of dominant social groups or a popular level. Instead, the region was riven with political suspicions and legacies of earlier hostilities: between China and Japan, between Korea and Japan, between China and Taiwan, etc. etc. While Western Europe had overcome hostilities at least as deep, partly with

American support in the early postwar years, no such evolution had occurred in Japan's regional hinterland.

The Bifurcation of the South

During the long boom in the postwar period the countries of the South on the whole also experienced high rates of growth: fifty of these countries had average growth rates of over 3 per cent per year between 1960 and 1975.[6] Total factor productivity growth was particularly high in the Middle East and Latin America: 2.3 and 1.8 per cent respectively – a better performance than East Asia whose annual productivity growth was only 1.3 per cent.

With the start of the Dollar–Wall Street Regime and the oil crisis, a bifurcation began on the basis of one criterion: how well the state concerned coped with the volatile and often savage dynamics of the new Dollar–Wall Street Regime. With the oil shocks and the onset of stagnation in the core, the overwhelming majority of countries of the South experienced strain on the current account. They could either borrow massively abroad under the new Dollar–Wall Street Regime, or they could make sharp domestic internal macroeconomic adjustments, tightening fiscal policy and devaluing their currencies. Borrowing abroad was the easy option: the Anglo-American banking systems were eager, as we have seen, to lend and borrowing allowed these states to avoid the domestic social conflict that macroeconomic adjustment required.

It is important to stress that borrowing from Wall Street was not only easy, it was *economically rational* for governments in the circumstances of the 1970s. In 1983, US Deputy Secretary of State Elinor Constable explained to Congress how US government policy created the conditions that would make governments in the South pursuing current economic rationality want to steer a course towards disaster: 'Our policy did not focus on the need to adjust. Rather, our primary concern was the encouragement of efficient "recycling" of the OPEC surplus – a euphemism for the assurance that countries would be able to borrow as much as they needed. The incentive to borrow rather than to adjust was strong. Interest rates were low or negative in relation to current and expected inflation; liquidity was abundant; and both borrowers and lenders expected that continued inflation would lead to ever-increasing export revenues and reduce the real burden of foreign debt.'[7] The critical failure on the part of the borrowing governments was to fashion economic policy within a framework of current economic rationality rather than grasping that the entire macroeconomic framework they faced could be transformed by *political decisions about the dollar price and interest rates of the US government transmitted through the world economy by the DWSR.*

Those countries which took the borrowing course – in the Middle East, Latin America and parts of the Soviet Bloc (especially Poland and Hungary, as well as Yugoslavia) – were then trapped in debt crises and long stagnations of fifteen years or more as they were dragged through the 'structural adjustment' ringer of the IMF/WB. Those countries which undertook internal adjustment and avoided the debt trap were mainly in East Asia and were able to weather the onset of the new regime and continued to grow.[8] Others were dragged down by the DWSR into a systemically induced series of financial blow-outs. During the 1970s, the number of financial crises never rose above five countries per year. Between 1980 and 1995 the number fell below five per year only in two years (1988 and 1989) and in some years the numbers ran at over ten countries per year. According to the IMF, two thirds of all its members have experienced severe financial crises since 1980, some more than once.[9]

It is important to underline one point about this experience. The ideologists of the DWSR claim that the debt crisis of the Latin American countries (and states in Eastern Europe) was *caused by* the bankruptcy of their earlier import-substituting development strategies involving large state sectors and protectionism. Thus, they had to embrace a new strategic paradigm – the so-called 'free market' one. Yet as Dani Rodrick has shown, the debt crisis and the attendant domestic financial crises in these countries had been caused *not* by their import-substituting, statist accumulation strategies – in mainstream terms these are *microeconomic* development devices – but by their government's failures of *macroeconomic* policy adjustment to the impact of the oil price rises and the new monetary-financial system of the 1970s. As Rodrick explains, Import Substituting Industrialisation (ISI) 'brought unprecedented economic growth to scores of countries in Latin America, the Middle East and North Africa, and even to some in Sub-Saharan Africa' for two decades. '. . . when the economies of these same countries began to fall apart in the second half of the 1970s, the reasons had very little to do with ISI policies per se or the extent of government interventions. Countries that weathered the storm were those in which governments undertook the appropriate *macroeconomic* adjustments (in the areas of fiscal, monetary and exchange rate policy) rapidly and decisively.'[10]

Thus, the real pattern of causality in the transformations following the adoption of the Dollar–Wall Street Regime was as follows: a successful development *strategy* faced sudden, large challenges to macroeconomic *tactics* produced by the orchestrated chaos of the new international monetary-financial regime. The macroeconomic tactical failure led to terrible currency and financial crises and these enabled Washington to impose a new strategic model on these countries. This model was then claimed to be a superior strategy to an earlier failed strategy. Yet the new model was nothing more than a combination of ad hoc solutions to pay off US banks plus a new vulnerability to the dynamics of US capitalism.

That this was indeed the case became starkly clear when the showcase of the new model, after a decade of stagnation and a short phase of growth, suddenly plunged into another terrible financial crisis: the Mexican crisis of 1994–95. Because, as a result of the usual ideological mechanisms, the high priests of the Washington Consensus really believed their new model was superior to the ISI model, as 'proved' by the earlier debt crisis, they genuinely could not notice Mexico's extreme vulnerability and fragility and the blow-out was a great shock. But its warning that the so-called Economic Reform free market model was a path only to increased vulnerability in the future was simply brushed aside. *It had to be a good model* because it was the *only model that fitted with the facts of a DWSR to which the biggest economy in the world, American capitalism, was increasingly hooked.*[11]

These crises, then, bifurcated the South into two zones: the new dependencies of the DWSR and the new growth centre in East and South-East Asia. The new dependencies themselves contained strong internal differentiations, between political economies which entered a path towards social disintegration (much of Africa) and others which entered a path of stagnation, punctuated by fitful growth (most of Latin America and the Middle East).

The story of the new, post-1980s dependencies has been one of chronic financial instability and stagnation, punctuated by fitful growth and further financial blow-outs. Since 1980, serious financial crises have been happening in one country after another, *seriatim* and affecting two thirds of the members of the IMF at least once. Each time, the Anglo-American media of the DWSR try to entertain us with juicy stories, full of local colour and details of local incompetence, corruption or whatever that just happened to cause each individual one of over half the countries of the world to turn out to be a basket case. But after a while these stories begin to pall as we realise that all the countries of the world seem full of corruption and incompetence causing blow-outs, while at the same time the same media assure us that the world as a whole is doing tremendously well, except for one country at a time!

As a percentage of GDP these financial crises can be extremely costly, especially where they take the form of crises at the heart of the banking system: in the Argentinian crisis 1980–82 these costs amounted to no less than 55.3 per cent of GDP; in Chile, 1981–83, 41 per cent; in Uruguay 1981–84, 31.2 per cent in; Israel 1980–83, 30 per cent and in Mexico 1994–95, 13.5 per cent.[12] The IMF has played a central role in distributing those costs, doing so in the active service of the United States but with the passive acceptance of the other G3 states.

East Central and Eastern Europe

The record of these countries under the DWSR since 1990 is overwhelmingly the same story of tragedy as that of most of Latin America in the 1980s. The propagandists of the DWSR have every reason to congratulate themselves on introducing capitalism into a number of these countries, given just how terrible the experience has been for the bulk of the population of the region. Ten years after the process started only one country, Poland, has clawed itself back to its statistical GDP per capita of 1989. And the deep gloom across the horizon of the entire region has been lifted only by flashes of lightning from financial crises, exploding in one country after another.

The New Growth Centre

The new growth centre in East and South-East Asia included China, South Korea, Taiwan and increasingly also the countries further south. They were unified not by the fact that they all shared the same internal development model but by the fact that their macroeconomic tactics enabled them to survive the new international regime of the 1970s, by the fact that they had access to the American market and, in the late 1980s, by the fact that many of them could enjoy an expanding influx not of hot money from New York but of productive investment from Tokyo. They constituted a new growth centre not in the sense that they had strong growth rates but in a much more fundamental sense: they were the one large centre of dynamic, sustained capital accumulation in the entire world.

At the start of the 1980s, the region (excluding Japan, Australia and New Zealand) accounted for only one sixth of world output. But by the mid-1990s it accounted for about one quarter of world GDP on purchasing power parity-adjusted terms. If this trend had continued, the region would have accounted for one third of world output by the year 2005. By adding Japan to the aggregate we can see that the centre of the entire world economy was, for the first time in about 500 years, shifting out of the control of the Atlantic region.

Similarly, over the last decade the developing countries of Asia have seen their share of world exports nearly double, to about one fifth of the total. These countries are also taking a growing share of industrial country exports, a factor that helped cushion the impact of successive recessions in the Atlantic area during 1990–93. During the 1990s to 1997, the region accounted for some two thirds of new global investment and for about half of the total growth of world GDP growth. Thus it was becoming increasingly important as a direct stimulator of the economies of the Atlantic world.

And it was achieving these results without clashing with the international logics of the Dollar–Wall Street Regime and the Anglo-American rentier interests entrenched within that regime. Thus Michel Camdessus liked to stress the wonderful opportunities offered by some of the stock markets of the region to western rentier capital: for example, in Hong Kong, Malaysia, and Singapore, stock market capitalisation, as a share of GDP, exceeds that of France, Germany, and Italy.[13] He also, of course, would make the spurious claim that the inflows of speculative Atlantic funds into these securities markets in the 1990s were a kind of net aid for the development of productive capital in the region. The reality was exactly the reverse; in his Per Jacobsson Lecture to the assembled central bankers and government officials in Hong Kong for the IMF/WB meetings in September 1997, the Chief Executive of the Hong Kong Monetary Authority explained the situation as follows:

> 'Much of Asian savings, in particular official sector savings and private sector savings that have been institutionalised, are still invested in assets of OECD countries . . . insofar as Hong Kong is concerned, in excess of 95 per cent of our US$85 billion of foreign reserves are invested outside Asia. Specifically, in the management of our foreign reserves, we work against a preferred neutral position of about 75 per cent in US dollar assets, mostly in US Treasury securities. I understand also that more than 80 per cent of total Asian foreign exchange reserves amounting to US$600 billion are invested largely in North America and Europe . . . It can be argued therefore that Asia is financing much of the budget deficits of developed economies, particularly the United States, but has to try hard to attract money back into the region through foreign investments. And the volatility of foreign portfolio investments has been a major cause of disruptions to the monetary and financial systems of the Asian economies. Some have even gone so far as to say that the Asian economies are providing the funding to hedge funds in non-Asian countries to play havoc with their currencies and financial markets. This comment is perhaps a little unkind . . . But *there certainly is a problem with the effectiveness of financial intermediation in this region, which is inhibiting the flow of long term savings into long term investment.*'[14]

The American Political Economy

The construction of the DWSR has had important feedback effects on the US financial system and economy, while endogenous US developments have exerted important and growing effects upon trends within the DWSR.

The American financial system has had one structural feature which has made it very different from almost every other capitalist system: the extraordinary fragmentation of its banking system. Whereas almost every other capitalist system tends to have large, national retail banks dominating the credit system and having a close inter-relationship with the state at a central level, this has not been the pattern in the United States.[15] In the changing economic conditions of the last quarter of a century, new forces have emerged in the American financial system, filling what one might describe as the void left by the fragmentation of the banks. And as these new forces have arisen, they have escaped from the kinds of regulation needed to prevent the most dangerous kinds of vulnerability from becoming pervasive.[16] We can list a number of the most significant changes.

First, there has been a dramatic decline in the role of the commercial banks in the supply of credit to the productive sector, with the rise of the so-called mutual funds. These organisations offered credit to companies in the form of bonds instead of bank loans. The company would issue bonds bought by the mutual funds. The mutual funds can then offer savers a higher rate of interest on their deposits than the banks could. The depositors would benefit also through the diversification of the mutual funds' holdings of bonds and other securities (paper claims for royalties that can be bought and sold in financial market places). Thus the supply of money-capital to American employers came to be tied in to the rise and fall of prices on the securities markets. And the savings of Americans of all classes came also to be tied in to price movements on these markets. The scale of the funds in these mutual funds has soared until it is as large, if not larger than the deposits within the entire American banking system.

The second major trend has been the breaking down of the walls between different sectors of finance. The rise of the mutual funds was followed by banks being able to develop their own mutual fund operations and thus become more and more involved in stock market trading. The American Savings and Loans institutions (the equivalent of Building Societies) were deregulated so that they could trade in securities and start acting like commercial banks. And in these ways the entire American financial system has been sucked into the vortex of the securities markets, a formula for opening the financial system to strong speculative pressures.

The third major change has been the development of a very large range of new types of securities. Mortgage contracts, for example, have become tradable bits of paper. So-called junk bonds with very high interest rates, used to amass huge quantities of funds for buying out companies, became very popular. And a whole new tier of securities, called derivatives, has grown enormously. They involve trading in securities whose prices are derived from the movements in prices in other, primary securities or currencies. The great bulk of derivatives trading is unregulated because it takes place 'over the counter' (OTC) between two institutions, rather than through regulated exchanges. One important effect of the growth of derivatives trading is that it links together price movements in one market – say, shares or bonds – with price movements in another – say foreign exchange. Shocks in one market thereby become much more contagious to other markets than in the past.

The fourth major change has been the rise of the hedge funds. The name is a euphemism: these are speculator organisations for making money through the buying and selling of securities on their own account to exploit price movements over time and price differences between markets. The biggest of these hedge funds are not marginal speculators. They are the offspring of the very biggest of the investment banks and the mutual funds. Hedge funds are not necessarily called by that name. Thus Goldman Sachs, which is a partnership, is largely a hedge fund: in other words the bulk of its profits in 1996 and 1997 derived from speculative trading on its own account. Salomon Brothers was also, in essence, a hedge fund. Since the banks are not allowed to engage in speculative activity, their managers have helped to establish hedge funds that *are* allowed to do so, because they are not banks but partnerships, often registered off-shore for tax-dodging purposes. The biggest of the banks then lend huge sums of money to what are, in effect, their creations, in order that the hedge funds can play the markets with truly enormous resources. This scale of resources is vitally important because it enables the speculator to shift prices in the market in the direction he wants the prices to move in through the sheer scale of the funds involved.

We will return to this issue of market power later. But it is important to stress the capacity of the hedge funds to use huge loans from the banks and from mutual funds to play the markets. These borrowings are known, in the jargon, as 'leverage'. According to IMF studies, hedge funds can be using, at any one time, loans twenty times their own capital. Soros, boss of one of the biggest funds, has said he was able to gain leverage fifty times his capital for his operations. But it now turns out that Long Term Capital Management was able to be leveraged 250 times its own capital. With a capital base of $2.5 billion it could, in other words, wield about $600 billion of funds. If we bear in mind that the total capital of US hedge funds in 1997 was estimated to be about $300 billion and assume that average leverage is fifty times the capital base, we get a total financial power of a staggering $15,000 billion – a speculative strike force of this dimension or larger has thus been built up at the very heart of the American system. And it is a force which is completely unregulated.

The final structural change in the US financial system during the last quarter of a century has been an enormous growth in its exchanges with the rest of the world. All the key players in the domestic market – the mutual funds, investment and commercial banks and the hedge funds – have become more or less heavily involved in international business. The most dynamic sector of growth has been the foreign exchange market and the foreign exchange derivatives markets, which are overwhelmingly unregulated OTC markets. At the same time there have been huge growths in the flows of funds into and out of the American financial markets from around the world and the big American institutions have spread their offices across the globe as other financial markets have been pushed open.

Two general conclusions can be drawn from this brief summary: first, the securities markets in the United States have become very large in terms of the volumes of business which take place in them in normal times. This gives them a quality which is highly prized by the holders of interest-bearing capital: the markets are, in normal times, highly liquid – in other words, anyone wanting to sell and leave the market can normally do so very easily, just as anyone wanting to buy can easily find a seller. But the second conclusion is that the inner structure of the whole financial system has become strategically very vulnerable to crisis. All the accumulated experience of credit systems under capitalism points to the fact that the American financial markets are far more vulnerable to a hideous collapse as a result of the disintegration of the regulatory order, the increasing centrality of the securities markets, the huge growth of extremely risky new types of securities and the extraordinary rise to dominance within the whole system of speculative funds. Even in the banking sector where stronger regulatory supervision is supposed to prevail, this control seems to have largely broken down. One recent survey found that only three out of 100 US banks were observing the regulatory rules fully.

The question therefore arises as to why the American state has allowed this set of developments to occur and continue unchecked. The most straightforward answer as to why this extraordinary strategic vulnerability has been allowed to spread through the US financial system is that the regulators themselves are closely linked to the big speculators. The US Treasury Secretary Robert Rubin is himself a speculator by profession, since he comes from the management of Goldman Sachs. Greenspan at the Federal Reserve has spent his whole life playing the markets when not in government. Federal Reserve Board members move continually through revolving doors between Washington and trading on the markets. This explanation no doubt contains an important truth, yet so much is at stake that one might expect the other areas of will formation within the American state to step in and assert control: the Presidency and Congress, for example.

A second explanation might be that these other instances of government have themselves become dependent upon the financial operators for campaign funds: they have in large measure become the cronies of Wall Street. This is factually true. As Rothkopf has demonstrated, Democratic Party Chairman Ron Brown pointed out to Clinton the importance of developing economic policies that would appeal to Wall Street in order to tap into huge pools of potential campaign funds there.[17] This again, no doubt, has force, but there are other immensely powerful centres of American capitalism outside the financial markets, which would surely cavil if the decisive control of the political establishment had been *captured* by speculative finance.

Yet another explanation might be that all the strategic social groups within American society have themselves been captured by the institutional dynamics of the financial markets. The income and wealth of the managements of the big corporations have become tied to future prices on the stock and bond markets, they have invested their savings in the investment banks, mutual and hedge funds and have been restructuring their own corporations to make the augmentation of 'share-holder value' their governing goal. And American workers also have come to rely upon the securities markets for their pensions, health care and even their wages, which have been increasingly combining cash with securities. Any regulatory drive would inevitably have a depressive effect on current activities and would therefore cut off the politicians involved in pushing for the regulation from important and broadly based political constituencies.

This political barrier is then powerfully buttressed by the rentier ideology of laissez-faire and free markets. But the power of ideology should not be exaggerated. The lives of workers in modern capitalism are tied to capital not only through the wage relation, but also through the savings relation. If the savings relation is mediated through the state, as in Western Europe, workers' security is less tied to market developments and rentier interests. But if the savings relation is in the direct control of private financial markets, then workers themselves acquire a rentier interest.

Such does, indeed, seem to be the political situation within the United States in the 1990s. It is in large part the result of the attempts by successive administrations to exploit the DWSR in supposed American capitalist interests. Whether it has strengthened the foundations of US capitalism relative to others we shall explore below. But it has had spreading narcotic and addictive effects through the US domestic political economy and has greatly encouraged the drift towards financial vulnerability.

And with the arrival of the Clinton administration the evolved DWSR has become more than an instrument for gaining quantitative molecular gains from US financial and monetary dominance. It has become radicalised as the activist programme for establishing a world imperium and it has also found its place at the very heart of the Clinton administration's political strategy for world order.

III   The DWSR and the Dynamics of Domestic Socioeconomic and Ideological Change

This account of the impact of the DWSR on political economies has at every stage pointed towards the way the regime, through the mediation of political economies, transforms socioeconomic structures within the states of the world. It does so by generating social conflicts within states, conflicts which the DWSR ensures do not take place on a level playing field: certain social groups within a state can exploit the DWSR in crisis situations in order to strengthen their domestic, political and social positions.

We can present the pattern very schematically: when a financial crisis occurs, certain social groups can gain from IMF/WB restructuring proposals. Money-capital can escape to Wall Street and the restructuring package will tend to strengthen its domestic social position; privatisations of state industries to restore state finances again benefit those sectors of the capital class with access to large funds of money. Export sectors can benefit from the restructuring package as well, and capital as a whole finds in the IMF package a way of imposing its rule over other, subordinate social groups. The sectors of domestic capital that are weakened are those engaged in import-substitution, while those supplying staple products for domestic markets will tend to be taken over by foreign multinationals provided with new access to domestic assets by the IMF package.

None of these outcomes is *automatic*: they depend upon domestic political struggles between social groups, political struggles whose outcome depends upon the political structure of a state and the balance of political forces within it at the time of the crisis. And despite the IMF/WB efforts to impose a one-size-fits-all standardised package, the exact algebraic forms (not to speak of the arithmetic ones) of these outcomes will vary from one state to another. To take an obvious example, there have been great variations in the algebra of privatisations in the former Soviet Bloc. And the impact of the outcome within the society is typically a new round of social and political conflict involving a backlash against the outcome. That is why the social and institutional engineers of the IMF/WB make great efforts to ensure that the package is robust against expected backlashes.[18]

Nevertheless, the general trend has been one of at least partial success in social transformation for the alliances of domestic social groups and the IMF/WB. This does not of course mean sustained macroeconomic success – far from it: new crises are typically just around the next bend in the road. But whatever the government thrown up by the backlash, it will face a new social balance of forces in its society and one which it will largely have to accept if it wishes to avoid new financial turmoil – panicking the markets. Thus a deepening social transformation of the internal social dynamics of states is produced by the DWSR.

These changes then feed back on to transnational ideological life. The deepening transnational social *Gleichschaltung* generates an increasing international convergence in the field of ideology, whose highest expression is the 'Washington Consensus'. The origins of the consensus at first sight appear to be a mystery. It is presented as the result of a purely intellectual learning curve: how people have learnt that so-called statist strategies do not work or do not work as well as 'free market' rentier strategies. Yet this explanation for the consensus cannot be true, since the old statist strategies seemed to work better in the past than the new free market strategies have worked in the contemporary period (the last quarter of a century). And the only really dynamic economies in the recent period have been those of East and South-East Asia, some of which have had highly statist strategic mechanisms.

The truth, of course, lies in turning the relation between the ideal and the material upside down: it was not the Washington Consensus idea that taught people to transform social relations; it was the material transformations of social relations which produced the power of the Washington Consensus idea. And the whole process was driven not by a quasi-legal regime of rules and norms and principles in an issue area, but by the mighty material forces of money and finance in the DWSR. As soon as this transnational socioeconomic regime started to crack so too would its reflection in the Washington Consensus .

Notes

1. Ruth Kelly, 'Derivatives – A Growing Threat to the International Financial System' in J. Mitchie and J. Grieve Smith (eds.), *Managing the Global Economy* (OUP, 1995).

2. The spontaneous rationality for German capitalism would have required a smaller mark union, without the Mediterranean countries, and with an eastward orientation. But Germany was pushed politically into the big EU monetary union, something which will require a major adjustment either by Germany (financial transfers) or by the Mediterranean countries.

3. On this see I. M. Destler and C. Randall Henning, *Dollar Politics: Exchange Rate Policymaking in the United States* (Institute for International Economics, 1989).

4. Under the DWSR governments except the US, Germany and Japan can have only two of the following three features: control over exchange rates, full financial mobility and independent monetary policy. On the general principles, see, for example, Charles Wyplosz, *Globalized Financial Markets and Financial Crises*, paper for Forum on Debt and Development, Amsterdam, 16–17 March 1998.

5. The huge expansion of the scope for private finance in pensions etc. would require a very large expansion of securities markets, would undermine bank-corporate sector linkages and open Europe's corporate sector for acquisitions by American finance capital.

6. The data used here are from Dani Rodrick, 'Globalization, Social Conflict and Economic Growth', revised version of the Prebisch Lecture delivered at UNCTAD, Geneva, 24 October 1997.

7. Statement by Elinor Constable in the US House of Representatives, International Bank Lending (Washington DC, GPO, 1983), p. 58, quoted in Kapstein, *Governing the Global Economy*.

8. A crucial factor in the capacity to make swift domestic adjustments is the domestic class balance of forces. It may be that the East Asian states had a far greater capacity to impose the costs of adjustment on the working class than countries that failed to adjust.

9. See Charles Wyplosz, *Globalised Financial Markets and Financial Crises*, paper for Forum on Debt and Development, Amsterdam, 16–17 March 1998.

10. Dani Rodrick, 'Globalization, Social Conflict and Economic Growth'.

11. The Mexican crisis was also interesting as the first big blow-out between the US and Western Europe within the IMF. Mexico was a vital US political interest so it was determined to stabilise it even if that meant using over $20 billion of West European money to do so. The West Europeans said there was no global threat from Mexico to the international financial

system so the US should pay and the BIS would grant only bridging money while the US hunted for funds elsewhere. But Treasury Secretary Bensten persuaded Michel Camdessus of the IMF to announce publicly that the West Europeans *were* fully committing the money, not providing only bridging money. This meant that if the Europeans publicly set the record straight, they could have tipped Mexico over the cliff and could thus have been blamed for a total collapse. For the first time in IMF history, the minutes of an IMF board meeting were made public because European officials leaked them to demonstrate that they had not voted for the bail-out (but had abstained).

12. Martin Wolf, 'The Ins and Outs of Capital Flows', *Financial Times*, 16 June 1998.

13. 'Globalization and Asia: The Challenges for Regional Cooperation and the Implications for Hong Kong', address by Michel Camdessus, Managing Director of the International Monetary Fund, at a conference sponsored by the Hong Kong Monetary Authority and the IMF on 'Financial Integration in Asia and the Role of Hong Kong', Hong Kong, 7 March 1997.

14. Per Jacobsson Lecture on Asian monetary co-operation by Joseph Yam, JP, Chief Executive of the Hong Kong Monetary Authority, Hong Kong, 21 September 1997.

15. This central role for very large national banks is true not only in Japan, France and Germany (which has also had strong Land banks) but also in the UK and in the former British dominions like Canada. Italy alone among the G7 countries approaches the US in its lack of strong national banking pillars in its financial structure.

16. It is, of course, true that some parts of the US financial system remain subject to what UK operators would regard as ferocious and tight control: the powers of the Securities and Exchange Commission are immense. But they regulate the activities of those involved in the stock exchange only from the angle of personal probity and not for the purpose of minimising macroeconomic risk.

17. Rothkopf, 'Beyond Manic Mercantilism', (Council on Foreign Relations paper, 1998).

18. For a detailed and fairly comprehensive survey of the tactics used for attempting to make the social engineering robust against backlash, see J. Williamson (ed.), *The Political Economy of Economic Reform* (Institute for International Economics, 1996).

5

Power Politics, the DWSR and the Clinton Administration

So far we have attempted to explain the mechanisms of the Dollar–Wall Street Regime, to show that it reproduces itself as a political as well as an economic mechanism, steered by the joint actions of US governments through their dollar policies and control of the IMF/WB and of the US-centred international financial markets. We have also tried to trace in rough outline some of its effects upon national political economies and the social structures of states. We also sought to minimally demonstrate, from the way both US dollar policy and the US attitude to international financial regulation and to the roles of the IMF/WB have operated, that the DWSR was run from the angle of US national interests. But the question we must ask is: how are we to understand national interests under contemporary capitalism? How can we arrive at a general conceptualisation of the political and economic interests of a leading capitalist state? This is the issue which we want to address now in order to try to provide a framework for understanding the radical activism of the Clinton administration in its efforts in the international political economy.

I National Interests and International Challenges

Mainstream Theories of State International Economic Interests

Mainstream economics and political economy tells us that the economic interests of capitalist states should produce no international political conflict whatever about economics as such, except for transitional adjustment frictions, provided a state's political leaders act in their own rational self-interest. These interests are defined as the following: first, growing long-term prosperity for their domestic population through raising domestic productivity – high productivity in one state does not weaken the drive for higher productivity in others; second, exploiting the advantages to be derived from the international division of labour by adhering to free trade; and thirdly, maintaining co-operation with other governments in an effort to manage effectively international macroeconomic flows. With growing prosperity, the state's own revenues will rise, giving it great international political power. So, according to this view, the international interests of states are essentially harmonious with those of other states, provided the others retain similar, open rational policies.[1] Thus, the mainstream theory suggests that the attempts by states to engage in political intervention in international economics are the result of certain special interests within the state trying to use their political influence on the government for 'rent-seeking' advantages which are actually damaging for the wider economic interest.

Mainstream economics does acknowledge that adjustment tensions can arise between states as a result of international payments imbalances. These can result in states being tempted to impose protectionist restrictions on imports or subsidies for exports in order to escape the need for domestic adjustments. A robust international set of rules is needed to prevent such ultimately self-defeating attempts by states to escape the need for internal adjustment.

Mainstream theory then adds extra sophistications connected to the supposed rise of economic interdependence, whereby the domestic actions of governments can have unintended transnational spillover effects within other domestic political economies and these then require the development of new international regimes for co-ordinating national policies in more and more fields. But such extra dimensions are presented essentially as technical responses to technical problems within a basic framework of deep harmony between the national economic interests of powers.

This mainstream economic theory dovetails well with mainstream pluralist political science. This views politics in a liberal democracy as a competition between parties for the votes of citizens whose preferences are guided by a self-regarding concern to maximise their own welfare. Since such welfare is concerned with increased individual prosperity, voters push governments to direct all their efforts towards economic growth and national prosperity. And governments will thus gain their optimum political pay-off by pursuing these goals in the ways prescribed by liberal economics, which holds the key to assuring their populations' prosperity and thus producing satisfied voters. Again, there are dangers that particular groups of voters will try to capture the political process in search of 'rent-seeking' advantages which will enhance the private welfare of sectional interests at the expense of overall welfare maximisation, but these special interests can be and should be suppressed through the appropriate design of systems of democratic accountability.

These mainstream economic and political science views sit slightly uneasily with the mainstream International Relations theory of 'neo-realism': this argues that states are driven by the inescapable characteristics of the inter-state system into a struggle for relative power – power relative to other states. Because states exist as isolated entities in an anarchic world where security can be guaranteed only by each state maximising its own power relative to other states, there is a ceaseless struggle between states for power.[2]

Reconciliation between these mainstream disciplines is achieved through the Neo-Realists' claim that in this ceaseless power struggle, states are inter-ested overwhelmingly in the coinage of military capacity: economics is of little interest to them.

But in recent years, neo-mercantilist theories have enjoyed a revival against mainstream liberal political economy. This is less a coherent body of theory than a view that international economic outcomes are profoundly shaped by international political conditions and forces.[3] But from this start-ing point the neo-mercantilists argue that the hierarchical international division of labour is 'path dependent' and is not the product of spontaneous free market outcomes. This path dependency is established through states manipulating markets to prevent the 'normal' operations of international markets, as envisaged by liberal international economics. As a result, then, of the impact of the inter-state system on international markets, there is an inevitable political struggle for national prosperity between states as each state tries to use its external political influence to manipulate its external environment for national advantage in trade. These kinds of views can accord with neo-realism but clash with mainstream neoclassical economics at a cognitive level (even if those holding a neo-mercantilist view of what actually happens share liberal views as to what should happen).

The problem with these different theories is that while they seem to pro-vide explanations of much of what goes on in international relations, they also seem to miss a great deal. Mainstream economics reminds us of the cen-tral importance of domestic productivity and of the value of international macroeconomic co-ordination. But it leaves an extraordinarily large burden on the idea of welfare-destructive 'rent-seeking' to explain the great swathes of activity in the international political economy which clash with its norms. To take a simple example which is completely irrational from a mainstream economic point of view: the wild dance of the dollar over the last quarter of a century has been completely irrational from a mainstream view: can it really be explained by certain groups 'rent-seeking'? And if it is to be explained like that, surely some groups seek rents from a high dollar and others from a low dollar. So how do we explain the seeming musical chairs among rent-seekers within the span of single presidencies?

As for neo-mercantilism, it offers an explanation of everything that the mainstream fails to explain but by the same token fails to explain everything that the mainstream does explain – the mixture of co-operation as well as conflict between the great capitalist economies. Neo-mercantilism would suggest that there should be a state of almost permanent economic warfare between the main capitalist states. Yet the degrees of tensions between them vary greatly through time and across space.

To make sense of the national interest in economics, we will suggest that these theories suffer from a common weakness: they lack any mediation between the 'economic' and the 'political', with the economic defined as 'growth', 'prosperity', 'jobs' or productivity. They thus take for granted what needs to be investigated: what kinds of social institutions actually control access to 'growth' etc.? What are their compulsions and how do their compulsions and interests operate in domestic politics to structure the definition of the national interest? We need a theory which includes these social mediations between the 'economic' and state political action on economic matters. One obvious such mediation is provided by the concept of *capitalism as a social system* which gives a twist to the behaviour both of the economy and the state.

We will not attempt here to furnish an alternative theory of the national interests of *capitalist* states: this would require a fully fledged theoretical alternative to mainstream social science. We will simply suggest some conceptual rules of thumb that may help to produce a more nuanced appreciation of the extent to which powerful capitalist states may define their national economic interests in ways that allow for both the co-operation sought after by mainstream economics and for the conflict stressed by neo-mercantilism.

A Rough Concept of Capitalist States' National Interests in International Economics

Within a capitalist economy, elected politicians surely do want what mainstream economics says that they should want: ever-higher productivity and growth. But such matters are not directly in the government's hands: they are in the hands of private capital which owns the productive labour. Democratically elected politicians, therefore, must serve the special needs of the employers of capital, because it is this group which takes the decisions about whether there will be investment and growth. Thus the national interest in economics has to be conceived as the national *capitalist* interest, insofar as the capitalist social group exercises sovereignty over economic life.

Private capitalists do not want growth as such: they want capital growth and security. And these goals do not have to come from actions whose end result is expanding national production. They can come from one capitalist concern extending its control over existing production in the sector. If they face competition, then one of the ways of tackling that competition is through a drive to raise their productivity, lower their unit costs, improve quality and thus try to sell more units and thereby attract a larger share of the market. But there are other ways of overcoming the competition: using the size of your capital for strategic action to destroy smaller rivals or potential rivals or co-opting your rivals into a cartel to control the market. And with monopolisation in a closed economy, it is by no means obvious that expansive investment for higher output is the royal road to further progress of capital growth. And if the market is already saturated and controlled, it is not obvious that very large new investments in new technologies (the key to rapid and sustained productivity growth) are rational.

The economic pressures towards monopolisation are very strong in advanced capitalist economies because advanced industry tends to have very high capital-output ratios (or, in Marxist terminology, a high organic composition of capital). Each extra £ of capital investment produces only a small extra-amount of value added. Very large investments in fixed capital are needed to enter the sector and capitalists who make such outlays need to be assured of long-term control of markets in order to realise an adequate return on their capital. This kind of capitalist enterprise has certain compulsions: to block new entrants to its markets; and to control prices to assure adequate long-term return on fixed capital investments.

Another very important feature of advanced industry is the fact that it tends to benefit from important economies of scale. Thus, the greater the market share a company can acquire, the more effectively it can compete with potential rivals. Thus companies have a compulsion to expand market share to assure maximal scale economies.

In earlier conditions of many small capitals competing within domestic, pluralistic markets, bankruptcies on the part of market leaders have few serious consequences for the state. But if big monopolies collapse and foreign monopolistic enterprises capture the market, this has serious consequences.

The productive sectors of the national economies of the leading capitalist powers are indeed highly monopolistic today. They seek to maintain control over their markets through blocking new entrants and through 'centralisation of capital' – big companies gobbling up small – and through concentration of capital – developing production systems to gain maximum scale economies. States are also enlisted to solve these problems both by providing large state-markets for monopolistic industries and by providing a very large range of support services (infrastructures, labour training, etc.) for these monopolistic companies.

In conditions where the main markets for such quasi-monopolistic industries are expanding internationally and where a state's capitals in those sectors face no serious international competition, there are likely to be high rates of investment and technological innovation as the companies concerned feel assured of future capital growth. But where new entrants challenge these quasi-monopolies successfully for market share, very great problems can arise: new large investments in fixed capital become extremely risky, profit margins are cut by the new competition and even the biggest companies can face the risk of bankruptcy – economic collapse.

If this is a roughly accurate picture then we can explore its implications at an international level. The capitals of the main capitalist states operate internationally for a number of objectives. First for raw materials needed in their production process and not available domestically. Some of these materials are so vital – energy and strategic goods like aluminium, bauxite, copper etc. – that they cannot leave matters wholly to the market: their state is enlisted to use political influence to assure supply. Another need is to control international markets in conditions often of acute competition. In the face of this, as with securing raw materials, national capitals will 'rent-seek': try to enlist their state in their cause, to help beat the competition. But the term 'rent-seeking' is hardly an appropriate one since it is *a necessary, systemic requirement in conditions of monopolistic rivalry*. And they have another international need: to gain access to external sources of labour – either very highly skilled labour sources in high-tech fields – or low-tech cheap labour for doing the labour-intensive parts of their internal labour process. The state can also help in these areas.

Against this domestic capitalist background we can ask what the rational role for the given advanced capitalist state is. The state is not, of course, simply its elected politicians: they come and go but the state must remain and it is the task of the top civil servants to present their political masters with the facts: the systemic facts of the state's situation and interests within a much longer time horizon than the electoral cycle. From this angle, the state must attempt to ensure the best possible conditions for its capitalists to want to invest and improve productivity and expand output – the material basis of the state's own resource strength. Since it is up to capital whether it does these things or not, the state has an overwhelming interest in serving its most important capitals. And since these operate internationally it must seek to serve their international interests. Insofar as they send streams of revenue and profits back to their home base and insofar as they extend their control over overseas markets, the state will consider its international position stronger: the better placed its capitals are in world markets, the stronger its position and influence.

This might suggest that in generally stagnant conditions in the core countries, there will be a war of each against all. If a state's main monopolies are threatened by the behaviour of the monopolistic enterprises of other states, there will be acute inter-state rivalries. But there tends to be an international division of capital as well as an international division of labour. Not every advanced capitalist state has a big international car company. Only some do.

The British state was prepared to give up the struggle to maintain its car companies: it had other international champions (it hoped), such as its financial sector, military industries, pharmaceuticals etc. Matters would be very different for Germany if its car companies were being shut out of international markets. But Germany in the postwar period has not made a central priority to build a large, internationally dominant set of financial markets. Both states will seek to ensure that the interests of their key sectors of capital are well protected internationally. Across most sectors there may be a 'capital fit' between two states. Then they can co-operate, perhaps each helping the other in a joint negotiating effort with third states.

The extent to which advanced capitalist states can co-operate in these ways is shown by the recent history of the EU, and most especially by the history of the Single Market. While presented as an attempt to break down barriers to international competition within the EU, the Single Market enabled each member state to encourage its national champions to extend their national monopolistic power and then to find ways to co-operate with others in their sector within the EU, so that they could work together in a monopolistic 'division of capitals'. Such efforts at co-operative cartelisation work more easily in some sectors than in others: the Single Market has not been fully implemented by any means and cartelisation tends to be unstable. Nevertheless, the programme has been far more successful in maintaining and deepening inter-state co-operation than any neo-mercantilist theorist would have predicted.

At the same time, the success of the EU states in achieving regional co-operation would have been impossible to achieve had it not been for the great value of the EU for its member states as a lever for international influence over the rest of the world economy. The EU acts as a powerful co-operative operation of European capitals for pressing together for a number of international objectives:

1)   Each member state can use the EU's trade regime to block competition from imports into the EU from the outside.

2)   The member state can use the EU as a very powerful lever in international diplomacy concerning the organisation of the international political economy: using the threat of exclusion from the EU market against those external states reluctant to open their markets.

3)   The EU trade regime does not cover export promotion on the part of member states, so each can take what measures it wishes to promote the interests of its monopolistic national champions abroad.

In conditions of stagnation within the core economies, the search for new openings outside the core is a central preoccupation and the EU provides a very valuable collective service for its member states in this task.

The National Interests of the Dominant Capitalist State

Against this background we can consider the interests of the dominant capitalist state within the international system, the United States. It gains enormous advantages from being the dominant military-political state as well as from being able to dominate the mechanisms of international economic management. This gives it far greater capacities to change its international environment to its advantage than any other state. The DWSR is a central example of the premiums of dominance. The whole world is its sphere of influence and it wishes to assure its continued dominance through the continued strength of its capitals internationally. And it has a far wider range of sectors than other capitalist powers in which it seeks to ensure the dominance of its capitals.

For the leaders of the United States, a capitalist map of the world looks very different from a natural geography map. Quantities of territory as such have little significance except in terms of geostrategy and the resulting basing and logistic requirements. What counts are, in the first place, localities with economically strategic raw materials (oil etc.). These must be firmly under control if possible: a sine qua non for maintaining dominance. But otherwise what stands out are quite small territorial areas: those with today's and tomorrow's key pools of labour and key markets, particularly for the decisive sectors of the US's capitals. Command over very highly skilled labour in the sectors of the future and over the machines that it produces is really vital. But the value produced by this labour can only be realised through international market sales. In the nineteenth century, the markets for the sale of goods produced, say, by British labour, tended to be scattered all over the world in the small wealthier classes of every country. In the contemporary world, on the other hand, the really big markets tend to be much more concentrated in small areas where the bulk of the skilled labour also lives: North America, Western Europe and Japan. It follows that for the leading capitalist state seeking to strengthen its capitals, dominance in these rather restricted areas is crucial. But the lead state must also view this issue dynamically and look at where the key skilled labour pools and markets of the next quarter of a century are likely to appear and gain control of the bulk of the streams of value from these. As for the great mass of the earth's territory outside these areas, it is of little significance and the people who live there can be of no more than auxiliary interest, or even of no interest at all, except insofar as one has to contain disturbances and a slide into forms of barbarism that may have international spillovers.

Within this framework, beyond the general principle of assuring the continued dominance of US capitalism, we cannot say the extent to which there will be conflict or co-operation between the US and other parts of the world. Answering that question will depend upon how much of a fit there is between the need for the American state to ensure that its capitals in key sectors dominate the key geoeconomic areas and what is going on in these areas. But we can say one thing: any attempt by any power to exclude the US from having assured entry for its capitals into these central pools of labour and markets, let alone an attempt to throw a ring around that area to develop it as a regional launch pad for an assault on US capitals in key sectors, would produce a savage American response.

Thus, the US interest is to ensure beyond serious doubt that the other main capitalist regions are securely, institutionally open to its capitals and that there is no risk of these regions suddenly becoming closed to US capitals, perhaps as a transitional step to that region acquiring greater strength in the international division of labour than the US has.

The US, in such circumstances, need not constantly fear that other parts of the world may be growing faster than the US domestic economy, as mercantilists would claim: after all this growth should be a growth for the US companies playing a decisive role in these areas. On the other hand, any region which exclude the US while it was growing dynamically would be an adversarial region.

One final point in relation to US strategy should, however, be mentioned. Insofar as the US retained dominance in the financial field, the US and its capital would want to be able to exercise that financial power in order to be able to take over capitalist companies in other regions, where possible. Financial strike power offers this opportunity for taking over competitors for market dominance, but it does so only if the legal rules in the other regions are such that hostile takeovers of companies are legally possible. Thus openness should mean more than just the ability of US companies to establish their own undertakings in other political economies. It should also mean that the relations of production, including the legal forms of corporate governance and the rules for takeovers, should be friendly towards such efforts on the part of US operators in key sectors for American capitalism to move in and take control of domestic markets.

Against this background, we can see that, contrary to the advice of current realist theorists of international relations, the US will want to cut its military cloth to fit its drives as a *capitalist* state: military power is not an end in itself. But we can also see that the great advantages which the United States could derive from the Dollar–Wall Street Regime through its dominance within it are by no means a sufficient condition for assuring US dominance. Dominance over international monetary and financial relations is not everything. It needs an anchor in dominance within the productive sector of the world economy and indeed without dominance in that sphere, control over international money and finance remains ultimately fragile.

We can thus try to use our rough theory as the basis for a set of hypotheses:

1)   That the US government, acting rationally, should wish to ensure that its capitals in its key sectors would gain control in the most dynamic regions of market growth.

2)   That it would want to ensure that the most dynamic pools of labour and of product markets should be maximally opened to its capitals.

3)   It would react with extraordinary and emergency measures to prevent the risk of exclusion from such markets.

4)   That it would require institutions to be built that could ensure structured dominance over the key geographical areas which were the main centres of international surplus-value extraction.

5)   It would gear its steering of the DWSR towards achieving these ends, unless it had other more appropriate instruments of statecraft for doing so.

The Pattern of International Capitalist Dynamics in the Early 1990s

In 1993 when Clinton came into office, after twenty years of the DWSR, the US's overall share of the world GDP was roughly in the same position as it had been in 1970. But there was a worrying new symptom of weakness, not present in 1970. This symptom lay in the US balance of payments. There had been a deficit in the late 1960s and early 1970s. But the deficit at that time could be explained by non-structural factors: the Vietnam war and the very large flow into Western Europe of US productive capital to take up large positions within the EEC market, positions which would generate a future stream of earnings into the US current account. But by 1993 there was a serious structural deficit in the current account. And it derived both from a trade deficit and from the need to service an ever-growing US international debt position. The American state had allowed its debt to grow to 70 per cent of GDP. The current account balance is not a trivial indicator. It demonstrates whether a state's capitals are earning more from the rest of the world than vice versa.[4] The trade deficit pointed to increasing US competitive weakness in its productive sector. If the current account is not in surplus, then the position of the state's currency can never be completely secure. Of course, seigniorage from dollar dominance gives the US far greater freedom from this payments constraint than any other state. But it is still a sign of weakness, one that could count in a crisis. And servicing those weaknesses in the current account had, by the 1990s, come to depend upon the co-operation of an 'ally' (though one increasingly branded in Washington as an 'adversary'[5]), Japan. The Japanese government was helping the US Treasury with a continual flow of Japanese funds into US Treasury bonds.[6] One of Bush's final acts as President had been yet again to try to bully the Japanese government into weakening itself to suit the US, this time over competition in the car industry. The result was humiliating for Bush and disquieting for US elites. The Japanese had simply brushed Bush aside and had shown self-awareness of their role in bankrolling the US government.

We must therefore look at what lay behind this current account weakness and summarise the general situation of US capitalism within the wider dynamics of international capitalism. A whole American literature has grown up around the thesis of what is called 'declinism' – the idea that the US is following in the footsteps of pre-1914 Britain down a primrose path to ever-lasting weakness. While this literature was much exaggerated, the comparison with Britain in the early part of the century is nevertheless instructive.

Indeed, the contemporary pattern of political-economic interactions bore significant parallels (as well, of course, as differences) with the dynamics of the international system at the turn of the century. The key units for analysis in both cases are the following: the lead country, the core competitors, the new growth centres, the dependent support-regions, and organised labour.

The respective lead countries were of course the UK and the US. In both cases, the lead countries' economies had grown for a whole historical period through interaction with the rest of the core: for the UK that had meant Western Europe during the nineteenth century; for the US it had meant Western Europe and Japan during the postwar boom. In both cases the end result was a strong competitive challenge from the rest of the core as it caught up and started eating into the market of the lead country. Stagnationist tendencies appeared within the core in the late nineteenth century and in the 1970s. Tensions also arose within the core, exacerbated by political shifts such as the unification of the German states into a single entity in 1871 and the development of bloc tendencies, notably in Western Europe from the 1970s.[7]

In such circumstances, there were powerful pressures from within the core, and notably from within its lead country, to look outwards beyond the core to exploit opportunities in the hinterland for solving internal problems in the metropolis. One part of the hinterland may be called dependent support-regions. For Britain, this was, of course, the Empire, above all the Indian empire. Products losing competitiveness within the core could be dumped in Empire markets, whose internal social relations of production could be restructured to accommodate them. On the eve of the First World War, textiles made up no less than 51 per cent of British manufactured exports. Whereas previously they had gone to Europe, they now went to the Empire. The Asian colonial market absorbed anything up to 60 per cent of these exports in the years before the First World War. As Eric Hobsbawm has put it, 'Asia saved Lancashire'. But it did more than that: by keeping Lancashire afloat it sustained demand in the UK market for exports from the rest of the world, thus easing tensions within the core. Even more important, India indirectly sustained the international monetary system of the day. If the Indian market had closed and Lancashire had collapsed, the pressures, already growing within the UK industrial heartland in the early twentieth century,[8] for protectionism would have been unstoppable. If the UK had opted for protectionism, the international monetary system would have been scrapped.

An analogous system has developed in the context of the core stagnation of the last quarter of a century. The US has sought to use the dependent support-regions as dumping grounds for US products through both an export drive and market-seeking FDI. It has used the IMF and the dynamics of the Dollar–Wall Street Regime to open up these states, to restructure their internal social relations of production to ensure that they could absorb these products. The resulting substantial increase in US exports has, in turn, sustained the US domestic product market, easing tensions in the core. In a similar pattern to the British case, over half of US exports in the 1990s went to countries of the South, not least Latin America. Yet even in its own Latin American hinterland, the US exported less than did the EU. And both in the earlier period and the current one, the dependent support-regions were very important sources of cheap, vital inputs into the productive processes of the core states.[9]

There is, of course, an important difference between American and British control mechanisms over the dependent support-regions: British direct imperial rule meant there was no balance of payments constraint on the colonies since their monetary system was sterling. The British could have them running permanent deficits with the metropolis without having to provide them with a market to cover their deficit-induced debts. For the United States, using the Dollar–Wall Street Regime, there is a constant need to provide the dependencies with a sufficient export market to cover debt servicing to the US financial sector. On the other hand, the British had to take direct responsibility for maintaining order in their dependencies, while the US system throws that responsibility on to the legally sovereign dependent state. So it is a case, probably, of swings and roundabouts, even though the function of being 'market of last resort' may seem a heavy burden for the US.

But as Patnaik has shown in his masterly and seminal study,[10] there was another actor in the world economy outside the core at the end of the nineteenth century whose role was also integral to the dynamics of the system as a whole. This other kind of actor was made up of the states which could be called the new growth centres. These could absorb surplus capital from the core as well as surplus labour for the purposes of productive capital accumulation. Between 1865 and 1914 the bulk of capital exports from the core took the form of British portfolio investments. And during that period as much as 68 per cent of total British portfolio investment went to the new growth regions, some juridically within the British Empire, others outside it.[11] This outpouring of funds from British rentiers to the new growth centres was itself a shift from their earlier destination towards the more backward West European core.

The same kind of pattern has occurred in the later period, though with significant modifications. In the first place, stagnation in the core has not enjoyed the safety valve of huge labour migrations outwards. And in the second place the outflows of funds from the core for productive investment in the new growth centres has come not only from rentiers in the lead country, but from productive capital in the rest of the core as well.

Another parallel is also important: in both periods, organised labour and the socialist movement seemed very weak and as a result strategies could be adopted for displacing tensions between the core countries not only towards the hinterland but also on to the working class (with labour emigration making this especially easy in the earlier period). Similarly, by the 1990s, it was hoped that labour was so permanently weakened by the collapse of the Soviet Bloc that tensions could largely be displaced downwards via so-called neo-liberalism.

Of course, there are important differences between the two periods as well. The internationalisation of finance out of London was more extensive and deeper in the earlier period than it has been in the current period. British banks alone had over 8,000 branches around the world. Secondly, the juridical empire form of external expansion is no longer viable: direct control of populations in the South can no longer be sustained by imperial centres: institutions like the IMF, the WTO, bilateral security Pacts and multinational companies must be used in combination with juridically sovereign states which are then required by the imperial system, as well as by international law, to shoulder exclusive responsibility within their territory for whatever the results of interacting with the core economies may be.

Thirdly, the internationalisation in the earlier period took place in a context of extraordinary stability of the international monetary and financial system of the core, unlike the chaos of the Dollar–Wall Street Regime.

But the big question for historically-minded American policy-makers in the 1990s has been whether there would be two more parallels between the earlier period and the current one. First, in the earlier period, a challenge to British power came from within the core in the form of the First World War; Britain survived this challenge, but was fatally weakened as a dominant power in monetary and financial relations. Could a similar kind of challenge face the US? But secondly, Britain faced a different kind of challenge from the new growth centres. The countries in this group included such dominions as Canada, Australia and New Zealand as well as other states such as Argentina, Japan *and the USA*. The USA took the exported funds from the core and seized control from Britain through helping it cope with its challengers in the European core. Could this happen again in, of course, a novel form?

It is not too difficult to perceive actors that could reproduce for the United States both the kinds of challenge that had faced Britain: the first could be described as the monetary-financial threat; the second, the new productive centre threat.

1) The financial-monetary challenge

This challenge could arise above all from the combination of the construction of the euro with financial instability within the United States itself. A serious American financial crisis could turn the Dollar–Wall Street Regime into its opposite: there could be a flight from US Treasury bonds, prompting a flight from the dollar feeding back into a really serious US foreign debt crisis: if something happened to produce a drying up of US financial markets for foreign borrowers, the latter might dump the Treasury bonds they had been using as a safe haven for their dollar reserves. There could be a double effect: the costs of servicing the US debt in the dollar market for Treasury bonds would soar, as interest rates shot up; at the same time interest rates in Europe would fall as people dumped dollars for marks (or euros). The US has to service its debt by borrowing in marks and yen, yet has a current account deficit with both these currency zones. At this point, people begin to worry about the medium-term future of the dollar, and the gigantic mass of greenbacks now all over the world after a quarter of a century of the Dollar–Wall Street system would give the crisis a new quality as people all over the world started to flee the dollar overhang: in such a situation the dollar could begin to resemble the rouble – a currency whose fall seemed to have no floor. This, of course, is a nightmare scenario, imaginable only in the event of a collapse of the American financial system of Mexican proportions. Yet the same results could occur over a longer period in a series of fairly small, incremental jolts. And the end result would be the same in either case: American policy-makers would wake up one day to face the inescapable fact that world leadership had passed elsewhere.

This trend could, of course, only occur if there was an obvious alternative global currency to the dollar. Such an alternative could not be the yen, because despite the unmatched size of Japan's financial surpluses, its domestic financial market is far too small to support the yen as a world currency and the Japanese economy is rather closed in trade terms – its exports and imports are a small proportion of its GDP. But the euro could be a very different matter. It could quickly establish itself as a major international currency, backed by large current account surpluses and large capital exports. And if its financial markets were integrated, they could quickly

rival Wall Street as sources of international finance. Were the EU then to
adopt tough interpretations of its laws on reciprocity in rights for foreign
financial services operating within the EU, it could curtail the operations of
US banks and other financial operators within the EU until its operators
gained equal scope in the US market (which they do not have at present).
This prospect is, to put it mildly, an uncomfortable one for any US
government.

2) The new productive centre threat

This is a seemingly less urgent threat, but a more dangerous one. It would
arise from the symbiosis of Japanese capitalism with the growth centre of
East and South-East Asia as both become the centre of gravity of the global
production system, making the profitability of American capital dependent
upon its links with the region, while simultaneously reorganising the international division of labour in such a way as to place US industry in a
subordinate position: the high prestige 'positional goods' – the high status
products for the international wealthy classes – and the fixed capital to produce them would be East Asian. This threat could materialise with special
force in the event that a ring was thrown around Japan and the region in the
form of a yen-zone cum trade bloc along West European lines. Suddenly the
US could find itself faced with collective resistance to its efforts to use its
political muscle to break into strong positions in the region. The DWSR
would be crippled by the yen-zone as a source of leverage while Japan, not
a debtor country, would be generating huge financial resources for productive investment. And the finance ministers of the South and even from
the US would be queuing in Tokyo for investment and financial support,
while the offices of the IMF and World Bank would be occupied only with a
dwindling band of exclusive US dependencies. And the Japanese regional
leaders could be happy to help the United States solve all its problems of
managing its decline, as the US had been with Britain earlier in the century:
they could even prop up a Dollar–Wall Street area analogous to the
Sterling–City of London area propped up by the US in the postwar years.

    Both these potential threats have been central preoccupations of US policy
intellectuals since the late 1980s. Of course, they were not the only topics of
discussion. The US had huge political resources for combating them and for
reshaping the post-Cold War world in ways that would entrench the US as the
dominant power throughout the next century. And since the US has the
lowest tax rates in the advanced capitalist world, it could take the needed
structural measures – a sharp increase in the share of taxation in GDP, to put
its state finances on a sounder footing.

    But the level of policy analysis and debate as the Clinton Administration
came into office was qualitatively different from the past: the issues to be

addressed were no longer those of incremental tactical adjustment within a largely given strategic environment. Fundamental, historical strategic review was on the agenda.

Of the two threats, the EU one looks superficially more menacing. Yet there were counter-balancing factors. First, the threat from the euro did not come from its creation, but from its being able to challenge the dollar as a world currency. Such a challenge would require a number of supports which the EU was unlikely to acquire quickly: a solid political base that could be counted upon to act as a single political unit in a crisis; a major military-political capability autonomous from the US, something on which there were few signs of progress; a unified and powerful financial sector, buttressed by a unified political authority – something a long way off; a coherent and politically acceptable domestic Euroland economic and social policy framework, something which spontaneous market forces would tend to undermine; a means of exiting the long European stagnation, something that the ECB was hardly likely to produce; a means of ending the politically disintegrative tendencies within Euroland politics, witnessed by the growth of the extreme Right and the deep splits on social policy and EU-wide democratic identity; perhaps most crippling, there was the patchwork of torn or shattered social and economic structures in the eastern part of the continent and the evident incapacity of the Euroland states to even begin to offer a coherent, serious answer to these problems. And finally, West European leaders had such an endless capacity to bicker among themselves that it did not take much on the part of a US administration to throw them into sixes and sevens. Meanwhile, US capital not only had very easy access into the EU market but the existing EU political structure was an extremely favourable one for US operators since at its heart was a Commission uncontrolled by EU internal democratic mechanisms, fixated on one problematic – deregulation to assist transnational business – and therefore easily captured by the influence of the US transnational corporations.

The East and South-East Asian region seemed at first sight to be less menacing because of its political fragmentation. Yet there were two sets of powerful and potentially complementary social networks tying the region's capitals together: the networks centring on Japanese business and the networks linking overseas Chinese business with the mainland. And these two networks were creating growing linkages and complementarities in the one region of the world with really dynamic accumulation. Furthermore, the networks were tending to leave US capitals out. Worse still, the more advanced economies, particularly South Korea, were directly eating into markets of core US capitalist sectors. And the region was becoming increasingly organic with Japanese capitalism. And in most of the countries there were barriers of various kinds to the US being able to establish its predominant influence within their political economies.

While from the angle of mainstream economics, the Clinton administration faced no political-economy threat at all, from the angle of neo-mercantilism, threats would be visible everywhere. But from the angle of our hypotheses, the direction of the threat for the Clinton Administration would be from East and South-East Asia. And it was potentially a very serious one because rooted in dynamic capital accumulation which was showing every sign of moving up the hierarchical international division of labour. Of course, there were incentives for US capitalism to swim with the spontaneous tide, since it was making large absolute gains in terms of exports, intra-structure investments etc. But this was also a kind of danger since the more these absolute gains loomed large, the more they would make it difficult for the American state to take tough action to prevail over the regional challenge.

II   The Strategy of the Clinton Administration

The Clinton Team and its General Stance

The atmosphere in the United States when Clinton came into power was one suffused with a sense of great historical drama, a sense that the United States was facing a great world-historical either/or. There was the awareness of America's gigantic power in the military field and in the monetary-financial regime; on the other hand, there was the challenge of East Asia and uncertainty about Europe. There was the sense that the United States was about to give birth to an entirely new set of global growth motors through the new information industries and a feeling that these could play the role of the motor car as a huge pathway to revived international accumulation which the US could hope to dominate; yet after very large investments in this sector its supposed transformative potential for US productivity has simply not materialised. And finally there was the triumph over the Soviet Bloc and the international Left; and yet paradoxically that collapse posed a major question-mark over the means that the US could use for exerting political influence in the world and consolidating that influence through institutions similar to the security zones of the Cold War.

Tremendous American intellectual energy was being devoted, therefore, to these strategic issues as Clinton came into office. As one policy intellectual put it, 'essentially, we have to erect a whole new conceptual basis for foreign policy after the Cold War.'[12] Others equated the tasks facing Clinton to those that faced Truman in 1945: Clinton, said one writer, is 'present at the creation' of a new epoch in world affairs and 'the next half century hangs in the balance'.[13]

The Clinton team itself was not, of course, going to spell out publicly how it conceptualised its strategic problem and its strategy and tactics for tackling it. The signs had to be read more indirectly, for example, through Clinton's appointments and institutional arrangements as well as through its policy statements and initiatives.

Clinton's top foreign policy appointments, like Warren Christopher (State), Anthony Lake (National Security), Madeleine Albright (UN), Lloyd Bensten (Treasury) were conventional, rather passive figures with links back to the Carter days.[14] Many observers wondered why Clinton had received a reputation for external activism when he made such personnel appointments.[15] But this perception was itself the product of old thinking whereby foreign policy meant what the Secretary of State or the NSC chief or the Secretary of Defence did. It ignored the instruments of economic statecraft, yet these were the instruments which Clinton placed in the hands of the dynamic activists.

The new team brought in to wield the levers of economic statecraft were a distinctive group: Robert Rubin, Ron Brown, Mickey Kantor, Laura Tyson, Larry Summers, Jeff Garten, Ira Magaziner and Robert Reich (as well as Vice President Al Gore) had distinctive general approaches to the defence of American power:[16] for them, it was about 'the economy, stupid'. And they believed that strengthening American capitalism was above all to be tackled through international political action. In line with this was their belief in the importance, even the centrality of state-political action in economic affairs: a conviction that the success of a national capitalism was 'path dependent' and the path could be built of institutions fashioned by states. And there should not be barren counter-positions of national states and market forces: they should work together, help each other, whether in technology, trade or finance. They were not classical national protectionists, but they were also not free traders. The term used to describe the school of thought represented by this team was 'globalists', promoters of a kind of global neo-mercantilism. The new concept was that competition among states was shifting from the domain of political-military resources and relations to the field of control of sophisticated technologies and the domination of markets.[17] The nature of the new game was also given a name: 'geoeconomics'. Lloyd Bensten may have been of a different generation and of a different background from the others, but he also shared a 'globalist' view.

The outlook of this new team was expressed in books like Laura Tyson's *Who's Bashing Whom* and by a host of other such works by those within or close to the administration.[18] The outlook was often expressed most bluntly by Clinton's new US Trade Representative, Mickey Kantor, who openly argued for a new kind of American Open Door strategy to ensure that the twenty-first century will be the 'New American Century'. As he put it: 'The days of the Cold War, when we sometimes looked the other way when our trading partners failed to live up to their obligations, are over. National security and our national economic security cannot be separated . . . No more something for nothing, no more free riders.'[19]

Kantor's linkage of external economic objectives and US National Security was reflected in Clinton's remoulding of institutions in the core executive: just after Clinton's inauguration he created a National Economic Council within the White House alongside the National Security Council. The choice of name was designed to indicate that the new body would acquire the kind of nodal role in US global strategy which the NSC had played during the Cold War. At the same time Congress instructed the Commerce Department to set up the Trade Promotion Co-ordinating Committee (TPCC) to co-ordinate nineteen US government agencies in the area of commercial policy. Instructive also was the fact that the head of the National Economic Council was to be a very experienced hedge fund speculator, Robert Rubin, former senior partner in Goldman Sachs, the hedge fund masquerading as an investment bank.[20] This gave the Clinton team prime links with Wall Street.

The way that the Clinton administration defined its approach has been summed up by someone who was initially part of it, David Rothkopf. He has characterised the Clinton administration's new international strategy as one of 'Manic Mercantilism'.[21] Stanley Hoffman makes a similar point, noting the new US activism in world economic affairs under the Clinton administration and its drive to open borders to US goods, capital and services.[22]

The Strategic Focus on East and South-East Asia

It has been widely suggested throughout the Clinton Presidency by many attentive observers that its efforts in economic statecraft have been mainly directed at one particular geographical area: East and South-East Asia. Rothkopf suggests this was the main motive for the entire drive, saying: 'Commercial diplomacy, however defined and practised, owes its developments as much to the rise of Asia's emerging economies as it does to any other factor.' East and South-East Asia were of decisive importance if the United States 'was to maintain its economic leadership'.[23]

The Clinton administration never admitted quite this, of course. It claimed instead that its target was to break into what it called the 10 Big Emerging Markets (BEMs): but six of the ten were in Asia: China, Indonesia, Korea, Thailand, Malaysia and India. Of the other four, the United States already had two: Mexico and Argentina. A ninth, Poland, actually fought its way on to the administration's list. That left only Brazil outside Asia as a major target of American interest. So basically, the list of BEM targets meant Asia. The Clinton administration targeted $1.5 trillion to $2 trillion of commercial opportunities in the world's emerging markets with $1 trillion in export opportunity targets. According to Rothkopf US 'intelligence agencies were drawn into the commercial fray, providing analysis and other forms of assistance for these efforts'.[24]

The BEM strategy was first outlined by Undersecretary of Commerce for International Trade Jeff Garten, in a January 1994 speech to the Foreign Policy Association in New York. John Stremlau, Deputy Director of Policy Planning at the State Department, 1989–94, pointed out that although it appeared unusual for Clinton to define his 'foreign policy doctrine in terms of special US interests in a limited number of key countries' Reagan had largely done so by targeting Afghanistan, Angola, Cambodia and Nicaragua. Stremlau pointed out that Indonesia had been singled out for special attention, not least because there the US was losing market share to the Japanese and the Europeans. He also explained that the US drive into Indonesia 'could complicate US relations with Japan, which views Indonesia as lying within its sphere of influence'. The key word was to bring about economic and political 'convergence' between the United States and the targeted states: in other words transforming the domestic economics and politics of these states to achieve a kind of *Gleichschaltung* between them and US capitalism. As Stremlau put it: 'Clinton administration strategists seem to have concluded that domestic imperatives and international realities require a new and more subtle version of "dollar diplomacy" – greater US economic and political convergence with the few countries that make up today's Big Emerging Markets. Success on all those diplomatic fronts is as daunting a foreign policy goal as any in the country's history, but success could lead to a century of unsurpassed prosperity and security for the United States . . .'[25]

The Clinton administration openly called for a partnership with US business to break into these markets and Commerce Secretary Ron Brown directly urged US companies to seek political help from the administration *on particular contracts*. In addition the Ex-Im Bank, OPIC and the Trade Development Agency were geared up for providing priority assistance to US companies seeking entry and domination in markets in the BEMs.

But this could only be a minor detail. According to a study conducted by the Dutch section of the international association of Atlantic councils (the civilian opinion-forming arm of NATO), the Clinton administration's key concept in its external economic strategy was that competition among states was shifting from the centrality of political-military resources to the field of control of sophisticated technologies and the domination of markets.[26] This view closely corresponds to our hypothesis as to the rational external strategy for the US in the 1990s, directed towards East and South-East Asia. The big problem was what mix of tactics the US could deploy to decisively open the region up to US hegemony.

Tactical Options

We can outline some options available to a state with the resources of the USA for bringing the pools of labour and markets of the region permanently under the sway of the US and its economic operators.

1) The old European imperial power approach: direct military coercion and subordination.
2) Brigading the states of the region into a US-led alliance against some external threat: the classic postwar US approach to gaining hegemony over key centres of production.
3) Launching all-round economic warfare against the region (including oil-war like that used by the Nixon administration against its 'allies' in the early 1970s).
4) A more radical, activist strategic use of the multilateral organisations.
5) Using a mix of carrots and sticks in bilateral and regional economic statecraft.
6) Seeking domestic social linkages in target states through propaganda.
7) Using the instruments available through the DWSR for currency and financial warfare.

We will briefly survey each of these possible instruments in order to gain some insight into the tactical dilemmas of the Clinton administration.

1) Direct military coercion and subordination

This, of course, was not a serious option, but it is instructive to see why not. Quite simply, despite the enormous advances in weapons technology and the overwhelming superiority of US military capacity, direct military coercion followed by effective colonial subordination is unthinkable in today's world. The first reason is that as the US military's capacity to kill rises towards infinity, its capacity to die sinks towards zero. And to directly control populations and deal with popular movements in the contemporary world requires that military forces have a substantial capacity to die.[27] The rise of the world's population to political awareness and their acquisition of some free time rules out the old nineteenth-century tactics of the gun-boat and colonialism. The alternative course is to achieve ascendancy through staging domestic political coups in order to impose dependent groups in power who will serve US business interests. But such activity cannot be conjured out of the air: it usually requires the existence of a perceived domestic threat (traditionally from the Left) which the government of the day is perceived by a group within the dominant class as failing to deal with. Such preconditions did not exist in a region enjoying unparalleled economic advance and faced by no significant domestic social threats.

Yet if both these tactics are unavailable, there seems to be an irresolvable dilemma: given that state sovereignty has to be accepted, the US has no choice but to achieve its goals within them states *through* the existing dominant social class within them. The problem thus becomes one of how to change the orientation of these dominant social groups.

2) Brigading states into a US-led alliance against some external threat so that in exchange for US protection the states concerned open their economic assets to US operators

This is the classic US tactic of the Cold War period. Samuel Huntington has explained how US tactics worked: 'Western Europe, Latin America, East Asia, and much of South Asia, the Middle East and Africa fell within what was euphemistically referred to as "the Free World", and what was, in fact, a security zone. The governments within this zone found it in their interests: (a) to accept an explicit or implicit guarantee by Washington of the independence of their country and, in some cases, the authority of the government; (b) to permit access to their country to a variety of US governmental and non-governmental organisations pursuing goals which those organisations considered important . . . The great bulk of the countries of Europe and the Third World . . . found the advantages of transnational access to outweigh the costs of attempting to stop it.'[28]

And as David Rothkopf has added, in the postwar years 'Pax Americana came with an implicit price tag to nations that accepted the US security umbrella. If a country depended on the United States for security protection, it dealt with the United States on trade and commercial matters.'[29] The efficacy of the tactic depended upon two conditions: first, the ability of the US to persuade the local dominant social groups that they faced an external threat; and secondly, the US's ability to persuade these same groups that the US and only the US had the resources to cope with the threat and the will to do so. In Western Europe the threat was, of course, the internal-external one of Communism and the dominant classes of the region needed little persuasion – on the contrary they were in many cases begging for US intervention.[30] The distinctive US organisational model of the giant corporation could thus enter foreign labour and product markets, spreading first to Canada then to Western Europe (facilitated by the EC's rules and redevelopment) and then on to other parts of the world. In this way, rather than in the primitive militarist conceptions of realist theory, military power played a central role in postwar capitalist power politics.

With the collapse of the Soviet Bloc, the Bush administration had still hoped that the United States role as controller of security zones and wielder of enormous military resources could remain a potent instrument for strengthening the position of American capitalism vis-à-vis its economic rivals. His great efforts to ensure that a united Germany remained in NATO were followed by his war against Iraq, one of whose main goals was to show the rest of the capital world that it had to treat the interests of US capitalism with respect. But this was a false dawn. With the collapse of the Soviet Union itself, the US's ability to make political use of its extraordinary military superiority was bound to diminish.

It has not, of course, disappeared. The fact that the US has military resources today greater than all of Western Europe, China, Japan and Russia put together is a fundamental fact about world politics. It is evidently determined to retain the capacity to fight and prevail in a war against the combined forces of Russia and China.[31] This is not, of course, because it wishes a war with these two states. But if these two states did form an alliance in hostility to the capitalist world, the US could cash in its strategic military power politically again, by being able to brigade the rest of the core more firmly under its influence. And this military power also has another very important function: it can deter its 'allies' from making international political alliances which might threaten US capitalism. When Germany and other parts of Western Europe seemed in the late 1970s to be moving towards a new regime of deepening economic co-operation with the Soviet Bloc (in the face of the economic stagnation and the chaotic conditions of the DWSR at the time), the US had been able to cut the movement dead with its battle cry against the 'Finlandisation' of Western Europe, with its missile deployments in Germany and Italy and with its general offensive in the second Cold War. This, in itself, rules out either of the two other triadic centres even contemplating mounting a direct challenge to American leadership of world capitalism. Neither Germany nor Japan has shown the slightest hint of an interest in such an adventure.

But the problem for the US has not been stopping the other triadic powers from mounting a direct political challenge. The problem has been losing political leverage to secure its economic interests within their new, post-Cold War hinterlands: East Central and Eastern Europe and East and South-East Asia. Insofar as such regions face no external threat whose tackling requires military resources such as only the US can supply, the instruments of Cold War diplomacy lose their efficacy.[32]

In 1993 the Clinton administration did attempt to use this Cold War-style diplomacy in East Asia through using a double-barrelled approach. It simultaneously raised two threats: first, the supposed danger to the region of a North Korean nuclear strike; and secondly, a lower-level kind of 'threat' – China's human rights behaviour.[33] Both, of course, had an anti-Communist flavouring. These démarches were coupled with a drive to brigade the non-Communist East and South-East Asian countries, including Japan, into a major drive to open their economies to the US within the so-called Asia Pacific Economic Co-operation (APEC), the aim of which was both to open up the economies of the region in ways which favoured US penetration and to weaken the impulses towards regional economic co-operation within ASEAN to the exclusion of the USA.[34]

But these efforts to use the old Cold War techniques for economic objectives failed. The confrontation with North Korea misfired as the US discovered that Pyongyang could be pushed into actual military conflict as a result of fear of an American strike – and military conflict was actually the last thing the US wanted – while the US simultaneously found that other states in the region preferred *Chinese* mediation *between* Pyongyang and Washington to lining up behind US bluster against North Korea. It was a diplomatic disaster and humiliation for the US. As for the attempt to mobilise political support in the region for an alliance against China based on human rights rhetoric, this overlooked the fact that most of the potential allied governments found US rhetoric about human rights distasteful, at best. After declaring early in 1993 that continuing US–Chinese trade relations would depend upon improvements in China's respect for human rights,[35] the Clinton administration felt compelled to declare a year later that 'we need to place our relationship into a larger and more productive framework' than one centred upon human rights.[36] This change of line came at a time when Washington needed Peking's help over North Korea. But it also came after a year in which Washington's European allies had refused to follow Washington's lead on the human rights card and were eager to gain as much extra business in China as possible.[37]

3) Launching or threatening all-round economic warfare against the region (including oil-war, like that used by the Nixon administration against its 'allies' in the early 1970s)

This idea has been intensively and publicly aired within the United States in relation to Japan since the mid-1980s. The seriousness of this was demonstrated by the way in which a public media campaign to identify Japan as an enemy and a threat was developed by some influential groups within the United States. Yet a direct, frontal campaign of economic warfare and blockade against the whole region or against Japan would have been enormously costly and counter-productive. The European powers would probably not have co-operated. The campaign could have destroyed the tissue of US-led international institutions and could have destabilised the American economy itself. Instead, the concept of all-round economic warfare was deployed by the Clinton administration as a threat, a potentiality, supported by the assembling of a battery of instruments and operational concepts. These instruments included mechanisms such as the Super-301 instrument for unilateral trade-war, created in the Reagan period, the strengthening of so-called anti-dumping actions, the declaration that US economic access to other economies was now a *national security issue* (thus an issue on which economic warfare could be used), and the doctrine of the existence of *economic adversary states* to which liberal economic principles should not be applied. Alongside these concepts, the Clinton administration dropped even lip-service to so-called GATT multilateral principles in trade issues, adopting instead as its key principle reciprocity and raising the slogan of 'fair' trade. And finally the threat that the US would build a regional fortress in the American hemisphere which would be used to exclude East Asian operators.

4) An activist drive to change the programmes of the multilateral organisations

Within the workings of the DWSR, US administrations in the 1980s had extracted gains from crisis-hit countries in terms of opening their financial markets to free flows of international funds, opening their financial markets to US financial operators, opening their asset markets for buy-out by US corporations and so on. But these were piecemeal gains associated with particular countries and crises. Some of the gains, particularly in relation to the free flow of international funds, were partially reversed, as occurred in Chile and other places. But the problem was that East and South-East Asia had largely escaped such treatment because these states had largely avoided financial crises.

   Building upon work already achieved under the Reagan and Bush administrations, the Clinton administration decided to radicalise the programmes of various multilateral organisations in order to commit them to the radical opening of national economies. This would then turn them into the functional equivalent of the role played by what Huntington called the security zones of the Cold War. States that wished to function within these multilateral institutions would, to paraphrase what Rothkoepf said in the context of bodies like NATO, have to deal with the United States – the controlling power within these organisations – on their domestic economic assets. And if a state tried to evade 'dealing with the United States' on these issues, it could be excluded from membership of the multilateral institutions. And if it was so excluded, it could be subjected to a full range of instruments of economic warfare and be denied secure insertion in international markets, since such secure insertion would increasingly depend upon a state's good standing in the multilateral organisations. The result was four interlinked campaigns to change the programmes of these bodies as follows:

1)   First, changing the programme of the IMF to commit it to the ultimate complete dismantling of controls on the capital account in every country, letting funds flow into and out of countries freely. The great political

triumph on this was the decision at the IMF/WB gatherings in Hong Kong in 1997 to change the IMF Articles of Agreement to commit the IMF to complete liberalisation in this way.

2) Second, adding a new programmatic package to the World Trade Organisation's programme through an agreement to liberalise financial services with the ultimate objective of complete freedom for financial operators to enter every financial system with the same rights as local operators (so-called national treatment). The great political triumph here was, supposedly, the deal achieved in the World Trade Organisation in December 1997 on the global liberalisation of financial services.[38]

3) Third, changing the programme of the OECD in two main ways: first, making the ending of controls on capital accounts and on the movement of financial service operators a precondition for OECD membership; and second, through adding a package of rules known as the Multilateral Agreement on Investment (MAI), which would grant complete freedom for industrial corporations to move into national economies and buy up local companies, set up their own operations and dominate local product markets: the great political triumph here was supposed to occur in 1998, with the final MAI agreement, although the OECD horse would, as it turned out, stumble at the last fence in the negotiations.

4) Fourthly, a whole battery of other measures, from the organisation of securities markets to the protection of technological monopolies (so called intellectual property rights), to be adopted by the multilateral organisations giving their (US) leadership the right to reorganise a state's internal social relations of production to fit with the require-ments of US operators, or, to put the point another way, to match the most recent 'scientific' advances in economic thought as expressed by the Washington Consensus.

The point about these campaigns was not actually to tear down all the insti-tutional barriers everywhere at one go. As a matter of fact, the Clinton administration would not necessarily have had the slightest objection to an ally like Chile re-imposing some element of capital controls. The point was to use these changes in the programmes of the multilateral organisations as what might be described as political can-openers to open the lids of *certain specific political economies*: those of East and South-East Asia.

It is important to understand the exact politics involved in the radicalisation of the programmes of the multilateral organisations. First, the drive could appear to respond to the great power of the idea of establishing a cosmopoli-tan system of global governance for its responds to deep, wide and thoroughly justified human yearnings in the contemporary world to overcome nation-state rivalries. The programme radicalisation seems to achieve this. Secondly, there is the great power of the idea of replacing the command politics of one state against another by the rule of law, universal laws by which all will be bound. The radicalisation programme seems to correspond to this desire since people assume that the multilateral organisations work in a rule-based way. But thirdly and most crucially, these two powerful ideas co-exist with a reality which entirely contradicts them: the multilateral organisations are supranational forces for most of their member states but not for all, not for those states, above all the USA, which control them. An organisation used by one state to govern the globe is not a supranational institution of 'global governance'. The US can block items it dislikes off the agendas of the IMF/WB and the OECD. It agreed to the WTO's creation on the explicit basis that if WTO rulings were 'unfair' to the US, then US governments would be duty bound to ignore them. And this leaves the WTO as a framework not of law but of bargaining. In cases where the US can strike a better deal bilaterally outside the framework of the WTO it will be do so and will strike such deals in violation of WTO principles. And as the Dutch Atlantic Commission's study of US trade policy shows, this policy was moving, under Clinton, under the code word 'fair trade', in the direction of managed trade, using the governing principle for the United States of reciprocity rather than multilateralism.[39] The concept of managed trade, systematically pursued by the US towards Japan, involves replacing a rule-based trade regime with a results-based regime. In other words, target states must accept certain quantitative targets for their imports and exports of particular sets of goods, as in Comecon-style trade planning.

But a final feature of the US politics of radicalising the programmes of the multilateral organisations should be noted. The entire drive could not have been accomplished without the support of the European Union and its member states. Following the conclusion of the Uruguay Round there were unmistakable signs of a new Atlantic Partnership for reorganising and resubordinating the world economy in the interests of these two centres. As US Assistant Commerce Secretary (for market access and compliance) Vargo has explained, 'Experience has shown that, large as we are, we cannot open the global marketplace on our own. We must have partners in that endeavour . . . No trade round or other major multilateral initiative has been achieved without the joint leadership of the United States and Europe.'[40] And Vargo goes on to explain how prior US–EU agreement was vital for the Uruguay Round, the Information Technology Agreement and the Basic Telecommunications Agreement. The same was also true of the WTO financial services agreement and, until the French government's revolt, over the OECD's draft MAI Treaty as well. Stuart Eizenstat, Undersecretary of State for Economic, Business and Agricultural Affairs, has also underlined the centrality of this co-operative effort, creating pressure on Asian and Latin American countries to fall into line.[41]

The institution which has played the central role in preparing the ground for such transatlantic coalition-building has been the so-called Transatlantic

Business Dialogue (TABD), proposed at the conclusion of the Uruguay Round in December 1994 by US Commerce Secretary Ron Brown and established in a first meeting in Seville in November 1995. As Assistant Secretary of Commerce Vargo has noted, his department advanced the TABD concept because it believed that 'given the enormous cross-investment by US and European firms in each other's markets, a single transatlantic business community already existed that could agree jointly on common solutions which would benefit both the US and European economies.'[42] The TABD meets regularly before the twice-yearly US–EU summit meetings to feed proposals into these summits.

5) Using a mix of carrots and sticks in bilateral and regional economic statecraft

By combining continuous manoeuvring between bilateral, intra-regional, inter-regional and multilateral moves in a very sophisticated way the Clinton administration has sought to maximise its gains. At one moment it seems to move towards a drive for a new economic Monroe doctrine to take over Latin America, weaken MERCOSUR and threaten to exclude Japan and East Asia or even Europe. When fear runs high in other regions, it then offers peace with say, East Asia in exchange for a big access deal of the right sort there. Europe then panics that the US is constructing a bilateral monopoly with Japan and offers either a bilateral EU–US monopoly or a global multilateral deal. Such offers are then taken back to Asia and turned into another threat of a bilateral monopoly unless ASEAN deals. And so on.

The Clinton administration thus used the tactic of threatened exclusion with skill: it laid enormous early emphasis on the supposedly massive strategic significance of NAFTA, making the EU and the East Asian countries fear Clinton wanted a regional fortress from which to wage trade war. This was an ideal atmosphere in which Clinton could finally lock horns with the French over the Uruguay Round. At the same time the Franco-American marathon neatly crowded out all other countries' concerns over the proposed WTO treaty since there was simply no time to tackle such problems: Asian concerns could be ignored. And armed with the WTO deal, the Clinton administration then agreed with Congress that the US would reserve the right to ignore the WTO if it started treating the US 'unfairly'. In the context of this anxiety, Clinton made much play of making APEC a mighty lever for constructing a US–Japanese bloc, provided, of course, the East and South-East Asians including Japan opened their economies up to the US.

The Open Door drive in East Asia was pressed by the Clinton Administration both bilaterally and through APEC. The APEC summit in Seattle in 1993 agreed to create 'a community of Asia Pacific economies' and spurred the successful conclusion of the Uruguay Round in the GATT.

APEC's Bogor Declaration in Indonesia the following year pledged 'to achieve free and open trade and investment in the region' by 2010 for the industrial countries that make up 85 per cent of APEC trade and by 2020 for the rest. The 1995 Osaka APEC summit adopted a so-called Action Agenda that sets out the principles, the menu of issues and the timetables through which APEC's political commitments would be translated into tangible results. The APEC leaders at Osaka pledged to start liberalisation in January 1997. The November 1996 summit at Subic in the Philippines demonstrated that the governments of the region were far from unanimous on the need to translate their high principles into practical liberalisation measures. But as preparations for the November 1997 Vancouver summit got underway, the mouthpieces of American financial globalisation interests were pressing more strongly than ever for the open door. Fred Bergsten, for example, from the Institute of International Economics in Washington, was still insisting: 'Liberalization and deregulation of financial services are essential to sustain economic development throughout the APEC region (as elsewhere).' Yet APEC's actual practical progress in the direction the Clinton administration wanted was minimal, even trivial.

Washington took an exceptionally tough stance for the radical demolition of controls on the movement of financial services, but it did so in a carefully targeted way, threatening to pull out of a WTO agreement and build its own network of liberalised financial services markets unless certain specific countries greatly liberalised entry of financial services: namely Thailand, Indonesia and other East and South-East Asian countries. At the same time, the Clinton administration ensured that the OECD committed itself to insisting any new members must first dismantle their capital controls or get a plan for their dismantling agreed and then used that as a weapon against Korea, which was seeking OECD entry.

The campaign to open up East Asia's financial sectors had begun in the 1980s, focused on capital account liberalisation and financial deregulation. During the 1980s, Korea removed many of its controls on capital outflows, including portfolio investment abroad, outward financial credits and bank deposits. But it retained many restrictions on various kinds of capital inflows, especially those resulting in debt obligations. Up to 1997 ceilings were placed on total amounts of domestic securities that could be issued abroad. There were also ceilings on levels of portfolio investments in Korean stocks. But foreign investors were given easier access to domestic bond markets. And before Korea's accession to the OECD in December 1996, it removed a number of restrictions, such as those on intra-company loans of an FDI character, and those on friendly mergers between foreign and Korean companies (though mergers of the biggest chaebols with foreign partners were still prohibited). By joining the OECD, Korea was obliged to design a schedule for implementing the

OECD Codes of Liberalisation of Capital Movements and Current Invisible Operations and to endorse the 1976 OECD Declaration on International Investment and Multinational Enterprises as well as the OECD's 'National Treatment' Decision. Another important dimension is the relaxation of restrictions on cross-border trade in financial services. The liberalisation schedule which Korea agreed with the OECD involved speeding up liberalisation measures to complete most of them by December 1998 and the remainder by December 1999.[43]

While repeated US attempts to engage in trade conflict with Japan had proved increasingly ineffective because of the Japanese capacity to resist and even retaliate, Washington was able to wage a vigorous trade war against Korea: it imposed anti-dumping actions against Korean TVS, imposed so-called 'voluntary export restraints' on Korean steel, textiles and clothing, used the Super-301 clause against Korean products because it claimed Korea was using unfair practices and demanded greater and greater opening of Korea to specific US products.[44] This wave of trade war against Korea worked. A Korean trade surplus with the USA of $9.6 billion in 1987 was turned into a trade deficit with the USA of over $4 billion by 1996.[45]

Meanwhile both Thailand and Indonesia substantially removed their capital controls, but they did not open up full rights for US financial operators to compete in their domestic economies. Malaysia took a similar line. These countries' resistance to US operators gaining free entry and national treatment in their financial sectors was treated as a cardinal international issue by the US government at the start of 1997. It threatened to block the entire WTO package deal on the liberalisation of financial services unless Thailand and Indonesia in particular but other East Asian countries as well fully signed up to liberalisation. In the spring of 1997, the British government on behalf of West European governments sought to mediate and persuade the US government to moderate its demands. But for the Clinton administration, these countries were the key and the key to them was opening up their financial sectors. This was the position in April 1997 when a new actor entered the bargaining arena: the big US hedge funds began their attack on the Thai financial market.

But the aim of these kinds of attack was not just a quantitative one. If so, by 1997 the USA should have been well satisfied: Korea had become the USA's fifth largest export market. The aim was a radical restructuring of the social relations of production within Korea in order to engineer an economic *Gleichschaltung* of Korean capitalism and of others in the region with the interests of American capitalism. And that required seeking internal allies within Korea and other states in the region, allies who could help to open the lid on their social relations.

6) Seeking domestic social linkages in target states through propaganda

The Clinton administration's mercantilist trade diplomacy was simply, there-fore, one tactical prong of a multi-pronged strategy. Another very important tactic was that of building and strengthening ideological linkages with strate-gic social groups inside the states of the region. At the level of mass propaganda, the key was the notion that all had to face the reality of an irre-sistible force whether for good or ill: the force was not, of course, the United States: if it had been, then it would have confronting the not insignificant force of Korean nationalism. No, the force in question was, of course, 'glob-alisation'. But for a more sophisticated bourgeois audience a different kind of more focused propaganda campaign was launched, appealing to the ren-tier side of the passions of local capitalists. To appeal to this rentier interest, economic life is reconfigured as the constant struggle of the saver against brutal 'financial repression', for freedom to place his or her funds where s/he likes and for his or her right to a just royalty on a nest egg.

In the mid-1990s a large US propaganda campaign was targeted at the Korean business class's rentier inclinations by the institutions of the Washington consensus, including not least the publications of the IMF and World Bank. A good example of such propaganda is provided by the Institute for International Economics in Washington, a tirelessly repetitive source of such transparently American-serving material. Their grandly titled APEC paper called 'Restructuring Korea's Financial Sector for Competitiveness' is a diatribe against 'financial repression' on behalf of the toiling Korean rentiers. It explains that without freedom 'savers are offered low rates of return'; with financial repression 'projects are typically not funded according to their rates of return, but rather on the basis of noneco-nomic considerations . . . In the case of Korea, this is reflected in the low average rate of return on bank assets, which is among the lowest of those observed in emerging markets . . . More generally, government intervention in the financial markets erodes the autonomy of the private sector which becomes increasingly vulnerable to policy decisions by government offi-cials . . . The result is income growth that is slower than needs be . . .' Furthermore 'Markets cannot work efficiently in the absence of reliable information. Simply think of the problem of trying to value shares in the stock market under such conditions' and 'Lastly, financial repression acts as an implicit tax on holders of government debt. By restricting capital flows, the government can in effect force domestic residents to accept government debt at lower interest rates than would be the case if there were no controls on capital.'[46] In short, for the authors, economics is mainly about the human rights of savers to earn that extra percentage point of interest, a roy-alty cruelly repressed for decades by South Korea's malign concentration on economic growth.

7) Using the instruments available through the DWSR for currency and financial warfare

By 1997, it was possible to argue that the US had chalked up a significant range of quantitative successes in its East and South-East Asian campaigns. It had achieved successes both in gaining new legal rights of entry and in gaining a greater quantity of profits from the region. Yet the relative weight of US capitals in the region's economy was still in decline.

The 1997 annual report of the American TPCC (Trade Promotion Co-ordinating Committee) showed a declining US share of the Asian export market. While the US had increased its share of exports to Mexico, Argentina and Brazil, the US's market share in China, India, and South Korea (as well as in South Africa and Turkey) had declined.

The share of total US exports that went to Asia increased from 15 per cent in 1990 to 20 per cent in 1996. But its share of total exports to the region in twenty-five key product categories fell from 13.5 per cent in 1990 to 12.3 per cent in 1996. Japan's share fell from 20.5 per cent to 18 per cent and the EU's from 16.4 per cent to 15.7 per cent. These declines can be explained for the most part by the rise of intra-Asian exports: their share rose from 34.2 per cent in 1990 to 38.6 per cent in 1996. 'However, in key instances, US share loss was due specifically to gains by Japan and the EU.'[47] Table 5.1, using a different definition of Asia and excluding intra-Asian trade, under-lines how weak the US position was, relative to Japan.

Table 5.1   G7 Exports to Asia in 1996

Exporting country	Percentage of Asian export market
USA	29
Japan	43
Germany	10
UK	6
Italy	5
France	4
Canada	2

Notes: Asia includes South Korea, ASEAN, India, Pakistan, China and Hong Kong. Total exports in 1996 = $350 billion.

Such statistics suggest that by early 1997 the US campaign towards the region was failing.

Or was it? There is one weapon in the locker of the US Treasury which we have not yet looked at: its ability to exploit the Dollar–Wall Street Regime as an instrument for currency and financial warfare. The use of the DWSR as such an instrument is easily explained. The region's political economies did not suffer from the usual kind of Third World vulnerability: domestically politically weak states whose weakness was expressed as high budget deficits leading to high borrowings and debts on international financial markets. The region's states were not indebted in this way. Their vulnerability to the DWSR arose in the first place at the currency pole of the DWSR. They were mainly reliant on export-led growth. This made them vulnerable to strong movements in currencies. Since their currencies were mainly tied to the dollar and they exported significantly to Japan, a low dollar against the yen boosted exports, but a high dollar against a falling yen hit their exports. During the early 1990s, as part of what many see as a deliberate politically inspired US campaign against Japan, the US Treasury supported a falling dollar against the yen. This put very great pressure on Japanese industries and they responded both by shifting new investment into the rest of the region to benefit from the low dollar, and through many voices being raised for the construction of a yen-zone tying the region together under Japanese leadership. This would have been a catastrophic blow to the interests of American capitalism.

But with the appointment of Larry Summers as Under Secretary at the US Treasury in 1995, Washington reversed its dollar–yen policy and allowed the dollar to rise ever higher against the yen. This started to exert great pressure on the exports of many of the region's economies. At the same time, large flows of hot money started pouring into the region from the United States. Those states in the region which had liberalised their capital accounts to allow such flows entry found their currencies being pushed still higher by this inflow of hot money, while simultaneously finding domestic inflationary pressures building up. In 1996 flows into Indonesia, Malaysia, the Philippines and Thailand increased by 43 per cent to $17 billion.[48] Private flows to Asian emerging markets in the 1990s are given in Table 5.2. The effects of the squeeze on exports was to cause difficulties in very important parts of their private sectors and they were tempted to borrow abroad from US and European as well as Japanese banks to tide themselves over the export squeeze.

In short, the combined effects of the two poles of the DWSR were, by 1997, ensnaring the region's economies in a trap. US dollar policy was the first critical precondition for the crisis. The success of the US government and of US financial operators in persuading a number of governments in the region to open their financial sectors to inflows of hot money was the second precondition. The actual flows of hot money that then occurred in 1995–97 were responding to the effects of falling interest rates in the US financial system in the middle of the US boom: they were seeking higher short-term royalties in the still rapidly growing economies of the region. They were the third critical precondition. All that was needed by the spring of 1997 was for someone to pull the trigger. That job was one for a handful of US hedge funds.

Table 5.2   Private Financial Flows to Asian Markets (billions of US$)

	1990	1991	1992	1993	1994	1995	1996
Total net private capital inflow	21.4	37.7	22.4	59.5	75.1	98.9	106.8
Net foreign direct investment	9.5	15.2	17.2	35.2	44.6	50.7	58.0
Net portfolio investment	0.9	2.8	9.6	23.8	18.5	20.1	20.1
Net other investment	12.9	19.7	4.5	0.5	12.0	28.1	28.8
Net external borrowing from official creditors	5.6	10.7	10.2	8.2	5.9	5.0	6.7

Source: International Monetary Fund: International Financial Statistics and World Economic Outlook databases.

Intention and Action in the Run-Up to the East Asian Financial Crisis

The question, of course, arises as to whether the Clinton administration was consciously using the DWSR as an instrument of economic statecraft against the East and South-East Asian economies. What is certain is that the dollar-yen exchange rate is in the policy gift of the US Treasury and Federal Reserve. Summers was deliberately organising a strong dollar against the yen and was fully committed to it. What we do not know is why he wanted the dollar to rise against the yen. One explanation is that he wanted to help out Japanese business and in particular to help it export more to the United States. Is there anyone in the world who would believe that? Another explanation is that he wanted to prevent any moves towards the creation of a yen-zone. But the Japanese government had never joined the movement for such a zone. We are thus left with a mystery over the source of Summers' policy, unless he was interested in squeezing Japan's dollar-linked hinterland economies in the region. Everything that we know about the Clinton administration's obsession with the challenge of the region also points in this direction.

   The Clinton administration was also, in the mid-1990s, concentrating its campaign to end controls on the capital account upon East and South-East Asia. Enormous pressures and inducements were being exerted to this end. There was no sign of such a campaign directed at Chile. The focus was on Asia. And so too was the focus on liberalising the entry of foreign financial services. This was directed especially at Thailand, Indonesia and Korea. The US government did not, of course, organise the flows of hot portfolio funds into the region. But they were bound to occur: the dynamics of such outflows of funds, linked to the domestic US business cycle, are well known. US Treasury Secretary Rubin is an old hand from Goldman Sachs and understands these dynamics perfectly. As Nixon had foreseen back in the 1970s, financial markets can be used as instruments of US external policy.

As to bank loans to East and South-East Asia, the US government always claimed during the Cold War that while German and Japanese banks worked hand in glove with their governments' political strategies, the US government approach was always different.[49] Yet there was, in fact, a strong element of government direction to US banks in the 1970s in the US banks' recycling of petrodollars to countries of the South.

But, of course, we can have no proof of intentionality and of co-ordination with the private sector on the part of the Clinton administration. This absence of proof is common to much work in trying to analyse the actual practice of economic statecraft. We must use circumstantial evidence.

Thus, to take a famous example, it might appear with hindsight that Paul Volcker, head of the US Federal Reserve, understood at the time that when he sharply raised US interest rates in 1979 he would plunge much of Latin America into a major financial and currency crisis. But did he think of that before he raised interest rates? And did he raise interest rates *in order to achieve that result?* He has insisted that the problem was not uppermost in his thinking and that the Fed anyway lacked the resources at the time to make a prior study of the impact of the interest rate rise on the region. We cannot just take his word for it. But circumstantial evidence suggests that we can believe him: there were obvious other domestic reasons for raising interest rates at least to some extent in 1979; and if he had realised he would cause a gigantic crisis in Latin America he would also, surely, have realised that he would bring the US banks to the brink of total collapse. Volcker would hardly have wanted that.

On the other hand, when analysts who may be assumed to have excellent access to US policy-makers claim that the Reagan team deliberately used a high dollar and high interest rates in 1981–83 with the aim of exerting pressure on 'Socialist France' we may well view that as a case of economic statecraft, using monetary policy.[50] The source is credible and the political importance of the goal is all to obvious: the failure of the French drive for growth between 1981 and 1983 was to be viewed in Western Europe as the final defeat of Keynesianism.[51] Here then we have a typical example of the US government using the dollar as a major weapon in a campaign for strategic political objectives. And the significance for the Reagan administration in defeating the French experiment cannot be doubted.

C. Randall Henning of the main Washington think-tank of the US international financial institutions,[52] claims that American governments have frequently used their control over the dollar price as a diplomatic weapon in dealings with Western Europe. Pointing out that the US is less vulnerable to exchange rate shifts than Western Europe, Henning writes: 'When clashing with European governments over macroeconomic policies or the balance of payments, American officials often took advantage of this asymmetry. In several instances, the threat of a precipitous exchange rate movement pressed European governments to reflate or dampen their economies in accordance with American preferences.'[53]

The circumstantial evidence in the East and South-East Asian case points overwhelmingly towards strategic design on the part of the US Treasury. But design for what exactly? To weaken these countries in macroeconomic terms, certainly, and to generate financial instability and currency vulnerability. But to set them up for hedge fund financial warfare?

The activities of the big US hedge funds in the East and South-East Asian crisis may seem to most of us to have been a bolt from the blue. Until the LTCM crisis of September 1998 most people had probably never heard of hedge funds. But for the leaders of the US Treasury they were a central part of their everyday furniture. They had been the central actors in all the major currency and financial crises of the 1990s, such as those of the Italian lira and the pound in 1992, that of the franc and the EU's Exchange Rate Mechanism in 1993, that of the Mexican peso in 1994 and a host of others. And when we speak of hedge funds we are not speaking of the more than 1000 such organisations scattered across the United States: we are talking about a handful of funds of this name which operate on the international currency markets and which have more or less unlimited access to really gigantic loans from the very biggest of the American banks. Although they are opaque and very secret about their operations, they are at the very summit of the American financial structure. And their power makes instruments like Super-301 or anti-dumping instruments look like pea-shooters. We must look a bit closer at how they operate.

Hedge Fund Financial Warfare[54]

The growth of hedge funds operating in foreign exchange markets and especially in foreign exchange derivatives is a direct outgrowth of the DWSR with its wild swings of the dollar against the yen and mark. Foreign exchange derivatives can be used for genuine hedging (i.e. insurance) against swift, large changes in the exchange rates of two currencies (foreign exchange risk). We will explain how this hedging can be used and then look at the kind of speculative operation used by hedge funds. You may be doing business that involves you committing yourself to making purchases over a long period of time in France and the price is denominated in French francs. At the moment sterling is, say, high against the franc at 10 francs to the pound. But something could happen within three months to make the pound fall massively against the franc to 5 francs to the pound. Purchasing at that time will cost you double what it does today. But in the derivatives market you can pay a bank a fee to gain the option of buying francs for pounds at 9.50 francs to the pound. If the franc stays at 10 to the pound all you lose is your fee to the bank. You only had the right to buy francs at 9.50 to the pound, but you didn't have to buy at that price. But if the pound does fall to, say, 6 francs to the pound in three months time, the option covers most of your losses because it allows you to get your francs not at 6 to the pound but at 9.50. So this so-called forward foreign exchange derivative market protects you to some extent.

The key for the hedge fund speculators being able to use these forward markets lies above all in the size of the funds that they can borrow relative to the size of the market. If the speculator's funds are big relative to the market, he can shift market prices with his own funds then gain a multiplier effect as other smaller speculators strengthen that price shift by following it, and as the multiplier effect proceeds, he can withdraw from his position, taking profits.

Using the same example of the franc-sterling exchange rate, the speculator starts in the same way, except that he takes out huge forward contracts to sell pounds for French francs at 9.50 to the pound in one month's time: say forward contracts totalling £10 billion.[55] For these he must pay a fee to a bank. Then he waits until the month is nearly up. Then suddenly he starts borrowing pounds again in very large volumes and throws them against the exchange rate through selling them. So big is his first sale of pounds that the currency falls, say 3 per cent against the franc. At this point other, smaller players see the pound going down and join the trend he has started, driving it down another 3 per cent. Overnight he borrows another vast chunk of pounds and sells into francs again, and meanwhile the word is going around the market that none other than the master speculator is in action, so everyone joins the trend and the pound drops another 10 per cent. And on the day when the forward contract falls due for him to sell pounds for francs at 9.50 the pound in the spot market is down at 5 francs. He takes up his forward contract and makes a huge profit. Meanwhile there is a sterling crisis etc. etc.

The official line of the Washington Consensus, of the IMF Managing Director Camdessus and of Stanley Fischer (Camdessus's deputy and the central operational designer in the IMF) is that the hedge fund speculators are of little significance except as triggers which essentially reveal trends already present in the so-called fundamentals of an economy. The argument is that no speculator can engineer structural shifts in prices on financial markets because there are so many players on these markets and these players act largely rationally, linking their buying and selling to their judgements about the underlying economy concerned. (Fischer has had to become somewhat more nuanced, acknowledging 'swings in market sentiment [which] . . . may on occasion be excessive, and they may sometimes reflect contagion effects, which may themselves be excessive on occasion.')[56]

This is a superficial view, that can be defended only on the basis of experience in large financial markets operating normally with high levels of liquidity in large advanced economies. But as Joseph Stiglitz, the chief economist at the World Bank, and many others have pointed out, this is far from being the case for smaller, much less secure financial markets in smaller economies. Nor is it true even in advanced markets in many circumstances: the sudden fall of the dollar against the yen, by a staggering 10 per cent in less than a week in October 1998, was widely put down to the action of one or two very large funds unloading dollars for yen. They had this effect because the market was thin: when few people are willing to buy (or sell), falls (or rises) are likely to be magnified.

The Camdessus view is also not shared by leading speculators in forward foreign exchange markets, for whom the size of the financial war chest of the speculator relative to the scale of activity on the given foreign exchange market is decisive. Bill Lipschutz, former top currency speculator for Salomon Brothers, explains this vividly in the following interview with Jack Schwager:[57]

'How is large size an advantage?
You're kidding.
No, I'm serious.
If a big buyer comes in and pushes the market 4 per cent that's an advantage.
He still has to get out of that position. Unless he's right about the market, it doesn't seem like large size would be an advantage.
He doesn't have to get out of that position all at once. Foreign exchange is a very psychological market. You're assuming the market is going to move back to equilibrium very quickly – more quickly than he can cover his position. That's not necessarily the case. If you move the market 4 per cent, for example, you're probably going to change the market psychology for the next few days. [In other words, when others see a big swing created by a powerful hedge fund, they follow its lead for the next few days, also buying, enabling the hedge fund to sell to them and take its profits.]
So you're saying size is an advantage.
It's a huge advantage in foreign exchange.
How large an account were you trading at Salomon?
That question really has no direct meaning. For a company like Salomon there are no assets directly underlying the trading activity. Rather, over time, the traders and treasurer build up greater and greater amounts of credit facilities at the banks. The banks were eager to extend these credit lines because we were Salomon Brothers. This is an example of another way in which size was an advantage. By 1990, our department probably had $80 billion in credit lines. However, no specific assets were segregated or pledged to the foreign exchange activities.' In mentioning $80 billion, Lipschutz was referring to the end of the 1980s. By the mid-1990s, the leverage

available to the top speculative operators could be ten times that figure.

And Lipschutz's last answer brings us to the huge financial strike power that these big hedge funds can mobilise from the US banks. One of the most dramatic revelations from the LTCM affair was the way it revealed that this fund had more or less unlimited access to loans from the biggest of the American banks. Although the activities of funds like LTCM, Soros's Quantum Group and Robertson's Tiger Fund are very secretive they operate right at the very centre of Wall Street networks. The IMF has suggested these funds can borrow twenty times their capital, Soros admitted to fifty times. But the LTCM was revealed to have borrowed 250 times its capital base.[58] The main hedge funds are supposed to have a combined capital base of $300 billion. Let us assume that their leverage is only 100 times their capital (and not the 250 times of LTCM). That would give them a collective leverage of $30 trillion. Of course, they don't all work together: only some of the top hedge funds do. Thus, attacks on currencies are usually the work of half a dozen of the biggest hedge funds operating together. They can mobilise funds far larger than the GDP of middle-sized rich OECD economies like, say, Australia.

The derivatives markets dwarf all other financial sectors and the biggest of these markets is that for foreign exchange derivatives. A 1995 study by the Bank for International Settlements put the total principal in foreign exchange derivatives at $16 trillion.[59] While daily turnover in the ordinary foreign exchange market was $520 billion in April 1995, daily turnover in the foreign exchange derivatives market in that month was $740 billion.

It might be thought that such a huge market would involve a large and diverse collection of operators. Yet this is not so. The centres of this market are in the US, in London and in Canada and no less than 75 per cent of business in these centres is handled, according to an IMF study, by just ten hedge funds.[60] And these ten companies work very closely together. The great bulk of their business is 'over the counter' rather than within exchange institutions and it is totally unregulated. And they are very secretive. According to the IMF, some 69 per cent of foreign exchange derivative business is conducted between these dealers. And collectively these companies can mobilise enormous financial resources. The IMF estimates that the foreign exchange derivatives hedge funds can mobilise between $600 billion and $1 trillion to bet against currencies in speculative attacks.[61] This is truly staggering firepower.

There is no doubt whatever that the hedge funds were the driving force of the attack first on the Thai baht, then on other regional currencies and the Hong Kong stock market. The first hedge fund assault on the baht occurred in May 1997, one month after the Clinton administration launched its campaign demanding that Thailand and Indonesia open their financial sectors fully to US financial operators. Thailand was the most vulnerable target for attack because it was actually the most open economy in the region, the one whose government had adopted a model closest to US demands. It was also suffering from that typical feature of American-style open financial systems – a large speculative bubble in its property market.

The central roles of the hedge funds in the triggering of the Asian crises of 1997 was fully reported at the time by the *Financial Times* and other financial papers.[62] Yet much of the mainstream Anglo-American media have treated this as if it was the paranoid populism of Malaysian Prime Minister Mahathir. Mahathir was simply stating a fact about the role of these operators. And he was not alone. A dispute amongst the IMF directors themselves has exploded into public view on this question, an unprecedented event. Under pressure from East and South-East Asian governments, as well, perhaps, as fellow directors of the IMF, Managing Director Camdessus agreed to carry out an investigation of the hedge funds' activities in the crisis. He then chose a mainstream American economist for the job. When the report came in, Camdessus agreed with it. But other IMF directors did not. They considered the report unsatisfactory because it underplayed the role of these institutions in the crisis. They did not just disagree. They insisted that Camdessus publicly record the disagreement in the main directors' report for the autumn 1998 Washington IMF conference. This is unprecedented in IMF history. It suggests much more than an analytical disagreement: a belief on the part of some directors that they were faced with some sort of cover-up on the issue.

Of course one of the reasons for the extreme sensitivity of this issue is because the US government must have been very well informed about the activities of these hedge funds. They would know this because the Federal Reserve would know that the big US banks were bankrolling the East Asian operations of these funds. US intelligence would also be informed. The main banks of any state work extremely closely with their state.[63] Commonly governments get their leading private sector banks to extend credit to a foreign government or large company in the furtherance of foreign policy objectives. And the top banks can in turn gain access to intelligence information from their governments, important for assessing political and other kinds of risk. All this is so to speak normal. US officials always used to argue that the US government was different from others in this respect. Such claims may have carried some force during the Cold War. But after the damage done by the US hedge funds to Clinton's Mexico policy in 1994–95, it is scarcely credible that the US government would have done nothing to bring some oversight, at the least, over what its hedge funds were up to. If US intelligence has, as we know, been largely switched towards economic and commercial intelligence we can doubt that this work is confined to the small change of negotiations on business deals while steering clear of the politically absolutely central field of international finance.

But whatever the exact relationship between the activity of these funds and the activity of the US Treasury, they were both acting in the same direction in the summer and autumn of 1997.

Notes

1. A useful restatement of these positions is found in Krugman, 'Competitiveness: A Dangerous Obsession', *Foreign Affairs* (March/April 1994).

2. The classic statement of this position is found in Kenneth Waltz's work.

3. The work of Robert Gilpin has done much to revive this trend of thought as a means of understanding international economics. His work in this field began at the start of the 1970s with 'The Politics of Transnational Economic Relations', *International Organization*, 25:3 (1971).

4. Because the current account combines both trade in goods and invisibles, including the stream of earnings from MNC production abroad and debt servicing, it is the most useful indicator of a state's basic economic relationship with the rest of the world.

5. In the draft US Senate trade bill, in 1986, one of its sections began: 'When trading with adversaries, like Japan . . .' Such language has become standard in Washington. See C. Michael Aho, 'America and the Pacific Century: Trade Conflict or Co-operation?' *International Affairs*, 69:1 (1993).

6. The inflow of funds didn't come only from Japan: the biggest inflow actually came from the UK and very large flows also came from Holland. But the Japanese bought a lot of the Treasury debt. With the fall of the dollar in the late 1980s, these mainly private Japanese holders of US dollars saw over $200 billion wiped off the value of their holdings as a result of this dollar devaluation and by the 1990s, the US government came to rely increasingly upon Japanese *state* funds flowing into Treasury bonds. Thus, the stability of the system came to depend upon the political commitment of the Japanese government to US stability. On this, see Susan Strange, *Mad Money* (Manchester University Press, 1998).

7. These began with the construction of 'European Political Co-operation' and the project of monetary union both launched at the start of the 1980s. Though both were largely abortive, the impulses behind them remained, and gathered strength.

8. These pressures were championed by Jo Chamberlain, the political leader of the West Midlands industrial bourgeoisie.

9. Although now intellectually discredited by the work of Walter and others, the American theory of so-called hegemonic stability which argues that the world needs one overwhelmingly dominant state if there is to be stability in the world economy (and especially its monetary system), had the great merit of pointing to the lack of automatic stabilisers in the core economy. Their question: who will provide the 'public goods' of stability is best answered by saying it is provided by the dependent support-countries of the South, even though the goods they provide are not really 'public' since they are enjoyed only by the core economies. On the theory, see Walter, *World Power and World Money* (Harvester).

10. P. Patnaik, *Accumulation and Stability Under Capitalism* (Clarendon Press, 1997).

11. Estimates by Matthew Simon, cited by Patnaik in Patnaik, *Accumulation and Stability*.

12. Will Marshall, head of the Progressive Policy Institute, *Washington Post*, 21 December 1992.

13. Roger Morris, 'A New Foreign Policy for a New Era', *New York Times*, 9 December 1992.

14. Aspen in Defence had a more activist, radical agenda.

15. See, for example, Anthony Hartley, 'The Clinton Approach: Idealism and Prudence', *The World Today* (February 1993).

16. Of this list one partial dissident was Robert Reich: he shared a belief in state action in international economics and his concern for labour standards and protection could be usefully instrumentalised in economic diplomacy over trade issues. But he lacked some of the America-First-in-Everything zeal of the others and dropped out of the administration eventually.

17. Gioia Marini and Jan Rood, 'Maintaining Global Dominance: The United States as a European and Asian Power' in Marianne van Leeuwen and Auke Venema (eds.), *Selective*

Engagement: American Foreign Policy at the Turn of the Century (Netherlands Atlantic Commission, 1996).

18. See Laura D'Andrea Tyson, *Who's Bashing Whom: Trade Conflict in High-Technology Industries* (Institute for International Economics, 1992); Ira Magaziner and Mark Patinkin, *The Silent War: Inside the Global Business Battles Shaping America's Future* (Vintage Books, 1990); Jeffrey E. Garten, *A Cold Peace: America, Japan, Germany and the Struggle For Supremacy* (New York Times Books, 1992).

19. USIS, 23 February 1996: 'Kantor says US to Fight Farm Trade Barriers.'

20. Rubin was later to become Treasury Secretary – his current position.

21. David J. Rothkopf, 'Beyond Manic Mercantilism', Council on Foreign Relations, 1998.

22. Stanley Hoffman, Martin Wight Memorial Lecture, LSE, June 1998.

23. Rothkopf, 'Beyond Manic Mercantilism'.

24. Rothkopf, 'Beyond Manic Mercantilism'.

25. John Stremlau, 'Clinton's Dollar Diplomacy', *Foreign Policy*, 97 (Winter 1994–95).

26. Gioia Marini and Jan Rood, 'Maintaining Global Dominance: The United States as a European and Asian Power' in Marianne van Leeuwen and Auke Venema (eds.), *Selective Engagement: American Foreign Policy at the Turn of the Century* (Netherlands Atlantic Commission, 1996).

27. The deaths of twenty US soldiers in Somalia was enough to abort the US mission there. In the Bosnian and Kosovo cases, the Clinton administration was not prepared to put the feet of US soldiers on the ground while fighting was going on. Air power can destroy states but cannot control populations.

28. Samuel P. Huntington, 'Transnational Organisations in World Politics' *World Politics*, vol. 25, no. 3 (1973) p. 344.

29. David J. Rothkopf, 'Beyond Manic Mercantilism'.

30. For the British, the threat came within their Empire (and indeed, partly from the USA's desire to open it up). But by getting the US to take over the battle against Communism in Europe, they hoped to free their own resources to save the Empire against a whole range of pressures, including American ones.

31. See Gilbert Achcar, 'The Strategic Triad: The United States, Russia and China', *New Left Review* 228 (March/April 1998).

32. Of course, great powers do not simply have to *respond* to locally created dangers and crises. They can *create* local crises and threats which then lead other states in the vicinity of the crises to welcome or at least accept the great power's intervention to tackle the crisis. Those who have followed attentively the Bush administration's operations in relation to Bosnia in 1992 can see the unmistakable signs of the US deploying such tactics in the EU's hinterland. See Susan Woodward, *The Balkan Tragedy* (Brookings, 1996).

33. This campaign dovetailed, of course, with the British campaign to keep Hong Kong's wealth-stream flowing in the right direction after the hand-over of the colony to China.

34. On US perceptions of ASEAN in the early 1990s as the embryo of a move towards a Japanese regional bloc, see C. Michael Aho, 'America and the Pacific Century'.

35. David Lampton, 'America's China Policy in the Age of the Finance Minister: Clinton Ends Linkage', *The China Quarterly*, no. 139 (September 1994).

36. Press conference statement, The White House, 26 May 1994.

37. Lampton, 'America's China Policy'.

38. The WTO Financial Services Agreement did not, in fact, go as far as the US had hoped. See Wendy Dobson and Pierre Jacquet, *Financial Services Liberalisation in the WTO* (Institute for International Economics, 1998).

39. Examples of managed trade are the emphasis since the 1980s on the part of the EC and the US on so-called Voluntary Export Restraints (VERs) and the US emphasis, particularly in East Asia and Japan, on Voluntary Import Expansion (VIEs). Both VERs and VIEs are 'results-oriented' instruments characteristic of managed trade. See Frank Buelens, 'US Trade Policy: Free Trade or Fair Trade' in M. van Leeuen and A. Venema (eds.), *Selective Engagement. American Foreign Policy at the Turn of the Century* (Netherlands Atlantic Commission, 1996).

40. Quoted in Robert D. Blackwill and Kristin Archick, *US–European Economic Relations and*

World Trade (Task Force on the Future of Transatlantic Relations, Council on Foreign Relations, April, 1998).

41. Ibid.

42. Testimony before the House Committee on International Relations, Subcommittee on International Economic Policy and Trade, Federal News Service, 10 September 1997.

43. See Robert Ley and Pierre Poret, 'The New OECD Members and Liberalisation', *The OECD Observer*, no. 205 (April/May 1997).

44. See Walden Bello, 'East Asia on the Eve of the Great Transformation', *Review of International Political Economy*, 5:3 (Autumn 1998).

45. Ibid.

46. Institute for International Economics: 'Restructuring Korea's Financial Sector for Greater Competitiveness' (APEC Working Paper 96-14).

47. *Financial Times*, 29 October 1997, p. 10.

48. UNCTAD, *World Investment Report, 1997* (UN New York and Geneva, 1997).

49. See J. Andrew Spindler, *The Politics of International Credit: Private Finance and Foreign Policy in Germany and Japan* (The Brookings Institution, 1984).

50. This claim is made by I. M. Destler and C. Randall Henning in *Dollar Politics: Exchange Rate Policymaking in the United States* (Institute for International Economics, 1989). This institute is the main think-tank of Wall Street financial institutions.

51. Interestingly, economic statecraft involving monetary policy, such as these examples, tend to be ignored in the literature, including in Richard Baldwin's otherwise important book, *Economic Statecraft*. But Susan Strange, without using the term statecraft, has illuminated a great deal in her writings on politics and international money.

52. The Institute for International Economics.

53. C. Randall Henning, 'Europe's Monetary Union and the United States,' *Foreign Policy*, no. 102 (Spring 1996).

54. I am grateful to Michel Chossudovsky for this precise and useful concept. See his 'Guerras financieras', *Vento Sur Numero*, 40 (October 1998).

55. The speculator's counter-party bank can cover its position by simultaneously taking out a forward contract to sell francs for pounds in a month's time.

56. Stanley Fischer, 'Capital Account Liberalisation and the Role of the IMF', paper to seminar on Asia and the IMF (19 September 1997).

57. From Jack D. Schwager, *The New Market Wizards: Conversations with America's Top Traders* (Harper Collins, 1992).

58. IMF, 'Developments and Prospects in Emerging Markets', *World Financial Outlook* (IMF Washington DC, November 1997), p. 33.

59. Bank for International Settlements, 'Central Bank Survey of Foreign Exchange and Derivatives Market Activity', May 1996.

60. Coenraad Vrolijk, 'Derivative Effects on Monetary Transmission', (Working Paper of the International Monetary Fund, WP/97/121, 1997).

61. 'Mahathir, Soros and the Currency Markets', *Economist*, 27 September 1997.

62. See the *Financial Times* for the last week of May 1997 and the first two weeks of July 1997.

63. See, for example, J. Andrew Spindler, *The Politics of International Credit: Private Finance and Foreign Policy in Germany and Japan* (The Brooking Institution, 1984).

6

The Politics and Economics of the Panic of '98

The Asian crisis began in Thailand at the start of July 1997. The next country to fall was Indonesia. But the really decisive financial crisis was that of South Korea. It was the South Korean crisis which ended the temporary stabilisation of Indonesia and which finally brought complete collapse there. And the South Korean crisis was responsible for plunging the whole region into slump.

The general pattern of the crises is easily summarised. Hedge funds attacked currencies, eventually breaking the Thai baht, then the Indonesian rupiah. These hedge fund attacks led the US mutual funds and the Triad's banks as well as other financial operators to pull their funds out of the countries concerned. As the funds poured out, currencies collapsed further and there were two immediate effects: first, local banks could not continue to roll over their dollar debts through new borrowing because the western institutions were no longer lending; and secondly, as currencies collapsed, the size of the dollar debt in terms of local currency resources leapt upwards. This double blow then fed through to the rest of the financial systems of the countries affected as local banks refused new credits to industrial companies, threatening them with insolvency. A vicious downwards spiral ensued threatening a complete collapse of the financial systems upon which any capitalist economy depends for economic activity.

Until the summer of 1997 the East and South-East Asian states had managed for a quarter of a century to avoid being entangled in the lethal, intersecting steel wires of what might be called the twin yo-yos of the Dollar–Wall Street Regime: the currency yo-yo of the dollar-yen-mark exchange rate, throwing trade and investment relations one way then the other; and the financial yo-yos of hot money and short-term loans whizzing into the financial nerve centres of regions' economies and then whipping back out again. No government in the region could do anything about the swings of the yen-dollar exchange rate: they could only try to adjust their

103

exchange rate policy and domestic macroeconomic conditions to try to cope. But those states which had succumbed to the pressures of the US government, the IMF and the Wall Street institutions to open their capital accounts and domestic financial sectors to some extent were allowing their economies and populations to enter a mortally dangerous trap: the inflows of the hot money and short-term loans arrived like manna from heaven, because they seemed to enable these states to evade the effects of currency fluctuations and thus to evade hard domestic adjustments through credits from the Anglo-American financial centres. But it was not manna: it was bait. When the financial sectors of the region bit into it they were hooked, trapped in the sights of the US hedge funds, sitting ducks for financial warfare. The hedge funds struck, the lines of credit were wrenched back into London and New York and economy after economy was dragged, writhing like a wounded animal, on to the operating table of the IMF and the US Treasury.

Of course, not all the East Asian economies were dragged directly into the crisis. Those which had refused to bow to American pressure to dismantle their capital account controls escaped the onslaught because the hedge funds could not hit them. The factor that turned a state's failure of macroeconomic adjustment into a catastrophe was the degree to which the Asian development model had been breached by liberalisation of the capital account. Those countries which had largely kept their capital controls were protected from the financial attacks which followed: China, Taiwan, Vietnam and India. Those that had liberalised in the key areas found their macroeconomic management failures exploited by devastating speculative attacks. And even Hong Kong, which could not have been said to have had serious macroeconomic problems but did have a liberalised capital account, was to be subjected to sustained, repeated hedge fund assaults for more than a year.

Despite this, as in the past crises in other parts of the South in the 1980s, Anglo-American leaders and propaganda media were quick to politically exploit the crisis, making the intellectually illiterate claim that failures to manage exchange rate volatilities and conjunctural financial sector instability proved the bankruptcy of the East Asian growth model and the universal validity of the Anglo-Saxon model of capitalism.[1]

As throughout the history of the DWSR, the East Asian crisis was to be a case of what might be called the teamwork between the spontaneous drives of the financial forces of Wall Street and the political will and ingenuity of Washington. As the crisis spread across the region, the US Treasury and the Federal Reserve were serene about its global consequences. They knew from a wealth of past experience that financial blow-outs in countries of the South provided a welcome boost for the US financial markets and through them for the US domestic economy. Huge funds could be expected to flood into the US financial markets, cheapening the costs of credit there, boosting the stock market and boosting domestic growth. And there would be a rich harvest of assets to be reaped in East Asia when these countries fell to their knees before the IMF.

But Rubin, Larry Summers and Alan Greenspan made four analytical errors. First they failed fully to grasp the fact that East and South-East Asia was no longer just the South: it was a dynamic and weighty component of the world economy. A deep crisis there would transform the economic equations of those economies outside the triad which supplied inputs for the East and South-East Asian boom. These commodity producers would see their export prices slump. This fact in itself need not have alarmed Rubin. On the contrary, the prospect may have delighted him. Declining relative prices of commodities from the South had been one of the keys to the non-inflationary American boom.

But if Rubin was taking this view of the likely fall in commodity prices, he was guilty of American-centred thinking and forgetting another context upon which the commodity producers' falling export prices would impact: the endemic structural financial fragility of these commodity producing countries as a result of the past triumphs of the DWSR. Countries like Russia and Brazil may have been turned successfully by the DWSR into a honey-pot for Wall Street financial operators but they were honey-pots precisely because they were so much weakened by debt burdens. A weakening of their and many other similar countries' trade prospects as a result of the East Asian crisis could tip them over the abyss as financial operators saw the threat and fled.

And the third problem that Rubin did not fully grasp was that the huge growth of speculative forces within the US financial system itself could only be sustainable through constant expansion. Like the pyramid funds of Albania, such speculative forces can sustain losses on betting with borrowed money on the part of some players only through the bulk of the others being able to throw more money on to the table and to make fresh gains. With multiple financial crises occurring simultaneously in many places, the speculative forces on Wall Street could find that the banks bankrolling them would lose confidence in continued expansion, fear collapse and then move to create it by refusing further lending.

Analytical failures of these kinds were to lead Robert Rubin to approach the Asian crisis not just with serenity but with excitement and enthusiasm. As we shall see, the US Treasury was to view the crisis as an historic opportunity which, if seized, could transform the future of American capitalism, anchoring its dominance into the twenty-first century. This was the fourth problem that Rubin failed to foresee: the problem of Rubin himself as an actor in the crisis.

We will not review the details of the course of the East Asian crisis.[2] We will focus only on the responses of the Japanese and American governments to the crisis and in particular on the stance of the US Treasury towards the decisive moment of the East Asian events: the South Korean financial breakdown. We will then look at the structural reasons for the transformation of the Asian crisis into a generalised international financial panic in 1998. And we will conclude by considering whether they may be a path away from 'globalisation'.

Tokyo's Crippling Defeat

As the Asian crisis spread across the region from Thailand in July and August 1997, the most affected states turned to other states for help. The US government refused to take any positive action to stabilise financial systems and currencies and kept the IMF on a leash. At the height of the Thai crisis in August, the US government's response was to send a delegation to Bangkok demanding further liberalisation of Thai markets to improve access for American capital.[3] Japan therefore faced a decisive test, the biggest political test it had faced for, perhaps, fifty years. It could take upon itself the task of leading the region out of crisis, but in doing so it would challenge the political authority of the IMF and the central strategic drive of the US. But if the Japanese government remained supine and let the Clinton administration dictate events and terms, the consequences for Japanese capitalism could be extremely grave. Its financial system, already in serious difficulties, could be dragged down by its very heavy exposure in the region and the US would be likely to exploit this weakness up to the hilt.

The Japanese government attempted to steel its will to intervene politically. It came forward with a proposal that it would manage an Asian consortium, an Asian Monetary Fund (AMF) to stabilise affected countries. This initiative drew strong support from governments in the region. Particularly striking was the Chinese government's support for the plan, an unmistakable sign that a regional coalition between Japan and China was a distinct possibility. The Thai rescue package was the result of the work of the Japanese government in putting together a coalition. But at the last moment the IMF and the US entered the scene to put their trademarks on it to prevent an open Japanese challenge to IMF global control. But still the Japanese government advanced its AMF proposal, suggesting that the fund could have $100 billion of financial resources. As one analyst explained '[US] Treasury officials accordingly saw the AMF as more than just a bad idea: they interpreted it as a threat to America's influence in Asia. Not surprisingly, Washington made considerable efforts to kill Tokyo's proposal.'[4] In this, the Clinton administration was able to enlist the support of the West European governments, who joined the campaign to exert the maximum influence on East and South-East Asian governments to turn away from the Japanese proposal. In an interview with Larry Summers of the US Treasury, *Institutional Investor* explains: 'Concerned that Japan was proposing the idea [of the AMF] as a step toward hegemony in the region, but unwilling to bring such a sensitive issue into the open, US and European financial officials worked the phones with South-East Asian officials, talking down the idea and hoping it would die quietly . . .'[5]

The later Indonesian IMF deal did include a substantial American and West European involvement, as a means of combating the Japanese threat. By November of 1997, the will of the Japanese government to offer the region a path out of the crisis which would evade the strategic goals of the US government was broken.

The full story of the dramatic diplomacy surrounding the failed Japanese démarche has yet to be told.[6] But Japan suffered a stunning political defeat inflicted by the US with the support of the EU. The basis for EU support for the US Treasury throughout the crisis is also a story whose details remain obscure, but one with great significance for the future.

American Government Tactics over Korea

The IMF's Indonesian package did, for a while, seem to work. In the first week of November 1997, Michel Camdessus felt confident enough to declare that the IMF had succeeded in breaking the vicious circles of financial collapse in the region.

But just at that moment, the financial problems in South Korea became critical and the Japanese financial system was simultaneously gripped by panic. This was the first really critical point in the transition from a purely East Asian financial crisis to a world financial panic. South Korea's economy is larger than those of Thailand, Indonesia and Malaysia put together. The evolution of the Korean crisis in November and December 1997 produced the shipwreck of both the Indonesian and Thai economies and triggered the transmission of the crisis to the financial centres of the West as well as Russia and Latin America.

But the central characters in the Korean drama of late 1997 were not simply or mainly international and Korean bankers. The denouement was produced by Robert Rubin and Larry Summers in the US Treasury Department. They have made no attempt to conceal the fact that they ran the IMF operation on Korea.[7] They decided that the IMF should be used not in the ways it had operated in the last fifty years but instead in the new ways in which it should operate in the twenty-first century. For the US government, Korea was going to be a first.

It is the behaviour of the American government in the terms it required the IMF to impose upon South Korea that has caused the most controversy amongst those who had formed part of what has been called the 'Washington Consensus'.

The reason for the debate about the US government's role lies in the fact that its policy for dealing with the South Korean crisis was not only not geared to stabilising the won and the Korean banking system: it was not even geared to stabilising international financial markets. Instead it made its governing objective a drive to transform the internal social relations of production within South Korea and to risk the *deepening* of the Korean crisis and the *continuation* of international financial panic in order to achieve that transformation.

In financial crises like that in Korea, the traditional task of the IMF is simultaneously to stabilise the exchange rate and to find a way of reassuring international financial markets about the solvency of the South Korean banks. This dual operation will then provide time during which domestic economic activity can continue thus providing a context in which a restructuring of the banking system can take place.

Yet in the case of South Korea, the IMF programme was not designed to restore investor confidence *in Korea* at all, nor was it designed to revive activity on the part of Korea's main economic operators. It was instead a domestic transformation programme that would inevitably undermine investor confidence in the institutions of Korean capitalism.

The siege of the South Korean currency, the won, began on 6 November, the day when IMF Managing Director Camdessus was explaining that the IMF package for Indonesia should break the vicious cycle of economic destabilisation in Asia. Between 6 November and 17 November the Korean government sought to defend the won, before abandoning the struggle on the latter date and closing the foreign currency market for three days. On 20 November the government asked the Japanese government to persuade Japanese banks to roll over their short-term loans to Korea. But the East Asian crisis was now plunging Japanese financial institutions, deeply engaged in the region, into crisis: one of Japan's four biggest securities houses, Yamaichi, would collapse four days later. So the Japanese government was paralysed. The following day, 21 November, the South Korean government announced that it was asking the IMF for a rescue package.

Negotiations with the IMF then dragged on for a full two weeks. On Monday 1 December the IMF and Korea had still not agreed a deal: they were disagreeing about the growth target for the following year and about the IMF's demand that twelve merchant banks should be closed. The following day US Federal Reserve Chairman Alan Greenspan said that the Asian crisis was likely to accelerate the move from large amounts of government-directed investment to a system that encourages more private sector involvement: this was a clear statement that the US authorities required a radical break with Korea's model of capitalism. Finally, on 4 December, agreement between South Korea and the IMF, totalling $57 billion, was announced.

Senior officials in the US Treasury Department were well aware that the IMF's Korean programme was something different from the usual IMF operations: something new. As reported by the *Financial Times* the programme was 'a strategy carefully crafted by the US and the IMF that was intended to provide the blueprint for what US officials have confidently claimed as a "genuinely 21st century response to the first 21st century financial crisis"'.[8] The details of the strategy were worked out by Treasury Under Secretary Larry Summers in Manila and US Treasury officials managed the extremely difficult negotiations with the Korean government from a suite within the same hotel in Seoul as the IMF delegation. It seems that the IMF officials within the region were ready to settle on the basis of more lenient terms with the Korean government, but they were prevented from doing so by the US Treasury officials who had the backing of IMF Managing Director, Michel Camdessus.

The US's Twenty-First Century Solution: Transforming the Social Relations of Korean Capitalism

The IMF programme for Korea had 2 main parts:

1) Protecting the interests of creditors and the stability of the international financial system.
2) Korean economic management and social transformation.

1) Protecting creditors and the stability of the international financial system

The central element in this part of the package was, of course, the provision of funds from G7 states and multilateral organisations to western financial institutions which were exposed to the Korean debt crunch. Formally these funds were, of course, advanced to the Korean government, but only in order for them to flow straight back into the hands of Korea's private creditors. Thus, the western lenders which had flooded the Korean market with loans and then suddenly withdrawn were to be rewarded with what the *Financial Times*'s leading commentator called 'vast bailouts of IMF money'.[9]

Yet sums advanced by the G7 and multilateral organisations did not cover the full amounts of Korea's short-term debt obligations and much of the IMF package – for example, the money committed by the US Treasury – was not supposed to be used for such pay-backs: it was last resort, standby money. Thus, the package envisaged that the Korean government would take immediate measures to generate domestic sources of pay-back funds. This new funding was to be generated by the Korean government sharply raising domestic interest rates and simultaneously sharply tightening domestic fiscal policy to strengthen its own financial position. It had to commit itself to massively increasing domestic interest rates while simultaneously tightening its fiscal policy. Short-term interest rates had to be raised to over 21 per cent – a real rate of 15 per cent – and there was to be a tightening of fiscal policy by a huge 1.5 per cent of GDP. Against this background, the American banks were preparing to come forward with a new loan to the Korean government at penal rates of interest but of sufficient size to cover the shortfall in the international support package.

Thus the protection of western creditors was to be achieved through the transformation of the Korean financial crisis into what would be likely to be a complete domestic financial breakdown within Korea itself. When domestic financial crises occur, the economic task of governments is to pump more money into the banking system and to lower interest rates in order to restore the creditworthiness of the banking system and in order to restimulate the industrial sector so that it too can maintain its creditworthiness. But the IMF package involved bailing out international creditors by making a bad Korean domestic crisis catastrophic. In the words of Martin Wolf of the *Financial Times*, the IMF demanded a 'damagingly tough squeeze on economic activity . . . If the illness is debt deflation, a significant economic slowdown must make the patient's condition worse.' The IMF package was 'little more scientific than for a doctor to bleed his patients'.[10]

The IMF package indeed included further requirements that would intensify the domestic collapse: thus, despite a devaluation against the dollar of 30 per cent, which would automatically push up domestic prices substantially, inflation was to be kept at 5 per cent. In a yet further squeeze, the Korean banks were required to switch rapidly to international standards, so they had to build their capital base and make bad loan provisions instead of offering credit to the industrial sector. The result was to be a severe credit squeeze.[11] Martin Wolf summed up this aspect of the IMF programme as follows: 'The conclusion: however sick Korean companies and banks may be now, they will soon be sicker.' This prediction proved accurate. A *Financial Times* editorial in May 1998 noted that 'the pain [of the East Asian crisis] is proving worse than many anticipated. The need to combat recession looks like becoming as urgent as the previous priority of restoring market confidence. There is no point in endorsing a cure that ends up killing the patient.'[12]

2) *Social transformation and foreign capital access measures*

The slump-generating elements in the IMF package should not be seen only as an internationally costless way of squeezing debt repayments out of Korea. They were evidently designed to create the necessary domestic framework of economic incentives for completely reorganising the institutions of Korean capitalism, destroying what Robert Wade has called Korea's Asian Development Model. A *Financial Times* editorial explained the general goal of the package: 'For Korea this must mark the end of an era of dirigisme that contributed to its extraordinarily successful development. But this crisis has shown that such interventionism cannot be combined with freedom to borrow abroad. Since the latter can hardly be halted, Korea has no choice: it must liberalise systematically.'[13]

Under the IMF package, the chaebols would be turned into western-style companies, placing short-term profits first, relying upon share issues and largely depending upon internal savings for their new investments. Thus, as the *Financial Times* commented: 'A reduction in Bank lending will force [the chaebol] to turn to capital markets, subjecting them to investor discipline as corporate transparency improves and family owners yield control. This process will come with a high cost . . .'[14]

The squeeze was carefully crafted to hit the chaebols very hard. Thus, it included a specific ban on public works programmes, something which the Korean government has traditionally used to help the chaebols, many of which have been engaged in government-funded public works construction.

The drive against the Korean Development Model was combined with requirements for sweeping Open Door measures allowing the fullest possible access for foreign capital. A major feature of the IMF programme was the insistence on faster and fuller opening of Korea's doors to entry and exit by foreign capital both in the banking and corporate sectors. Specifically, foreign investment in domestic financial institutions and domestic equity were to be liberalised; domestic money and bond markets were to be opened to foreign investors, and restrictions on foreign borrowing by domestic corporations were to be lifted.[15] The ceiling on foreign ownership of shares in Korean companies was to be raised from 26 to 50 per cent as from 15 December 1997. Japanese products were also to be given bigger access to Korean markets. (Previously Japanese exports to Korea had been limited because of Japan's large trade surplus with Korea.) Under the agreement $5.5 billion was to be delivered to Korea the following day and a further $3.6 billion would be disbursed on 18 December assuming that the first review of Korea's programme of internal changes was satisfactory.

The Failure of the US Government's Drive for a Twenty-First Century Solution

The relief in international financial markets when agreement was finally announced between the IMF and the South Korean government lasted less than twenty-four hours. When international operators actually read the agreement, they fled from Korea in panic, so that the following day the country was plunged into a downward spin. But this did not surprise or alarm the US Treasury. Indeed, they indicated when the package was announced that they were not expecting any quick restoration of confidence. For the next two weeks, as the Korean crisis deepened as a result of the IMF programme, Treasury officials remained unbending and confident about the package.

On 5 December, the day after the IMF agreement, the won started plunging again so that by 8 December it had fallen about 16 per cent since 3 December. The reason for the fall was very simple arithmetic: the IMF package did not cover Korea's short-term debt servicing and a new wave of contagion spread across the entire region. On 10 December an IMF document was published showing that the Korean deal involved closing some of Korea's big commercial banks and this created new waves of panic. On 11 December there were huge losses in stock markets across the region[16] and the panic spread to Wall Street and to Latin America. On 12 December the Korean won fell to 1,891.40 to the dollar whereas it had been 1,170 to the dollar at the time of the IMF package nine days earlier. In short, the IMF stabilisation package was no such thing: it further destabilised the Korean economy.

Yet the US government calmly indicated that it was not prepared to change its stance. Treasury Secretary Rubin stated that implementing the IMF programme was 'the absolute key to . . . re-establishing confidence in the financial market.' This again was a new concept: in the past, *the announcement of agreement* on a rescue package was supposed to stabilise an economy in payments difficulties: implementation came later. But Rubin was saying that confidence and thus stability would be restored in Korea only after a first wave of implementation of the transformation programme. Rubin's Treasury officials and those of the IMF said South Korea must carry out the reforms before there could be any talk of new money. The IMF would release a further $5.6 billion by 8 January only if Korea stuck to its schedule of promised domestic changes.[17]

But on Friday 12 December, the Indonesian crisis acquired catastrophic proportions as the rupiah fell 11 per cent in a single day and lost 22 per cent during the week (54 per cent during the year).[18] At the same time, signals from Seoul suggested that South Korea was going to break with the IMF deal and simply default on its private sector's debts. And this threat of a Korean default in turn raised fears in Wall Street and London of a systemic crisis in the international financial system.

It was only at this point that the US Treasury finally itself panicked and drew back from its '21st century solution'. On Monday 15 December the US Treasury backtracked and the IMF said that its executive board meeting would consider that day the speedy delivery of further money to South Korea. The IMF said it was responding to a request from the Korean government, but Korean government officials said they were unaware of any such request having been made.[19] The 'request', in other words, seems to have come from Wall Street. The following day the won soared up 16 per cent against the dollar, the stock market rose by nearly 5 per cent and equity markets across the region also revived. On 16 December, the US Federal Reserve Open Market Committee shifted its own policy guidelines by failing to raise interest rates as US domestic indicators would have required. And on 17 December, the Japanese government gave a stimulus to the Japanese economy with a $15 billion tax cut. The dollar fell sharply lower against the yen, while stock markets across the Asian region shot up. And on 18 December the IMF disbursed the second tranche of $3.5 billion out of its loan package, despite the failure of South Korea to fully comply with the schedule of reforms in the original package.

Yet the crisis was sill not over. On Monday 22 December after Moody's rating agency downgraded the foreign currency ceiling for Korean bonds and currency, the won fell from Friday's 1,550 to the dollar to 1,715. The Tokyo and New York stock markets fell. On 23 December the World Bank disbursed a $3 billion loan to South Korea – its share of the IMF-led rescue package. By 24 December, US financial markets were gripped by the fear that South Korea would still have to declare a debt moratorium. The *Wall Street Journal* reported that the US government's part of the IMF-led package – $5 billion, which was supposed to be a back-up sum to be used only as a last resort – might now be thrown into the breach; it also reported that US banks were discussing restructuring their loans to the South Korean private sector, providing debt relief. Later that day, the IMF, the US and twelve other governments pledged to send a new tranche of $10 billion but said that for a South Korean recovery it was critical that international commercial banks agree a 'significant' rescheduling for Korean financial institutions. The IMF said it would be disbursing a further $2 billion (from its $21 billion total) to South Korea on 30 December and a further $2 billion on 8 January. The US and twelve other OECD countries said they would be sending $8 billion (out of their pledged $24 billion) by early January – this was money pledged to be used only as a last resort. Of this total, $1.7 billion would come from the US, $3.33 billion from Japan.[20] US Treasury Secretary Robert Rubin said: 'This is a major world event . . . It seemed appropriate for the [G7] industrial countries and other nations involved in the second line of defence to move their aid effort forward.' The 'major world event' he was referring to was not a Korean one but a threatened breakdown in American financial markets, unable to stand the strain of the US Treasury's political démarche on Korea.

The US Treasury's climb down was, in fact, a stunning defeat. As the *Financial Times* reported, US Treasury officials 'know that the critical decision to add an extra $10 billion from the IMF, US, Japanese and other government resources and to engage the banks in a debt rescheduling exercise is a stunning policy reversal that could have big implications for the way future financial crises are tackled . . . "The fact is, the official sector looked a default by Korea in the face, and blinked," said Morris Goldstein, a senior economist with the Institute for International Economics.'[21] The US Treasury itself claimed that its climb-down was no such thing because the extra money and the involvement of the US private banks in rescheduling Korean loans was combined with further conditionalities being imposed on Korea for faster and deeper restructuring of its capitalist system. But nobody else saw matters in that way.

The backtracking by the US government did prevent the Korean default. But it did not end the wider financial panic: Indonesia was left with a complete credit crunch and effectively a complete default on its debts. The whole region was galloping into a deep depression which in turn would spread the effects of the Asian crisis to other parts of the world, particularly commodity producing countries like Russia which would find world demand for their exports slumping and would thus face an exchange rate and financial crisis of their own.

But the important point about this central episode is the fact that the US government *sought to use panic in the private markets dealing with Korean currency and debt as a political lever* to further its policy objectives within Korea. And it was the American financial market's leading operators which exerted pressure upon the US government to stabilise the Korean economy. It was, of course, embarrassing for the US Treasury to be sitting down with private bankers to agree the rescheduling of private loans to Korea. But for the US and other western banking communities, rescheduling the Korean debt with the US Treasury was a welcome relief.

As the shocks from the financial crisis worked their ways through the Asian economies, the IMF's predictions about the region's growth prospects for 1998 turned out to be wildly out of line with realities. Deep slumps gripped much of the area with the most appalling suffering being experienced in Indonesia. But the hopes of the US government that it could reap substantial benefits for its capitals in the region as a result of the crisis did seem to be coming true. The battle for the future character of Korea's relations of production as a whole has continued to rage and it is by no means clear yet what the final outcome of that struggle will be.

But already in December 1997, American capital was looking forward to making a killing in Korea. The *New York Times* of 27 December reported that 'Korean companies are looking ripe to foreign buyers.' The *Los Angeles Times* of 25 January 1998 reported, 'US Companies See Fire Sale in South Korea.' The *Chicago Tribune* reported on 18 January that 'Some US Companies Jump into Asia with Both Feet'. And the *Wall Street Journal* reported Coca Cola's purchases of companies in Korea and Thailand under the headline, 'While Some Count Their Losses in Asia, Coca-Cola's Chairman Sees Opportunities' (6 February). The gains in terms of US companies being able to take control over Asian assets have been substantial. As Hiromu Nonaka, secretary-general of Japan's ruling Liberal Democratic Party, put it in the summer of 1998: 'There is an invasion of foreign capital, especially US capital, under way. A type of colonisation of Asia has started.'[22] During the first five months of 1998, US companies had bought up double the number of Asian businesses that they had bought in any previous year, spending $8 billion in total. Significantly the main target was the Japanese financial system, followed by South Korea and Thailand. The purchases in South Korea have also been targeted especially on banking and finance. Securities Data, a US-based monitoring agency, described the surge in asset purchases as an 'historic moment'. European companies, especially those of the UK, Germany and Holland have also been very active, spending about $4 billion. This centralisation of Asian capital in Atlantic hands was intensifying as months passed. According to Goldman Sachs, the pace was 'certainly picking up'.[23] As Paul Krugman pointed out, the fact that the US purchases of business have been spread across many sectors including those where the US companies could not be thought to have a competitive advantage shows that the fire-sales are the product of weaknesses produced by the financial crisis.[24]

From Asia to the Wider World

It is worth underlining the point that the big US investment banks were far from happy with the drive by Rubin and Summers (supported by Alan Greenspan at the Federal Reserve). Wall Street's dislike of Rubin's aggressive line had a simple explanation: his behaviour had created panic at the very heart of the international financial system, was dragging the Indonesian political economy into oblivion and was bringing some important speculators at the heart of the system close to collapse. The link between the DWSR and Asia would turn out to be two-way. While the centre of the international financial system stabilised in early 1998, this was only a temporary release. For the weight of the East Asian growth centre in the world economy would ensure that there would be an indirect boomerang effect on Wall Street via the effects of the Asian financial crisis on the product markets of the world.

This was the linkage that the US Treasury and Federal Reserve failed to foresee. As so often in the past the initial effects of the Asian crisis were beneficial for the US economy where things mattered most: in the bond and stock markets. Flight finance from Asia poured into New York, lowering bond yields and thus making speculation in shares on the stock market more attractive than ever.

But in the early months of 1998 it did indeed become clear that East and South-East Asia were heading for a deep economic depression. And because the region was the dynamic centre of the international productive economy, its depression quickly affected those economies producing the key commodity inputs for the world economy, such as oil. The collapse in oil and other commodity prices was swift and it was soon reflected in great difficulties for oil-producing states like Venezuela and Canada and, of course, Russia. Between September 1997 and September 1998 the price of oil dropped 33 per cent, that of wheat fell 39 per cent, that of copper fell 22 per cent. The main indicator of commodity futures prices, the CRB-Bridge Futures Index, which covers seventeen commodities, fell 18 per cent between September 1997 and September 1998. The overwhelming proportion of the exports of so-called emerging markets are commodity-based and since most of these emerging markets were heavily indebted and thus their financial systems and currencies were vulnerable to sharp deteriorations in their current accounts, the crisis spread.[25]

The Russian collapse was the next decisive phase of the crisis and the next big test for the US Treasury. Yet again it put together an IMF package and yet again this was inadequate; in August 1998 the rouble collapsed. The US Treasury could have stepped in at the last minute with some sort of emergency rescue. If it had been able to understand the real situation it was in it would certainly have done so. But Rubin again failed to grasp the reality. Now he looked at Russia through a speculator's eyes. Russia's assets had been a bonanza for six years but the economy had been a steadily worsening disaster, shrinking without limits and now tiny and largely irrelevant in the world economy. Why, he must have reasoned, bother about the rouble collapse?

But he overlooked two facts. First, the Russian elites were not rooted capitalists at all. And secondly, a quarter of a century of the Dollar–Wall Street Regime had left much of the rest of the world with fragile and vulnerable financial systems. In just about every financial crisis since the start of the 1980s, the governments which were hit felt that they could not risk repudiating their debts for one very fundamental reason: their financial systems were only the nerve centres of whole capitalist economies with multiple links with the international economy. To have simply repudiated debt would have jeopardised interests across much of their economies by threatening a period of isolation. Russia was different. Economic life in the country had been in tragic and uninterrupted decline throughout the 1990s. Russia did have a thoroughly 'modern' set of internationalised financial markets, but their prices bore no relation to actual activity in the economy. They were purely speculative markets in ownership titles and the Russian banks were the same: useful for sucking resources in financial form out of the Russian economy into the Anglo-American financial centre and otherwise engaged in pure speculation. The only significant link between Russia and world product markets was energy and strategic raw materials.

Thus, when the July IMF plan for Russia failed and new western money was not forthcoming, the rouble was ready to plummet. This time Soros did not even need to enter the forward market in the rouble. He simply had to open his mouth and say that the rouble would collapse and it did. But what had not been expected was the response of the Russian government. It simply repudiated its debts on the bonds it had issued to international speculators. It did not seek negotiations, it did not beg for more help. It simply stated that although western investors thought they had short-term government bonds at a certain rate of interest, they were wrong: they now had long-dated bonds at a much lower rate of interest. And although western investors thought that they had hedged their currency risk (of the rouble collapsing) attached to their bond holdings by buying derivatives from Russian banks, they were wrong again. The money would not be forthcoming.

Since the Yeltsin government represented a very narrow layer of speculators whose money was safe in the Anglo-American financial centre, this was the rational course of action for the government. So narrow was the fiscal base of the Russian state – in other words, so weak were its roots in the real life of the Russian economy – that to hand over its meagre tax resources to western bond holders would have been suicidal anyway. And the production links between Russia and the world economy were tiny.

The Russian Default and the Fragility of Economies Weakened by Two Decades of the DWSR

The Russian default was an enormous international shock because around the world there were so many economies whose public sectors and banking systems were full of international debt, built up over two decades of monetary and financial volatility and crisis. And this debt was now no longer locked into medium-term bank loans as in the old Latin American crisis of the early 1980s. It now took the form of securities – bonds and stocks – that fitted in neatly with the interests of US rentiers and mutual funds, enabling them to escape markets instantly by selling up.

The question they faced after the Russian default was: should they sell now? There might be no contagion from Russia to Brazil, with its large public debt funded by short-term bonds. But what if there was a failure in Brazil? This would drag down the whole of Latin America and spread further. Therefore, these speculative investors had every incentive to behave prudently and withdraw their funds. And by doing so they would, of course, provoke the crisis that they were guarding against. These kinds of thoughts were suddenly transforming the patterns of security prices all over the world and this sudden shift was what seems to have brought a central US financial institution, the so-called Long Term Capital Management (LTCM) hedge fund to its knees. It had been betting on what it had assumed to be a one-horse race: that as a monetary union approached in January 1999, the Italian bond market would converge with the German. But the Russian default suddenly moved the Italian bond market the other way despite the approaching start of the euro.

But the LTCM crisis was an accident waiting to happen. And the pressure on Latin American financial systems was also an accident prepared by the steady strengthening of ties across the world's financial markets in the form of hot money. The ties of hot money were themselves a reflection of the basic fact that so much of the world economy had become too fragile and risky for the long-term commitment of funds by the rentiers of the core economies. There was also a power relationship at work, of course. Governments desperate to roll over their debts would take whatever they were offered by Wall Street: if they were offered hot money, so be it. But this power relationship was itself an expression of fundamental economic weakness and vulnerability outside the core. Wall Street would not have been so powerful, if these economies had not been so dependent. So we are driven back to the origins of this dependency and they lie in the fact that the growth paths of many of the world's economies in the 1960s and early 1970s had been broken by the rise of the DWSR, plunging economies into crises which left them with chronic weaknesses and vulnerabilities.

And the same regime had fed back to the American economy itself. It had been able to 'benefit' from the DWSR by opening up Latin America and strengthening its exports to the region. By 1998 about half of US exports were going to Latin America and Asia. This had been a handy escape route for the American productive sector faced with the competitive challenge of Japan and Western Europe. The DWSR had offered a way out from the hard, domestic task of raising productivity levels and reorganising the linkages between savings and productive investment in the US economy. And the DWSR had another 'beneficial' effect as well: it offered paths to link the ordinary American to a speculative-rentier system whose power stretched ever deeper into the economies of the world. This was revealed with stark clarity by the Mexican crisis of 1994–95 as *Time* magazine explained at the time: 'What many Americans discovered last week was that for all the beltway rhetoric pitting Wall Street against Main Street, Wall Street long ago intersected with Main Street. At risk in [Mexico] were not only US banks and giant investment firms but mutual funds held by tens of millions of little-guy investors who bet their savings on double-digit yields in emerging markets like Mexico. "This wasn't about bailing out Wall Street" a congressional staff member said [of the rescue package], "but about mutual and pension funds and that means average Americans."'[26]

Time magazine was right about the facts, but the growth of powerful speculative forces within almost every sector of the US economy was greatly stimulated by the evolution of the DWSR. And by 1998 the US economy was inflated by very large and socially all-pervasive speculative distortions: the stock exchange, despite the falls in 1998, remains the central inflated bubble.

The American bull market has continued, with a couple of notable interruptions, for fifteen years and has become absolutely central to American capitalism. In the last fifteen years equity prices have risen tenfold.[27] In the last three years the stock market has created more paper wealth – in the sense of inflated asset prices – than in the previous three decades.[28] During this three-year period, the cumulative gain on the Standard and Poor's 500 index has been 111 per cent.[29] This amounts to $3 trillion. By the spring of 1997, the value of US stocks finally exceeded the US's annual economic output of about $8 trillion.[30] As Paul Krugman put it, these leaps in share prices could be justified only 'if the US economy is poised to begin decades of extraordinary growth'.[31] The bubble had been rising in the housing market in many parts of the USA as well and by October 1998 there was evidence that it was about to burst.

The entire US economy is now locked into the bubble. As the director of US Economics Research at Goldman Sachs put it: 'The importance of the stock market in keeping this virtuous circle [in the US economy] intact cannot be overstated.'[32] The banking systems on Main Street and Wall Street as well as the mutual funds and pension funds are all hitched to the bubble. And so too is an extraordinarily wide constituency of ordinary Americans. Personal household debt ratios in the USA have never been higher and large parts of the middle classes have borrowed to invest in the bubble.

David Levy of the Jerome Levy Economics Institute in New York gives the following picture of how an uncontrolled expansion of fictitious credit money and of speculative forces in the US stock market were sustaining the US boom as of the start of 1998. In four of the last five years, consumption has grown faster than personal income. This has been a key factor in widening profit margins. In 1997 the personal savings rate in the US was at 3.8 per cent, a fifty-year low. A consumer borrowing boom helped spending outpace income in the mid-1990s, but by 1997 households faced record debt and debt service burdens. Households are carrying an unprecedented 85 cents of debt for every dollar of after-tax income. Credit card delinquency rates are hovering near the previous all-time high and personal bankruptcies keep breaking records. 'Euphoria over stock market gains has powered the consumption spree.' Consumers have been spending not only in response to portfolio gains but also in anticipation of future gains. 'Never in the postwar period have consumers been so influenced by the stock market.'

Stock market speculation has also done its bit for what President Clinton considers to be his greatest domestic achievement so far: getting on top of the US budget deficit. Capital gains tax receipts to the Treasury are up from $44 billion in 1995 to $100 billion for 1998: a direct indicator of the volumes of speculative trading in US securities markets.

But by the end of October 1998 the signs of a mounting financial crisis were multiplying. A credit crunch had already started in the US financial system. Institutions in debt were not able to find easy access to new credit. If the credit crunch were to spread to Main Street, demand in the US economy could collapse very swiftly. In short, the American people are at the time of writing at risk of being swept into the vortex of a crash generated by the speculative boom which they had hoped signalled a better future.

When the American Central Bank, the Federal Reserve Board, intervened in late September 1998 to save the Long Term Capital Management Fund (LTCM), it threw a beam of light into the black hole at the heart of what has come to be called globalisation. Federal Reserve Board Chairman Alan Greenspan was issuing a simple, clear set of messages: that, since the Fed steps in only to tackle 'systemic risk', the safety of the entire American credit system was apparently threatened by the behaviour of a single, speculative hedge fund; that the international constellations of financial markets revolving around their American centre were in fact subordinated to a centre of speculators; that the welfare of literally billions of people, whose livelihoods depend in one way or the other on the functioning of credit systems, was potentially jeopardised by a couple of Nobel Prize winners and a former deputy chairman of the Fed who had been engaged in an orgy of reckless speculation; that the macroeconomic policies of the rest of the world should be shifted by lowering interest rates to help bail out a Cayman Islands company. Globalisation had come to this.

And while we were absorbing this set of messages, Greenspan proceeded to supply some more: he did not start moves to wind down and close LTCM. He also rejected an offer from a big mid-western speculator, Warren Buffet, to take the problem off his hands by taking it over. Instead Greenspan brought all the biggest American investment banks together to jointly run LTCM indefinitely, creating the mother of all speculative institutions. This prompted the Chairman of the House of Representatives Banking and Financial Services Committee, James Leach, to remark: 'Working as a cartel, those running LTCM potentially comprise the most powerful financial force in the history of the world and could influence the well-being of nation states for good or for naught, guided by profit motive, rather than national interest standards.'[33] Leach was right, as we already knew by the autumn of 1998. A handful of American institutions like LTCM had already demonstrated their capacity *to engage in full-scale financial warfare against states.* They can plunge a state in to economic ruin, leaving tens of millions of people utterly destitute. And as Joseph Stiglitz, chief economist at the World Bank, pointed out, many smaller economies in the world can be ruined in this way, regardless of their so-called 'fundamentals': their fundamentals are not as fundamental as these hedge funds.

Most of the biggest of these speculative organisations are completely opaque and unregulated because Alan Greenspan and US Treasury Secretary Robert Rubin have wanted them kept that way. This was Greenspan's last message during the LTCM crisis: he claimed that such hedge funds could not be regulated because if they were, they would only escape to places like the Caymans! Instead, he proposed to make *the targets* of some of these organisations – the financial systems of countries in the South – much more transparent. As a *Financial Times* editorial remarked, this will simply make them even more vulnerable to speculative attack.

It is painful for mainstream economists to face this bizarre reality. We know that if a big bank at the heart of a financial system goes bust, it can pull down other banks through its defaults on debts and it can cause panic amongst savers when they see deposits in the bank being wiped out. But a speculative trader on securities markets or foreign exchange markets is surely something quite different. These operators are speculating in the sense that they are making profits through betting on price movements in a market or price differences between two markets. We know that such speculative activity is endemic in stock markets, bond markets and foreign exchange markets as well as in the so-called derivatives markets – markets in instruments 'derived' from these more basic markets. But we take speculation to be the froth on the top of markets which are playing an indispensable role as 'capital markets' which help to ensure that capital goes to the most profitable sectors and places. So if a speculative operator bets wrongly and goes under, this should neither affect the underlying operations of these markets, which supposedly largely reflect real trends in economies, nor should it have anything to do with the banking system which is engaged in supplying credit to governments and the corporate sector.

Yet Greenspan's rescue of the LTCM revealed a different picture. It has turned out that top American banks have been pouring enormous loans into speculative hedge funds and doing so while claiming not to be interested in knowing anything about the bets which operators like the LTCM were engaged in on international financial markets. More, the Federal Reserve Board must have known for years that this had become a central feature of the activities of the core institutions of the US banking system. A one-line bill in Congress could have banned such lending but no move whatever was made by the US government to take such action. Thus we come to some inescapable conclusions: that for the leaders of American finance and of the US state, gigantic speculation on international financial markets was basically safe. Second, that it was extremely profitable. Thirdly, that it was a rational way to relate to these international financial markets. And fourthly, that it was good, in some way or other, for the health of American business.

These propositions could be minimally true only if the summits of American finance engaging in this speculation could, in some way or other, rig the markets. This at first seems improbable. It would require some or all of the following conditions: that they had enormous market power, huge mobilised funds that could dictate short-run price movements in these markets; but if they were competing against each other they could cancel out each other's attacks; so a second condition could be that they worked together, either by carving up markets into different spheres or by co-operatively entering a given market; a third possible condition also existed: that they could individually or collectively have access to insider information about future events on these markets, information that could enable them to win.

In LTCM's case, all three conditions seem to have been met. First, it was able to mobilise really enormous sums. IMF studies had indicated that hedge funds could mobilise loans amounting to twenty times their capital. But as we have seen, LTCM could mobilise 250 times its capital of $2.6 billion, in other words $650 billion. This is enough to shake prices in any market. Secondly, LTCM turns out to be the instrument of a cartel of US investment banks, of *all of the top ones*, plus the biggest of the European banks, UBS, so competition was not a significant problem. And thirdly, it appears that LTCM had excellent channels to insider information. Congressman Leach pointed out that LTCM had links with governments. Italy's central bank has been a big investor in LTCM at the very time that it was playing the Italian bond market! This is a startling revelation. Since the actions (and words) of the Bank of Italy can directly tilt prices in the Italian bond market, co-operation between the LTCM and the Bank looks like a winning, though criminal, combination. But that was not all. According to an internal report within Europe's largest bank, UBS, written in 1996, at that time no less than eight state banks were 'strategic investors' in LTCM. And the UBS report, a copy of which was obtained by Reuters, suggests there was collusion, for it explains that LTCM's links with these state banks gave it 'a window to see the structural changes occurring in these markets to which the strategic investors belong.'[34] That is a polite way of saying LTCM had enough insider information to foretell the future. Is it any wonder that when UBS read that report, it decided to 'get a piece of the action'?

The final ingredient in LTCM's success was its public relations management. Journalists, academics or small-time traders, reared on neo-classical theories of how financial markets work, might press the following question: since markets not traders set prices, how can a speculator like LTCM be sure to win? And LTCM's answer was, with the highest tech computer software designed by two Nobel Prize-winning number crunchers!

The reality was that it would take a lot more than a power failure at LTCM's computer centre to put a stop to its winning run at the casino. Bringing down the mother of all hedge funds would require action by the mother and father of all 'exogenous shocks', the kind of shock, or series of shocks that hit the world in 1997–98. These shocks were not, actually, exogenous to the system that produced operators like the LTCM. They arose from the evolution of the inner dynamics of what has come to be called globalisation.

Globalisation's Dialectical Twist

The revelation that the summit of the US financial system consists of a handful of speculative hedge funds supplied with almost limitless credits by the American money-centre banks indicates that globalisation has worked itself out in a dialectical fashion over the last quarter of a century. It began in the heady days of the Nixon administration as a liberation of US economic management from the constraints of subordinating the American economy to the global economy of the Bretton Woods regime. International financial liberalisation did indeed increase the leverage of the American state over international economic affairs. But this expanded *political freedom* to manipulate the world economy for US economic advantage has ended by deeply distorting the US economy itself, making it far more vulnerable than ever before to forces that it cannot fully control.

Washington's capacity to manipulate the dollar price and to exploit Wall Street's international financial dominance enabled the US authorities to avoid doing what other states have had to do: watch the balance of payments; adjust the domestic economy to ensure high levels of domestic savings and investment; watch levels of public and private indebtedness; ensure an effective domestic system of financial intermediation to ensure the strong development of the domestic productive sector. The DWSR provided an escape route from all these tasks. And as a result, by all normal yardsticks of capitalist national accounting the US economy has become deeply distorted and unstable: unprecedentedly high levels of public and household debt, a deep structural balance of payments deficit and a business cycle dependent upon asset price bubbles.

And to keep the US economic show on the road, the United States has become deeply dependent upon Wall Street financial markets' ability to maintain huge inward flows of finance from all over the world. If these inward flows of funds were to come to a halt, or go into reverse, the structural weaknesses of the US economy would be starkly revealed, with potentially catastrophic consequences. In the jargon, Wall Street is a 'liquidity-driven' market whose constant resupply of funds from abroad plugs the hole of the

US economy's low level of domestic savings and keeps the US domestic boom going.

This structural pattern means that American governments have acquired a vital interest in maintaining an international pattern of monetary and financial relations which is extremely volatile, unstable and crisis-prone, because it is these features of the international economic system which maintain the vast inflows of funds into New York. And it is in this context that we can see the way in which the big US hedge funds are not an aberration but are rather financial institutions in the (deeply distorted) American national interest. Every international act of hedge fund financial warfare in any part of the world acts like a shot in the arm for the liquidity of the US financial markets, maintaining downward pressure on interest rates and stoking the stock market boom.

This dialectical twist of globalisation has not been the product of some planning unit in the American federal government. No evil group of conspirators sought to construct a system in which the macroeconomic health of the US economy required monetary and financial chaos to be perpetually recreated in the international economy. The whole pattern is the result of a chain of blundering gambles. But the pattern remains, nonetheless, a structural one.

It is also, ultimately, an unsustainable one, if for no other reason than because the US economy depends not only upon constantly reproduced international monetary and financial turbulence. It also depends increasingly upon expanding economic growth, especially in the so-called 'emerging markets' of Latin America and Asia. The US productive economy is ever more open and ever more dependent upon macroeconomic developments in these economies. And thus does Washington find itself in a vicious contradiction: the US domestic economy depends upon Wall Street which depends upon chaotic instabilities in 'emerging market' financial systems; but at the same time the US domestic economy depends upon growing 'emerging market' economies able to absorb US products and generate high streams of profits for US companies operating within them.

Notes

1. An exception to this truculent and illiterate triumphalism which partially saved the professional honour of Anglo-American journalism was to be found in the honesty and moral courage of Martin Wolf's writing in the *Financial Times* and in many, though not all, of the *Financial Times*'s editorials.

2. But see Robert Wade and Frank Veneroso, 'The Asian Crisis: The High Debt Model versus the Wall Street–Treasury–IMF Complex', *New Left Review* 228 (March/April 1998); Robert Wade and Frank Veneroso, 'The Gathering Slump and the Battle over Capital Controls', *New Left Review* 231 (September/October 1998); Bruce Cumings, 'The Korean Crisis and the End of "Late" Development', *New Left Review* 231 (September/October 1998); See also Walden

Bello, 'East Asia on the Eve of the Great Transformation', *Review of International Political Economy*, 5:3 (Autumn 1998). A very full chronology as well as a large and very useful archive of other material on the crisis can be found at N. Roubini's web site at http://www.stern.nyu.edu/~nroubini.

3. Michael Vatikiotis, 'Pacific Divide', *Far Eastern Economic Review* (6 November 1997).

4. Reic Altbach, 'The Asian Monetary Fund Proposal: A Case Study of Japanese Regional Leadership', *Japan Economic Institute Report*, no. 47A, 1997.

5. *Institutional Investor*, December 1997, quoted in Ron Bevacqua, 'Whither the Japanese model? The Asian economic crisis and the continuation of Cold War politics in the Pacific Rim', *Review of International Political Economy*, 5:3 (Autumn 1998).

6. But see Bruce Cumings, 'The Korean Crisis and the End of "Late" Development'. See also Walden Bello, 'East Asia on the Eve of the Great Transformation'.

7. Interviewed on the US TV programme *News Hour*, Rubin was asked by Jim Lehrer why he had been working so hard on the Korean IMF programme. Rubin replied: 'Jim, American leadership has been absolutely central to this effort . . . in today's world the United States is really the only country that is in a position to provide the kind of leadership that is needed to deal with issues of this magnitude and importance to our country.' *News Hour*, 13 January 1998 (http://www.pbs.org/newshour).

8. *Financial Times*, 2 January 1998, p. 3.

9. Martin Wolf, 'Same Old IMF Medicine', *Financial Times*, 9 December 1997, p. 18.

10. Martin Wolf, 'Same Old IMF Medicine'.

11. Quoted in the *Financial Times*, 11 May 1998, p. 19.

12. 'Agony sets in for Asia', *Financial Times*, 7 May 1998, p. 19.

13. 'Korea's Rescue', *Financial Times*, 4 December 1997, p. 25.

14. *Financial Times*, 4 December 1997, p. 6.

15. Martin Wolf, 'Same Old IMF Medicine'.

16. HK down 5.5, Malaysia 7.4, Indonesia 4.6, Singapore 2.3, Philippines 4.9, Thailand 4.9 per cent, and there was a new wave of pressure against the Hong Kong dollar.

17. N. Roubini, 'Chronology of the Asian Crisis' (stern.nyu.edu/~nroubini). p. 31. This involved lifting restrictions on foreign investment and making its banking system 'more accountable to market forces'. Another key IMF condition was for the Korean government to curtail public spending – in other words public works projects, the lifeblood of the construction companies around which many of Korea's chaebols are built.

18. The subsequent collapse of the Indonesian financial system, followed by the collapse of the Sukharto regime, should be seen as an unintended by-product of US policy towards Korea at this time.

19. N. Roubini, 'Chronology of the Asian Crisis' (stern.nyu.edu/~nroubini).

20. Robert Rubin explained that the US contribution would come from a special fund administered by the US Treasury that did not require Congressional approval.

21. *Financial Times*, 2 January 1998, p. 3.

22. Quoted in the *Financial Times*, 2 June 1998, p. 16.

23. Tony Walker, 'US Buys $8bn of Asian Business', *Financial Times*, 15 June 1998.

24. See Paul Krugman, 'Fire-Sale FDI' (http://www.stern.nyu.edu/~nroubini).

25. See Michael M. Phillips, 'Plunging Commodity Prices Spread Turmoil in the Global Economy', *Wall Street Journal*, 27 August 1998.

26. Cited by Adam Harmes, 'Institutional Investors and the Reproduction of Neoliberalism', *Review of International Political Economy*, 5:1 (Spring 1998).

27. David Levy, 'Praying for a Soft Landing', *Financial Times*, 2 January 1998, p. 10.

28. Gerard Baker, 'Is This Great, or What?', *Financial Times*, 31 March 1998, p.25.

29. Barry Riley, 'An Old Bull That Won't Die', *Financial Times*, 3/4 January 1998.

30. Richard Waters, 'Where the Money Is', *Financial Times*, 3 December 1997.

31. Paul Krugman, 'Pity Alan Greenspan', *Financial Times*, 3 June 1998, p. 18.

32. William Dudley, 'From Virtuous to Vicious', *Financial Times*, 6 May 1998, p. 18.

33. Quoted in Garth Alexander, 'Bank America Joins Hedge Fund Casualties', *Sunday Times*, 18 October 1998.

34. Ibid.

7

Conclusions

The main argument in this essay has been that the central features of what has come to be called globalisation have their origins in deliberate decisions of the Nixon administration taken in order to secure the continued international dominance of American capitalism. While the original spur to the creation of the DWSR was a perceived threat to US dominance from Western Europe and Japan, the most malign consequences of this regime have been inflicted upon the populations of the South and on those of the former Soviet Bloc. They have paid for the regime through appalling financial and economic crises which have had devastating consequences for hundreds of millions of people. Today it is the turn of tens of millions of people in Indonesia who are experiencing the effects of this barbaric regime.

The DWSR's disastrous economic consequences for the majority of humanity have at the same time been accompanied by astonishing political success. Every financial and economic blow-out has been successfully blamed upon its victims and has been used to destroy the earlier development strategies of countries plunged into crisis. Whatever the weaknesses of earlier strategies, whether in Latin America or in Asia or in the former Eastern Bloc, their results were at least less damaging to the health and welfare of the majority of their populations than is the case under the frameworks devised by the US Treasury and transmitted through the IMF and the World Bank.

At the same time, what began as part of a battle by the Nixon administration against its triadic 'allies' has become increasingly a joint project of Atlantic capitalism – the US and the EU – against the rest of the world. We have made no attempt to investigate the underlying causes of the long stagnation in the advanced capitalist countries, but a growing theme in the 1980s and 1990s has been the formation of an Atlantic coalition for a new drive southwards, using the DWSR to re-engineer social systems outside the core in order to co-ordinate them with the interests of Atlantic capitalism.

This campaign should not be seen as being driven by a single compulsion, such as the search for cheap labour or the search for markets. It is better viewed as an exploitation of power over the international political economy by the US and the EU in order to extract every possible useful advantage through re-engineering societies outside the core; or, to put matters the other way round, to expel as many problems as can be expelled outwards from the core societies. Financial crises in the South, dependencies on US and EU markets, inherited debt burdens, inabilities to steer economies in the face of bewildering changes in the international economic environment – all these factors have been seized upon by the Atlantic powers as instruments for gaining positions in the countries concerned: for seizing control of product markets, for buying local company assets to centralise capital under Atlantic control, for exploiting huge pools of cheap labour (shut out by ever-stronger immigration barriers from access to core economies), for taking effective control of financial systems for speculative purposes, gaining higher marginal yields for the pension funds of the populations of the North and for engaging in orgies of speculation and frequently corrupt and criminal activities. Most of these activities are presented as the very opposite: as teaching the supposedly ignorant and incompetent governments of the South how to run their affairs properly, as helping them to pay off debts, as supplying them with aid through FDI etc.

The pattern of Japanese capitalist expansion has been different in the 1980s and 1990s simply because Japanese capitalism has been far more genuinely productive as a national capitalist system than the capitalisms of the Atlantic world. While the bulk of so-called Foreign Direct Investment in Eastern Europe or in the South by Atlantic capitals has been a matter of taking over companies and market shares, Japanese capitalism's huge surpluses of value have been channelled into the creation of new productive assets in East and South-East Asia and have been compatible with very rapid rates of growth and substantial industrial development in the region. The rapacious mercantilism of so much of EU's trade policy towards the South and towards East Central and Eastern Europe, and the drive of the US to compensate for competitive weaknesses in its productive sectors through taking predatory advantage of its monetary and financial sector dominance, has contrasted with the Japanese capacity to stimulate and feel comfortable with rapid growth in East and South-East Asia. But the result of the combined dynamic growth of China and the rest of the East and South-East Asian region, in relative harmony with Japanese capitalism, has been a perceived threat to the future dominance of the US over the world economy, a threat-perception fully shared by the West Europeans. The result was the gamble of the Clinton administration culminating in the so-called Asian crisis of 1997. The direct target of that gamble was the countries of East and South-East Asia. But its indirect but more fundamental target was the possibility of an emergent regional bloc centred economically in Japan but potentially including China as well.

There is, as yet, no conclusive evidence that the Clinton administration acted strategically from 1995 to use the dollar price rise, pressure to dismantle controls on the capital account, inflows of hot money and financial warfare by the US hedge funds to bring countries in East and South-East Asia to their knees. There is much circumstantial evidence to suggest strategic planning. But the question remains open. What is not in doubt is that once the hedge funds had struck, the US Treasury launched a dramatic assault against the social relations of production in South Korea with the aim of achieving a *Gleichschaltung* of Korean assets and US capitalism.

But the very success of that assault was too much for the scarred tissue of the political economies on the rest of the periphery to sustain. Those wounds inflicted by earlier triumphs of the DWSR, in Russia and other parts of Eastern Europe and in Latin America, had not healed sufficiently to withstand the strains from the East Asian crisis and the resulting panic of '98 revealed the heart of globalisation to be an extraordinary black hole of rampant Wall Street speculation. The G7 package of so-called reforms of the international financial system is nothing more than an attempt to keep the whole speculative show on the road.

It may be thought that the US government and the European Union are seriously campaigning to dismantle all controls on capital accounts and to completely open all economies to the complete freedom of movement of all forms of core capital at all times. If they were attempting to do this it could only be described as lunacy. Their aims have been much more limited, namely to gain *the right* to open up any economy as they please and to use multilateral treaties as a basis for laying siege to any political economy whose government is attempting to protect assets against capture by powerful Atlantic capitalist groups. The Atlantic powers have to balance their thirst for control over markets and assets and pools of labour against their need to preserve the stability or at least the viability of states and political economies outside the core.

There are many in the Atlantic world and elsewhere who would hope, for the best of reasons, that the political fragmentation of the world into a Balkanised patchwork of states could be overcome by steps towards genuine world government. This would, indeed, be a desirable goal. But it would be a grave error to assume that the current IMF/WB structures are a genuine step in that direction. The reality is that these structures are less genuinely supranational in their functioning than they were under the Bretton Woods regime and are far less so than was envisaged by Keynes and Dexter White when they negotiated the Bretton Woods regime during the war. What is overlooked by the proponents of developing these institutions further along their current lines is the fact that the principal obstacle to the construction of genuine organs of global governance lies in the most powerful states themselves. It is they who have the most to lose from such a development because at present they control these multilateral organisations for the purpose of furthering their own power and interests. And the entire IMF/WB system is designed to shift the costs of the power-plays of the Atlantic world on to the bulk of humanity, which lives in the South.

It is dispiriting for many to have to face the prospect of returning managerial autonomy to nation states in order to advance towards a more genuinely unified world. It might be thought possible to envisage a coalition of medium-sized states being formed to take dominance out of the hands of the United States government and organise a system of global governance which is at least based upon a broader kind of oligarchic co-operation between, say, the largest twenty countries (largest, that is, in population terms). This could be seen as a genuine step forward. But simply to state it is to see how distantly utopian such a programme of reform currently is, despite the fact that the Atlantic powers could still have the initiative within such a forum on most issues. They are addicted to maintaining their grip on the world economy and world politics, come what may.

Relations between the capitalist core and periphery have undergone extraordinary transformations during the twentieth century. In many ways the optimal form of the relationship from the angle of core economies was that of the European empires, with the British relationship to India being the paradigm. The inability of the core states to handle their own internal relations during the twentieth century produced paradoxical results. The combination of two devastating European wars and new, far more productive American production technologies generated a new phase of postwar growth in the core. And the rising American capitalism needed to break up the European empires rather than build a new exclusive empire of its own. But with the return of stagnation in the Atlantic economies, it has been the United States which has felt itself to be in need of a functional equivalent of Britain's Indian Empire: a large source of cheap inputs for US industry and a vital destination for ever larger shares of US exports and local market control, and one that would, in addition, pay for its own administration and, like nineteenth-century India, pay a handsome tribute to the imperial power. All these requirements have been sought by the US using the DWSR and the social engineering activities of the IMF/WB during the 1980s and 1990s.

Japan in the 1980s and 1990s, like the US at the end of the war, has had no need for such an imperial system: it could have sustained continuing and expanding growth in its region of the world, sorting out minor difficulties like a property bubble in Thailand, currency misalignments etc. without significant difficulty. But it could have done so only if the US had been so locked in conflict with the EU as to have let Japan carry on without disruption.

The determination of successive US administrations since the 1970s to put

America first has derived from the rational appreciation of the enormous privileges and benefits which the top capitalist power gains from being on top within an international capitalist system. But the struggle for power between capitalist states can no longer be a zero-sum game. This is not because the United States needs a booming Japanese or German economy for the prosperity of the American people. American leaders would be happy to accept slower US growth of, say, 1 per cent per year for five years in exchange for Japanese growth of –1 per cent per year for five years, rather than have US growth at 3 per cent in exchange for Japanese growth at 5 per cent. The real basis for inter-capitalist co-operation lies in the increasing difficulty the leaders of all three parts of the triad will have in managing an increasingly unruly world. This is the truth that has been temporarily eclipsed during the first post-Cold War phase but remains fundamental for any sober political leadership.

As this essay has suggested, the United States and the other Atlantic powers seek to strengthen their grip on other parts of the world mainly by capturing powerful social constituencies within the political economies concerned. There is a basis for such social linkages in the rentier interests among the dominant social groups outside the core. The *reductio ad absurdum* of such interests has been the class of predatory money-capitalists that was enabled, with great help from the western financial sector, to seize control of the Russian state. But throughout the world, powerful rentier groups can enjoy great benefits from the ability to move funds out of their state into New York or London and thus insulate themselves from social breakdowns and developments within their own countries. These money-capitalists can also benefit from IMF/WB regimes which entrench the dominance of local financial sectors over political and economic life. And for rentiers it matters not in the slightest whether their royalties come from local business or from transnational corporations: if anything, the latter would be the preferred option.

The 1990s has been a very peculiar moment. During this decade, it appeared that labour as a social force had vanished for good. Into this momentary vacuum came what will, in future, be looked upon as a bizarre international social movement, the neo-liberal globalisation movement. Many may believe that this movement was created *ab initio* by the American mass media. But it was created at least as much by the yearning of tens of millions of people throughout the world to hope that somehow the collapse of Communism would lead to a better world. In parts of the world like Eastern Europe, people simply had to believe such a thing in order to cope with cognitive dissonance. The result was the most absurd infatuation with diseased, speculative international financial markets and with equally absurd Washington Consensus nostrums about development through deflation leading towards depression. Whatever the outcome of the Panic of '98, this international social movement is intellectually finished. It is shrinking before our eyes into a narrow ideology of rentiers and speculators. They remain, of course, extremely powerful, but they have lost the capacity to present themselves as the bearers of any modernisation programme for the planet.

In the next phase of development the energy and élan of the rentiers will decline and labour will begin to regain its balance, despite the efforts of the World Bank and the financial sectors of the West to subordinate labour to rentier interests by destroying public welfare provision and introducing the euphemistically named 'social safety' net for the deserving destitute under private fund management. The long battle will begin to rebuild a modicum of public control over economic life and the social welfare of the mass of the populations of the world.

Is There an Alternative?

The Dollar–Wall Street Regime has tended to produce a new Atlantic alliance, shown in action for the first time in a really dramatic way during the East Asian crisis. In relation to strategies for organising the world economy there has been sufficient common ground between the US, Germany, British and Dutch capitalisms to design common programmes for advancing mutual interests internationally. Yet the creation of the euro casts doubt on the political sustainability of this alliance. Independently of the intentions of EU leaders, the euro could undermine the capacity of the US to maintain the DWSR quite quickly. The result of this development could be serious transatlantic strains, strains that will tend to be all the greater if they occur in a context of international economic stagnation or worse.

On the other hand, the euro is coming into existence in an extraordinary political and institutional vacuum. There is, for example, not even an obvious institutional mechanism for running the euro's exchange rate policy towards the dollar. And the likelihood of any genuinely democratic leadership over the economy of the European Union looks extremely remote, since to create one would require unanimous agreement from all fifteen EU governments. It would appear, indeed, that there is a strong will to prevent democratic and accountable leadership from emerging. If so, this is another way of saying that speculative and rentier interests in the financial systems of the EU – the social groups with the strongest links to their Central Banks and to the European Central Bank – will exert predominant influence and will seek a close alliance with the United States. There is a widespread assumption in Western Europe that somehow the European Union is bound to have a more 'civilised' attitude towards the IMF/WB and the countries of the South than the attitude of American administrations. Yet evidence for this is almost impossible to come by, and at least as far as the general

approaches of British, German and Dutch governments have been concerned, their records in the 1980s and 1990s towards North–South
economic issues have often been worse than that of US governments. And in
trade policy, the European Union has had an increasingly strong emphasis
on neo-mercantilism, achieving maniacal proportions on occasion, partly, no
doubt, because of the European Commission's desire to prove itself valuable
to member states by responding enthusiastically to almost any call for protectionist measures – an attitude which is very understandable since the
Commission as yet lacks any democratic credentials and must thus constantly prove its value as an instrument in the main policy area where it
wields power, that of trade policy.

Nevertheless, the arrival in power of the German Social Democratic government alongside the Socialists in France and the PDS in Italy, may give
hope for a change of direction in EU policy. It would therefore seem possible to imagine a change of orientation at the level of the Council of
Ministers. If so, it is not very difficult to propose measures which would
help to tackle many of the malign developments which are grouped under
the name of globalisation.

A first step would be an end to the attempt to extend the power of the
dominant capitalist powers over the conduct of economic and social policy
in other states throughout the world. The EU should simply declare that all
states should have the right to decide how they wish to manage their financial systems, what controls they wish to have on their capital accounts, what
rights they wish to provide for or deny to multinational companies, financial
services etc. and indeed what trade policies they wish to pursue. The EU may
wish to continue to accept all the international obligations it has entered
into with the US in the WTO, the OECD etc., but it would oppose attempts
to brigade other states into accepting these regimes and it would oppose
attempts to exclude states from the application of GATT principles because
they did not wish to subscribe to this or that liberalisation programme.
Secondly, the EU should declare that financial institutions lending internationally must be supervised and protected by their home governments, who
should bear the full costs of bailing them out. The IMF will provide bridging
loans to such governments to help them bail out their banks, hedge funds
etc. but their tax-payers must ultimately foot the bill. Thus, if US banks or
hedge funds are facing collapse through a payments crisis either at home or
abroad they must turn to their domestic lender of last resort for help. They
should no longer expect the poor of Indonesia or Brazil or Russia to foot the
bill. Thirdly, lenders must understand that sovereign governments have the
right to unilaterally repudiate debt. This is a risk that lenders must build into
their calculations when lending funds abroad. Fourthly, the EU must take
steps to initiate a new system of public EU insurance of loans to other governments whether made by EU, private or public financial institutions on

the basis of EU approval of the purposes of these loans. Such loan insurance operations should be transparent and democratically accountable. All other private lending activities abroad would not be covered at all in the event of borrower default. And finally, the EU would *temporarily* continue to participate in current IMF/WB operations but only on the understanding that all IMF/WB conditionalities would be published and on the basis that an international conference was convened to reorganise the international monetary financial system in line with recommendations such as those suggested here. If such ideas were not adopted by the other main powers, the EU should adopt a policy of international pluralism in the handling of international economic management. Those states which desired to continue within the IMF framework would be free to do so, while other states might prefer to operate within the EU framework. At the same time, the EU would seek to negotiate agreements with other countries establishing regimes of fixed but adjustable exchange rates.

Proposals of this sort should be combined with the reassertion of an EU financial system centred on bank intermediation of finance, strong public regulation and a preference for public or co-operative saving institutions. The tax systems of member states should be adapted to ensure the taxation of flows of hot money into and out of the EU and to ensure that speculative trading on securities markets was penalised through taxation. Tax havens should be abolished throughout the EU and the EU should work to eradicate them internationally. One way in which this could be done would be through ensuring that information about persons or companies maintaining funds offshore are made available to the relevant tax authorities within the EU and such persons or companies should be made liable for the payment of taxes on these funds in their EU country of citizenship.

For some such reform programme to be carried through would require a very substantial exercise of political power over rentier and speculator interests within the EU itself. The speculators often try to claim that a reassertion of public control over international finance is technically impossible because of technological change. But these claims have force only in the sense that it is technically impossible for states to prevent crimes. This is true: most of the work of the judicial system is ex post facto: first the crime, then the investigation and prosecution. It is the same in the case of private international finance. Regulators cannot stop companies from switching funds around the world, legally or illegally. But they must be able to find out what has been happening after the event. If they cannot do so, then this is because the top managements of the companies concerned cannot themselves find out what their operational staff have been doing with their funds. Of course, managerial controls are often poor – witness Barings and many other similar disasters. But if managements can keep records of what their companies have been up to, then states can keep track of what has been happening through the usual requirements for 'transparency': they can inspect the books. Of course, they cannot do so 100 per cent: there will be a great deal of fraud and corruption at the very top of the financial system. But states can still exercise great sway, if they have the political will to do so.

But the problem of mustering political will to re-subordinate money-dealing capital to public policy goals for economic development lies at root in the area of strategies for economic revival. What gives the private financial sector its social and political dominance is above all economic stagnation. Under conditions of stagnation, governments go into fiscal deficits and public debt mounts. This makes governments dependent upon conditions in bond markets. The private financial operators demand deflationary retrenchment of public finances, thus deepening the cycle of stagnation and rentier dependence. A strategy for re-imposing public order over economic and social life thus depends upon combining such measures with an economic growth strategy.

This brings us to a fundamental question which has been deliberately avoided throughout this essay, namely the causes of the long stagnation in the production systems of the core over most of the last quarter of a century. We will not begin a serious exploration of that issue here. But most ways of explaining the reasons for the long stagnation would tend to do so by suggesting that there has been some sort of saturation or overproduction crisis within the triadic economies. If that is the case, then given the right financial and monetary environment, there should be the possibility for a dynamic process of catch-up development in the new regions opened up to capitalism in East Central and Eastern Europe, in other words for these economies to play the role of a catch-up growth centre which had been played by East and South-East Asia. If such a catch-up growth were to take place, it would not resolve the deeper historical problems of stagnation, but it would substantially ease them. During the 1990s, this potentiality in East Central and Eastern Europe has been squandered by the combined efforts of the capitalisms on both sides of the Atlantic to engage in short-term predatory tactics towards the region. The United States has been obsessed with integrating the region into its Dollar–Wall Street Regime for international monetary and financial manipulations, without the slightest interest in the establishment of favourable conditions for regional development. Meanwhile West European governments, mired in stagnation and internal social and political tensions, have viewed the region basically as a source of problems and political-economic threats: a source of pressures for the restructuring of industries in Western Europe, a source of population migration threats and a source of budgetary threats if a country like Poland were to enter the European Union. No serious international strategy for the economic revival and for the economic development of the region has been attempted.

The obvious place to begin the search for such a strategy is in Western Europe amongst the parties of the social democratic Left. For fifteen years European social democracy has been a political nullity, with its leaderships in France, Italy, Spain and Belgium sharing as much in common in the field of direct financial corruption as in anything else. As for Blair's Labour leadership, it is bought and paid for. But the new German Finance Minister, Lafontaine, is certainly different. He is a determined European Keynesian with a strong will and a political following in a political economy that is absolutely central. This raises the possibility of a Keynesianism not so much rooted in the Keynes of redistributing income within a national economy to boost effective demand – although such redistribution would be a good thing in itself – but in the Keynes of ideas for organising the postwar international economy for growth: the Keynes who sought to propose the kind of 'financial repression' and statist development strategy for the world, placing productive growth in the saddle and organising euthanasia for the rentier – a model that is now rather bizarrely thought of by many as an East Asian invention.

I think that this is a theoretical possibility. Just as capitalism found a way out, in the end, from the crisis of the 1930s and the war, a way out that offered a greatly improved deal for a large part of humanity, so I believe it could, in principle, do so again. But I doubt that it will, not because of the nature of capitalism as such, but because a solution would require a *tactical radicalism* and an intransigence of political will which it is difficult to imagine European social democracy as being capable of.

A European social democratic answer to the present crisis, led by the new German government, would have to take very bold steps, with the support of other governments like those of France and Italy, for a pan-European strategy for economic revival. The key to such a strategy must be to tackle the payments weaknesses and vulnerability of the East Central and East European economies. This is where the euro could be used as a powerful lever, backed by the financial power of the ECB. With the arrival of the euro, the member states of Euroland will no longer have to worry about their current account balance because they won't have one. They should therefore become less mercantilist about trade issues. Secondly, the euro will give seigniorage privileges to Euroland in the East. The latter economies will denominate their trade, their accounting, their reserves in euros. Euroland can buy as much as it wants in the East and just pay for everything in the currency which they produce: euros. Euroland can do for the East what the USA did for Japan after the war: open its market wide.

But that is not the most important way in which the euro could be used. The vital task is first to secure the currencies of the East against speculative attack so strongly that they can greatly enlarge their current account deficits without worries about the sustainability of these deficits. This task of securing their currencies is not a significant problem for Euroland's Central Bank because of the enormous financial resources in its hands, now dwarfing tiny banks like the Bundesbank. The Bundesbank offered guarantees of unlimited very short-term support for the franc. The ECB can with ease offer the same only much more so to the currencies of the Eastern region. These governments can then forget their worries about hedge funds and ignore the IMF. And even if Euroland does not impose new capital controls, it should certainly urge East Central and East European governments to do so, so that Wall Street can never 'short' their currencies in the forward foreign exchange markets again. The Euroland authorities could declare that for a five-year period they are aiming for the states of East Central and Eastern Europe to run trade deficits of 10 per cent of their GDPs and the ECB will underwrite their currencies while they are doing so. Secondly, these economies should use their deficits for infrastructure projects and investment in fixed capital projects of their choice. They will have the resulting deficits funded out of the current very large trade surpluses of the EU (or Euroland).

This means large, serious, very long-term credits or even grants (funded through a 'tax' in the EU current account surplus). They do not have to be at non-market 'aid' rates although they could easily be. But they must be long-term and big and should be handled by public authorities in Euroland. The US and European investment banks, speculators and rentiers have already had their sport in the Eastern region. It is now time to clear out their Augean stables. Either large public offerings of long-term bonds issued by the European Investment Bank or long-term loans to the region offered by the same bank (actually a bank made up of the states of the EU) should be advanced.

These mechanisms could at last begin a virtuous circle of productive interaction between the two halves of the continent. The East could import the plant that it needs and expand its domestic markets and exports West. The expanding streams of income in the east could provide the effective demand for expanded imports from the West. Speculative fevers could subside across the continent and full employment could return, aided no doubt by Lafontaine-style large transfers of wealth back from capital to labour through the tax system. If big capitals in Europe still wish to emigrate, let them go. But where to? From the biggest integrating market in the world to the shattered tissue of economies in the South being managed under intellectually bankrupt 'development models' of rentier capitalism, 'liberated' from the 'financial repression' that served the capitalist world so well in the days of the Communist threat.

If the new German social democratic government in Germany could embark on a path like that and largely pull it off, then Euroland could begin to offer a way out for other parts of the world as well. But it would be a bitter political battle against enormously powerful financial interests which have thrived on the DWSR and which have the strong support of the US government. It is a course that would wreck the international strategy of American capitalism, challenging its entire ideology. It would require the German social democrats to build a *political coalition* across Europe and one that could genuinely fire popular enthusiasm. And such a coalition would, if necessary, have to be prepared to break the great taboo of the entire Cold War period: it would have to be prepared, if necessary, to mobilise public opinion in Europe *against* the American ally, simply in order to defend the strategy against US disruption. And those who have followed the Bosnia crisis closely know how far the US is prepared to go when high political stakes are involved. So do those who have followed the East Asian crisis closely.

But the major impediment to such a strategy lies not within the United States or with the social power of rentier interests. It lies in two other directions: first, in the deep nationalist subordinations of the social democratic parties of Europe themselves. A plan for West European revival through a Marshall-type plan for East Central and Eastern Europe would be viewed in Paris (or London) as a plan to strengthen Germany rather than France or the UK. This would be the first stumbling block. The second would be that there is no effective institutional structure for actually pursuing such a plan: there is no economic government for Euroland, no responsible democratic leadership for using the euro as an instrument of economic revival and no easy path to achieving appropriate institutional mechanisms: gaining them would require an EU Intergovernmental Conference at which unanimity was achieved not just to supplement the Maastricht Treaty but to substantially modify it to make the ECB more like the Federal Reserve Board of the United States: an institution with the explicit task of serving socially useful development purposes. Such changes could be achieved. But the record suggests that they will not be. The Blair government, for one, would, on its past record, wish to play a wrecking role since Blair himself is a passionate enemy of what he calls the 'tax and spend' European social model. On the other hand, it could be argued that Blair is not really attached to any idea whatever, and might be won over to such a project of reform. Or alternatively the institutional mechanisms could be developed informally through the committee of Euroland finance ministers from which the British government is currently excluded.

If there is no effective European social democratic challenge to the globalisation drift, the next phase of international politics will be a turbulent and ugly one. The lesson of the East Asian crisis that will be drawn in many parts of the world is that the Atlantic powers are prepared to use economic statecraft to block capitalist catch-up development. The assumption of the 1990s that after the collapse of the Soviet Bloc the world would unite under

American leadership will be shown to have been a ridiculous illusion. The 1990s were a unique moment when real global institutional reform for sustainable development, based upon global political co-operation and international institution-building, could have been achieved under Atlantic leadership. But that opportunity has been utterly squandered as so often in earlier moments of victory.

Nothing demonstrates the vapidity of the 'new thinking' more graphically than the current catchphrase of 'The Third Way': this is simply a slipway to enable European intellectuals, whether liberal or social democratic, to abandon their social liberal or social democratic values, for the sake of overcoming their cognitive dissonance with an Americanised Europe. Insofar as they abandon the struggle for egalitarian and cosmopolitan solutions to international problems, these banners will be taken up by more radical currents. They will draw the conclusion that Marx was right about capitalism being ultimately incapable of providing a viable framework for sustainable human society on this planet.

PART II

Politics in the Globalisation Period

8

The Gulf War, Iraq and Western Liberalism

The states of the North Atlantic have, since the days of Palmerston, frequently hoisted the flag of liberalism on their way to war. But rarely since 1945 have the principles of right, law and justice been invoked as strongly as in the call to arms for Desert Storm. The populations of Britain and America were encouraged to believe that half a million troops and one hundred billion dollars were being committed to affirmative action on behalf of the rights of the people of Kuwait and, indeed, to the inauguration of a new global order of justice.

In the first part of this chapter, I try to untangle the disparate strands that make up this language of rights used by western leaders to vindicate Desert Storm. I then bring together the principles of evaluation deployed by the liberal current dominant in Britain and the United States today – rights-based individualism – with an analysis of the Gulf conflict. This enables an exploration of the degree to which goals and actions in the war can be justified in liberal terms, and reveals the severe limitations of a conventional rights-based approach. In the second part, I turn to the 'enemy' – Iraq – in order to examine the evolution of this state, so many of whose people have been killed by the military forces and economic blockades of Britain and the US, and to challenge the most influential, liberal account of the development of modern Iraq and of its Ba'athist regime.

I Liberalism and the Invasion of Kuwait

Most versions of Anglo-American liberal and natural-rights thinking employ a universalist standard of judgement to evaluate international politics. They repudiate the normative stance of the realists, who insist, in the words of their postwar doyen, Hans Morganthau, that the national interest is 'the one guiding star, one standard of thought, one rule of action' in such matters.[1]

141

Rights-based liberals readily acknowledge, of course, that much of what states – including their own – actually do bears little relation to the professed ideal. Indeed many would agree that the political culture that shapes the executives of these states is far closer to the norms of Morganthau than to their own, although they would deplore that fact.

Within this setting, the leaders in both the US and UK sought to mobilise liberal opinion following the Iraqi invasion of Kuwait by appealing not simply to national state interests but, above all, to general principles. While some opinion-formers debated the issues in the language of utilitarianism, adopting a universalist welfare criterion for assessing the costs and benefits of alternative policies, the dominant language of public debate was that of rights, justice and law. This discourse was triggered primarily by the use the Bush administration made of UN Security Council resolutions. These were interpreted in an idiom that was in fact metaphorical: the transfer of the discourse that serves the domestic legal system within a liberal-democratic state to the realm of world politics. In the perception of millions, international affairs became a depoliticised process of crime and judicial punishment. This single displacement transformed not only the way people judged the political background to the Gulf war, but above all how they *perceived* it: namely, as a criminal act with juridical consequences. Thus the complex fields of force that constitute global politics were magically transformed into the image of a world enclosed within a constitutional state order, run according to the liberal theory of law. The metaphor passed itself off not as a moral truth but as the explanation of actual events.[2]

Firstly, the sufficient and necessary cause of the US attack on Iraq was presented as the act of a villain: Saddam Hussein, personifying the Baghdad government. This act 'forced' the US to send half a million troops and its global arsenal in response, just as a domestic crime triggers the standard procedures of police response. The Anglo-American blockade and attack was thus reduced to the status of a depoliticised, purely judicial action, from which any political motives, methods or aims would be expunged, just as they would in the work of a local law-enforcement agency. Desert Storm was to be as much a work of nature as the impersonal, blind justice of the law – or, indeed, as a storm in the desert. Thus the actual course of events was turned on its head: contrary to the judicial logic of the metaphor, the US administration in fact decided it must 'prevail' over Iraq and *therefore* campaigned to criminalise the Saddam Hussein regime. (Just as the US first decided to support the regimes of Israel or Indonesia and *then* ensured the decriminalisation of those countries' actions in occupying or annexing.) This process involved anthropomorphising the Iraqi state and its political-administrative organisation into a single person – Saddam Hussein, criminal. And the more his human features were enlarged, the more other

men and women in the 'criminal' state were dehumanised. The army of conscripts became the murder weapon, the lives of millions of Iraqis the various
limbs and resources of their leader. Hence they were fair game; or else they
became collateral, in the sense of standing alongside the criminal –
bystanders in the police shoot-out.[3]

This anthropomorphism enabled the weaving of a powerful theme of
human-rights abuse into the legalist discourse. The war against Iraq became
a campaign against a serial killer and torturer, military action being presented as a mere consequence of the original 'crime', the annexation of
Kuwait. Furthermore, the war-making itself could be portrayed not as a tidal
wave of political violence, killing tens, perhaps hundreds, of thousands – an
act unleashing the passions of millions across the globe, and bearing
unknown and unpredictable long-term political consequences – but as a
technical means of enforcing an end – namely, the rule of law.

As a mobilising ideology for war, then, this metaphor was a formidable
construction: an absolutised 'either/or' – one the monstrous criminal, the
other the very embodiment of justice. It provided a thorough integration of
theory and practice – cognition, evaluation and necessary action. Indeed,
the metaphor was to prove in some respects too efficacious, too powerful,
when the war ended with the monster criminal still in place and butchering
further victims on a larger scale – Shia rebels in the South and Kurds in the
North. However, as an explanatory theory or criterion of judgement the
metaphor could not, of course, be taken seriously.[4] World politics is not
enclosed within a constitutional state order with a fully fledged legal regime
and law-enforcement agency. Legal thought and practice are no doubt a significant element in international affairs (valued especially by small, satisfied
powers), but international public law remains rather a half-formed, perhaps only embryonic, force. Indeed, for some of the biggest powers the
legal element is often no more than the small change of politics.
Furthermore, when powers like the US or UK go to war they do so for reasons of national interest, in pursuit of state objectives. As for the idea that
attacking a country is equal to enforcing a law, the greatest of classical liberal
rights-based philosophers, Immanuel Kant, long ago taught us that war is
inherently anti-law.[5]

Although no one could claim that the legalist metaphor adequately
describes reality, some may nevertheless maintain that UN backing for force
against Iraq provides a democratic political legitimation for the war (as
opposed to a liberal, rights-based justification). After all, has not the Left
repeatedly used the authority of the UN's Charter and resolutions to attack
the United States and its allies in other conflicts – some still current – such
as Nicaragua, East Timor, Israel, South Africa, Grenada, Panama? The fact
that none of the five permanent Security Council members vetoed military
action against Iraq was certainly of great political significance, but this fact

confers not the slightest *democratic* legitimacy upon the subsequent attack. UN Security Council resolutions embody merely a Hobbesian, positivist form of law as the command of the most powerful – namely, the will of the five permanent members who happened to be the victors of 1945 plus a small, circulating collection of other states. Even the 'states' democracy' of the UN General Assembly was not reflected in the crucial resolutions of the Security Council. Indeed the entire thrust of these resolutions, as inter- preted by the US and Britain – that there should be no diplomatic negotiations with Iraq – contradicted the overwhelming majority of the General Assembly, who desired a negotiated solution. And in any case, the resolutions did not even legalise the attack in the formal procedural sense; that would have required a positive vote by all five Security Council mem- bers, but in fact China abstained. Also the Charter requires parties to a conflict to take steps toward reconciliation – in other words, to negotiate: precisely what the Americans (and the British) resolutely refused to do throughout. And in the name of 'liberating Kuwait' the British and Americans interpreted the final UN resolution as legitimising any and all means – not exactly a liberal juristic maxim.

Thus, any principled political stance on the war-drive against Iraq cannot be based upon acceptance of UN Security Council resolutions, as the embodiment of either judicial or democratic principle. We are required, therefore, to make a political judgement based upon our own understand- ing and prognosis. Such judgement cannot abdicate before UN decisions.

Two Traditions of Rights

Liberal theory offers a number of disparate approaches to the evaluation of political events, ranging from the Hegel-inspired liberal idealism of Green, through the historicism of Croce, to utilitarian viewpoints. But one per- spective dominates all others at present in the US and, increasingly, in the UK: namely, that of natural-rights, or Kantian deontological theory of rights, based on a universal principle of justice rather than welfare. But this approach in fact conflates two incompatible traditions of *political* thinking on international relations, traditions that share a common source in the dis- course of universal rights: one, the old natural-rights tradition, which predates liberalism, not to mention democracy, and has its source in medi- aeval debates and its highest expression in the international-relations theory of Grotius; and two, the modern tradition of Kantian liberalism. I will briefly examine these in turn.

Grotius, a Dutch Protestant writing during the Thirty Years War and just prior to the birth of the modern state system (marked by the Treaty of Westphalia in 1648), was confronting the problem of whether, in a hitherto

Catholic European system, Protestant princedoms had a right to exist and to impose their religion upon their subjects. To resolve this problem he insisted that every state should be treated as a sovereign in relation to other states, as well as to the Papacy and the Empire. He then argued for a law-governed relation between these sovereign entities. Grotius's thought concerning domestic politics was, like most strong rights-theorists of the day, trenchantly authoritarian, insisting upon the absolute power of the state over its citizens. He defined liberty as dominion in material things and argued that man has a natural right to punish wrongs, especially wrongs against liberty (that is, property), and further, that this right of punishment should be transferred to the state. Grotius also transferred the notion of liberty-as-property to the state in international affairs, viewing the character of state boundaries as that of a private estate. Grotius was also the founder of the modern idea of a rights-based legal system. His *Introduction to the Jurisprudence of Holland* (1620) was the first construction of a legal system based upon a conception of rights. And his later *De Jure Belli* laid the foundation stone of modern theories of 'just war'.[6]

The Grotian view of inter-state politics may be hundreds of years old, but it nevertheless remains the official doctrine of the international state system today, thanks to its implementation after the Treaty of Westphalia and to the way in which the intra-European principle was extended across the globe through imperial expansion. The doctrine invests sovereign states with legitimate power within the international system and grants each state the right to total (negative) freedom to do what it desires, provided only that it does not infringe upon the freedoms of other states to do likewise. States are thus the only morally relevant actors in world politics. It follows that a world political order in which each state's sovereignty is respected is a basically just order. The US and the UK officially subscribe to this doctrine (while unofficially frequently flouting it – the recent US adventures in Grenada and Panama serving as examples) although it should also be said that the concept of a 'superpower' tends to grant the US additional rights commensurate with its extra 'responsibilities'. The world's diplomatic fraternity has a strong professional interest in the continued vitality of this approach.

The doctrine, then, gives rise to the conventional theory of a 'just war'. War is just under the following conditions: first, when it is launched by a legitimate body – namely a state; secondly, when that state has a just cause, and overwhelmingly this means that the state concerned is defending the principle of its territorial integrity (in Grotian terms, its property) against aggression; thirdly, when the state has 'right intentions' – in other words, when it is not using one violation of sovereignty in order to perpetrate another; and finally, to be just, a war requires the use of 'correct means'.[7]

What I have called the 'legalist metaphor' draws much of its power from this Grotian official doctrine of the inviolability of states: from a crime-and-punishment view of their relations, and from their collective right to exclusive possession of the field of international relations.

The predominant liberal school of thought today, at least in the Anglo-American world, derives from Kant.[8] Yet Kant's thought on international relations was constructed in sharp polemic against Grotian ideas. Kant questioned the Grotian ethical basis of international law since it could be used to justify acts by states which had at best a dubious moral foundation. He pointed out that no government had ever been persuaded to refrain from an action on account of some rule of international law banning it. And, in the words of Parkinson, 'Kant was particularly hard on those who considered . . . the doctrine of "just war" had any bearing on the maintenance of peace or on the improvement of international relations generally.'[9]

Modern Kantians give overriding priority not to the rights of states but to the rights of individuals. They formally single out one key instance of good, accord it absolute primacy, investigate whether it is violated, and prescriptively work for its restitution, repudiating the notion that this priority right may be sacrificed for the greater welfare of all. The good in question is usually that of individual freedom, on the grounds that if individuals have freedom they possess the means of achieving all other goods. The task of political analysis and action is to work out the least costly means for restoring this overriding right to freedom. But this, it must be stressed, is freedom for individuals and not for the fictitious legal persons known as states.[10]

There is, of course, a basis from which liberals may derive rights for states – namely, through the collective rights of nations to self-determination. But we should note that some are uneasy about such collective rights, and especially about their derivation from the notion of a collective democratic will. For the right to self-determination is, in reality, a democratic rather than a liberal-individualist right. My aim here is not to explore all the nuances of this Kantian rights-based liberalism, but to apply its main principle to the Gulf crisis.

The Invasion and Annexation of Kuwait

The invasion of Kuwait on 2 August was carried out with very little military resistance or bloodshed. Initially the Iraqi government said it would begin withdrawing from Kuwait on 5 August, while demanding negotiations. It then remained, set up a provisional government, and altered course; after the imposition of a military blockade through a UN resolution, Iraq formally annexed Kuwait as its nineteenth province.

The occupation of the country by force was accompanied by considerable repression and suffering, by no means only among the minority of the population holding Kuwaiti citizenship. There occurred first the rounding up and transportation to Iraqi prison camps of thousands of soldiers and police (estimates vary between seven and thirty thousand). In addition, many thousands of foreign workers were deported and detained in Iraq. Then there was the use of torture against, and on occasions the killing of, those suspected of having engaged in acts of armed resistance. In its report of 19 December 1990, Amnesty International estimated these killings in the hundreds.[11] In addition, some 300,000 Kuwaitis – a majority of the country's citizens – felt impelled to flee or to remain outside the country, along with large numbers of other permanent residents. It is not clear to what degree this exodus was caused by fear of the Iraqis or by fear of an American attack. Kuwaitis leaving would have suffered a significant drop in living standards, despite receiving money from the government in exile. Average income in the country before the invasion was higher than that in the United States, with a standard of living considerably better than that of the American middle classes, many citizens employing servants and often not having to work.

Condemnation of Iraqi aggression, variously expressed, was issued worldwide. This opposition to the invasion and annexation in the main conflated two quite different principles: the violation of states' rights and the violation of people's rights. Within a Grotian, states' rights perspective, annexation involved what we might call the killing of a sovereign state – the greatest injustice that could be committed within the terms of states' rights theory, and an act of state murder unprecedented in postwar history. Kuwait, a fully-fledged member of the United Nations, was, effectively, liquidated. If states' rights are sacrosanct, this was a uniquely heinous crime.

There is no need to examine the factual details of the Gulf crisis in order to justify Desert Storm within the terms of states' rights doctrine. Iraq gave just cause. What is more, the attack on Iraq was launched by an alliance of legitimate state authorities (backed by UN Security Council resolutions – a fact with no bearing on this theory's guiding principles). The motives of the US-led coalition were 'right' provided we accept – as we should – the temporary character of the occupation of southern Iraq by coalition troops; only the introduction of US troops into Iraqi Kurdistan without the prior authorisation of the Iraqi government raises a doubt over US intentions. The Bush administration's refusal to march on Baghdad or to assist militarily the uprisings in the South or in Kurdistan is a plus, not a minus, in terms of the principles of states' rights. Finally, there is the question of 'correct means'. If such means are governed by international conventions embodying the rules of war, they pose few problems of justification to the US – extending even to the use of napalm or the bombing of civilian targets if such could be shown to be deliberate policy decisions by the authorities. Those who object to the use of certain means by the US usually do so on the basis of principles other than those of states' rights – for example, human rights or human-welfare principles.

It is nevertheless the case that states' rights doctrine and its 'just war' corollary have no basis in liberal or democratic theory. Nothing in liberal, democratic or socialist political philosophy gives primacy to state power or state rights as such. These philosophies are, in fact, quite prepared to countenance the disappearance of this or that state, including its violent overthrow and the redrawing of territorial boundaries. Moreover, states have rarely acquired their supposedly sovereign rights and powers by democratic means. They have usually gained them through recognition by other states and the granting of a seat at the United Nations – a mechanism not necessarily tied to the assertion of democratic political principle. Indeed, a large proportion of existing, legitimate states assumed their form and rights through the direct impact of imperialism upon their region and subsequent recognition by the dominant imperial powers of the day. Iraq is a case in point, and so is Kuwait. The peoples' rights and will in both cases played no part, quite the contrary. In the case of Kuwait, sovereignty was achieved, above all, due to the strength of British military power and political influence throughout the period up to 1961 when international recognition was granted. Such recognition of state sovereignty is, in theory, a matter of international law, settled not by simple force but by legal title to territory. As it happens, Iraq had a very strong claim, in legal terms, to the territory of Kuwait.[12] But such claims are far from being decisive for liberal democrats or socialists.

It is significant that rights-based liberalism does not, in fact, speak with one voice on the key question of Iraq's denial of rights in Kuwait, although there is a common stress on the infringement of individual liberties by the Iraqi armed forces and police. (According to Amnesty's findings this infringement applied particularly to the imprisonment of former members of the Kuwaiti security forces and to the savage repression against suspected armed resisters or spies, with no respect accorded to the due process of law. Expressions of civic resistance – such as the refusal to use Iraqi number plates on cars – were also punished. Kuwaitis fleeing invariably suffered, though their welfare was probably not greatly affected. On the other hand, the sufferings of the fleeing or deported non-Kuwaiti settled population were often considerable.) But what about the injustice of the annexation itself? This did not actually involve a loss of civic and political rights for the majority because, being debarred from holding citizenship, they had no such rights under the al-Sabah regime. Yet it did mean loss of statehood for the minority with Kuwaiti citizenship. Many strands of individualist liberalism would be suspicious of any collective claims to statehood – true, say, of the Isaiah Berlin of *Two Concepts of Liberty*, and also of the Bertrand Russell of *Political Ideals*.[13] And a Wilsonian notion of national rights for all ethnic groups entails serious difficulties due to the problem of Arab national identity. Mill, on the other hand, did strongly defend national self-determination on the grounds of the right to political participation.[14]

The decisive principle for most liberal democrats here is, surely, not a liberal principle of justice or freedom but a democratic one: that of popular self-determination. The people of Kuwait were brutally and flagrantly denied the right to decide for themselves whether they wished to be integrated into Iraq. None of the Iraqi government's subsequent justifications for the annexation can override this fact. That the people of Kuwait had been living under an autocracy has no bearing on the matter. Thus on democratic principles alone the Iraqi government should have been opposed. But democratic principle, at least on Mill's grounds of political participation, requires respect for the rights of all the settled population of Kuwait, not just the minority granted citizenship (34 per cent) or the tiny proportion with voting rights under the al-Sabahs (some 7 per cent) – that is, before the abolition of such rights in the 1980s. If the Iraqis had organised a genuinely free referendum of all the people, and this had produced a vote in favour of fusion with Iraq, the attitude of liberal democrats might have been very different. But they did no such thing, and there is every reason to suppose that the great bulk of the settled population would, in any case, have voted against annexation. The Iraqi occupation of Kuwait therefore had to be opposed as a matter of political principle by both liberal democrats and socialists. The question then became a programmatic one: how to end the occupation, and what positive aims to advance in the struggle for self-determination. But this last goal, as we have seen, has a special twist because of Kuwait's unique character: the fact that the majority is denied any civil recognition. It must surely include what we take for granted in other cases of self-determination: namely, the right of all its settled residents to full citizenship.

A rights-based liberalism, privileging individual freedom, tends to underplay other critical political issues raised by the invasion. One of these was who should control and who should benefit from Gulf oil. This was central not only for western policy-makers but also, of course, in the politics of the Arab world, and for liberal social egalitarians and the socialist Left. Hundreds of billions of dollars worth of oil revenue was channelled by the Kuwaiti ruling families into western investment – generating substantial profits, particularly in the UK and the USA. This income could have been used directly for economic development in the Arab world, to transform the lives of people in Amman, Damascus, the Nile Delta and, of course, Iraq.

Another issue, closely linked to the oil factor, was the social structure of Kuwait: that it represented, in the words of an authoritative study of the region, a form of 'new slavery' with a 'viciously reactionary character'.[15] Of the capital generated from oil for investment abroad, 90 per cent was concentrated in the hands of eighteen families. The manual work in the state, and much of the managerial and professional work, was carried out by non-Kuwaitis, especially Palestinians who had settled in Kuwait in large numbers since the 1950s. Yet such people, denied citizenship because they lacked a family connection with the territory traceable to the 1920s, were entirely without civic rights, despite forming the majority of the population.

Such issues would have to be traded off in some way against the injustices of the invasion, particularly in the context of evaluating the US-led military attack on Iraq and its consequences.[16] Yet they were mostly ignored in the mainstream public debate on the crisis, although one American senator quoted a remark in the *New York Times* that pithily encapsulated these concerns, dubbing Kuwait 'an oil company with a seat at the United Nations'.[17]

Achieving Self-Determination

We will now examine the means that were available for ending the occupation of Kuwait against the yardstick of liberal theories of individual rights. The main options were: (1) a negotiated diplomatic solution; (2) popular resistance backed by external moral and material aid; (3) trade and other embargoes; (4) military action. A rights- based approach could, in principle, support any one of these options. But it could support option (4) only if this could be shown to be the sole realistic means for freeing the people of Kuwait. And even then this school would have to be convinced that the instrument chosen for war – the state(s) waging it – would not itself produce new political oppression or injustice in place of the old. Utilitarian theorists might very well, on the basis of their factual analysis and prognosis, wish to rule out option (4) on the grounds that military force would inevitably create greater suffering than it would produce any gain for the people of Kuwait. I will assess each option in turn, in terms of both its realism and its consequences.

1) A negotiated diplomatic solution

The doctrine I have called 'states' rights' theory does not necessarily favour the diplomatic solution to ending an occupation because, by investing states with the qualities of persons, this doctrine may favour punishing an aggressor state for 'killing' a 'brother' state, as one punishes a murderer. Such punishment may be retributive, or may be justified on grounds of example or deterrence. But this approach is at variance with all humanist varieties of liberalism, let alone socialism, for it adopts a nihilist, or at least an agnostic, attitude towards the rights and welfare of real human beings, whether as individuals or communities.

For rights-based liberals (and for utilitarians), a negotiated solution must be a preferred means, provided, of course, that such a solution is possible and does not compromise on the issue of principle – complete freedom from occupation for the people of Kuwait. There *were* negotiations immediately after the invasion; and the Jordanian government, along with the PLO and Algeria, have always insisted that a negotiated end to the occupation of Kuwait acceptable to Iraq was possible. None of these early diplomatic efforts made progress. And it is vital to establish why not. There seem to be two reasons: first, because various Arab governments preferred to see Iraqi power destroyed; second, and crucially, because the United States put enormous pressure upon King Fahd and President Mubarak to prevent any negotiated settlement.

Baghdad then proposed that the UN should tackle the occupation of Kuwait and the Israeli occupations within the same terms of reference. This remarkable proposal corresponds exactly to a rights-based liberal-universalist approach to problems of political justice. It was not suggesting that nothing be done about Kuwait until the Palestinians' right to self-determination was tackled; rather, it was a call to the UN to apply a common principle to both occupations. Yet not only did the US administration bluntly reject the proposal, but it outlawed the idea of diplomatic negotiation altogether, opting instead for total military blockade and subsequent all-out attack. This repudiation of diplomacy demonstrated that the American (and British) policy-making establishment was far from allowing its political operations, following the Iraq invasion, to be governed by liberal, rights-based principles. Iraq repeatedly called for negotiations.[18] The UN Charter requires them. The US utterly ruled out any such diplomacy. The war party in the US and UK denounced negotiations with Iraq as 'appeasement', but this analogy was inappropriate. For the negotiations that produced the Munich Agreement opened Czechoslovakia up for German conquest; it was a case of negotiating for German *expansion*. The negotiations over Kuwait would have been precisely on the terms for Iraqi *withdrawal*.

Some say that Iraqi offer was insincere, but this view is not credible. After all, had the offer been taken up, Baghdad would have pulled off an unparalleled political triumph in the Arab World as the leadership that had achieved a great political victory for the Palestinians – ample compensation for withdrawal from Kuwait. Indeed, it was precisely on these grounds that the US rejected any action on Palestine: Saddam Hussein would gain from it. But this was a price the US should have been prepared to pay, for its failure to support justice for the Palestinians for twenty years. Rights-based liberalism is not governed by considerations of tactical advantage for a given political leadership that adheres to liberal principles of justice. It can be argued that the Iraqi state was rightly denied any gain in political status after its action in Kuwait. It is surely true that the contest for positional goods like status and political prestige in the hierarchy of states is something liberals should deplore. But a principled liberalism concerned with justice for all human beings has no interest in tailoring its policy to the apportionment of such goods or their withdrawal from one state or another. That entire approach is a relic of states' rights thinking.

The view that attacking Iraq would have the salutory effect of deterring future aggression is unconvincing. The most it would do is demonstrate that aggression without US approval does not pay, for we have abundant evidence that aggression or annexation *with* US approval does pay (in the case of the US – Panama, Grenada, and in that of its allies – Morocco, Israel, Indonesia, Turkey and so on).

The Iraqi offer was extremely embarrassing to Washington because the US had been supporting *injustice* for Palestinians. But a principled, rights-based liberalism rejects any relativisation of the right to political freedom. That Saddam Hussein had proposed a joint solution to the questions of Kuwaiti and Palestinian oppression should, therefore, have strengthened the case for the Baghdad offer, rather than weakened it.

2) The resistance movement

It might be argued that the US should be condemned for its failure to negotiate, but that, given this failure, we had no choice but to support the blockade and/or all-out attack. This logic assumes the existence of only one kind of force in the world: state military force. But as the Vietnam War demonstrated, this is not the case. Popular-resistance movements are another, potentially very powerful, agency for achieving national freedom. Furthermore, in almost every conceivable instance, this agency is far preferable in ethical terms to the appalling destructiveness of state military force.

The importance, indeed the primacy, of popular-resistance movements for political freedom is given especial emphasis by John Stuart Mill in his article 'A Few Words on Non-Intervention', written in the same year as 'On Liberty'.[19] For Mill, popular resistance to achieve liberation is superior to external military intervention not on the utilitarian ground that the latter may be more costly or may not achieve political freedom, but because a people must 'become free by their own efforts'. In this instance we find that the option of external pressure and support for popular resistance was simply excluded in line with states' rights ideology – which expressly precludes all agencies other than states from having a legitimate role in international politics. There is thus a presumption in favour of state action.

A popular-resistance movement in Kuwait did exist; and it had the support of significant groups within Iraq for a struggle for self-determination. And if, for once, such a movement had been given political/moral support from the West, there is every reason to expect that a powerful political force could have been built. (The Palestinian *intifada* against Israeli occupation is a striking case in point: despite military subjugation, killings, torture, detention without trial, reprisals against civilians, and mass expulsion, the Palestinian resistance, with a population about the size of Kuwait, became a powerful political force. What is more, it achieved this in the teeth of permanent ferocious hostility toward the 'terrorist' PLO from the world's most powerful states, but also in the face of majority Israeli hatred of the movement.) The Iraqi opposition rejected both Saddam Hussein's forcible annexation of Kuwait and the bombing and invasion of their country. In March and April they showed that they had considerable forces in Iraq. In the context of a commercial embargo targeted on the Iraqi military and oil industry, this opposition could, in conjunction with Kuwaiti resistance and pressure from the Arab world generally, have greatly increased the negotiating pressure on the Baghdad regime.

However, the Kuwaiti resistance movement would have had to confront two serious obstacles. The first was the social structure of Kuwait under the old al-Sabah regime; the second was Kuwait's oil wealth. The necessities of popular resistance would have forced the movement to call on the people of Kuwait to join a common struggle. This would not have been hard vis-à-vis the Palestinians since they too face occupation, but it would also have required a programme of civil rights and social justice for all the settled residents of Kuwait – an end to the old helotry. The resistance would also have had to advance a blueprint for the future use of Kuwaiti oil revenues. But far from being a problem, this could have been their political trump: the redirecting of oil revenues away from the Anglo-American financial circuits into economic development for the entire Arab region, including Iraq, Egypt, Jordan and Syria. This would, of course, have reduced – to put it mildly – the enthusiasm of the Bush and Major administrations for the resistance, undoubtedly persuading those tied to the al-Sabahs to break with the movement, while the Kuwaiti ruling families retired to their residences abroad; but such a programme would have guaranteed the existing living standards of Kuwaiti citizens. It is clear, however, that this popular-resistance strategy would have been anathema to the US and UK governments, not to speak of the Saudi royal family, threatening to undermine everything the West was seeking to defend in the region.

3) Economic embargo and military blockade

I have argued that a diplomatic settlement fully satisfying rights-based liberal criteria of justice was perfectly possible. Some, however, may hold that Iraqi offers of a negotiated settlement – immediately after the invasion and then following annexation – were extracted only under the coercive pressure of embargoes and blockade. This may be true. Possession of Kuwaiti oil certainly conferred wealth and power that the Ba'athist regime would have preferred to retain. And even though the regime itself had not engaged in a long internal propaganda campaign, doubtless many Iraqis had long believed that Kuwait should belong to Iraq – thereby adding nationalistic support to the case for annexation. Yet there is no exclusivity of options between embargoes, exploratory negotiations and support for the Kuwaiti popular-resistance movement and Iraqi opposition. But the use of what has come to be known by the blanket term of 'sanctions' requires careful scrutiny.

First, we should note the peculiar terminology. 'Sanctions' in this context simply mean measures to enforce a command: there can be military or non-military types of sanctions. However, within public discourse in Britain during the Gulf crisis a semantic slippage occurred: the word 'sanctions' came to mean all measures short of direct military attack on Iraq – including a full-scale blockade of the country. There was undoubtedly some strategic justification for counterposing 'sanctions' to 'war': the anti-war movement wished to maximise the coalition opposed to military attack, rightly seeing the decisive task as prevention. Nevertheless, it is incumbent on us to examine very carefully the various measures grouped under the heading of 'UN sanctions', and to register the qualitative difference between various embargoes and a military blockade of Iraq.

Two kinds of embargo possessed a powerful rationale: that on oil exports, denying the Iraqi government the possibility of profiting from Kuwaiti oil and facing it with a substantial cost for its continued occupation, and that on arms supplies to Iraq. Arguably there was a strong case for a total embargo on Iraqi exports. But all such measures were different in kind from a full-scale blockade in two key respects. First, the blockade was a form of siege warfare against the civilian population of Iraq and Kuwait. Supplies of food and medicines, specifically excluded from the earlier embargo, were interdicted by the blockade, an escalation that was bound to hurt the civilian population in a country so dependent on trade. And secondly, the blockade involved, and legitimated, the build-up of US military forces for an all-out attack.

And what was the purpose of such a blockade as an instrument of pressure on the Iraqi government? If American demonising of the Ba'athists was accurate, then this regime was presumably indifferent to the sufferings of its people. Assuming that the regime did seek and require some degree of popular consent – a more realistic assumption – the blockade remained an indiscriminate weapon likely to harm the poor, the elderly and the infirm. As an intervention within Iraqi politics it was likely to draw politically aware Iraqis closer to the regime, which in turn could – and did – attack the blockade as a savage weapon against the most vulnerable people.

4) The US-led attack

Even according to classical just-war theory the impossibility of other means – popular resistance, embargoes, negotiations – did not produce adequate grounds for an attack on Iraq. Two further conditions were necessary: the attack should confine itself to those means minimally necessary for the liberation of Kuwait; and the 'intentions' of the attackers must not, in turn, entail injustice. The US administration did seek to legitimate its war against Iraq in such terms as the attack was being launched. Of course people were well aware that the American state was launching the war for reasons other than political principle: US interests in the region were directly involved (interests often reduced simply to 'oil'). But many were led to assume that such interests did not conflict with the US military acting as the instrument of justice responsible for administering the minimum force necessary to liberate Kuwait.

Once again, however, we find a tension between states' rights theory and liberal approaches based upon the inviolability of the person. The former requires of good intentions little more than a renunciation of territorial acquisition, while its prohibition on means applies only to the deliberate slaughter of non-combatant civilians. The latter, on the other hand, has great difficulty in squaring its injunction against violation of the person in domestic life with the total relaxation of this injunction in the external military activity of states. No doubt there exist supposed solutions to this problem by anti-consequentialist rights theorists, but such thought is now largely discredited. Rights-based theorists who do recognise the need to take consequences into account must justify the attack by implicating Iraqi conscript soldiers in their government's unjust act of invasion. This seems a difficult argument to sustain, given that the Iraqi soldiers were not volunteer professionals – indeed many risked death trying to evade the draft. (American and British forces, on the other hand, did comprise solely professional soldiers.)[20]

As the war progressed and it became clear that more destruction was being wrought than was necessary for liberating Kuwait, efforts were made by military public-relations personnel to justify this excess by deploying the concept of 'collateral' damage. But in the war's aftermath it was impossible to treat the US war effort as having been governed by the means-rationality of liberating Kuwait: it became clear that the excess destruction was of a qualitative, rather than quantitative, nature. We must remind ourselves of what in sum the military effort against Iraq entailed: (a) A total military blockade. (b) Bombing of the crucial life-support systems for the entire population of Iraq – water and energy supplies, sewage systems – all of which produced what the UN's deputy secretary-general called a 'near apocalyptic catastrophe for the people of Iraq', involving starvation and epidemics of killer diseases. (c) Destruction of the vital irrigation systems on which Iraqi agriculture depends. (d) Bombing of the country's industrial and transportation infrastructure, driving it, effectively, back into a pre-industrial era. (e) Refusal of Baghdad's offer to withdraw from Kuwait, made over a week before the ground war started – an offer welcomed by some European NATO states but discounted by the US. (f) Rejection of the Soviet peace proposal, accepted by the Iraqi government, before the ground war was launched. (g) 'Collateral' damage: the killing of civilians, not only in the Baghdad bunker but in the proximity of bridges and other non-military installations far to the north of the so-called Kuwaiti 'theatre of operations'. (h) Use of weapons of mass destruction in order to achieve wholesale extermination of the Iraqi conscripts in the Kuwaiti theatre: napalm, cluster bombs, and above all the 'fuel–air explosive' dubbed in the US the 'poor man's nuclear weapon'. (i) The 'turkey shoot' at the Matla Pass and prosecution of a war of annihilation against forces that scarcely returned fire. It is simply beyond credibility that 'means' of this sort can be justified within any form of rights-based liberalism as commensurate with the end of freeing Kuwait.

There was also the 'liberation of Kuwait'. Only the narrowest Grotian view, which interpreted 'liberation' as the return of property title to the Emir and his family, could present the defeat of Iraqi forces as a liberation for the people of Kuwait. The rule of the al-Sabahs and some eighteen satellite clans is dependent upon their suppressing democratic, constitutional reform. Kuwaiti oppositionists seeking the return to a constitution far short of western liberal democracy have been harassed, threatened, and even subjected to assassination attempts. And the liberal-democratic principle of civil rights for non-Kuwaiti residents has been rejected in favour of a regime of terror, torture and killings, directed especially against the Palestinian community. According to the PLO, by mid-March, three weeks after the ceasefire, two hundred and fifty Palestinians had been killed in Kuwait. The New York-based Middle East Watch had by the end of March documented over one thousand cases of torture, forty resulting in death. By late April, US government files recorded three hundred and fifty Palestinians missing – feared dead at the hands of the Kuwaiti government.[21] These actions were overwhelmingly the work of the security forces, with the direct participation of members of the al-Sabah family. An epidemic of rape attacks on non-Kuwaiti women residents heralded the reimposition of a 'helot state' regime of severe social oppression.[22] And the government announced plans, even before it had returned to Kuwait, for the expulsion of about half a million formerly settled Arab residents of Kuwait, mainly Palestinians.[23] And all this was, of course, combined with the re-establishment of the grossly inequitable circuit of oil capital from Kuwait into the Anglo-American banking system.

Such were the direct consequences of the US decision to operate through the al-Sabahs in Kuwait. Their aim since late August 1990 was not the restoration of the constitutional order, far less political support for democracy, but rather full political backing for this dynastic autocracy. Not a word was spoken by the US administration on behalf of the political rights of non-Kuwaiti residents. What is more, US special forces were initially working with the Kuwaitis in their sweeps through Palestinian districts and were present in police stations while torture was being practised, often, allegedly, quite indiscriminately on young Palestinian men. It was for these ends, then, that the killing and destruction in Iraq was to be justified.

Liberal Means Versus American Goals

I have been prepared so far to go along with the assumption that the American (and British) states may *in principle* have constituted instruments for implementing liberal principle in the Gulf crisis. The predominance of realist moral precepts in the core executives of these states has been noted, as has the evident fact that the administrations were straightforwardly pursuing state interests. Discussion of their behaviour has, nevertheless, been confined to the means of liberating the people of Kuwait and has merely noted how their actions have (repeatedly) departed from preferred liberal norms. But measured against these states' actual conduct in the war this analytical and evaluative framework simply breaks down. It is therefore necessary to re-examine the facts of Desert Storm and try to analyse what its results say about the goals of the US-led operation.

The central puzzle for many has been the combination of two elements: (1) A drive toward war (as opposed to pursuit of a negotiated solution) and subsequently to a crushing military victory, including the wholesale destruction of civilian life-support systems and maintenance of the blockade after the end of hostilities. (2) The failure of the US to press home its military victory to the occupying of Baghdad and overthrow of the regime or, once the war was over, to support the rebellions in the Shia South and in the Kurdish North. These elements appear inconsistent: the destruction of Iraq during the war suggests a drive to topple the regime; behaviour afterwards suggests support for it. The attack on the civilian infrastructure seems gratuitous and aimless. Only through a political analysis of US interests and goals can we make sense of this seeming inconsistency.

United States rejection of a negotiated solution and of the option of economic sanctions plus support for the Kuwaiti resistance cannot be deemed an accident. Nor can US dismissal of the Iraqi withdrawal offer and the Soviet peace proposal before the land war began. All were deliberate acts of policy, but with what objectives in mind? One of these can be expressed crudely, and rather misleadingly, as the 'oil factor' – a long-term structural interest; and the other has to do with global factors not directly related to the Gulf or Middle East.

The 'oil factor'

Since the late 1970s the US has made explicit its determination to exercise overall influence in the Gulf, laying down the parameters for all political forces in the region through the so-called 'Carter Doctrine'. According to Zbigniew Brzezinski, the doctrine's architect, US interests were three-fold: first, guardianship of the oil industry 'with all its political, economic and military ramifications'; second, keeping the USSR out; and third, protecting 'the moderate states in the region, which could be toppled by local upheavals, as happened with Khomeini's ascendancy in Iran'. This latter threat is 'perhaps the most elusive, and yet potentially the most dangerous' to US interests, whether the attack 'be from the left or from Islamic fundamentalism . . . As the Iranian revolution graphically demonstrated, it is very difficult for Western policy-makers to develop an effective response once new and powerful social, religious and political attitudes gain widespread acceptance, the hold of a leader of government begins to slip, and a crisis erupts.'[24] These three interests form a hierarchy of US concerns: at the apex is 'oil'; from this derives the commitment to the 'moderate' regimes and to excluding the USSR.

Viewed as a purely commercial matter, oil interests could fit easily with the liberal objective of removing Iraq from Kuwait (thereby ensuring that Iraq did not control too high a percentage of supply and thus carry too much weight in the oil market). However, one might wonder why a simple shift of ownership would provoke the US into sending half a million troops against Iraq: after all, sellers of oil need buyers, and the long-term price of Middle East oil is dictated by the price of substitutes, and thus has a limited range of fluctuation.[25] But control of Middle East oil is vital for the Americans in two other respects: first, the double economic value of oil revenues, and second, the importance of oil control for US global political power.

Gulf oil provides a very large international market for important sectors of advanced capitalist industry (construction, engineering, military equipment and so forth) and this is overwhelmingly a *state* market, since the revenues are in the hands of the ruling dynasties. Therefore the power that exercises a dominant *political* influence upon the sheikhdoms in effect governs the market. Secondly, oil revenues become great lakes of rentier capital, the flow of which, influenced critically by political factors, is vital for the entire structure of global finance-capital and banking interests. And thirdly, oil money talks politics directly, through the uses to which it is put. This is the case, for instance, right across the world – especially the Islamic world – with Saudi money, which cements regime after regime, from Pakistan to Morocco. And the passages of that money are ultimately controlled by the power which defends the Saudis – the USA.

If the regime of Saddam Hussein had controlled the flow of much of that oil capital, dozens of countries around the world would have had a simple choice between two world politico-economic authorities: on one side, the IMF/WB, the 'official', American-controlled institution governing the world economy; on the other side, Baghdad, the undoubtedly unofficial but equally efficacious centre for capital and loans. And would this investment capital have flowed as readily through the American banking system and the City of London? Who can tell? One certainty is that political financing by a Ba'athist regime would not coincide with the funding of Islamic theocratic or dynastic currents. The same factors would apply to the Iraqi-controlled market for western industrial products. Directly threatening to US interests in such a scenario would be the impact on the dollar; for Saddam Hussein might have preferred to denominate his capital in marks or yen. As the world's biggest debtor, with its debt denominated in dollars, the US economy would clearly be vulnerable if a significant proportion of Middle East oil revenues were switched to another currency. For the United States to concede such political power to Saddam was unthinkable.

And finally, the control of oil supplies to both Japan and the countries of Western Europe has always served the US as a crucial political lever in relations with these states. They are, after all, more reliant upon Middle East oil than is the United States, and would undoubtedly increase their independence if their sources were not under the latter's 'protection' but under that of a regime not itself dependent on the US.

These oil factors – the revenue market, capital, and control of the 'allies' supplies – make direct political suzerainty over the region by the United States essential. To shore up its own political position in the Gulf and that of its client regimes like the Saudis it was necessary for the US to demonstrate its supremacy over Iraq, to repudiate all diplomatic discussions and negotiations, to ban Arab or West European regimes from resolving the crisis peacefully, and finally to dictate to Baghdad: either climb down humiliatingly before your own population and the Arab world or we will crush you. A negotiated end to the Iraqi occupation would have suggested US weakness.

The features of the Iraqi state that threatened US dominance were quite different from those stressed by liberals – the dictatorship, the cult, the repression, torture and killing of oppositionists, the use of chemical weapons against the Kurds in Halabja in 1988. The threat lay primarily in the fact that it was not a socially weak and subaltern dictatorship tied to the West through the nature of its ruling class, as was the case with both the Shah and the Saudis, and indeed the Egyptians. The rentier/comprador character of such dictatorships and the social gulf between them and their lower middle classes makes them easily controllable by the West. Ba'athist Iraq, with its ferocious disciplines over the governing elite itself, was different: it sought to base its power on the capacity to mobilise politically its domestic population behind transformative goals, unlike any other regime in the Fertile Crescent. It was not, therefore, dependent on western powers to maintain its internal security.

The regime's mobilising capacities were demonstrated after the invasion of Kuwait. Saddam Hussein was not especially popular as an Arab leader, but Baghdad's post-occupation calls for social justice against the reactionary sheikhdoms and plutocrats of the Gulf evoked a powerful response. A Professor at the American University in Washington DC who toured the Middle East after the invasion of Kuwait reports that Iraq raised 'the class question, the "haves" and "have nots" . . . on a pan-Arab level as it never has been raised before . . . [Saddam] managed to tap into tremendous resentment, and this has immense medium and long-term implications. The national question remains to the fore, but the connection with the class question has been made . . . [E]ven the press financed and controlled by the oil states in the region and in Europe [covered] the fabulous oil-wealth of individuals: tales of corruption, gambling and squandering. The corresponding impression is that even if corruption does occur on some scale in Iraq, the surplus has largely been plowed into the country for its development.'[26] Not that the Ba'athist regime was seeking to stimulate popular movements to overthrow the sheikhdoms. But it was threatening to pull these regimes within its regional sphere of influence as a means of insuring them against subversion from below; none of these ruling groups, including the Saudis, can feel safe in their own societies without an outside protector. Saddam Hussein could no doubt have lived quite happily with the sheikhs and even the Saudis in place, but only on his terms – a potential challenge to the established role of the US. It therefore follows that a crushing US military victory over Iraq, with no concession to negotiation, was intended to demonstrate unequivocally to all groups in the region who ultimately controlled their destiny and who did not.

US global power interests

This does not explain, however, why the US administration repudiated both the offer to withdraw from Kuwait ten days before the ground war started and the subsequent Soviet peace plan, in favour of bombing Iraqi forces in the Kuwaiti theatre and a ground campaign – a response in no way demanded by the interests set out above. To understand US aims we must, then, appreciate a further factor fuelling the Bush administration's desire for a crushing military victory: the need for a 'demonstration war'. Let us note two repeated themes of President Bush: the New World Order and the

Vietnam syndrome. Both signalled global motivations for the war. And as far as the Vietnam syndrome was concerned, the US had to demonstrate that it was no longer just a nuclear super-state with feet of clay when it came to fighting a conventional war against an enemy in the South. It had to show the will and the military capacity *on the ground as well as in the air* to prevail against a substantial conventional force. But to achieve this the US needed to effect by air the liquidation of Iraqi forces in and around Kuwait, in order to make the ground war safe for a largely unblooded US army, rebuilt since the Vietnam debacle. The outcome, a triumph for all wings of US conventional forces, was to make America's main power asset, its military capacity, once again central to world politics.

The features of the Iraqi regime described above also partly explain why so much military effort was directed towards the destruction of civilian life-support systems. To understand this strategy fully it is necessary to consider the intended political consequences: namely, to make the Iraqi regime that emerged from the war utterly dependent upon the US without the need for military occupation. The success of this policy was soon apparent. Throughout Iraq people have been suffering malnutrition, starvation and various epidemics, including cholera. To deal with the most serious and urgent damage to its infrastructure the Iraqi government has needed equipment it does not possess. It has been unable to export and it lacks funds to purchase even necessary food imports. In short, the only sphere in which it has not been severely crippled is that of internal military security. This dependence on a largely American-controlled external environment would not have occurred without the destruction of the framework of civilian life. What, then, have been the objectives of this subordination to American power?

One purpose was spelt out in the allied peace terms: the destruction of Iraq's capacity to strike at Israel. But a second has been to destroy the dynamism of the Ba'athist regime and hence the domestic source of its independence from the US, thereby rendering it as beholden to the US as the ruling groups in the Gulf states. The strategy, in sum, has been to guarantee the regime's subservience to the US and yet simultaneously to maintain Iraq as a coherent political force in the region. This brings us to what is seemingly the most incoherent aspect of US policy: did it want, during and after the war, to overthrow the Baghdad regime, or to support it?

Much confusion about US policy here derives from a failure to distinguish the Ba'athist regime from its leader. The Bush administration has had one key policy objective: to achieve Saddam's downfall. The official Iraqi and Arab understanding of Desert Storm must be brought into line with US interests in order to prevent any possible future Nasserisation against American action posing a serious challenge to the US in the Arab world. The US desperately needs a leader in Iraq who, while obviously not

supporting their action, could declare Saddam Hussein's policy an unjusti-
fiable mistake, and one directly responsible for the attack. Without the
removal and discrediting of Saddam *by Iraqi elements* Arab politics may yet
polarise around the stance taken on Desert Storm. In addition, the successful management of domestic public opinion in the West requires the
disappearance of the 'Monster of Baghdad'.

Yet to destroy the Ba'athist regime with its hundreds of thousands of supporters in the state apparatus and satellite organisations is quite another
matter. That would have meant backing the only popularly rooted alternative
political force in the Arab part of the country: the Shia opposition, grouped
within the Supreme Council of the Islamic Revolution, and the Iraqi
Communist Party. The US supports neither of these; and since the rebellion
in the south of Iraq, which started on the day of the ceasefire, was led by
Islamic currents, the US sanctioned its suppression by Iraqi security forces.
The reason for this lies, as Brzezinski stressed, in the fact that the American
administration perceived Islamic fundamentalism to be a mortal threat to
the Saudi regime and therefore to US dominance within Saudi Arabia. This is
not a specifically Shia threat; the danger lies, rather, in the fact that the Saudi
regime is held in power by its claim to lead and guard Islam. This claim had
been seriously undermined before this Gulf crisis by the Iranian example, one
whose Islamic credentials are more authentic than the evidently rotten Saudi
dynasty, and which is certainly more popular and politically pluralist. The
Saudis' acceptance of half a million US troops into their country has shocked
the Islamic fundamentalist current in Saudi Arabia to a degree not registered
by western public opinion. An Islamic regime in Baghdad – and one with
democratic legitimation in the country, given the majoritarian status of the
Shia community – was not an acceptable prospect for the Bush administration.
Precisely the same factors had led the US to shun the united Iraqi opposition:
Kurdish support for a Shia-led government in Baghdad would have been a disastrous political outcome to the war for American regional interests.

The position in Kurdistan has been more straightforward for Washington
since the link between the Kurdish and Shia leaders was broken. The
Kurdish nationalists on their own cannot take power in Baghdad. But the
stronger their representation within a formally unified Iraqi state, the more
dependent the Baghdad regime is on whoever controls the Kurds. There has
been a long political association between the US and the Barzani, tribalist
wing of the Kurdish movement. The CIA was evidently giving covert support
to the Kurdish *peshmerga* forces at the end of the war.[27] On the other hand,
Saddam Hussein's agreement with the Kurdish leaders, Talabani and
Barzani, is a negative development for the US. If the agreement is finalised,
it could strengthen the very ruler they wish to topple. The Kurdish leaders
have an incentive to make a deal with Saddam unless they are absolutely
convinced of a long-term US guarantee of their power position. The ques-

tion at the time of writing is whether the US is ready to make that commitment, thereby producing a de facto splitting of Iraq, with Kurdistan 'protected' by Turkey and their own military forces (while maintaining the de jure unity of Iraq, Lebanon-style), or whether the Bush administration will draw back in the face of such a dangerous, open-ended commitment.

Not one US political objective bears any positive relation to liberal criteria of justice or freedom. The aim of demonstrating American dominance in the Gulf would be classed as wholly unjust by rights-based theory. The same would apply to the aim of asserting US world leadership through a demonstration war. Protecting Israel against the Arab states and against the Palestinians' claims over annexed and occupied territories cannot be justified. The rhetoric of humanitarianism towards the Kurds bears no relation to American objectives in the north of Iraq; and the linchpin of their political strategy in the region – protecting the Saudi regime – is a goal that necessarily entails the suppression of liberal and democratic rights.

There is only one conclusion to be drawn from this analysis – a very disquieting one for rights-based liberalism. It is that the entire framework within which liberal discourse situates the American attack on Iraq does violence to reality: it subsumes American behaviour under the category of an instrument – albeit one among other possible instruments – of liberal justice following the invasion of Kuwait by Iraq. Yet American state power has been and is being used to support and to further injustice and continuing oppression in the region. We are thus obliged to adopt a radically different framework for analysing the Gulf crisis from that with which we began: a framework for evaluating the injustices of the Iraqi regime, but also for evaluating those of the far more powerful United States and its allies. Those who present the US war drive as a force for liberal values and a move toward restoration of justice in the Gulf are complicit in the carnage and destruction wrought by Desert Storm to buttress a regional regime of oppression and economic exploitation.

II   Understanding Modern Iraq

Western liberal public opinion has sought to understand the modern Iraqi state through one interpretation above all others: that of Samir al-Khalil in his book *The Republic of Fear* (1989) and in a number of recent articles.[28] Although Khalil's book has been used to legitimatise the war against Iraq, it was of course intended for no such purpose, being a serious and important reflection on issues well beyond the fate of Iraq; it is the work of a humane ex-Marxist sickened by his experiences of the Ba'ath and seeking a better future for his people. Articles written in response to recent events show Khalil to have been shocked by the slaughter perpetrated by US-led forces. Nevertheless, Khalil's study is deeply rooted in the tradition of classical Anglo-American liberalism.

Khalil organises his history of modern Iraq around two sociopolitical paradigms: one is the monarchist regime of British times, and the other is 'totalitarian' Ba'athism, described essentially as 'Stalinist' on account of its political structures. This model is combined with another: that of traditionalism versus modernisation and modernity. Within this conceptual framework he constructs his pathos-filled equations on modern Iraq: a modernising monarchy committed to transforming a traditionalist society, but ineffective because opposed to state-forced change; and, subsequently, great social transformation by the Ba'athist regime at the cost of brutal totalitarianism.

In the following analysis of modern Iraq – in part a critique of Khalil's study, of its political and ethical presuppositions and value-judgements – I use a broadly chronological frame. The first section considers the period of monarchical rule: from the British-imposed regime of Faisal I to the revolution of 1958. The second section follows the post-revolutionary narrative from the first decade of military rule, through the early state-building and reformist period of Ba'athist rule in the seventies, to the regime of Saddam Hussein, turning finally to an appraisal of the disastrous war with Iran and the annexation of Kuwait.

The Monarchy and Imperial Design

Khalil presents a very favourable evaluation of the Hashemite monarchy imposed on Iraq by the British at the start of the 1920s. Faisal, he says, was 'prepared to do virtually anything in the effort to encourage . . . [the Iraqis] to change themselves and then society, except to use force'. There is, however, a slippage here: namely, the implication that the monarchy adhered to the liberal principle of restricting the use of force to the protection of individual, or at least traditional, rights, though strictly speaking Khalil only claims an absence of forced *modernisation*. Commitment to historical accuracy should have prompted him to add that in fact excessive force was used against the people.[29] Initially, to impose the regime on the people of Mesopotamia the British inflicted 98,000 casualties,[30] gassing and bombing the local resistance into subordination. Although he bore no direct responsibility, Faisal willingly accepted the leadership of a state constructed in this way. Most historians agree that Faisal's regime, imported from Mecca, had no significant constituency of popular support, and that, consequently, throughout the 1920s and 1930s, the monarchy was engaged with the British in fighting one revolt after another.

Let us take as our source not some leftist anti-imperialist but the conservative, anti-nationalist Elie Kedourie. He writes that 'The North as a whole had to be coerced by the Royal Air Force' into submission,[31] a more or less continuous task: 'Bombing . . . until the very eve of independence alone sub-dued them [the Kurds].'[32] In 1931 the Kurdish leader Sheikh Mahmud started another rebellion. The British decided that the Iraqi army itself should tackle this so that it might be 'blooded' before independence. However, their action was unsuccessful, so the RAF had to intervene.[33] This pattern of revolt and bombing was reproduced in the Shia South – one rebellion after another having to be put down during the 1920s and 1930s.[34] For his part, Khalil extends his support for the regime past Faisal's death, through the 1930s and beyond. Kedourie records the crushing of protests against military conscription as late as 1936: 'the killing, it seems, was indiscriminate, and the old men, women and children were the victims of machine-gunning and bombing from the air'; and a revolt in 1937 over agrarian issues and conscription was 'put down with the help of indiscriminate aerial bombing'.[35] The regime responded to this insurgence by forcibly expelling Shia religious leaders on the grounds that they were Persian.[36] The monarchy also introduced the public hanging of political opponents, the first chosen by Nuri es-Said being the leader of the long-established and popularly based Communist Party. He and others were strung up in a Baghdad square for allegedly continuing political activity while serving a three-year jail sentence. Kedourie summarily characterises the monarchy as despotic, its record 'full of bloodshed, treason and rapine'; 'however pitiful its end', he remarks, 'we may know that it was implicit in its beginning'.[37] A conclusion that renders Khalil's claim for the virtues of monarchical rule somewhat hollow, to say the least.

Khalil develops his analysis by counterposing the notion of a modernising British–Hashemite state with that of a very traditional society – a world of ancient Mesopotamian institutions commanding deep popular attachment. Now it is certainly the case that the British brought modern technological culture to Iraq and that the Hashemite regime – to the irritation of the British – spread some modern, pan-Arabic nationalist ideas, particularly through the efforts of people like Husri in education. But to make sense of the respective roles of the British and of the Iraqi monarchy they controlled, it is necessary to go beyond the simplifying contraposition employed by Khalil and to examine each element in some detail.

The thesis that the British represented a dynamic modernising force fits a general defence of the progressive aspect of British imperialism – an argument used, perhaps rightly, with regard to, say, India. Kedourie, for example, greatly admired British imperial administration. Khalil, for his part, extends such admiration to British policy in Iraq, writing: 'The British mandate and the institutions it gave rise to in Iraq, were the agents of a modernisation that did not arise gradually or indigenously as the outcome of a population's own resourcefulness and engagement with the world. The British in Iraq were modernisers more than colonisers, despite acting out of self-interest.'[38] Kedourie's judgement of the British role in Mesopotamia is different: 'When we consider the long experience of Britain in the government of Eastern countries, and set beside it the miserable polity which she bestowed on the populations of Mesopotamia, we are seized with rueful wonder. It is as though India and Egypt had never existed, as though Lord Cornwallis, Munro and Metcalf, John and Henry Lawrence, Milner and Cromer had attempted in vain to bring order, justice and security to the East, as though Burke and Macaulay, Bentham and James Mill had never addressed their intelligence to the problems and prospects of oriental government. We can never cease to marvel how, in the end, all this was discarded . . . [in] Mesopotamia.'[39] As for Khalil's view that the British-formed elites were agents of modernisation, this is not shared by the British themselves after the Second World War. A report from Chancery in Baghdad to the Eastern Department of the Foreign Office on 16 July 1946 declares: '[W]ith the old gang in power this country cannot hope to progress very far.'[40] If by 'modernisation' Khalil means economic development, the bal-ance-sheet outside the oil industry, of course, was not impressive. In by far the most important sector, agriculture, the British achieved the remarkable feat of regression: Iraq's productivity declined from 275 kg per acre in 1920 to an average of 238 kg per acre between 1953 and 1958.[41]

To turn now from the activities of the political regime to changes in soci-ety under the monarchy, Khalil describes a thoroughly traditional world of inert, ancient institutions – like Merry England before the totalitarian Tudors set to work. But this is a flagrant misrepresentation, at least with regard to the main institutions concerned with the reproduction of daily life and the maintenance of social order. For these were brand new mecha-nisms – modern structures built on the ruins of Ottoman society.

Economic and social change under Ottoman rule had been gradually erod-ing tribal structures. British policy involved a conscious effort to reverse this trend. In the words of the Administration Report of the Revenue Board in Baghdad for the period 22 March to 31 December 1918: 'Settled agriculture and extended civilisation have tended to disintegrate the tribe and to weaken the influence of the Sheikhs. To restore and continue the power of the tribal Sheikhs is not the least interesting of the problems in land administration which the Baghdad wilayet presents.' The solution chosen by the British was to create an almost entirely new social structure by distributing huge estates – the biggest in the Middle East – to tribal heads who demonstrated their political loyalty to London. Thus, at a stroke, a new ruling class of 'government sheikhs' was established. In the words of Major Pulley, reporting to the civil commis-sioner in Baghdad on 6 August 1920: 'Many of them were small men of no account until we made them powerful and rich.' The Civil Commissioner of that time, Wilson, wrote later: 'The Shaikhs were in most cases directly depen-dent on the civil administration for the positions they held; realising that their positions entailed corresponding obligations, they co-operated actively with the political officers.'[42] So much, then, for Khalil's image of an organic relationship between the sheikhs and ordinary members of their tribe or peasants; their real organic relationship was with the British.

On the basis of this new landowning class, the British sought to reimpose and strengthen tribal identities and divisions at every level. They set up a new legal system, codified in the Tribal Criminal and Civil Disputes Regulation, which remained in place until the revolution of 1958. Also, rather than allow that bugbear of individualist liberalism, the state, to possess tax-levying powers and the responsibility for administration and police, these were transferred – privatised – into the hands of the new ruling class. And to cap it all, mechanisms were established under which the rural masses were tied in semi-serfdom to the estates.[43] To repeat: all this was a new, modern imperial invention. And, as Batatu shows, as the monarchy decayed in the postwar years, it strove to strenghten and further entrench tribal divisions.[44]

Thus we have a complex picture: the creation of *new* foundational institutions of landownership in order to *revive* dying traditional authority relations, resulting in economically and socially regressive consequences, undertaken for thoroughly modern imperialist political purposes – namely, to create a ruling class dependent upon British military power and therefore committed to imperial interests in the region.[45] This use of imperial power to effect extensive social engineering for narrow strategic ends is beyond the comprehension of a liberal political theory like that of Khalil, blind as it is to the interrelatedness of state and class interests, and content as it is to reduce complex historical process to a struggle between 'tradition' and 'the modern'.

Parliamentarism and Coercion

Khalil sees only virtue in the British-imposed parliamentary system in Iraq. Consequently, for him its abolition in 1958 was a lamentable development.[46] Against the charge that parliament was ineffectual, he declares that, on the contrary, 'the Iraqi parliament before 1941 was astonishingly vibrant as a mechanism for drawing out individuals from their communities'.[47] He does not, however, spell out what this vibrant mechanism was. Nevertheless, a British official reported to London in 1928 on exactly how the system worked: the government's provincial governors acted as election agents with the task of drawing up lists of those who had to be elected *and* of those who could do the electing.[48] The Report on the Administration of Iraq for 1928 admitted that elections and representative government were a mockery. Kedourie thus offers the following simple judgement on the vibrant mechanism: '[E]lections to the chamber of deputies and appointments to the senate were an additional weapon in the hands of the government wherewith the better to control the country.'[49]

For Khalil, then, the Kingdom of Iraq was parliamentarism in politics plus traditional *Gemeinschaft* in the village – in short, a world free of the rootlessness and violence of modern mass society. Here is his idyll: 'In King Faisal's time a peasant had his tribe, his religion, his sect, his village, and his allegiance to the sheik whose lands he tilled. His entire world was constructed from these elements.'[50] There is no mention here of oppression, of the fact that the peasants of the great estates were reduced to little more than chattels; the monopoly of coercive force resides a priori with the state. And although the landowners controlled state administration, the subjection of their peasants occurred in the private sphere of civil society and is therefore of no ethical significance to a liberal champion of individual freedom.

It is instructive to counterpose to Khalil's idyll the insight of a British military man, an RAF pilot who was busy contributing in his own way to what Khalil calls the peasant's 'entire world'. In current parlance this pilot 'had a job to do' on those peasant villages. Nevertheless, he understood a good deal more about the life of ordinary Iraqis under the monarchy than Khalil. He writes of Iraq in the 1930s:

> Government is not, as with us, a machine which grinds out laws . . . It enters into the house here. It knows that you have four sons and that one of them is a post office official in Mosul. It knows that you have Turkish leanings, and that, as a natural consequence of such, you are not to be trusted. It knows that you were friends with Hamid Khuluf before his exile, that you are therefore probably sending information to Persia, and that it must on that account consider in a fresh light what you do with your claim for water-rights against Muhamed Derwish . . . It is this grossly personal element in the all-pervading activities of government which evokes from the uneducated people that quality which we are too apt to dismiss as insincerity, but which is, in reality, nothing but the inevitable compromise of any simple man chased by the bogey of insecurity. For an Englishman with a clear conscience there are few occasions when, in facing an acquaintance, he is tempted to express views at variance with his true ones. But the Iraqi before an official, or even another of his own kind, is in doubt. He must propitiate, and speak fair words. His position is unstable. There is no permanence. He knows that the fact as to whether the official has a good or bad opinion of him will affect his private life vitally. He feels the ground shifting beneath his feet. It is the same with the official himself when addressing his superior. He too feels the ground quaking beneath him, feels his confidence welling out. He may be sacked because his enemies have spoken ill of him. There will be no redress for him, no rehabilitation, unless he has influence in high places.[51]

Here, then, was a set-up that lacked the technical sophistication of the later Ba'athist political-police apparatuses, but which had something far more cost-effective: a *social* dictatorship over the mass of Iraqis by a landowning class that directly controlled their entire means of survival, in addition to the government machinery and local administration. This power was 'all-pervasive', even entering their dwellings. And it was a world unregulated by law: where those below had no recourse to legal rule to challenge abuses of power, even in non-political spheres. But the quality of everyday social relationships, including that between rulers and ruled, is nowhere considered by Khalil. What matters to him is that the monarchy displayed lofty liberal values by refusing to intervene on the peasants' behalf by abolishing the great estates. This perspective blinds him to the burning sense of injustice that fuelled the revolt against the landlords and the monarchy in the 1958 revolution.

Post-Revolutionary Upheaval

Khalil is not a reactionary. Yet there is no escaping his view that the revolution of 1958 was a disaster, or his identification of the source of that disaster: the entry of the mass of Iraqis on to the political stage, bursting through the integument of ruling-class power – or, in Khalil's gloss, 'the eruption of the undifferentiated structureless mass into politics'.[52] He declares that 'The parliamentary form of government was the only institutional mechanism that might have provided a countervailing measure to the emergence of the masses as a force.'[53] Thus Khalil betrays what other liberal writers like Kornhauser, using mass-society theory but seeking to remain within a liberal-*democratic* frame of reference, prefer to obscure: namely, a strong bias against popular democracy and a desire for institutions that will block, fragment and control popular political involvement.[54] When Khalil speaks of the mass being 'structureless' he should name the real controlling structures over the mass of people (as opposed to the parliament in which the people were not involved): the institutions of landlordism, sheikhly control of civil administration, tribalist legal coercion and so forth. Furthermore, he should register the absence of any structures for involving the people in civil life, far less for channelling their energies in the public sphere – no inclusive local government institutions, no legal industrial-relations organisations, no welfare-state or educational facilities, no civic, cultural or leisure centres. The only large inherited civic institution touching the whole population was the army.

What the old regime *had* bequeathed was a confusing set of political identities. Emerging from an artificial (British) construction, it followed that post-revolutionary Iraq was a geopolitical concept to which people felt no attachment or loyalty. Khalil registers this fact but fails to grasp its significance: 'Iraqi nationalism understood as a sense of identity with a territorial entity known as Iraq does not exist.'[55] This touches upon a central problem for liberal political theory: a deeply embedded notion that the liberal state, and thus any sound state, is held together by law rather than by deep *political* identification with the national state as well as structures of social power. The only positive identifications that the British and the monarchy infused into everyday life were loyalties to clan, tribe or sect. The alternatives to this bequest were loyalties to the Arab nation – fostered by the intelligentsia, and later politically expressed by the Ba'ath Party – and commitment to communism, fostered by the Iraqi Communist Party (ICP). States that lack popular loyalty find it extremely difficult to institute within themselves political division and opposition. Without loyalty to the whole, such division threatens to destroy the whole, a problem greatly exacerbated when existing loyalties along tribal, ethnic, religious and class lines are as myriad and complex as they were in Iraq. The problem was not that the masses were undifferentiated and amorphous in their loyalties, but quite the reverse.

While the old ruling classes were crippled by the revolution, succeeding military regimes between 1958 and 1968 proved incapable of carrying through the programme of positive social transformation demanded on all sides in the popular movement: namely, thoroughgoing land reform, nationalisation of the oil industry, and planned economic development, with the aim of improving the lot of the mass of people and promoting social justice and egalitarianism.

Regional Conflicts

The fundamental rifts in the state have been those involving the Kurdish North and the Shia South. Neither problem of political integration was seriously addressed by governments in this period. The Kurdish question involved a combination of ethnic, social and tribal conflicts. The Kurds, comprising 23 per cent of Iraq's population, were split between urban centres and villages spread through mountainous country, very much under the control of landlord tribal chiefs. From this latter sector came the leadership of the Kurdish nationalist movement, headed by Mulla Mustafa Barzani, a powerful landowner. This leadership, threatened by Qassem's land reform at the start of the 1960s, and demanding national autonomy for the Kurds – which Qassem refused – launched an uprising. The regime, supported by the Iraqi Communist Party, sought to crush the uprising militarily, but the war continued throughout the 1960s, with Barzani gaining material support and training from the Shah of Iran and Israel.[56] The other, more modern, nationalist movement, based in the urban centres of Iraqi Kurdistan among the middle classes and intelligentsia, and under the leadership of Talabani, at first refused to support the Barzani revolt. But eventually it did so, while opening links with the Ba'ath Party in the hope of a better deal from Baghdad should the latter overthrow Qassem.[57] (The Ba'athists did gain power for a few months in 1963, but the fighting dragged on until they returned to power in 1968.)

The problems of the rural communities of southern Iraq at the time of the 1958 revolution were principally those of social oppression, poverty and backwardness. But in addition they felt excluded from national public life through the dominance of the Sunnis from the Baghdad region. In 1958 both the Ba'ath Party and the much stronger Communist Party were predominantly Shia in composition, and the latter in particular commanded enormous support among the Shia population. But the split between the ICP and the Ba'ath over the issue of Arab national unity involved ICP support for the anti-Nasserite Qassem regime; while, for its part, the nationalist Ba'ath sought the overthrow of that regime and participated in bloody repression against ICP attempts to defend it against the 1963 coup. When the Ba'ath revived, it had lost much of its Shia base. Meanwhile the Communist Party – overwhelmingly the major political party in Iraq after the 1958 revolution – split, with the more radical wing attempting a Che Guevara-style guerrilla war against the military governments of Baghdad, centred in the river valleys and marshes of the Shia South.[58] This attempt at insurrection was crushed, and the ICP's strength amongst the Shia was weakened.

Meanwhile, one section of the Shia clerical leadership, alarmed by post-1958 secularism – in particular, the strength of atheistic communism and the declining hold of Islam amongst Shias – sought to reverse the tide by launching a movement of theocratic reaction in the late 1960s, 'al-Dawah' (Islamic Call), a clandestine party aided, after the Ba'ath came to power in 1968, by the Shah of Iran, and oriented towards terror tactics.[59]

Lacking a strong, established bourgeoisie that could control and steer popular aspirations, Iraq's ruling class possessed only the armed forces as an instrument of political integration. But the centrifugal forces within the state threatened the military itself with fragmentation. Such, then, were the compound challenges to any attempt to integrate the state politically after ten years of post-revolutionary turmoil.

Before examining life under the Ba'athist regime that came to power in 1968, we should ponder Elie Kedourie's prognosis following the 1958 revolution: 'Iraq under the monarchy faced two bare alternatives: either the country would have plunged into chaos or its population should become universally the clients and dependents of an omnipotent but capricious and unstable government. To these two alternatives the overthrow of the monarchy has not added a third.'[60] The aim of the Ba'athist leadership was precisely to find that third alternative: to build a modern, stable, politically integrated state.

Ba'athism in the 1970s: State-Building and Reform

Khalil is not blind to the social transformation achieved by the Ba'ath Party since its seizure of power in 1968. He acknowledges that the regime dramatically modernised Iraqi society, led by its drive against illiteracy and for free education for all – a revolution that produced, according to Khalil himself, one of the best-educated intelligentsias in the Arab world. He also credits the regime with giving women the right to careers and participation in public life; thus by the end of the 1970s women formed '46 per cent of all teachers, 29 per cent of all doctors, 46 per cent of all dentists and 70 per cent of all pharmacists'.[61]

Of even greater importance, however, was the fact that this Ba'athist regime finally carried through the land reform promised by the revolution, utterly transforming the social conditions of the peasantry. It also created a modern welfare state for the urban working classes and poor. And it did what other regimes feared to attempt: it took on the oil companies and nationalised them, turning to the USSR for help. This was not the first nationalisation of Arab oil, being preceded by moves in Libya and Algeria, but such action in 1972, before the Yom Kippur war, was still a perilous undertaking, strongly resisted in the West until the French broke ranks. Finally, the government launched an ambitious programme of industrial investment and development.

During the early 1970s the regime made a serious effort to integrate the Kurdish North by offering the most far-reaching settlement any government had proposed to its Kurdish population. The Ba'ath – unlike the Turkish government, for instance – had always recognised the Kurds as a separate nationality. Saddam Hussein proposed a Kurdish autonomous region with its own parliament as well as ministers in Baghdad, recognition of Kurdish as an official language, and Kurdish teaching in schools. Barzani rejected this offer, worried by the renewed push for land reform and, above all, encouraged by the Shah of Iran (who, incidentally, offered no such rights to his own Kurdish population) that he could gain a far better deal by waging war against the Ba'athist government. In 1973, Kissinger, preoccupied by the task of isolating Syria in the peace process, gave further substantial assistance to the Kurds in order to bog down the Baghdad regime in a costly war. The tactic worked, costing the latter two billion dollars a year until Saddam Hussein persuaded the Shah to end this aid in 1975. (One week after the Shah had informed him of this, Barzani offered unconditional surrender and went into exile in the USA where he died.) Of course, the Ba'ath could have easily satisfied the Kurds if it had offered them full self-determination and control of the northern oil fields. But all states in the modern world are extremely grudging and cautious when secession and vital economic interests are at stake.

In the South, the Dawah denounced the Ba'athist government not because it was Sunni-dominated but because it was atheistic, because its leader, Michel Aflaq, was a Christian, and because it was allied with the Communist Party and the USSR.[62] The Dawah fulminated against such issues as the secular Ba'athists' tolerance of alcohol consumption, even in the holy cities of Najaf and Kerbala. The regime hit back with savage repression combined with a major programme of public spending on the Shia shrines and on social development. The policy seems to have had some success until it was seemingly threatened by the Islamic revolution in Iran.[63] The regime's approach to the difficult relationship between Islam and secularism was a good deal more sophisticated in matters of principle and policy than that of many governments facing similar problems: namely, recognition of the cultural centrality of Islam and of the requirements of religious practice, combined with a resolute defence of the secular framework of public life. At least formally, the regime sought to extend tolerance to the significant Christian minority.

Controlled Participation and Repression

The leadership worked successfully to subordinate the armed forces to the Ba'ath Party itself, thereby ending the role of the officer corps as the sovereign state authority. Political decision-making was concentrated in the hands of the party and its leadership. Some have viewed the party as merely an empty façade behind which the politics of clan and tribe have prevailed. It is certainly the case that clan fissures are present within the Ba'ath, as indeed they were within the Communist Party; these are partly an expression of the currents that permeate the organisation, but testify also to the presence of nepotism and rivalry such as is found in any ruling party. Ultimately such factors must pose a threat to the party's own stability and legitimacy, and are, therefore, a symptom of crisis.

The Ba'athist regime committed itself to the principle of popular sovereignty and to a constitutional, representative state, but declared that the need for a state of emergency made the introduction of such a democracy impossible. It consequently vested supreme authority in a Revolutionary Command Council (RCC) on the basis of a provisional constitution: a body able to rule by decree and veto government decisions. After the civil war with the Kurds in 1975, the government organised elections and established a parliament. But the emergency institutions remained in place, as did the RCC. (We might note that Egypt has also been ruled by decree under a state of emergency more or less continuously since before 1967, though under Sadat and Mubarak Islamic *Sharia* law has also been introduced, unlike in Iraq.) Although the party had thus made certain of retaining its absolute position of power, it had at the same time made efforts to involve other parties. For much of the 1970s, for example, the Communist Party was in the government; at various times the Talabani wing of the Kurdish nationalist movement has been in alliance with the regime.

At the level of institution-building, the Ba'ath created local councils with elected representatives. These proved to be a key instrument, along with the trade unions, for drawing people into public life; another has been the local militias. Yet in these realms, too, the party exercised control, severely restricting their degree of effective political autonomy. This stifling party presence was especially evident in the political police and repressive apparatus, which threw a blanket of surveillance over the entire population. The first task of these organisations was to crush those believed to be working actively to overthrow the regime. Methods have invariably been brutal and victims often murdered. For instance, those Communists who continued the guerrilla war in the South after the Ba'ath came to power could not expect to leave prison alive. Since most organisations are permeated with family and clan links, the brutality was often directed at relatives.

The second task of the repressive apparatus was to act as a tool of political coercion against other parties or movements. Thus, while seeking to cajole the Communist Party leaders into a united front and participation in government, the regime would apply pressure by persecuting and sometimes even killing Communist militants at the base of the party. The ICP, legalised by the regime of Saddam Hussein, probably suffered more killings from its hands after 1968 than it had suffered in the decade 1958 to 1968, with the exception of the period immediately after 1963.

Ba'athism in the 1980s: Saddam Hussein

By the late 1970s, the Ba'ath had a formidable achievement of state-building behind them and had largely stabilised the new institutional structure. As a result of social reforms, egalitarian policies and a thoroughgoing modernising drive – all helped greatly by the mid-seventies oil-price increases – they felt strong enough to call elections and establish a parliament. We can, therefore, reasonably assume that the party had achieved a degree of popular support despite the absence of free party competition.

The picture, of course, looks very different today; and the rot set in long before the US-led attack of January 1991. What went wrong? The short answer is the Iraq–Iran war, started by the Ba'athist government. As well as inflicting a dreadful toll in human suffering on the Iraqi people, it reopened the civil war with the Kurdish nationalists and generated a more brutal style of politics – one that resulted, for example, in the Iraqi army's gassing of civilians in Halabja and the slaughter of thousands more Kurds after the war was over. At the end of hostilities the Iraqi state was heavily in debt – a position worsened by the oil-price slump – and the regime prey to the manoeuvres of the Emir of Kuwait. Conditions thus conspired to make Iraq vulnerable to a re-opening of the deep fissures in the state which the Ba'ath had spent the 1970s seeking to close.

It is arguable that the trigger for this disastrous chain of events was the replacement in 1979 of Bakr by Saddam Hussein as president. This move was certainly resisted within the Ba'athist leadership, though nothing is known about the disagreement, and therefore whether or not the appointment represented a policy turn (perhaps doubtful, since experts agree that Saddam Hussein had been the driving force of the regime throughout the 1970s). One negative effect of this change in leadership was the rapid growth of a personality cult. Such cults inevitably alter the decision-making mechanisms of a regime, replacing collective party bodies with the authority of one man, thereby concentrating power in absolute fashion. As a consequence, the regime's policy-making capacities may have been weakened, although Saddam Hussein's very survival suggests a resourcefulness and command that is evidence to the contrary. Notwithstanding this development, the decision to wage war against Iran was not merely the whim of the president, but appears to have had both party and popular support.[64] In point of fact, the weaknesses in Ba'athism that led directly to the attack on Iran were its nationalist ideology and petty-bourgeois roots, factors present from the start of the regime. During the 1970s they did not cripple its progressive, modernising project, though nationalism will certainly have helped to prevent a democratic settlement with the Kurds. However, the change in external environment brought about by the Islamic revolution focused new pressures upon the Ba'athist project at its most vulnerable point.

The Ba'ath Party in Iraq, like that in Syria, had its roots neither in the urban capitalist classes nor in the industrial working class, but in the large middle class of intellectuals, state employees, artisans and small merchants – very important strata in the Fertile Crescent. On the whole these groups did not stand in an antagonistic relationship to the working class. For this reason Batatu is fully justified in including the Ba'ath Party along with the Communist Party among the revolutionary forces of modern Iraq. The split between these two groups under Qassem derived, as we saw, from their lack of common ground on the national question. The ICP failed to support the national movement's aspiration for immediate unity with the United Arab Republic embracing Syria and Egypt, and this ensured Ba'athist leadership of the movement. Yet the party's experience during the 1960s told them that a programme simply calling for immediate Arab unity was insufficient, and also that there existed formidable obstacles to achieving a stable unification of the Arab states. The post-1968 party had not abandoned the latter as a long-term aim, but its priority was first to construct a powerful, integrated Iraqi state. This was, above all, the project of Saddam Hussein, the Iraqi party's general secretary.

The Ba'athist programme of nationalisation, economic development and establishment of a welfare state benefited both workers and the middle class. The scale of accruing oil revenues undoubtedly made a decisive contribution to the success of the modernisation programme in education and health. It also helped to sustain a pattern of state-dependent industrial development. The Iraqi state was not portrayed as a means of emancipation for the country's working population, but as the resource and authority best able to construct a strong Iraq, capable of leading the Arab nation. There is nothing unusual, of course, about such statist politics; most of today's imperialist powers went through just such a phase. Nevertheless, in a region like the Gulf, where the world's strongest superpower has important interests, this project was fraught with great risks.

Response to the Iranian Revolution

In Iran, the Shah's drive to dominate the Gulf had produced a military build-up and growing hostility to Iraq. This had caused the Ba'ath to develop its own military strength in the 1970s, funded by its oil revenues. The subsequent fall of the Shah in the Islamic revolution transformed the political equation in the region and presented the Ba'athist leadership with an irresistible temptation. The centre of that equation had been the protection of American interests in Saudi Arabia and the Gulf. Iraq, shut out of this security structure, had been on the defensive regionally and impelled to concentrate upon its domestic programmes. The Iranian revolution did not just remove America's regional policeman; it created a state claiming leadership of the Islamic world and therefore posed a mortal threat to the Saudi order. Thus the opportunity arose for the Iraqi regime to become the military linchpin of America's new security system in the Gulf, a role which the social weakness of Saudi Arabia prevented it from playing. There also existed, of course, a powerful domestic incentive for the Ba'athists to intervene militarily in the region: for clearly the Islamic revolution posed a direct threat because of the religious appeal of Shia Iran to the people of southern Iraq. A military victory would serve decisively to bind Iraqi Shias into a common political identity with the rest of Iraq.

The Ba'athist leadership, politically sophisticated and keen to exploit this regional development, could also spot a further set of incentives. By becoming the sword defending the interests of the West in the Gulf, it would escape the pariah status given it during the 1970s, and thereby gain access to the metropolitan centres of Western capitalism: loans, new technologies, investment expertise, training and so forth, as well as entry into the world of legitimate international diplomacy – something solely in the gift of the Atlantic states.

Only one question remained: would it work? The Americans assured Baghdad that it would: that the Iranian armed forces were in chaos and a quick war would present few risks. But this turned out to be nonsense. Eight years of atrocious suffering were the result. By 1982 Saddam Hussein had realised that his plan for a quick victory had been a delusion and he sought to extricate his regime from the war through a negotiated settlement. However, the Iranian government made the removal of Saddam Hussein the precondition for peace, which provoked in turn an ever more brutal Iraqi military response against the more powerful state, including the use of poison gas on front-line Iranian troops. By the time a negotiated peace was in place, in 1988, it was abundantly clear that the decision to attack Iran had been a grave political and military miscalculation. A million people had died, oil wealth had been squandered, and the government had lost control of Kurdistan. Economic recovery had the reconstruction of a damaged and overburdened state and social fabric – not to mention the repair of shattered lives – would make tremendous demands of the Ba'ath, and take many years to effect. And the government could count on few allies within Iraq. Efforts to rebuild links with the ICP were rejected and the regime had no political means of integrating the South effectively. A policy of terror was finally applied to integrate the Kurds. The regime's only asset was a powerful, battle-hardened military machine. Nevertheless, the scale of this modern Iraqi army – very large for the Gulf region – could only be considered a threat by surrounding states, and by their allies. Thus, by the end of the 1980s all the main historical forces both within and outside Iraqi politics were uniting against the Ba'ath. The stage was set for the catastrophe of 1991.

As is usual after a war, the Arab people of Iraq demanded a new and better deal in 1989. The regime did not have the resources to provide such a deal and the al-Sabahs presented an ideal target-cum-solution. Heavily in debt and hard-hit by the oil-price slump, the regime had been victim to the Emir of Kuwait's endeavours against OPEC quota and price decisions. It therefore risked a strike at the al-Sabahs and invaded, undoubtedly hoping that this would be followed by a negotiated way out of its debt problems. When the US blocked such negotiations and demanded a total public capitulation, the regime understood that this could lead to its domestic collapse. It decided to stand, like Nasser in 1956, and defend its dignity as leader of the Arab nation against the enormous military power of the West, no doubt calculating – correctly as it turned out – that the US was still unable to turn to Iran as its surrogate power in the region and thus could not risk the break-up of Iraq.

Lessons for the Left

I began this section with a polemical engagement with Samir al-Khalil, criticising in particular the reductive nature of his conceptual framework and the limitations this imposes on his analysis of modern Iraq and the Ba'athist regime – limitations at the heart of the liberal tradition within which he works. I hope subsequently to have shown that Iraq's recent history, bearing directly on the events that led to defeat in two immensely damaging wars that radically changed the geopolitical map of the Gulf region, was an infinitely more complex narrative than Khalil allows. Notwithstanding this criticism, *Republic of Fear* represents an honest and important reflection on Iraqi politics, a reflection unrestricted by narrow strategic concerns and possessing greater insight than the attenuated arguments typical of most liberal commentary on the Gulf crisis. Most significantly of all, Khalil's work addresses questions of great import to the Left.

The central problem is that the Iraqi Ba'ath did carry through a fundamental social transformation, adopting for this purpose an economic programme almost indistinguishable from that of the Marxist Left: namely, radical land reform, nationalisation of industry, the encouragement of cooperative farming, and state-led economic development. The Baghdad regime, what is more, stood for a secular public life without taking a negative stance on Islam; it even formally recognised the national identity of the Kurds. Notwithstanding this progressivism, it has also been an extremely repressive regime, using political police as its main instrument of control. It finally imposed on its people a misguided effort to become the imperialist guardian in the Gulf, before leading them into the Kuwait catastrophe. The leaders of the Iraqi Communist Party have responded to this experience by calling the Ba'athist regime 'fascist'. This, however, does little but explain the problems away. For Ba'athism was not a counter-revolution against democracy and the labour movement; it was an alternative to military rule, and in its socioeconomic policies a left-oriented regime with which the official Communist Party cooperated through most of the 1970s.

Khalil, for his part, has responded in another way: he sees the Ba'ath as the product of a deficient and degraded Arab political culture, and consequently as a totalitarian movement analogous to Stalinism. His solution has been to reject that model in favour of the theoretical culture of Anglo-American Cold War liberalism, and to denounce all goal-oriented activist regimes seeking to transform social conditions. His solution in short is: liberal-democratic constitutionalism now, whatever the social correlates and consequences. But this stance is not acceptable to the Left, entailing as it does a capitulation before social injustice and the evasion of political choice and strategy. It drives Khalil, ultimately, to the belief that American military strength could constitute a liberal *deus ex machina* – a wild illusion.

The Ba'ath came to power as a tiny organised party, by way of a military coup. It sought to sink popular roots through greatly expanding the party, and was acutely aware of the need to extend the base of its political support, reaching out to the ICP for this purpose. But when the extended state of emergency ended in the mid 1970s, the Ba'ath leadership, awash with huge oil profits and aware of its wide popular support, turned increasingly towards a de facto one-party dictatorship, eschewing the need for pluralist institution-building. This was a fatal turn, yet one easy to accomplish, not only because the use of policy apparatuses to carve up political space was effortlessly simple, but also because there was no other political model available. This is where Khalil's reference to Stalinism is very much to the point. The party leadership, including Aflaq and Saddam Hussein, were not simply corrupt adventurers. Indeed, they were passionately committed to the Ba'athist cause; they also sought to overcome the failings of the earlier Ba'ath and of Nasser, and were looking for models, not least in Eastern Europe and in Cuba, for a way forward. They found nothing there to urge them against the course of one-party dictatorship. If their middle-class nationalism made the regional imperialist temptation irresistible, the Stalinist experience made their domestic course equally so. Their critique of Nasserism did not extend beyond the need for a powerful hegemonic party. The lesson from Eastern Europe was that a one-party dictatorship was assisted, in its formative phase, by the deployment of political police.

The Left's answer to this Stalinist experience does not consist of pitting society against the state; it involves building popular, pluralistic state institutions with sovereign powers over the executive. The sovereignty of such popular institutions must lie precisely in their pluralism and be underwritten by a ban on political violence as a method of resolving disputes amongst elected parties. This does not preclude the temporary concentration of great powers within the executive, including the right to rule by decree; but it does entail the ultimate subordination of all parties and agencies to the will of the elected assembly.

The political culture of twentieth-century Iraq has been shaped more by British-imperialist social engineering than by the people of that country, excluded for decades from the political system. The Ba'athist project has its derivation more in the political traditions of the North, both in its nationalist and in its socialist values, and has nothing in common with the political culture of such Arab neighbours as Saudi Arabia or the Emirate of the al-Sabahs. And its critical weaknesses owe far more to the deficiencies of Stalinism and to the external temptations of the American-constructed incentive system in the Gulf than to the supposedly closed discursive universe of some putative organic 'Arab culture'. This latter is, in fact, nothing more than another mythical western construction useful for explaining away the disastrous, destructive consequences of Anglo-American military intervention in the Arab world – today, as well as yesterday and tomorrow.

Conclusion

Desert Storm was justified before a liberal-democratic public in the West in the language of rights. However, this discourse is one shared with an older tradition of states' rights theory, the substantive principles of which differ radically from, and indeed are largely antagonistic towards, those of contemporary liberalism. As a consequence, the shared language readily serves to obscure this antagonism and the disparateness of the two traditions. The application of universal rules to cases, abstraction from context and history, the attempt to transform political complexities into juridical questions of crime and punishment – such common modes of thought and representation can translate a domestic liberalism into an ideology for justifying statist militarism abroad. Moreover, the contemporary revival of Kantian political theory, the full development of which has been achieved in the work of Rawls, has not on the whole taken its universalist mission seriously. Liberal justice in the latter's work remains, in a theoretically unconvincing manner, confined within national boundaries, thereby leaving the field of international politics to the Grotians, if not the realists.

In the first part of this article, I attempted to apply the principles of rights-based liberalism to the Gulf crisis by employing the problem-solving approach that has characterised most commentary and discussion in the West. The problem was defined simply: how to end the injustice produced by the Iraqi invasion of Kuwait. And the issue explored was whether the response – culminating in Desert Storm – could be justified as the instrument of liberal justice. The conclusion reached was that this response was in fact directed toward objectives, and was the expression of interests, that run counter to liberal-democratic principles – at the expense of the Iraqi and Kuwaiti populations. Thus the barbarity of war was the price not of justice but, rather, of defending oppressive regimes and thereby fulfilling imperial design in the Gulf and the wider Arab world.

This judgement calls in question the problem-solving framework with which we began. To establish the invasion of Kuwait as the central problem, and then to subsume the British and American states under the category of possible instruments of justice, is to presume that the social order disrupted by the invasion embodied a minimal principle of justice. Yet no such order did exist prior to the invasion; instead there was oppression and inequity, in which the West – and, above all, the USA – had a primary stake. It is therefore behoven upon any liberal politics that takes its values seriously to identify the western powers as the central obstacle to the pursuit of popular interests and democratic goals in the region.

This in turn raises fundamental questions about the international order over which the western powers preside. Throughout this chapter I have criticised the normative side of what I have termed 'states' rights' theory. The cognitive aspect of this theory presents us with a world of independent nation-states that are only related externally. Such juridical sovereignty precludes the possibility that some states might penetrate the internal economic and political life of others. This possibility, of what could be called 'states' rights imperialism', would seem a contradiction in terms within the framework of the theory. Nevertheless, for hundreds of millions of people in the South this scenario is all too real: the legal sovereignty of their states sits easily with a situation in which most economic, social, and indeed political, relationships in their daily lives are governed by centres of power – 'private' and 'public' – located in the North.[65]

The Iraqi revolution of 1958 was impelled by the aspiration to throw off the yoke of social oppression constructed by the British and their subaltern collaborators early in the twentieth century. And it led to the project of the Ba'ath Party to transform Iraq into a modern, secular, egalitarian and constitutional state. In the decades since the collapse of the European empires this aspiration has been shared by a variety of political movements in the South. The difficulties of attaining these goals do not by any means derive mainly from the characteristics of leaders like Saddam Hussein. More fundamental obstacles include the fissures in the new territorial entities bequeathed by the European powers, the external economic and geopolitical environments designed in the North, the local social structures and comprador regimes they favour, and the absence of tested alternatives to the evidently bankrupt Stalinist model of development. Any critique of the nationalist and authoritarian politics of the Ba'ath should show awareness of these overlapping contexts.

The appeal of liberalism resides, above all, in its emphasis upon the overriding importance of subordinating political power to respect for the person and for the rights of the individual. Yet in so far as it singles out the individual's relation to the state as its primary concern, liberalism can display a double blindness: towards the oppressive relationships governing the real, everyday lives of the majority; and towards the potentially progressive role of popular movements for radical change, of political force and of state action in modernising and transforming people's lives. This blindness is exemplified by the liberal perspective from which Samir al-Khalil observes the history of modern Iraq. And it was exploited to the full by the western coalition which seized upon the dictatorial form of the Iraqi state in order to represent a drive to secure imperial interests as a struggle between liberal respect for persons and political oppression. The real stakes in Desert Storm were very different, as has become all too evident in its aftermath.

Notes

1. Hans Morgenthau, *In Defence of the National Interest* (Knopf, 1952), p. 242.

2. Legal metaphors are, of course commonly used in political discourse. When a government performs an injustice, we frequently call it a 'crime'; but this is not meant literally: we know we are using a metaphor. Thus, to say that the West's policy on Third World debt is 'criminal' because it leads to millions of deaths in the South means it is grossly unjust, politically and morally wrong. We do not use the word literally and order the arrest and execution of Mr Camdessus and the other officials of the IMF and World Bank.

3. The projection of Saddam Hussein as a monstrous criminal could also result in an assumption that the US military was actually being used on behalf of the Iraqi people against its government. The notion that because many Iraqis oppose their government they will therefore condone the killing of 100,000 of their fellow countrymen and the destruction of their social infrastructure lies at the source of the notion that justice demanded that the allies march on Baghdad. Overlooked is the fact that the organised Iraqi opposition (not to speak of the population as a whole) opposed any attack upon Iraq, issuing a statement to this effect at their Damascus meeting of December 1990.

4. Amongst its most vigorous opponents would of course be the realist Right, which dismisses (correctly) the notion that law is dominant in international affairs from the *normative* standpoint of imperialism. They glory in US and western allied domination of the globe, insisting that nothing, such as the details of this or that legal covenant, should challenge this primary virtue. It is, nevertheless, important that wholesale rejection of the values of the realist Right – directly counterposed, as they are, to those of the Left – does not lead to a denial of the factual truth contained in their current view of the world. For, how could they be out of tune with world political realities when their school of thought has to a great extent been *calling the tune* by way of a dominating presence since World War II in the core executives of the most powerful western states?

5. See W. B. Gallie, *Philosophers of Peace and War: Kant, Clausewitz, Marx, Engels and Tolstoy* (Cambridge University Press, 1978), chapter 2.

6. On the history of natural-rights theories and the place of Grotius within their development, see R. Tuck, *Natural Rights Theories* (Cambridge University Press, 1979). On Grotius's role within the history of international-relations theory, see F. Parkinson, *The Philosophy of International Relations* (Sage, 1977).

7. For an account of this theory, see Telford Taylor, 'Just and Unjust Wars', M. M. Watkin, ed., *War, Morality and the Military Profession* (Westview, 1979), pp. 245–58. As Michael Walzer points out, Marx, in his First and Second Addresses of the International on the Franco–Prussian War of 1870, uses the language of states' rights and legalism. But these addresses cannot, of course, be used as the basis for an exposition of Marxist theory on war. Marx was acting as the secretary of an International the leaders of which in the UK were trade unionists who by no means accepted Marxist theory – a fact Waltzer fails to mention. See M. Walzer, *Just and Unjust Wars* (Westview, 1978), pp. 64–66.

8. Particularly visible in the journal *Philosophy and Public Affairs*.

9. Parkinson, *Philosophy of International Relations*, p. 69.

10. This is the view held most clearly by those we may describe as 'global Rawlsians', like Pogge. But it is strikingly not the view held by the greatest reviver of Kantian liberalism in the contemporary Anglo-Saxon world, John Rawls himself. Rawls's entire theory, for all its seeming universalist generality, is, in fact, a theory premised upon the justice of existing international relations and to be applied only within an existing state. As Brian Barry points out: 'Rawls does have a brief discussion of international relations, which he conceives in the spirit of a pure 19th century liberal like Gladstone, not even making concessions to 20th century ideas to the extent of catching up with Woodrow Wilson.' B. Barry, *The Liberal Theory of Justice* (Oxford University Press, 1973), p. 130. Thus Rawls makes concessions to states' rights theory and even to the legalist metaphor, writing: 'The basic principle of the law of nations is a principle of equality. Independent peoples organised as states have certain fundamental equal rights. This principle is analogous to the equal rights of citizens in a constitutional regime.' Rawls, *A Theory of Justice* (Oxford University Press, 1972), p. 378.

11. See the *Amnesty Report* 'Iraq/Kuwait', December 1990. It was impossible to verify such figures: the Iraqi government sealed off Kuwait from western journalists on the grounds of military security in the face of an imminent allied attack. Thus Amnesty relied upon testimony from people who had left Kuwait. This led to inaccuracies, notably the allegation that the Iraqis had deliberately killed hundreds of babies by removing their incubators. This story, repeatedly used by President Bush to justify war preparations, turned out to be false: it was supplied by an agent of the al-Sabah regime, the previous rulers of Kuwait.

12. Iraq's legal claim to Kuwait derived from the territory's integration into the province of Basra under the Ottoman Empire. The Ottomans never recognised British 'protection' of Kuwait and neither did the Iraqi monarchy set up by the British after the dismemberment of the Empire. (The British, incidentally, threatened to take the whole of Basra province out of Iraq unless the Iraqi government approved the treaty ensuring effective British control over Iraq, as Hanna Batatu explains in *The Old Social Classes and the Revolutionary Movements of Iraq: A Study of Iraq's Old Landed and Commercial Classes and of its Communists, Ba'athists and Free Officers* (Princeton University Press, 1978), p. 189. The British also threatened to take the Kurdish area and Mosul out of Iraq unless King Faisal granted Britain control of the oil there.) In 1938 the Kuwaiti Legislative Council unanimously approved a request for Kuwait's reintegration with Iraq; in the following year the British suppressed an armed uprising which had this as its objective.

13. See V. Held, S. Morgenbesser and Thomas Nagel, eds., *Philosophy, Morality and International Affairs* (Oxford University Press, 1974). This collection, evidently designed to present the authoritative liberal view on key issues, as interpreted by the editors of *Philosophy and Public Affairs*, includes an article on this topic: 'The Principle of National Self-Determination' by S. French and A. Gutman.

14. The overwhelmingly dominant form of national consciousness in the Arab world throughout the twentieth century has been that of pan-Arab nationalism. The existence of an Arab nation was a belief shared by a spectrum of opinion stretching from King Faisal of Iraq to the Communist International throughout the 1920s and it included the Arabists in the British Foreign Office. However, the British concern for oil and for geopolitical security (the route to India) led them to an almost unique policy in the Gulf region, namely establishing or fostering states based upon tribal-dynastic identities. Kuwait under the al-Sabahs is a case in point.

15. Fred Halliday, *Arabia Without Sultans* (Penguin, 1974), pp. 431, 434.

16. This trade-off would not simply be between socioeconomic rights and civil-political rights, but one between the civil-political rights of the majority of Kuwait's settled population and the minority. Liberalism, particularly in those forms hostile to the entire notion of collective national will, would surely weigh the civil-political rights of the non-Kuwaiti settled population of Kuwait very heavily. It is interesting to note that the major work of liberal theory of the last two decades, John Rawls's *A Theory of Justice*, simply does not address the issue of how to define a civil-political community. As Brian Barry observes: 'The odd thing about Rawls's treatment of the question how a particular community is to be defined for the purposes of a theory of Justice is that he does not discuss it . . . Rawls . . . may believe that he can dodge the question how the community is to be defined. But it seems to me that this is an arbitrary move which cannot be defended within the theory.' Barry, pp. 128–29.

17. Quoted by Ralph Schoenman, 'Iraq and Kuwait, A History Suppressed', mimeograph, New York, October 1990.

18. The American rejection involved a classic replacement of political principle with legal metaphor by insisting on the idea that two separate 'cases' were involved.

19. J. S. Mill, 'A Few Words on Non-Intervention', J. S. Mill, *Dissertations and Discourses* vol. III (New York 1873), pp. 238–63.

20. The anti-consequentialist argument – that you should judge an action without regard to its consequences – has been largely discredited among liberal ethical philosophers concerned with public policy. See Robert E. Goodin, *Philosophy and Public Policy*, (University of Chicago Press, 1983). Rawls displays an uncharacteristic irritation in dismissing anti-consequentialism in *A Theory of Justice*.

21. See the article by Robert Block in the *Independent*, 21 March 1991, p. 10; and the articles by Robert Fisk and Robert Block in the *Independent*, 27 April 1991, p. 1. See also Michael Simmons in the *Guardian*, 19 April 1991, p. 11.

22. See the *Observer*, 28 April 1991.

23. The Kuwaiti government has subsequently declared a reduction in the number of Arabs (mainly Palestinians) it will expel. Palestinians have formed a large proportion of the managerial and professional middle classes in Kuwait, in the public as well as the private sector, and they cannot easily be replaced.

24. Zbigniew Brzezinski, 'After the Carter Doctrine: Geostrategic Stakes and Turbulent Crosscurrents in the Gulf', H. R. Sindelar and J. E. Peterson, eds., *Crosscurrents in the Gulf: Arab, Regional and Global Interests* (Routledge, 1988), pp. 2, 3.

25. This is not to deny the importance of such fluctuations for domestic macroeconomic management in Western Europe or Japan. And any power able to control such fluctuations can exert a significant influence on, for example, attempts to harmonise economic policies among the members of the EC in preparing the way towards monetary union in Western Europe. This control thus gives political leverage over other governments.

26. See the interview with Samih Farsoun in *Middle East Report*, no. 168 (January–February 1991), pp. 5–6.

27. See George Joffe, *Marxism Today* (May 1991).

28. Samir al-Khalil, *Republic of Fear* (Hutchinson, 1989); see also his article in the NYRB, 11 April 1991 (published in *Libération*, 18 April 1991).

29. Khalil, NYRB, 11 April 1991. There is actually a further slippage: Khalil's belle-lettristic separation of the person of Faisal I from his political regime, and consequent evasion of a factual account of what Faisal's regime did, in favour of an inquiry into what Faisal's supposed personal inclinations and motives were. But Khalil's readers could not be expected to spot this and would take his remarks to mean that the monarchy *as a political regime*, decisively controlled by the British, had a progressive, modernising project.

30. Fran Hazelton, 'Iraq to 1963', in CARDRI, *Saddam's Iraq: Revolution or Reaction?* (London 1989), p. 3.

31. Elie Kedourie, *The Chatham House Version and Other Middle-Eastern Studies* (University Press of New England), p. 256.

32 Ibid, p. 258.

33. See the dispatch from Sloan, Baghdad, 11 June 1931, 890g.00/1501, quoted in Kedourie, *Chatham House Version*, p. 438.

34. Kedourie, *Chatham House Version*, p. 250.

35. Ibid., pp. 237, 238.

36. Ibid., p. 250.

37. Ibid., p. 239.

38. Khalil, *Republic of Fear*, p. 174.

39. Kedourie, *Chatham House Version*, p. 262.

40. FO 371/52315/E 7045, quoted in W. R. Lewis, *The British Empire in the Middle East 1945–1951: Arab Nationalism, The United States and Post-war Imperialism* (Oxford University Press, 1984), p. 309.

41. M. S. Hasan, 'The Role of Foreign Trade in the Economic Development of Iraq, 1864–1964: A Study in the Growth of a Dependent Economy', in M. A. Cook, ed., *Studies in the Economic History of the Middle East from the Rise of Islam to the Present Day* (KPI, 1970), p. 352. And such socioeconomic regression in agriculture did not generate, by way of compensation, a class of urban entrepreneurs. The landlords, who generally lived in the cities enjoying their new wealth, consumed it rather than invested, and as M. Farouk-Sluglett and Peter Sluglett explain, they 'played an essentially parasitic role in the economy while bearing down heavily on the peasantry. It is important to stress that these tendencies were the direct result of British policies during the mandate and that, in addition, the policies had been elaborated at the time in order to produce this overall result.' M. Farouk-Sluglett and P. Sluglett, *Iraq Since 1958: From Revolution to Dictatorship* (KPI, 1987), p. 33.

42. India Office LP & S 10/4722/1920/8/6305, quoted in Farouk-Sluglett and Sluglett, p. 277. For Wilson's views, see Sir A. Wilson, *Mesopotamia 1917–1920: A Clash of Loyalties* (London 1931), p. 96, quoted in Farouk-Sluglett and Sluglett, p. 277.

43. FO 371/3406/139231, quoted in Farouk-Sluglett and Sluglett, p. 276. As the latter explain: 'The policy of bolstering the powers of the shaikhs continued throughout the mandate and monarchy periods, and large landownership became the social base of the regime . . . in the provinces of Kut and Amara . . . some of the largest private estates in the Middle East came to be located, mostly created by the stroke of a pen between 1915 and 1925 . . . This process resulted in the formation of enormous private estates.' (Ibid., p. 31). In the country as a whole, eight owners held 855,000 acres – about 107,000 acres per person. In 1958 2,480 individuals owned 55 per cent of all land.

44. See Batatu, *The Old Social Classes and the Revolutionary Movements of Iraq*, pp. 73–128.

45. As to the precise nature of these interests, anti-imperialist authors tend to stress oil; others point to the strategic dangers of leaving Mosul and Kirkuk out of British control. See Marian Kent, *Oil and Empire. British Policy and Mesopotamian Oil 1900–1920*, (Macmillan, 1976), especially ch. 8; and, on the strategic dimension, John Darwin, *Britain, Egypt and the Middle East. Imperial Policy and the Aftermath of War, 1918–1922* (Macmillan, 1981), especially ch. 9.

46. See Khalil, NYRB, 11 April 1991.

47. Khalil, *Republic of Fear*, p. 163.

48. Dispatch by Randolph, 21 May 1928, 890g.03/9, quoted by Kedourie, *Chatham House Version*, p. 438.

49. Kedourie, *Chatham House Version*, p. 438; see also Batatu, *The Old Social Classes and the Revolutionary Movements of Iraq*, pp. 102–4.

50. Khalil, NYRB, 11 April 1991.

51. A. D. MacDonald, *Euphrates Exile* (Rochester, 1936), pp. 54–56. Kedourie's evocation of the attitude of the Iraqi state under the British towards the population of that country is all too familiar from allied treatment of Iraq today: '[T]hey were the government in its exalted and boundless power, the others were the subjects who must be prostrate in obedience. The texts of proclamations to the tribes in revolt are characteristic and revealing: The government desires to spare you, come therefore with all speed to the offices of the government and offer your obedience; otherwise the government will punish you, and yours will be the responsibility.' *Chatham House Version*, p. 261.

52. Khalil, *Republic of Fear*, p. 241.

53. Ibid., p. 254.

54. It is not clear from the book whether Khalil himself aware of the sources of mass-society theory in the politics of the European counter-revolution against democracy: namely, the writings of Gustav le Bon and of Catholic anti-liberal corporatism from the days of Pio Nono to the clerico-fascists of the 1920s, as well as 'aristocratic liberals' of the counter-revolution such as Ortega y Gasset. Ultimately the sources go back to Burke and de Maistre. A classic contemporary statement of these reactionary positions is to be found in Leonard Schapiro's *Totalitarianism*, which hasn't a good word to say for democracy and sees Nazism as one of its outcomes.

55. Khalil, *Republic of Fear*, p. 120.

56. Israel had started supporting the Barzani leadership in the 1950s, training Kurds in sabotage techniques at a base near Ramleh. Rafael Eitan, later Israeli Chief of Staff, even paid a clandestine visit to Barzani's forces in Kurdistan. By the mid 1960s Israel had become one of Barzani's main props. This and other details were revealed by Menachem Begin on the Israeli Home Service, 29 September 1980 (BBC Summary of World Broadcasts, ME/6537, 1 October 1980, cited in Patrick Seale, *Asad*, London 1988, p. 243).

57. On this and other aspects of the labyrinthine politics of Kurdistan, written from a position sympathetic to the Iraqi CP and hostile towards the Ba'ath, see Peter Sluglett, 'The Kurds', in CARDRI, *Saddam's Iraq* (London 1989).

58. Many of the militants from this wing of the party subsequently joined the Palestinian movement in Jordan, especially the PDFLP. On the history of the Iraqi Communist Party, including its roots in the Shia South, see Batatu's monumental work, *The Old Social Classes and the Revolutionary Movements of Iraq*.

59. See Dilip Hiro, *The Longest War* (Routledge & Kegan Paul, 1989), p. 24. On the ideology of the Shia current, see the very informative article by Hanna Batatu: 'Iraq's Underground Shi'ite Movements: Characteristics, Causes and Prospects', *Middle East Journal* (Autumn 1981).

60. Kedourie, *Chatham House Version, p.* 260.

61. Khalil, NYRB, 11 April 1991.

62. Hiro, *Longest War,* p. 24.

63. Ibid.

64. If we accept Phoebe Marr's account in her chapter on the Iran–Iraq war in P. Marr, *The Modern History of Iraq* (Westview 1985).

65. For an illustration of how these mechanisms operate in relations between the Western powers and Eastern Europe today, see Peter Gowan, 'Western Economic Diplomacy and the New Eastern Europe', *New Left Review* 182 (July/August 1990).

9

The Theory and Practice of Neo-Liberalism for Eastern Europe

Eastern Europe's market for policy ideas, suddenly opened in 1989, was swiftly captured by an Anglo-American product with a liberal brand name. This policy equivalent of fast food swiftly erected barriers to other new entrants and established a virtual monopoly on policy advice in most target states in the region. While some critics view it as having as much connection with West European liberalism as a Big Mac with beouf bourgignon, it has made up for any deficiency in nutritional value by superb advertising and aggressive salesmanship.

The public launch was handled by the *Economist* on 13th January 1990 with a long article by Professor Jeffrey Sachs of Harvard. Under the significant title of 'What is to be Done?', Sachs wrote in the style of a Lenin of decollectivisation against all the assorted Menshevisms of half-measures. Yet the article is worth re-reading for it reminds us of the status of the debate into which Sachs was intervening. It was about how the West should seek to reshape the life of the entire East European region. Only one aspect of the debate and of Sachs's policy concerned the sequence of domestic changes to be required of governments in the various individual states. Indeed, Sachs's programme was about creating an international environment in which the domestic aspect of his policy would become the only rational course for any government to pursue.

Sachs's proposals were enthusiastically supported by both American and British policy-makers and they have become household names in Eastern Europe: every Russian schoolchild learns about the '3 Zatsias'. Such popularisation is also widespread in western universities where the policy is boiled down to an abstractly universal toolkit for DIY construction of market economies out of Communism: an immensely attractive format for university teaching. At the same time, Sachs's ideas have received the very highest accolades from the Anglo-Saxon academic world. The Harvard Professor gave a famous series of lectures on his paradigm at LSE. These were subsequently published by MIT. He is widely credited with founding a new discipline, The Economic Theory of the Transition. Since Harvard and LSE professors would buy it and even sell it, few policy intellectuals in the defeated East could have the self-confidence to doubt its scientific credentials.[1]

In truth, Sachs has never presented his policy as either a toolkit or as a new theory. But like all rigorous policy his does contain a more or less explicit model of the behaviour of relevant actors and of the ways in which they will interact in given contexts, faced with given constraints and incentives.

We will first try to clarify what Sachs's policy model has actually been. We will then try to examine the extent to which the main relevant actors identified in the model have behaved in the way the theory predicted. And in the light of that experience we will attempt to draw some conclusions about the real relationship between western policy and the ideas propagated by Sachs and his followers and suggest an alternative model for understanding what has happened.

Sachs's policy has had various names: shock treatment, radical Economic Reform, Big Bang, the '3 Zatsias' or Shock Therapy (ST). Sachs himself has not been happy with any of these names but has come to accept the latter and we will follow him in this.

I   Shock Therapy

Sachs's model has the characteristic problem-solving form familiar in policy analysis: it says, if you want to achieve outcome A, then you must get actor X to produce output Y, which will then interact with its environment in such a way as to achieve outcome A. The model makes assumptions about the behaviour and motivations of the relevant actors, about how they will respond to given negative or positive incentives and about the context in which they act. We evaluate the model by judging whether it really will achieve outcome A and, if so, whether it will achieve it at least cost.

Sachs formulated his model to solve one big problem: how should the entire ex-Communist region of Eastern Europe and the USSR be reorganised in order to achieve, in Sachs's words, 'a recovery of human freedom and a democratically based rise in living standards'.[2]

A very broad spectrum of opinion, at least in the West, would accept this problem-definition and desired outcome. Yet many would be suspicious of a concerted, western-directed plan for regional social engineering to achieve this outcome. Ralph Dahrendorf expressed two worries on this score. He argued that 'the countries of East-Central Europe have not shed their Communist system in order to embrace the capitalist system – whatever that is . . . If any creed has won . . . it is the idea that we are all embarked on a journey into an uncertain future and have to work by trial and error within institutions which make it possible to bring about change without bloodshed.'[3] Dahrendorf's rejection of the whole idea of a western system is an implied warning against social engineering to achieve a forced decollectivisation. Sachs defends such grand planning on the grounds that the world is governed by systems (Communism and capitalism) whose main structural features of socioeconomic and power relationships are perfectly understandable: however variable in detail they nevertheless have, so to speak, the same basic genetic codes.

But Dahrendorf's second concern is the primacy of respecting the existing tissue of social institutions and to strengthen social institutionalisation by introducing openness: the free circulation of ideas and the building of consensus through debate, negotiation and compromise. This approach would place the development of a legal state and political liberalism above schemes for systemic change: the latter should grow out of the 'open society' or 'civil society'. Sachs rejects this, saying that if the states of the region adopted Dahrendorf's approach 'of open experimentation, I doubt that the transformation would be possible at all, at least without costly and dangerous wrong turns'.[4]

Thus, what might be called Sachs's inverted Leninism is more than a matter of style: it relates to the entire methodology of his model: he is a strong believer that he – or at least the West – can plan in such a way as to enable the peoples of the region to avoid costly wrong turns and he simultaneously believes that left to their own collective efforts they would take wrong turns or indeed might not opt for his goals at all. The corollary of these views is that the policy he advocates will entail a sequence of events in which institutional consolidation and democratic stabilisation bring up the rear.

1) Path and Output at a Regional Level

Sachs's policy has had as its object not individual states but the entire post-Communist region of Eastern Europe. He advanced his ideas in line with the views of the American and British governments as to how to transform Eastern Europe as a region. And he counterposed his regional goals with an alternative solution which dovetailed with the French government's general approach. We will summarise the regional policy which Sachs opposed before turning to his alternative:

1)   Encouraging the former CMEA region, including the USSR, to remain linked economically.
2)   Leaving the evolution of socioeconomic forces in each country to the

interplay of forces within the country concerned, without using western pressure to impose a particular system.

3)   Making the emphasis of western policy that of economic revival in the region as a whole, using, for example, a regional development bank for that purpose.

4)   Rejecting a pespective of bringing some ex-Communist countries into the EC in the short or medium term. Instead, offering a pan-European Confederation embracing both the EC and the East, including the USSR.

The alternative, American approach, of which Sachs was a passionate advocate, involved:

1)   Breaking up the Comecon region and above all, breaking East Central European countries from the USSR.

2)   Making a root and branch switch to a particular form of capitalist institutional structure in each state a precondition for normalising relations with that state.

3)   Therefore imposing a hub-and-spokes structure on the relationship between the West and East Central Europe,[5] with each target state in the region relating to the others principally via its relationship with the western hub.

4)   Starting the process of regional transformation in the states with the most politically sympathetic governments and then using both negative and positive incentives to extend the required mix of domestic policies across the region as a whole.

5)   The entire process would be carried forward by the capacity and will of western states to provide, in the main via their multilateral organisations, the necessary positive incentives for co-operative governments and constraints for unco-operative governments.

6)   The revival of economic activity in co-operative target states would take the form of trade-led growth directed toward Western Europe, compensating for Comecon's collapse.

7)   Co-operative states would gain full access to the market of the EC (partly through radically changing some of its key institutional pillars, such as its trade regime and Common Agricultural Policy), very substantial economic assistance and eventual membership of a greatly enlarged EC.

Sachs's 1990 article outlined this entire approach with cogency. He claimed that keeping the Comecon region together would be sub-optimal: the 'East European common market that some suggest as a precursor to integration with the West would simply be a poor man's club'. He therefore urged its break-up and in effect the start of a competitive race by East European states to prepare themselves for direct entry into the West European market. Secondly, he rejected mixed or hybrid forms of socioeconomic system on the grounds that Market Socialism had proved to be unworkable: the East European states 'must reject . . . ideas about a . . . 'third way . . .' and 'go straight for a western-style market economy'.[6] He urged radical reform in the EC to accommodate an export surge from target states and called for an unprecedented degree of funding for co-operative states from western sources, especially from Germany.

Sachs was able to point out that his model was already being applied by two states in the region, in 1990: Yugoslavia and Poland: as Sachs, who had been advising the Yugoslav government in 1989 and had then transferred to Poland, explained: 'Poland will bring in the first comprehensive market-oriented reforms in Eastern Europe. Yugoslavia will undertake a similar programme.'[7]

The American approach as articulated by Sachs was, of course, adopted by the G7.[8] Its key element – the fragmentation of the Comecon region and its replacement by hub-and-spoke relations between isolated eastern states and the West, has subsequently been largely naturalised in western public and academic discourse. Debate about ST has thereby been reduced to cost-benefit analysis of whether the spokes should accept western conditionality or attempt an isolationist policy, or try some possible halfway house between the two.

The fragmentation of the Comecon region may seem as natural as, say, the hostility of Serbs, Croats and Bosnian Muslims in the 1990s or the hostility of the French towards the Germans in the late 1940s. But to believe that is to ignore the capacity of the West to shape outcomes. This capacity was used by the US to bring France and Germany together. As Richard Holbrooke, the American Assistant Secretary of State for European Affairs, has recently pointed out, this capacity was not used in Yugoslavia and the result was, in his view, 'the greatest collective security failure of the West since the 1930s'.[9] And western influence was used to encourage the fragmentation of the Comecon region in 1990–91. Sachs was part of that effort of encouragement and he justifies the break-up not on the grounds that it was bound to happen, but on the grounds that it was desirable from an economic point of view. The policy did not oppose a slide towards national autarchy: it encouraged a condition of national autarchy from which it hoped that agreeing western terms for hub-and-spoke integration would appear not only the best but even the only rational exit.

Thus, at a regional level, the path lay through the gradual absorption of the states concerned into the western economy, institutionalised in the various multilateral organisations and especially the EU. The end product would be a unification of Europe in a single (reformed) EU market. This would generate, on a regional scale, the desired outcome of prosperous capitalist democracy.

2) *The Key Output of Shock Therapy in Each State*

If ST's projected outcome in each state is democratically-based increased living standards and freedom, the output of Sachs's policy is institutional.[10] Sachs has often named it as a 'market economy' or 'capitalism'. Yet closer examination reveals that specific state-institutional forms are the central output goals of ST at the level of a single country, not capitalism as such. He puts matters as follows: 'At the base of all of this transformation [is] . . . the idea . . . that the post-Communist world have the potential to grow more rapidly than the develop[ed][11] world and thereby to narrow the gap in living standards, if they harmonise their economic institutions and join their economies to the global economic system.'[12]

Even on the occasions when Sachs says his goal is simply 'capitalism',[13] we discover that he means the very particular institutional matrix which excludes most capitalisms throughout history from qualifying as capitalist at all.

Sachs tells us that 'the main precepts of capitalism [are] open trade, currency convertibility, and the private sector as the engine of growth.'[14] By this strange formula, Western Europe was not obeying capitalist precepts before 1958 (no convertibility) and the USA was not following capitalist precepts in the highly protected interwar period. These are thus the precepts not of capitalism but of Sachs, and two out of his three precepts could in theory be applied without a capitalist economy at all: they are to do with the external economic relations of states.

His desired output is further revealed by the six 'core reforms' that he tells us must be achieved: '(1) open international trade; (2) currency convertibility; (3) private ownership as the main engine of economic growth; (4) corporate ownership as the dominant organisational form for large enterprises; (5) openness to foreign investment; and (6) membership of key international economic institutions, including the IMF, the World Bank, and the GATT . . .'[15] Thus, four of his six planks (numbers 1, 2, 5 and 6) are about changing a target state's external politico-economic relations and one (number 4) is about a particular form of capitalist ownership: the form which enables companies to be bought and sold easily. Only number 3 refers to what would normally be meant by capitalism. In short, the output of Sachs's model is a very specific political economy: a state as open as it is possible for it to be to the forces of international economic operators: a state with a globalised institutional structure, through which the resources of what he calls 'the global mainstream economy can flow'.

It is this output which lays the basis for the desired outcome: 'In effect, by rejoining the rest of the global economy, they [i.e. the countries concerned] are able to import some of the prosperity from the rest of the world, usually through the importation of new technologies, organisational patterns and finance'.[16] Or again, when the target states are 'opened wide to international trade' and to international capital, they will gain 'the new technologies, managerial talent, organisational methods and financial capital needed to overcome the dismal economic legacy of the past 40 years'.[17]

Creating the free trade regime and the right institutional and economic conditions to attract foreign direct investment (FDI) are the core output goals for generating the desired outcome: prosperous capitalist democracies. Together, they will produce the efficiencies for growth.

Sachs's theme has been repeated tirelessly by American diplomats and the officials of the International Financial Institutions. As the US Ambassador to Hungary put it: 'I have often been asked why there isn't a new Marshall Plan to help Central and Eastern Europe. Well, there is – it is here – and it is called private foreign investment . . . Foreign investment creates jobs, enhances productivity, generates economic growth, and raises the standard of living. It brings new technology, new management techniques, new markets, new products, and better ways of doing business.'[18]

Another ST enthusiast, John Lloyd, has been particularly critical of those (on the Left) who fail to grasp the link between ST and the reality of global capital. All states must create open institutions that can tap into the huge, mobile capital resources in the world economy: 'The world in which choices are made a hundred times a day as to which economy millions or billions of dollars are invested in, the world in which commodities such as cars and computers and planes are put together in one location from parts made in a thousand; the world in which rivers of data flow to and fro across "borders" bearing information that a wilderness of KGBs could not analyse, or even capture – that is the world into which the Russian reformers had to struggle to insert their country.'[19]

Failure to adapt to the reality of globalisation will lead, in Lloyd's view, to disaster. 'The World,' he says 'would not tolerate a "special" Russia if specialness meant an unconvertible currency, an unreformed industrial structure and a hostile investment climate . . .'[20]

The vision of tapping into the resources of global capitalism to modernise the economy was a powerful motive for Eastern supporters of ST, as Yegor Gaidar illustrated in an interview with the *Economist* in early 1992, just after he had taken charge of the Russian economy.

When the *Economist* asked him whether the Russian people would accept the likely 'economic shocks' of 'an extraordinarily difficult transition', he seemed unaware that they were referring to the slump which his policy would cause and thought that the shock would be the flood of FDI that would engulf Russia. He therefore responded by saying: 'It is hard to feel threatened by a possibility that, say, Germany or France will buy up the entire country . . . We are also different from East Europeans. We don't have so much xenophobia. The social and political problems connected with foreign investment are easier here than, for instance, in Poland, which is preoccupied with its relationship with Germany. That is why I think that our opening and integration into the western world is a historical and sociopolitical chance for the West and for Russia also.'

But the really ingenious aspect of Sachs's work has been the way in which he has justified the sudden opening of target economies to global capital as the necessary first steps in government policy for what we would normally think of as capitalism. He justifies a sudden switch to free trade; early convertibility is justified as a means to anchor world prices in the domestic context and as a springboard to economic revival through trade; and FDI is indispensable for privatisation and restructuring. All western authorities have joined Sachs in insisting on these aspects of his policy. The role of FDI is particularly stressed. Thus the joint study by the IMF, the World Bank, the OECD and the EBRD of the Soviet economy, carried out at the behest of the G7 in 1990–91, pointed out that foreign direct investment would be 'crucial in the transition'.[21] The OECD concurs in its own study that it is 'crucial to the process of transition to a market economy'.[22] It also adds that 'the privatisation process must extensively rely on FDI'.[23] Creating the institutional conditions for FDI is thus not only the omega of ST; it is the alpha as well.

3) The Key Shock Therapy Actors

It is precisely because Sachs's goal is an institutional order radically open to global capitalist forces that the central actors in ST are governments. As Sachs explains, 'markets spring up as soon as central planning bureaucrats vacate the field'.[24] But to achieve the right kind of capitalist market institutions requires the sustained application of political and social engineering by governments in the target states and in the West (the latter operating in the main through their multilateral institutions). The joint action of eastern and western governments is needed to breed the right brand of capitalist private sector and to attract the interest of western global capital.

Sachs insists on the centrality of western governments: 'success in the economic transformation will depend not only on the East, but quite fundamentally on the West as well'.[25] He endlessly lists the West's power resources:[26] the capacity to open or close their markets to East European products; to decide on debt, on grant aid, on loans, and on the terms for loans for political as well as economic purposes, on technology transfers, on currency support etc.; to decide on entry or exclusion from international institutions, to allow eastern workers to flow westwards. All these give western governments tremendous bargaining power.[27]

The power political element in his policy is frankly acknowledged by Sachs: 'the problem of reform is mostly political rather than social or even economic'.[28] The task is to change an entire social/institutional order and power and conflict will be absolutely central to the process.

This centrality of western power has provoked sharp debate amongst ST supporters over the precise articulation of negative and positive incentives, a debate largely centred on differing appreciations of the motivational factors governing the behaviour of East European governments. Some say the only effective incentives are negative, exclusionary ones.[29] Sachs himself disagrees, insisting that once a government has publicly committed itself to ST and launched the programme, it will have the will to follow through but inadequate means. At this point the West must provide large funds to help the government with economic and political crisis management. ST thus requires that western governments will provide grants for target states' foreign exchange reserves, money for social security payments, 'Cancellation of most of the debt owed to Western governments and banks', long-term development finance for which 'Grant aid is again needed.' So too is free movement of labour westwards. They must also throw open their markets to the East. Failure by western governments to deliver at this point, says Sachs, will lead to 'criminality, political extremism, civil unrest, hyperinflation, capital flight, and, in the worst cases, civil war'.[30] Thus for Sachs, once ST is launched in a target country, the West quickly has effective power over the fate of the target state's population.

Yet there is one large gap in ST in this area. Lengthy discussion of the right mix of carrots and sticks to ensure compliance by eastern governments sits beside an almost complete silence on the carrots and sticks to make western governments' behaviour also comply.

There are two possible explanations for this silence. One would be that the end product of ST in the East would bring such large economic gain for western interests that no sticks are needed to ensure the West offers generous assistance. Yet Sachs does not argue this: he remains silent on the direct economic benefits to the West of his policy. Instead he has suggested that western governments can be driven more by political ideals even when they entail some economic cost. Thus in 1990 he suggested that EC governments would end the Common Agricultural Policy because of the dream of a united Europe: 'The EU will just have to accept that free trade in Polish hams is a price to be paid for living in a united and democratic Europe.' And he explains why the German government in particular will be motivated to transfer very large sums to Eastern Europe: it will be because of America's cancellation of FRG debt in 1953, an act which laid the basis for Germany's 'spectacular economic recovery'.[31] But we should probably not take these remarks at face value. Sachs is more plausibly implying here that the EU and Germany will respond in the ways required by his policy because America will effectively exert the required pressure upon them to do so. In other words, for Sachs, the USA will play the role assigned to it in hegemonic stability theory: in its own hegemonic interests, it will force the West European states to be true to their own long-term interest in achieving a globalised world economy.

As far as economic operators are concerned, the same pattern emerges: the need for rather brutal coercion of state enterprise managements and employees in the East while we can expect large flows of money and technology into the target economy from western TNCs once the right kind of institutional framework is in place. The motivational factors in the behaviour of western TNCs are left unexplored.

4) The Interlocking Wheels of the National Policy Cycle

ST has been popularised by Sachs, the IMF and others as the three '-isations', now familiar to every schoolchild in Eastern Europe: liberalisation, stabilisation, privatisation. More recently a fourth, final step has been added: institutionalisation. But this is to express ST as a linear set of steps by a single actor – the target state's government. If we are to recast the policy as a model of interaction of actors with each other and with their environment we get the following sequence:

1)   The liberalising/stabilising shock.
2)   The international shock.
3)   Privatisation and FDI.
4)   Trade-led growth.
5)   Political/institutional consolidation and growth.

We will examine each of these interlocking wheels in turn.

1) The domestic liberalising/stabilising shock

The domestic shock of ST is a double one: first, the sudden liberalisation of prices and slashing of state subsidies, coupled with the imposition of wage controls and second, a very tight monetary and credit squeeze.

Sachs follows neo-classical orthodoxy in viewing the sudden imposition of decontrolled prices, combined with wage controls, as being a creative process to provide a more allocatively efficient distribution of production factors than was provided by Communism. Thus the price liberalisation shock is a stimulant to growth, not a depressant. The credit squeeze and tight monetary policy does have a depressant effect, but it is designed above all to ensure that enterprises are forced to restructure by laying off workers rather than borrowing their way out of difficulties.

An interesting feature of the policy cycle is the fact that the liberalisation/stabilisation shock is to occur before the development of either a domestic group of money-capitalists – people who have accumulated large quantities of money to be used as capital – or a domestic system of financial markets. Thus state enterprises will not be able to respond to the shock by combining 'downsizing' of the work force with borrowing for investment in new plant. All their restructuring efforts will therefore be concentrated upon one production factor: labour and its price.

Although Sachs says little about this there is thus a central social dimension to the liberalisation shock: a sudden, dramatic weakening of the social power of the industrial working class: the end of state subsidies while wages are controlled involves a large fall in living standards; price decontrol deepens this fall and the start of unemployment consolidates the shift in the entire balance of social power.

2) The shock international integration of the target state

Simultaneous with the domestic shock, there should be the double action to tie the economy into the global economy through two steps: the radical liberalisation of trade and the making of the currency convertible. The key justification of the trade liberalisation is to ensure competition from western companies in domestic product markets to prevent local oligopolies from raising their prices excessively. Sachs calls this his 'greatest conceptual breakthrough'.[32] Trade liberalisation involves ending quotas and having very low tariffs: a free trade regime. And by making the currency convertible for trade purposes the link between local enterprises and the world economy will be consolidated.

These changes would go hand in hand with the fragmentation of the Comecon region, which would have a temporary depressive effect but would rapidly be overcome as western Europe opened its markets and the IFIs helped to stabilise the local currencies.

3) Privatisation, FDI and restructuring

An absolutely basic component of ST is the transfer of state enterprises into private hands. Yet curiously enough, this is the issue on which Sachs has been most vague. Of only one thing is he convinced: that handing enterprises over to the people who work in them as managers or workers would be absolutely wrong. But even on this issue he changes his mind as to why it would be wrong. In his book on Poland he says at one point that handing ownership over to managers and workers would be 'stealing'.[33] At other times he has said that handing ownership to the workers 'puts workers at excessive risk', presumably because they would bear full responsibility for the enterprise.[34] At other times, he says it would put the enterprise at risk from the workers because they would pay themselves too much instead of investing.[35] His clinching argument, however, is that worker-owned companies would not be trusted by capital markets. But this only begs the question as to the form of the banking system in the target country.

In his 1990 article, 'What is to be Done?', Sachs urged that 'the firms should be sold for cash', through auctions,[36] with a board of western financial advisers and legal experts checking on the deals. He seemed unaware of the ethical difficulties with this proposal: that those in the target state with the cash to buy a steel mill would be very few in number and without question former or current crooks at the head of Mafia pyramids.

He later dropped this idea on the grounds that it would be too slow a process. And instead of solving the problem of where the money-capital would come from to buy the enterprises, he wrapped the process up in a mystery: 10–20 per cent of the shares would go to the workers, 'another fraction' of ownership rights would go to households. They would not get the enterprise shares but would get unit trusts in 'investment funds'. These private 'investment Funds in turn would own the shares of the industrial enterprises', appoint the directors and monitor performance.[37] There would be ten to twenty such Funds. He assures us that criticism on the lines that foreigners would end up running the Funds and their enterprises is false, but he does not explain how or why it is false. Nor does he address the fact that ST requires privatisation in the midst of recession and that therefore the assets will go at very low prices.

Another major issue is whether the state enterprises should be restructured via a state industrial policy before they are privatised or whether they should be sold to the private sector first and restructured by the new private owner. Sachs tackles this by saying that the target state will lack the expertise to do it, while his nebulous investment funds will have such expertise. This will be the case presumably because the investment funds will be private and only the salaried employees of the private sector possess what it takes.

4) Trade-led growth

As with IMF Structural Adjustment Programmes, the target economy's economic recovery is designed to develop above all through trade-led growth, rather than a strong domestic recovery. A large flow of imports will be needed to retool industries and dynamic export growth will follow.

5) Political/institutional consolidation

It has been widely understood and accepted by the supporters of ST that the consolidation of a democratic regime brings up the rear of the ST process as its final outcome. The other side of this coin is that during the process of ST the rule is political crisis management by the executive, blunting and blocking popular pressures for a halt to or reversal of ST.

II A Balance Sheet of Shock Therapy in Practice

Sachs has rightly claimed that most governments in post-Communist Eastern Europe have to some degree tried to lock themselves into the hub-and-spokes structures of ST and have tried to combine the demands of the International Financial Institutions and the EC/EU with the often conflicting domestic pressures upon them. Some governments have drifted, without any coherent policy, and only a very few, like the Romanian government, have consciously sought a different road to a different form of capitalism.

We will argue five main charges against the policy:

1) That its macro instruments of regional fragmentation and domestic shock change have been immensely costly in the short and medium term.
2) ST's free trade-led policy for economic revival was largely misconceived.
3) Its micro policies for sustained economic revival have also tended to weaken rather than strengthen longer-term revival.
4) The practice of ST on the part of western actors has sharply diverged from the theory in that they have damaged the East European states.
5) In terms of its own criteria of success ST has been a failure.

We will also suggest that the elements of an alternative strategy contained in the positions of both the Gorbachev government in 1990 and the French proposals at that time would have been far less costly and would have offered far better prospects for the future: keeping the Comecon region united in its own reform project, developing new trade and payment arrangements for that region, and removing Cold War trade barriers to East–West trade, while letting each government move forward experimentally at its own pace. The western powers had the capacity to structure such an alternative, but the dominant western powers had no interest in pursuing it.

1) The Double Depressive Shock

The implementation of ST has brought a savage double depressive shock to
the entire region. Part of this has been the result of the ST model's insistence on breaking up the Comecon area, rather than maintaining regional
trade and production linkages through a customs union and new payment
arrangements. And part of the shock has come from the implementation of
the first elements of the ST Domestic Policy Cycle.

Every serious commentator on the region knows about these effects.
When Sachs first published his ST programme in January 1990 in the
Economist, that magazine had already explained to its readers what the projected effect of ST would be in Poland: it said that officially the government
forecast 400,000 jobless, but unofficially 'economists expect up to 3 million'.[38] The actual outcome was, in fact, in many respects worse, as Table 9.1
illustrates. In Russia, after six months of ST in 1992, real incomes were
reduced to 40 per cent of their 1991 levels and production was plummeting.

The OECD's study of the depression pinpoints four causal factors, all
deriving from ST. It says that the 'stabilisation' aspect, especially the credit
squeeze via credit ceilings, 'was identified as the important element contributing to the recession, especially at the beginning of the reform
process'.[39] It says the fragmentation of the Comecon region's trade had a
disastrous impact on industrial output: 'According to some calculations,
this volume effect alone can explain most of the fall in output in Hungary
and the former CSFR and about one third of the decline in Poland.'[40] It also
stressed that key institutional vacuums, as pointed out by critics of ST, such
as the absence of a financial system, meant that 'all countries suffered from
an inadequate supply-side response', in other words a downward spiral into
protracted depression.

Sachs has responded by first of all attempting to distance himself and his
policies from the fragmentation of the Comecon region and then blaming
the slump on that fragmentation. He has claimed that 'the decline in industrial production in 1991, and to some extent in 1990, was the result of the
collapse of trade with the former Soviet Union, not the result of economic
reforms in Poland'.[41] But he actively championed that collapse in favour of
a hub-and-spoke linkage with the EC. He must have been fully aware also
that the IMF was resolutely opposed to preventing such a collapse through
a payments union for the region. And he must surely also have been aware
of the fact that his fragmentation policy would be consolidated through
regional bloc arrangements for cutting East Central Europe off from production linkages with the USSR. As in the case of NAFTA, the EC would
consolidate this bloc through rules of origin arrangements, severing their
production linkages with countries to the East. The Association Agreements
between the EC and the East Central European countries, which Sachs has

commended, devote between one fifth and one quarter of their entire text to this topic.[42]

Sachs's second line of defence has been to claim that Communism was to blame for the slump.[43] He says that there were crises in a number of these economies before ST started. This is true. But the OECD study's charge is that ST made a bad situation catastrophic: Gomulka, a defender of the IMF, calculates that the average fall of GDP during what he calls the contraction phase of the transition was about 40 per cent.[44] This figure signals a devastating reality in human suffering for most people in the region. Even in 1998 only one country in the entire region had returned to its 1989 level of GDP per capital. Yet for Sachs, such issues are a detail not worthy of serious analysis.

The *Economist* tried to justify Sachs's view in the case of Russia by making the bold claim that Communism caused too much supply for demand levels and too much demand for supply levels! 'The transition from the rationing of central planning to the allocation of goods by the market was bound to require such a sharp fall in real wages: queues, in effect, reflect excess demand caused by prices that are too low in relation to wages.'[45] And having explained that goods had been too much in demand, it went on to explain that goods had also been too much in supply: not enough people wanted them! The government, it said, should not provide credits to enterprises, because to do so 'will buoy the production of unwanted goods'.[46]

Table 9.1   Indicators of Slump

Real GDP

	1989	1990	1991	1992	1993	1994
Poland	0.2	−11.6	−7.2	1.0	4	5
Hungary	−0.2	−4.3	−10.2	−5.0	−2	1
CSFR	4.5	−0.4	−15.9	−0.5		
Czech Rep.				−7	0	3
Slovakia				−7	−4	1

Industrial production

	1989	1990	1991	1992	1993	1994
Poland	−0.5	−24.2	−11.9	3.9	5.6	N/A
Hungary	−1.0	−9.2	−21.5	−9.7	4	N/A
CSFR	0.7	−3.5	−24.7	−10.4		
Czech Rep.				−10.6	−5.3	0
Slovakia				−14	−10.6	−4

Sources: H. Schmieding, 'From Plan to Market', *Weltwirtschaftliches Archiv.* no. 2 (1993); European Bank for Reconstruction and Development, *Transition Report* (1994).

There is one argument that some, like Gomulka, have sought to mount for the view that the ST slump simply revealed the waste under Communism. This argument begins by saying that by measuring the inputs and outputs of some East European enterprises at world prices, they were actually subtracting value from inputs. So the introduction of world prices would drive these sectors to the wall: hence the ST slump, though triggered by price liberalisation, was caused by the economic irrationality of Communism.

For this to have been the cause of the slump, the falls in production would have occurred in the value-subtracting sectors. Yet the production falls were across the board and in the Hungarian case we find that sectors identified by Hare and Hughes as the most efficient were in many cases hit harder than the big value subtractors, as Table 9.2 indicates.[47] Indeed, Hare and Hughes identified alcoholic beverages as one of the biggest value subtractors, yet it was the only sector to continue to grow during the slump!

Table 9.2   The Relationship Between Falls in Output and Industrial Competitiveness in Hungary, 1987–1991 (1987 = 100)

Industry	DRC ranking[1]	Competitive ranking[2]	Percentage output fall[3]
Fur, shoes	1st	2nd	50.8
Clothing	5th	5th	29.9
Precision instruments	12th	3rd	44.2
Electrical engineering	15th	8th	42.3
Rubber	23rd	12th	39.2
Building materials	6th	14th	36.4
Food industry	2nd last	2nd last	11.9
All industries	33	33	29.4

Notes:
1) DRC = Domestic Resource Costs.
2) Competitiveness ranking as measured by value added at world prices less labour costs and depreciation as a percentage of world price by industry.
3) The percentage fall in output in 1991 from 1987 levels.
Sources: J.C. Brada, I. Singh and A. Torok, 'Firms Afloat and Firms Adrift: Hungarian Industry and the Economic Transition', *Eastern European Economics*, (January–February, 1994), and G. Hughes and P. Hare, 'Competitiveness and Industrial Restructuring in Czechoslovakia, Hungary and Poland', *Commission of the European Communities: European Economy*, special edition, no. 2 (1991).

In any case, this argument is theoretically muddled. As Schmieding has pointed out,[48] price liberalisation is about altering relative prices and thus falls in some sectors would be compensated by rises in others whose products would at the same time leap upwards in relative value. And the overall value of output should remain the same or nearly the same as before, on one condition: that factor prices really did move flexibly in line with relative prices on the world market. The shift to world-relative prices would then quickly move from a no-change output level[49] to a surge of growth as the supposedly more allocatively efficient distribution of factors in the world market was reflected in a redistribution of factors in the economy.

Some IMF economists seized on the issue of factor price flexibility in 1992, claiming that the depression was caused by the failure to introduce world prices fully for labour. They thus said wages had not sunk low enough and fast enough. In short, the depression was caused not by ST but by the failure to implement it fully on the wages front.

Sachs could hardly adopt this argument since it would imply that ST has not been tried, particularly as wages have picked up a bit in most countries since 1992. But in any case, it is unsustainable. Real wages in Poland fell 33.6 per cent from the beginning of 1990 to the end of 1992. In Czechoslovakia in the same period they fell 21.5 per cent and in Hungary by 14 per cent. In all cases the falls were heaviest in the crucial first phase of the depression. The *Economist* noted that after six months of ST in Russia, real wages had dropped to only 40 per cent of their average for 1991.[50] By any standards these figures show extraordinary downward flexibility. As Schmieding comments, 'In a trivial sense, all economic crises can be related to a downward rigidity of real wages in a neoclassical framework. The negative impact of all possible disturbances on the profitability of production could always be compensated by a further decline in the real wage.'[51]

At the domestic level these slumps were, in fact, the direct consequence of two aspects of the ST shock: the collapse of effective demand – emphasised strongly by Kornai – and the credit crunch to impose a hard budget constraint upon enterprises. This credit crunch was exacerbated by the absence of any viable co-ordinating mechanism for redeploying factors of production: the old planning mechanism was destroyed and a capitalist mechanism – viable financial markets and a financial system – did not exist.

What concerns us here is not the continuing debate as to the relative weight of the two factors, but simply the undeniable fact that the depression was a core feature of the entire ST programme. ST supporters have advanced a host of other arguments to justify the depression effect of the model. They have claimed that Communist industrial goods were worthless; that there was a need for a growth in services; that the goods were no longer 'necessary'.

The 'worthless' argument has been nicely expressed by Garton Ash with his remark that returning the region to capitalism is like transforming a fish soup back into the aquarium from which it was made.[52] But this argument seems to be based more on anti-Communism than hard evidence. What the evidence shows is that when the EC lowered its Cold War barriers in 1990–91 to imports from the Visegrad countries, the latter's exports surged as follows: taking 1989 as 100, Poland's exports to the EC rose to 208.2 in current US dollars in 1992, Czechoslovakia's jumped to 250, and Hungary's to 178.6. These gains were not confined to traditional export sectors (which were in any case more diversified than typical middle-income country exports), but applied right across the board. As Richard Portes says: 'The explosive growth of Central and East European exports to the West in 1990–92 does conclusively refute those who claimed that these countries couldn't compete – that quality was unacceptable, marketing was poor and so on.'[53]

The argument that the service sector was underdeveloped is used by Sachs to suggest that a drastic reduction in industrial output was necessary. But this neither explains the slump in industrial output – the industrial slump was not caused by workers flooding into new service industries! – nor does it justify it: the service sector can grow without causing or requiring an output decline in industry.

The key justification is in fact one that is usually not stated bluntly and publicly: namely that there was no need for this industrial output in the East since Western Europe's economy was already saturated with overproduction in one sector after another. In other words, East European industry stood in the same relation towards Western Europe as the European airbus industry stands in relation to Boeing: it is worse than unnecessary: it is a competitive nuisance.

The Human Costs of the Slump

The human costs of the ST drive for rapid decollectivisation are probably not yet on a par with those of the original postwar collectivisation of Eastern Europe, if the political repression of the late 1940s is taken into account; and, of course, any comparisons with the USSR in the 1930s would be absurd. Nevertheless, the price paid for ST in human terms has been colossal.

According to UNICEF, the excess mortality in Russia, Ukraine, Bulgaria, Hungary and Poland between 1989 and 1993 was 800,000.[54] This figure includes excess deaths in the USSR before the start of ST in January 1992. Michael Ellman gives the figure for excess deaths in Russia alone in that year as 82,000 and says there were 'substantially more' such deaths in 1993.[55] The crude death rate in Russia rose from 11.4 in 1991 to 14.4 in 1993 and 16.2 in the first quarter of 1994.[56]

UNICEF explains that the transition has generated the health crisis in three ways: by increasing the levels of stress-related heart and circulatory diseases – these varied from 32–80 per cent in accounting for the rise in deaths in the region as a whole; by producing dietary deficiencies, and by causing sociopsychological tensions which have sharply increased murder and suicide rates. It comments that the East European health crisis 'has no historical precedents'.[57]

In Russia the number of murders rose by 42 per cent in 1992 and a further 27 per cent in 1993.[58] Between 1989 and 1991 homicides in Hungary increased by 43 per cent. In 1993 the suicide rate had increased from its 1989 level by 133 per cent in Poland, by 150 per cent in Romania and by 153 per cent in Russia.[59]

The problem of poverty and malnutrition has become very serious in many countries. A study in Russia by Goskomstat and the World Bank defined the poverty line as the income needed to maintain food consumption sufficient to maintain a normal body weight at an average level of activity – an austere definition by western standards. The study showed that in 1992 37 per cent of the Russian population fell below this line, while the figure for children under fifteen was a horrifying 46–47 per cent. A study carried out by CARE and the US Centre for Disease Control in 1992 found that on average Russian pensions were below what the World Bank estimated to be the minimal nutritional support level for a person living alone.[60] Using UNICEF's definition of mild malnutrition (less than 2,300 calories) the percentage of Poland's population suffering such malnutrition was negligible in 1989 but had reached 17.9 per cent in 1992.

If we define the poverty line as 40 per cent of the average wage in 1989 and the extreme poverty line as 24 per cent of the 1989 average wage, then by 1992 those in extreme poverty amounted to between 15 per cent and 26 per cent in Poland, Bulgaria, Romania, Russia, Ukraine and Albania; those in poverty were an extra 28 to 38 per cent. Life-threatening diseases have increased sharply in Russia. Typhoid and paratyphoid increased 13 per cent in 1992 and 66 per cent in 1993; diphtheria increased 109 per cent in 1992 and 290 per cent the following year. Deaths from tuberculosis increased 15 per cent in 1992.[61]

2) The Failure of the Shock Therapy Trade Regime

What Sachs called his 'conceptual breakthrough' of throwing target economies open to an almost completely free trade regime was justified in the first place to address the problem of oligopolies in the East responding to price liberalisation by raising prices while reducing output. But it was also designed to prepare the way for trade-led recovery. These goals neatly dovetailed with the ultimate goal of creating open door economies in the region for trade and for FDI. As it turned out, state enterprises were not the main culprits in raising prices. The most aggressive price increases were in the service sector and were carried out by private enterprises.[62]

But in any case the view that the Visegrad economies were heavily monopolised seems to be false. There was not, of course, perfect competition, but they were roughly as monopolised as the free market in the USA, according to the findings of Alice Amsden and her colleagues. Even Czechoslovakia, particularly singled out as monopolised, has had little more concentration than the USA. Thus in 1990 the largest 100 Czechoslovak companies accounted for 26 per cent of industrial employment while in the US the figure was 23.8 per cent.[63] In Poland, the degree of concentration was on a par with the USA. And given the fact that small economies, far more trade-dependent than the USA, could be expected to have higher levels of concentration in key sectors, Amsden's view is that the real problem for much of industry in the region was too much fragmentation, rather than too little.

Amsden et al. take sectors where East Central European economies have had growth potential and demonstrates the overfragmentation problems. In detergents, 80 per cent of the market is controlled by two companies in the UK and by three in Germany. But in Poland there were seven, none big enough for scale efficiency. In crude steel output Czechoslovakia ranked fourteenth and Poland seventeenth in the world, yet the biggest Czechoslovak steel producer (VSZ Košice) ranked only thirtieth and the biggest Polish enterprise (Huta Katowice) ranked only thirty-second in size. UNIDO reported in 1991 that the steel industries of the region generally faced the problem of undersized plants. The same fragmentation problem has existed in machine tools and in pulp and paper.[64]

Sachs is well aware of this, saying that 'the giant firms in Poland are small players in the European market'.[65] There are also lots of alternative ways of preventing monopoly price rises without throwing open the door entirely to imports – most obviously through regulatory bodies. But he ignores such possibilities.

The trade regimes established in 1990–91 in the Visegrad region are presented by Sachs as being on the West European model. But they were very different: quotas were abolished, other Non-Tariff Barriers were not established, anti-dumping instruments and safeguard instruments were not created, export promotion instruments were not set in place. Instead a one-club trade regime consisting of very low tariffs was introduced.[66]

The result was a predictable export bonanza into the region by West European companies which, as Giles Merritt of the Philip Morris Institute warned in 1991, 'could do irreparable harm'.[67] The assault on domestic producers was especially devastating in the consumer goods sectors. Between 1989 and 1991 consumer goods imports into Hungary nearly doubled and in Poland, in the first eight months of 1991 alone, they rose from 18.2 per cent to 31.6 per cent of total imports. The trade figures of the target countries do not necessarily accurately reflect events. Thus while Czechoslovak statistics show a mere 2 per cent growth in imports from France in 1991, the French figures show a rise of 180 per cent. During the 1990s, the traditional EU deficit in trade with the region turned into a surplus. Systematic studies have not been published yet on the extent to which these western exports involved the dumping of products in the East. But there is ample anecdotal evidence of this.[68]

The overall value of imports to Visegrad countries rose in the first half of 1993 by 7 per cent as compared with the corresponding period in 1992. This was the highest import surge since the mid-1980s. Imports to Hungary increased by 6 per cent, to the Czech and Slovak Republics by 18-22 per cent and to Poland by 27 per cent.

This export bonanza was the result of more than market forces. It was strongly subsidised by western governments through export credits and credit guarantees to their own exporting firms. These supports were presented as Aid for the target countries of the export drive. Indeed, according to Sachs virtually all western Aid to Russia has been in such export subsidies. They enable exporters to make risk-free breakthroughs into target markets while leaving the country concerned burdened with extra debt. An important dimension of this effort has been attempts by West European states to seize the markets in the Former Soviet Union previously supplied by East Central Europe. Anthony Solomon, former President of the New York Federal Reserve, calculated that western export credits were enabling about $4 billion of East Central European export trade to the USSR region to be diverted to western suppliers.[69]

A particularly damaging dimension of these policies for Poland and Hungary has been their impact on agriculture. At a time when the IFIs were demanding an end to agricultural subsidies in the Visegrad countries, the break-up of collective farms and very large wage reductions bringing falling food demand, the full force of heavily subsidised EU agricultural exports was dumped in the Visegrad markets. The EU's so-called humanitarian food aid programme for Poland in 1989–90 had prepared the way by destabilising demand conditions for peasant suppliers. The result has been that the most important private business group in the region, when Communism ended, the Polish peasantry, has become the most powerful social group in the country opposed to ST and to the EU.

Meanwhile, as far as eastern target states were concerned, efforts on their part to engage in direct export promotion were banned by the World Bank.[70] By 1991 the Visegrad governments were under mounting pressure to reverse their open door policy, and in general, tariffs and import surcharges were imposed. In Poland President Lech Walesa publicly accused westerners of trying to ruin Polish industry.[71]

Granting Market Access to the EU

The notion of trade-led revival of course meant an export surge to the EU. The IMF shock depression combined with currency devaluation was designed, as in Latin American Structural Adjustment Programmes, to turn the target states towards trade-led recoveries. Sachs's model therefore laid cardinal importance on the swift dismantling of the powerful trade barriers blocking eastern exports to the EU. The issue of EU market access was incorporated into negotiations on so-called Europe Agreements with the East Central European and Baltic states and on Partnership and Co-operation Agreements with the other, former Soviet Republics. The basic exchange involved the supposed granting of access to the EU's goods markets in exchange for opening both goods markets and fixed asset markets in the country concerned to West European companies.

The results of the negotiations with the Visegrad countries were strongly asymmetrical in the EU's favour,[72] although the EU presented them as asymmetrical in the target states' favour, by focusing only on tariffs rather than NTBs. While they reduced tariffs on most items the EU did not significantly reduce its Non-Tariff Barriers (NTBs) on the goods that mattered to the Visegrad economies. At the same time, the Visegrad economies were required to get rid of their NTBs by the GATT and the OECD. The EU built into the Agreements a battery of protection instruments – notably anti-dumping and safeguard instruments which did not conform to GATT rules,[73] while the Visegrad economies largely lacked such instruments. At the same time, the EU preserved its right to use the Cold War protection instruments against State Trading Countries against the Associated states – a clause which does not require comparison of domestic and export prices, and gives protectionist measures a free hand.

Given the slump, the credit crunch and investment collapse in the Visegrad countries, their export effort would have to be concentrated in their traditional export sectors, with low capital-output ratios. To appreciate how asymmetrical the Europe Agreements were, we must therefore focus on the treatment of those sectors.

Without exception they faced severe protectionist barriers from the EU under the Europe Agreements. The CAP was not modified significantly and the bulk of agricultural exports from Poland and Hungary – grain, livestock and dairy products – was in core CAP sectors. Chemicals continued to be subject to State Trading Country anti-dumping measures; textiles and apparel were subject to a form of managed trade which would be very damaging to the Visegrad textile industry, steel faced restrictive price agreements and anti-dumping instruments, and other sectors like Polish cars were subject to so-called Voluntary Export Restraints (i.e. quotas).

Table 9.3   Sectors of Export Strength in Early 1990s

Sector	Country with Export Strength
1. Food/agriculture	Poland, Hungary
2. Textiles/clothing	Poland, Hungary, CSFR
3. Iron and steel	Poland, Hungary, CSFR
4. Chemicals	Hungary
5. Coal	Poland
6. Fuel	CSFR

Source: C. Mastropasqua and V. Rolli, 'Industrial Countries' Protectionism with Respect to Eastern Europe: The Impact of the Association Agreements Concluded with the EC on the Exports of Poland, Czechoslovakia and Hungary', *The World Economy*, 17:2 (1994).

The trade aspects of the Europe Agreements came into force on an interim basis in March 1992. By the second half of the year, East Central European exports to the EU were in decline and during 1993 these exports slumped in an alarming way. In the first half of 1993 the combined value of exports from all the East Central and East European countries fell by 13 per cent in dollar terms as compared with the first half of 1992. The decline affected exports to the West, to transitional economies and to LDCs. This reversed the earlier pattern of a counter-balancing of declines to the CMEA area with rises to the EU.[74] The overall result was a trade deficit of some $7.2 billion in the first half of 1993, compared with a deficit of $1.5 billion in the same period in 1992.

Although the Czech Republic's trade deficit worsened as its imports grew by 21 per cent, its exports grew by 13 per cent. By contrast Polish exports fell by 7 per cent and Hungarian exports fell by over 23 per cent. The fall in Hungarian exports was especially strong in industrial consumer goods (down 30 per cent), in foodstuffs (down 17 per cent) and in agricultural products (down 59 per cent).[75] The dollar value of exports of clothing, textiles and footwear declined by 48 per cent in Hungary. In iron and steel products, Hungarian exports declined by 20 per cent. Thus traditional export sectors were losing their position but new manufacturing exports have not emerged: among the few exceptions was car production in Poland. The UN Economic Commission for Europe concluded: 'Until new investments are made on a large scale, prospects for sustainable export growth are slim.'[76]

These very bad trade results for Poland and Hungary in the first half of 1993 are no doubt partly explained by the EU recession and especially that in Germany, where imports from Eastern Europe as a whole went down by 10 per cent in the first half of 1993. But the western recession cannot be the entire answer, because Polish exports had already dropped substantially in 1992, when the German economy was not yet in recession.

The UN *ECE Bulletin* stressed that in 1992 and 1993 EU importing countries resorted more frequently to the use of anti-dumping and safeguard actions against ECE imports. During 1992, France, Germany and Italy imposed new quotas on steel imports from the region and the EU itself imposed anti-dumping duties on Visegrad steel products.[77] Following an outbreak of foot and mouth disease in Italy allegedly deriving from illegal Croatian cattle imports, the EU banned all cattle imports from the entire East Central European region (some of whose countries have not had incidents of the disease since at least the early 1970s). This led to threats of retaliatory measures until the ban was dropped. Hungary's main meat export to the EU – pork – was totally banned on an indefinite basis following an incident of swine fever.

It should, in this context, be stressed just how much was at stake for the EU in its trade relations with ECE. Even in the most sensitive sectors, a total liberalisation of imports would have produced a decline in the EU sector's output of only 2 to 4 per cent (agriculture and apparel). The most highly protectionist sectors in the EC were therefore not mortally threatened.

A final aspect of the EU's market access policy has been very important: the role of its rules of origin clauses in the Europe Agreements, which impose the hub-and-spoke pattern on economic linkages between economic operators in the target states and the EC/EU. They do so by blocking the re-export to the EC of products partly produced outside the target state (whether in a neighbouring Visegrad state or in the FSU). For most industrial products (e.g. those subject to Annex II in the EC-CSFR Agreement), the Europe Agreement protocols give a rule in the form of a threshold expressed in terms of value-added to the products in the Associated country: imported inputs should not represent more than 40 or 50 per cent of the value of the production. Thus the Agreements impose a local content requirement of 60 per cent. Although this threshold is the main form of rule, two other sets of definitions are also applied to some products:

a) products originating in an Associated country are those wholly obtained in that country.

b) products originating in an Associated country can be those 'obtained in the Associated country in the manufacture of which products (not wholly obtained in the country and not obtained in the EU) are used', provided that the said products have undergone 'sufficient working or processing'. The basic definition of 'sufficient working' for this purpose is a change in customs headings at the four-digit level of the Harmonised System, differing from that in which all the non–originating materials are classified. These kinds of arrangements embrace these economies in a condition of trade dependency towards the EU, locking the development of the division of labour in the target state into EU requirements.

The tragic result of these politico-economic interactions has been that the domestic depressive shocks policed by the IMF and designed to lay the basis for an export-led revival have largely led these countries up a blind alley, prolonging the depression. For the origins of the revival, insofar as it has come, have been led not by foreign trade but by domestic consumption.[78] *Yet the policies of the IFIs have been overwhelmingly directed at reducing domestic demand pressures, stamping out inflation, lowering wages and reducing government deficits through spending cuts.*

Fiscal Crisis and IMF Policy

The ST slump plunged most governments in the region into a deep fiscal crisis. This is a normal by-product of slump, though made far worse by the fact that ST did not prioritise a transformation of tax systems and a strengthening of administrative apparatuses. Thus a fall in industrial production which approaches 50 per cent for the region as a whole, during the slump in conditions where in most countries the tax system was almost exclusively focused on the turnover of industrial enterprises, was bound to create a severe fiscal crisis. Since, again, ST downgraded the importance of building a capitalist financial system, governments could not fund their deficits by borrowing on domestic bond markets. Thus deficit spending would directly fuel inflation.

As with the slump, Sachs tries to avoid responsibility for these fiscal crises: he says there was 'a nearly generalised fiscal catastrophe in the region' before ST with 'huge budget deficits'.[79] In fact the Czechoslovak government had a slight surplus in 1990 and went into deficit only in the first two years of ST. The Hungarian budget followed the same pattern from a slight surplus in 1990 to deficits in the following years. Poland did have a serious state budget deficit in 1989, of −6.1 per cent, but the deficit shot up higher than ever to 7 per cent in 1991 and 6.8 per cent in 1992 as a result of ST. Fiscal information for Russia is not available before 1992, but Gaidar's first year of ST left the budget deficit at 18 per cent of GDP. And these ST deficits occurred despite the slashing of state price subsidies.

The ST fiscal crisis presents a choice: either to opt for inflationary funding of the deficit, or to gain western funds to plug the hole in the deficit, or to massively cut back on government spending. The IMF has strenuously pressurised governments to take the last course. It has justified this by the argument that the overriding priority of policy is the need

to combat inflation. This has been the policy of the IMF during the historically almost unprecedented slump that has devastated the lives of
hundreds of millions of people during the last five years. Insofar as the
policy has been followed by target governments it has deepened the
slump and caused long-term damage to the social and administrative as
well as economic infrastructure of the region.

There has, however, been one major exception to this rule, an exception
which goes far to explain the country's beginnings of a return to some
growth: that exception is Poland. Here alone has the IMF supported really
major western financial support, in the form of a cancellation of half of
Poland's debt to both public and private creditors. This has transformed the
financial position of the government and has also created the basis for
stronger confidence in the future on the part of private capital. (Hungary
has had heavier per capita debts and has not defaulted, unlike Poland,
Bulgaria and Russia; yet it has not even gained debt relief, much less forgiveness.)[80] But even in Poland, recovery has still been undermined by the
IMF's drive in the early 1990s to make the fight against inflation through
government spending cuts the centrepiece of policy. Its catchphrase has
been that there is no trade-off between financial stabilisation and growth.
But in an Eastern Europe whose recovery has had to be domestic-con-
sumption-led the causality has flowed in a diametrically opposite direction
from the IMF's policy: without growth there could be no financial stabilisation. IMF policy for financial stabilisation tended to deepen recession and
thus further destabilised finances.

Gomulka has tried to explain this slump-deepening policy by the fact
that the IMF's mission is supposedly the world-wide fight against inflation.[81]
In other words, economic recovery in the region is not part of the IMF's job.
This does not explain why the IMF was opposed to plugging deficits by
Polish-style debt reduction or the recent Mexican-style transfer of macroeconomic support funds. Gomulka, very much an IMF insider on its East
European operations, explains the IMF's thinking on this. He is worth quot-
ing at length: 'The impact of foreign assistance can be substantial, even
vital, only on a few occasions, especially when it is in the form of grants and
debt reductions. However, large grants, if not linked to performance, reduce
the financial discipline of local economic agents, and may have an impact
on transition economies similar to that of a soft budget constraint on state
enterprises . . . Most of these economies are already heavily indebted, and
this gives them little room for contracting new debt. A far more important
foreign impact may come from the inflow of Western private investment and
know-how. However, internal reform efforts rather than external financial
assistance seem needed for this inflow to take place.'[82]

Gomulka, though slightly evasive, does acknowledge that debt reductions
and grants can make a vital impact. But his basic point belies his own earlier

suggestion that the IMF was simply fixated on inflation: helping governments ride the slump would not put sufficient pressure on them to push through to the end the institutional engineering to gain FDI, and this FDI would be the real lever of recovery.

The meaning of this is clear: the IMF was using the slump as an instrument for rapid social engineering at a micro level to create the desired goal of a state open to FDI. The IMF's domestic neo-liberal agenda could have been displaced debt cancellation or macroeconomic grants. Sachs himself has nicely summarised the resulting policy in the case of Russia: 'the sums [transferred from western public bodies] have been derisory . . . Virtually all western "aid" has come in the form of export credits to Russian enterprises, with short periods of repayment, rather than in the form of grants and long-term loans to the Russian budget . . . Overall support from western governments for the Russian budget, vitally needed for stabilisation, has been essentially nil . . . In 1994, there was essentially a complete collapse [of] . . . international assistance from governments on behalf of Russian reform'.[83]

Sachs has not supported this policy. His ST model presupposes massive debt cancellations and grants for macroeconomic assistance as well as for more political purposes. He predicts the catastrophic consequences in many parts of the region from western failure to deliver this aspect of the policy, even warning of civil war. Yet he does not acknowledge the obvious corollary: that his ST model was built on sand as regards his assumptions about the driving forces within western governments and IFIs. His ex post attempts to shift blame on to people like Gomulka, for thinking like 'bureaucrats' pre-occupied by waste, cannot absolve him of 'bureaucratic' intellectual errors in not grasping the political drives governing the western powers and the IFIs they control.

3) Shock Therapy's Micro-Policies for Restructuring

At the level of micro-economic restructuring, the ST model and the IFIs have shared a common approach. The restructuring should not be carried out by government industrial policies. It should be left to 'market signals' and 'market forces' and especially to western market forces entering through FDI. The task of target governments is simply to depress wages, to impose hard-budget constraints upon state enterprises and to privatise for cash. Market signals and forces will do the rest. Public sector interventionism would certainly be necessary, but it would take the form of the World Bank and the IMF exerting the necessary leverage to ensure this approach was followed.

The Primacy of Market Forces

It is now generally recognised that the 'market signals' of slump conditions were thoroughly distorted and could give no guidance as to which enterprises could survive and prosper in normal market conditions. R. Vintrova's study of the CSFR confirms this: she shows that there was a significant downward restructuring 'toward simple energy and material-demanding production processes, which are becoming much more advantageous to export, especially due to the rapid devaluation.'[84] Vintrova comments: 'While certain economists characterise the current economic decline as a "curative" structural crisis, they are unfortunately very far from the truth.' Domestic demand was now greatly distorted by the swift decline in the population's real income: 'if we were to respond to market stimuli at the moment, it would be necessary to shut down even industries with a promising demand'.[85]

Brada sums up the Hungarian experience by pointing out that the 'dramatic losses of output mean, as a matter of fact, the quasi-disappearance of whole industries. To give just one example: in the consumer electronics field, the two major domestic players on the market . . . had to declare bankruptcy in 1991 and 1992.' In iron and steel major producers were 'coming very close to disappearing from the market'.[86]

Collapsed markets and the ST credit crunch meant that enterprises faced a desperate liquidity crisis. The result was an investment collapse further undermining efficiency. In the CSFR investment activity dropped 29 per cent in the first three quarters of 1991. There was a capital famine for modernisation. Vintrova comments: 'No major investment has yet begun in this direction, and the necessary climate for it will not exist in the immediate future . . . An upsurge in investment would only be seen in the monopolised branches of the raw materials and energy complex.' The investment goods industry 'begins a self-sustaining recessionary spiral, gaining speed as it goes on. This is hardly a curative restructuring of production.'[87] Brada explains that in Hungary this investment collapse led to a dramatic undercapitalisation of many industrial firms. The share of gross fixed investment in GDP fell, in Hungary, from 28.8 per cent in 1980 to 17.8 per cent in 1990. Another factor stressed by Brada was the desperate struggle for market share by state enterprises, subordinating all other goals to that priority. Managers of loss-making industries also used up the firm's assets to cover current losses and keep the company going at any price.[88]

In a normal western capitalist economy such a catastrophic slump would lead to crisis management by the government. During the comparatively very minor recession in western Europe in the 1990s, the German, Italian and French governments provided massive targeted subsidies to particular industries and enterprises. In addition, credit conditions would be eased and the budget would go heavily into deficit. The governments of Poland, Hungary and elsewhere therefore turned towards an industrial policy which would involve helping state enterprises to restructure.

But the IFIs opposed such efforts. Thus while in a country like the Federal Republic of Germany government subsidies to industry are over 3 per cent of GDP, the IMF and WB have campaigned vigorously and effectively against such subsidies in the Visegrad countries. They dropped from 5.4 per cent of GDP to 2.4 per cent in Hungary by 1991 while in Poland they were reduced to a mere 2.4 per cent of budget expenditures by 1991 and in Czechoslovakia to 2 per cent of GDP in the same year.[89] These results were achieved by threatening to withhold IMF or WB loans.

The WB has also blocked governments from restructuring state-owned enterprises before privatising them. Sachs has claimed that this was unrealistic because governments lacked the resources in personnel to do this. But the WB took no chances and banned them from applying what resources they had. It explained that 'Such physical restructuring is best done by private owners.'[90] It therefore required the financial capacities of Poland's Industrial Development Agency be prohibited. The WB's agreement with the Polish government on this matter explains: 'IDA's existing financial portfolio will be transferred to financial institutions. Loans to enterprises will be sold or transferred to financial entities capable of managing credit risks . . . IDA's equity investments in enterprises will be transferred to equity holding entities, such as independent companies, private funds, privatisation funds or private equity holding companies. It was confirmed during negotiations [between the WB and the Polish Government] that transfer of IDA's financial portfolio will be completed by June 30th, 1992.'[91]

The WB stance was the same in Hungary. The MDF government had decided to pursue an industrial policy through the Ministry for Industry in the typical West European manner. The fact that the MDF had made this a centrepiece of its election programme in 1990 did not weaken the political will of the World Bank. It would not allow it. Matters were resolved in 1992 in the following way: 'The government is committed [to the World Bank] to reducing the role of the ministry [of Trade and Industry] in the economy rapidly, and the restructuring, revitalisation and government of the bulk of industrial enterprises is to be left to market forces.'[92]

The World Bank has similarly sought to emasculate national development banks, so central not only in Western Europe where the European Investment Bank plays that role but also in China and many other parts of the world. The Polish government established a Polish Development Bank in 1990 to lend funds to enterprises on a long-term basis. The WB intervened and ruled that this body must limit such lending to 15 per cent of its capital. The rest of its lending should be only to commercial banks.[93] In

Romania the WB's adjustment loan has been made conditional upon Romania's government privatising the Romanian Development Bank and a second state bank.[94]

Another field of economic policy where western public bodies have been decisive has been in seeking to end significant subsidies to agriculture in target countries. The impact of this in the trade field was noted above.

The significance of this campaign to ensure that the future structure of the economy should be determined by market forces needs to be underlined. Since most of these countries lacked private capitalists with the financial resources to buy large enterprises, these decisions were to be largely transferred to foreign capital. As we have seen, all the IFIs knew this and stressed how central foreign capital would be in privatisation.

Yet this foreign capital would come overwhelmingly from western Europe, a region already saturated with overproduction and facing historically high levels of structural unemployment, fiscal strain and social tensions. Any insertion of East European companies into West European product markets would therefore provoke West European resistance since it would produce an undesirable need for structural adjustment in the EU. At the same time, EU companies were driving to capture ex-Soviet markets from their previous suppliers in Eastern Europe. In short there was not a single West European productive sector that would welcome strong exporting in high value-added products by East Central European countries. Yet the planning, *ab initio*, of the new industrial (and agricultural) forces in the East was to be left largely to western operators.

This is not a debate about the gains to be made in technological transfer or other areas from FDI. Such gains can without doubt be important, but only on condition that there are strong national infrastructures and policies for controlling, directing and absorbing such transfer as is the case in the West. Yet what was being fought for was for the controlling and directing to be largely left to western actors.

4) Western Government Subsidies for Western Purchase of East European Assets

Western public bodies have pushed for the swift opening of state assets in the East to FDI and for full rights for foreign companies to participate in privatisation.[95] Eastern governments which failed to take such measures could not expect the western institutions, especially the IMF and the EU, to ease exclusionary embargoes on their participation in the western product or capital markets. Thus, the IMF and WB loans to Romania were blocked because its privatisation scheme limited participation by foreign investors. Western political pressure was used to gain the only two major deals concluded between Romania and western multinationals.[96] Equally important has been IMF pressure for governments to sell state assets, including the public utilities, to western companies in order to reduce fiscal deficits.

Such western pressure on the asset supply side has been combined with western state subsidies at all stages in the process of privatising to western multinational companies. In East Central Europe, the EU has largely funded the state privatisation agencies, it has set up units in the target state's relevant ministries and staffed them with EU nationals on the EU payroll, it has paid for the studies by western accountancy firms and investment banks of the industries of target states and it has given subsidies for the actual purchase of assets by EU firms, thus giving them an edge over competitive bids. The main instrument of this effort has been the PHARE Programme.[97] While other forms of Aid funds related to the region take the form of loans, PHARE, the great bulk of whose funds go to West European companies, takes the form of grants.

This programme was decided upon in 1989 and came into operation at the start of January 1990.[98] Its name is an acronym for 'Poland, Hungary: Assistance for Restructuring Economies'.[99] PHARE has been subject to a torrent of criticism largely because the EU has sought to dissimulate its purpose. The EU has presented it as both a partnership with target governments – recipient-driven – and as a means of transferring funds for people in the East. When it was set up, its main priorities were said to be transferring funds and other forms of aid to assist agriculture, environmental protection, the restructuring of industry and small businesses and educational development. Since PHARE has not in fact been about these things the criticism has been inevitable.

Table 9.4 PHARE and other Western Grant Aid[1] to CEEC (Millions of Ecu)

CEECS Year	PHARE Committed	Paid	Total G24 Grants
1990	500	171	960
1991	775	283.9	1,120
1992	1,015.5	433.9	1,120
1993	1,040	443.6	1,120
1994	835	492[2]	—
1995[2]	—	770	—

Notes: 1) Excluding debt reduction. G24 grants converted from $ to Ecu at $1=0.8 Ecu. 2) Projected in EC budget.
Sources: UN Economic Commission for Europe: Economic Bulletin for Europe, vol. 45 (1993), p. 94 and EC Commission, and EC budget for 1994, *Official Journal of the European Communities* (7 February 1994).

PHARE policy-making powers are not shared between the Community and the recipient country's government: they lie exclusively with the Community, although the regulation setting up PHARE does say 'account should be taken, *inter alia*, of the preferences and wishes expressed by the recipient countries concerned'.[100] The EU Commission has claimed that the target governments do, nevertheless, control implementation, citing the fact that PHARE units are in all the recipient countries' relevant ministries, and PHARE money is in large part disbursed by these units. But according to the EU's Court of Auditors the purpose of this decentralisation is not to give control to the target governments' officials since 'almost none' of the leading personnel in these management units are nationals of the recipient countries: they are from western Europe, appointed by EU bodies and work under the supervision of the Commission and of EC/EU Delegations.[101] The real effect of this administrative decentralisation has been to make it impossible even for the Court of Auditors to trace how PHARE money has actually been spent, since the Commission has given advances to these management units in the recipient countries and has been unable to supply the Court with information on how this money has been spent. Thus, although the Court's reports can be taken to be the most reliable source on PHARE, it also is in the dark about much of the programme.

Thus, one of the biggest early PHARE projects was 50 million ecu for pesticides for Poland. The Auditors were unable to trace where this actually went though the Court did establish that some at least was re-exported to the EU.[102] Also in the agricultural field, at the start of 1990 a project was started to supply loans for private farmers in Poland and Hungary, but two years later no loans had been granted. The Polish fund was, in 1990, quite large – 160 million ecu. But as late as January 1993 the Commission was still unable to give the Court information about the fund's activities even though it had promised a first report on it would be published in 1991.[103] The same pattern applied to another big PHARE project: to provide loan facilities for small and medium-sized businesses in Poland and Hungary. But at the end of the second year of this project no actual loans had been paid to SMEs in either country.[104]

The chief of the EU Commission's staff of economic advisers on Eastern Europe has explained why he thinks giving recipient governments a role in PHARE would have been a bad idea by claiming: 'typically it takes much longer for the recipients to specify their priorities than it would for the donors to impose theirs; demand-led aid is prone to exploitation by rent-seekers and hence may not be cost-effective'.[105]

These views are not shared by the EU's Auditors nor confirmed by the facts. Thus Portes seems to assume that rent-seeking is an East European rather than a West European problem. In one of the biggest PHARE projects, Tempus, for exchanges in higher education, East European rent-seeking was dealt with by, in the words of the EU Auditors, ensuring that there was 'prac-tically no involvement of the educational authorities of the recipient country'.[106] On the other hand it seemed to favour western rent-seeking: it handed the implementation of Tempus to a private organisation, the European Co-operation Fund (ECF), which has itself been devoted to the business of educational exchanges and has been bidding for Tempus exchange money.

Portes's readiness to raise the issue of delay is also curious. Thus from the start of PHARE in 1990, the governments of Poland, Hungary, Bulgaria, Czechoslovakia and the GDR had made environmental improvement mea-sures a priority. The EC Commission agreed. But in Poland, after three full years of the government's making this sector a priority, the Commission had carried through no single pilot investment project that would directly improve environmental conditions. The Hungarian government had pro-duced proposals for some 200 priority projects for tackling environmental problems, but the Commission did not select a single one of these, while it did fund the construction of a wildlife park and even supplied a central management building for it.[107] Projects regarded as urgent by recipient states, such as the construction of sewage purification plants in highly pol-luted areas such as the Black Sea, the Baltic, Warsaw and Northern Budapest were rejected by the Commission.[108]

In January 1994, the European Parliament criticised the Commission's lack of action on environmental issues and its failure to back recipient gov-ernment proposals such as those for the Danube Basin, Black Sea and the Baltic Sea. It criticised the fact that PHARE funds were used only for studies and it urged the Commission to use local consultants more often for PHARE.[109]

Yet within an ST framework, most of these criticisms can be dismissed, provided the purpose of programmes like PHARE are devoted to aiding privatisation and FDI. Since within the framework of ST FDI is crucial to pri-vatisation, modernisation and growth, western governments would be justified in helping in these tasks. And much of PHARE has been geared precisely towards that. There was a great deal of criticism of the fact that PHARE was devoted in the early years mainly to studies of the target economies by western consultants. The fact that in Poland the only product of the so-called loans for farmers project was a study of co-operative bank-ing caused some ridicule for telling Poles what they already knew.[110] But for FDI the task was not so much transferring western information East as transferring eastern information West. A study like that may have been valuable for, say, Crédit Agricole in encouraging it to try to take over agri-cultural banking in Poland. Or again, some forty studies by western consultants of Polish industries were carried out during 1990 and 1991. These kinds of studies were carried out in their hundreds across the region and transferred vast quantities of economic information westwards. The charge was made repeatedly that East European consultants were never used and should have been. Yet it is surely not obvious that such eastern consultants would have known the kinds of profitable opportunities that western multinationals would have been after in the region. And even if they did have an inkling of this, they might not have been sympathetic. The Slovak ministry of privatisation criticised these PHARE consultancies on its industries for not corresponding to its specific needs.[111] But this criticism again would be beside the point from an ST perspective since the specific needs to be met would be those of potential western investors. And their needs depended upon their global strategies, not on what, from an ST point of view, were narrowly national perspectives.

From this viewpoint, the only criticism of such studies would have been if they were used not to further western FDI but to undermine East European enterprises that posed a competitive threat in western markets. But because of PHARE's lack of transparency it is difficult to gain information on this front. One such case became a scandal: the Commission's spending of just under 950,000 ecu on a study of how to restructure the Czechoslovak iron and steel industries.[112] The sum was not even included in the programme for PHARE aid to Czechoslovakia. This was one of a number of such contracts for amounts of between 800,000 and 950,000 ecu not directly covered by any particular programme. Studies of this sort were very obviously of great political sensitivity when the Community was engaged in protection measures against a competitive threat from the Czechoslovakian steel industry.[113]

The Commission has, in fact, increasingly sought to motivate PHARE as a support programme for FDI rather than pretending it is about transferring funds into the hands of East Europeans. In the words of A. Mayhew, the Director of the Commission's Directorate General for External Relations: 'The countries of Central-Eastern Europe have criticised the [PHARE] programme for providing too much technical assistance, too many studies, if you want . . . we are now trying to move much more into the area of investment and away from studies which do not lead to any investment.'[114]

PHARE has also been the principal funder of the Privatisation Agencies set up as government bodies in Eastern Europe.[115] The PHARE commitments here have been detailed and thorough: thus in Poland and Hungary they have included paying for official cars and official equipment and, in the Hungarian case, for a financial adviser.[116] The fact that target governments do not always appreciate this Aid produces ridicule on the part of supporters of ST. As was the case with its attitude towards western export credit 'aid', the Polish government in 1994 refused to touch an EU grant fund designed to match the amount of money invested by EU companies in privatised Polish companies. Under the title 'Looking at gift horses', the *Economist* poured scorn on this rejection of 'free money' by a government 'running a budget deficit of more than $3bn'. For the *Economist* the advantage of giving the EU company a rent that could enable it to beat a Polish (or American) competitor was evidently too obvious to warrant justification.[117]

Table 9.5   PHARE Programmes by Sector (Millions of Ecu)

	1990 C^1	per cent	1992 C	per cent	P^2	per cent
Agric/Rural Development	136.0	27.4	273.0	11.9	167	18.8
Economic Restr/Priv/ finance	112.3	22.6	445.2	22.9	164.6	18.5
Environment	102.5	20.6	273.5	11.9	59.8	6.7
Human Resources[3]	36.8	7.4	488.3	21.3	226.9	25.5
Infrastructure	139.2	6.1	21.5	2.4		
Humanitarian aid	66.5	13.4	340.7	14.9	202.1	22.7
Miscellaneous	42.9	8.6	252.1	11.0	46.9	5.3
Total	497	100	2,290.3	100	888.8	100

Notes: 1) C = Commitments. 2) P = Payments. 3) This covers education and training, the social sector and public administration.
Source: EC Court of Auditors' Reports.

5) The Theory and Practice of FDI

It is no exaggeration to say that FDI has been offered to the peoples of the region as a deus ex machina bringing a universal panacea for all their ills.

FDI was presented both by ST theorists and the western multilateral institutions as both the key means for restructuring state enterprises in the East and as the lever for bringing dynamic growth and prosperity to the target country. The first of these claims risks becoming circular: FDI was to be the key means of privatisation because western conditionality and pressure would be geared to ensuring it was the only allowable means. The real argument is that FDI is the best, the optimal means of restructuring, because it transfers technology in a whole range of ways and can thus dramatically upgrade enterprise performance in the crucial higher value-added and technology intensive sectors. The second claim is more quantitative: it is that FDI will be the lever of growth and prosperity because of the sheer quantitative scale of the capital inflows which some countries can attract.

Both these claims can, in certain conditions, be true. It is striking that the first claim is advanced by ST supporters as unconditionally true: FDI is bluntly presented as the royal road towards technological upgrading, as if these economies were almost pre-industrial. The second claim, on the other hand, does have an important qualification attached to it: that FDI will flow in freely only if the target country provides the correct institutional framework and policy framework to attract FDI: failure to produce the institutional structure open to global capital will mean that FDI will not flow in.

We thus have a number of particular hypotheses:

1)   That the key variable affecting the size of FDI flows is the target state's institutional and policy framework.
2)   That FDI is a growth motor capable of generating national prosperity.
3)   That FDI will modernise production systems, in other words that it will be production seeking and it will upgrade technological potential.
4)   That without such flows, the transition to a modern economy capable of competing in the new world of globalised capitalism will be difficult, if not impossible.

These propositions are unfortunately either false, or grossly one-sided.

1) Institutional and policy frameworks and FDI flows

Universal experience suggests that an IMF-approved institutional and policy framework does not in itself generate substantial flows of FDI. UNCTAD's very thorough work on this subject does not treat institutional or policy orthodoxy as a significant factor, as Table 10.6 shows. Indeed, the factors which would attract really large FDI flows are precisely the factors which the ST experience of depression-led transformation in a fragmented regional context would undermine.

Table 9.6   Host Country Economic Factors Stimulating FDI

1.	Host country economic growth, especially growth outstripping population growth.
2.	Size of the domestic market.
3.	Degrees of regional integration.
4.	High profit rates.
5.	High skilled–low cost labour.
6.	Improved infrastructure.
7.	Exchange rates.

Source: UNCTAD: *World Investment Report,* 1994 (Geneva and New York, 1994).

This general experience of FDI has been amply proved in the case of the entire East Central and East European region. The whole region has attracted very small flows of FDI, without macroeconomic significance. And as the structural transformation deepened in both the Czech Republic and

Hungary in 1993 FDI actually fell instead of growing. On the other hand China, which has not at all followed IMF prescriptions and has failed to do such allegedly vital things as clarifying property rights and guaranteeing contracts, has attracted massive amounts of FDI. In 1992 alone China attracted more FDI than the whole of the Soviet Bloc attracted between 1989 and 1993. The following year China's inflow of FDI doubled over the previous year!

Table 9.7   FDI Flows into the Visegrad Countries, 1990–93
(net inflows in millions of US dollars)

	1990	1991	1992	1993
CSFR	199	594	1054	—
Czech Republic			983	561
Slovak Republic			71	100
Poland	88	117	284	850
Hungary	377	1459	1471	1200
Memorandum items:				
China			11,100	25,900
All East Europe & NIS 1989–93				11,000

Source: DG for Economic and Financial Affairs, Commission of the EC, *European Economy*, Supplement A, no. 3 (March 1994), and, for China, UNCTAD, *World Investment Report*, (Geneva and New York, 1994), p. 13.

China's institutional structure is, of course, exactly the kind of 'third way' market socialism that Sachs set out to discredit back in 1990. And international experience leaves little doubt that if the Comecon region had remained integrated, if the ST slump had been avoided and if an adequate trade protection regime had been in place, FDI in the region would, by now, have been several times higher than it has been.

2) FDI and growth: the causal direction

The causal relationship between FDI and growth runs in the opposite direction from the propaganda of ST supporters. The precondition for FDI on a large scale is domestic economic growth, not the other way round.

There are, of course, other kinds of international financial flows that do not depend upon growth: the vast speculative flows of hot money engaged in casino capitalism. This is undoubtedly the most dynamic aspect of the loose label 'globalisation', and it can dovetail perfectly with broken-down economies which are open to speculative flows. The debt-laden governments of such economies, desperate for new funding, can be driven to bond issues with very high interest rates and very short redemption rates. Such economies can be extremely attractive for global finance. Their very shakiness involves offering high yields to US pension funds and high-rolling investment banks. These operators have been making their presence felt in the Visegrad countries. In 1993 the Polish stock market soared tenfold. In January 1994 the *Economist*, believing the surge to reflect economic fundamentals, devoted an editorial to what it called the 'breathtaking' stock market boom and added: 'This expansion is no one-day wonder: it reflects a fundamental and remarkably rapid change.'[118] But the rise was not so rapid as the crash of the following month, when western banks walked away from the market with some $250 million of speculative profits.

3) FDI as market capture or technological upgrading?

The ST vision of FDI bringing new, modern technology into production processes in East European economies presupposes that FDI is mainly production seeking. Yet this has not been true. Empirical studies of FDI in the former Soviet Bloc have confirmed the previously known causes of large flows: in former Communist countries FDI is principally 'market seeking'.[119] Statistical analysis by the OECD Secretariat has confirmed this for East Central and Eastern Europe.[120]

The bulk of the flow into the Visegrad countries has gone into food, cigarettes, chocolate, soft drinks and alcohol sectors, consumer durables and cars as well as into the service sector.[121] Despite the overall collapse in purchasing power, there has been a rapid social differentiation producing a new market among what Anthony Robinson has called 'the growing class of new-rich traders, entrepreneurs and professional people'.[122] FDI in the manufacturing sector has overwhelmingly meant one or two big deals in the host country's car industry. More than half of Poland's and Czechoslovakia's industrial FDI went into a single car industry project: VW's Skoda project in the Czech Republic, and Fiat's FSM project in Poland.[123]

4) FDI and Czech engineering: a flagship?

The car industry is, of course, important, and new investment has taken place in this sector. But the Skoda experience illustrates some painful realities. First, progress in ST was irrelevant to VW's arrival. Five months after the fall of Communism and before any ST of any kind had been launched, Citroen, GM, Renault and Volvo were clamouring for Skoda. VW won the bid by promising DM7.1 billion of new investment and by promising to raise production to 450,000 cars per year by the year 2000. It also agreed that a new engine plant for Skoda would be built in Bohemia. Another key attraction of the deal was that VW would use Czech suppliers. VW also

Table 9.8 Sectoral Distribution of Joint Ventures at End of 1992
(per cent distribution)

Sector	CSFR	Hungary	Poland
Primary	3.9	1.5	4.3
Agric., forestry, fishing	3.5	1.5	4.0
Other	0.4		0.3
Secondary	32.0	46.0	74.6
Technology intensive	15.7	19.3	19.0
Other	16.3	26.7	55.6
Tertiary	64.1	52.5	21.2
Trade	19.7	15.8	3.2
Hotels, restaurants	2.1	0.9	3.2
Business-related services	19.7	20.6	5.2
Infrastructure	14.1	13.2	7.6
Other	8.2	2.0	1.9

Source: UN ECE, quoted in P. J. Buckley and P. N. Ghauri, *The Economics of Change in East and Central Europe* (San Diego, 1993).

pledged to retain Skoda's 21,000 workers. This was a serious package for substantial technological upgrading and for really significant technological transfer: not a mere bid to capture Skoda's existing market. In return the Czech government gave VW trade protection, ensuring it a monopoly position in the Czechoslovak market (as well as a two-year tax holiday and the writing-off of Skoda's debts). The WB's affiliate, the International Finance Corporation, which is supposed to offer low-interest loans to Third World enterprises, also stepped in with a sweetener for VW in the form of cheap money.

But in 1993–94 VW reneged on its promises.[124] Its investment plan was reduced from DM7.1 billion to half of that: DM3.8 billion. There would be no Czech engine plant, and no commitment to 450,000 cars by the year 2000. Employees have been cut to 15,000 and more redundancies will follow. And VW turned increasingly to using its West German parts suppliers rather than Czech subsidiaries, bringing more than fifteen such firms in to replace their Czech competitors.

When companies are unable to compete in world markets, such cutbacks can be necessary. But the interesting lesson of Skoda is that it could compete profitably, which its German parent could not. As the *Economist*'s subsidiary, *Business Central Europe*, explains, 'In 1993 Skoda was VW's star performer, the only profitable operation at a time when the concern was racking up world-wide losses of DM2.3 billion. VW President Ferdinand Piech described Skoda as the "loveliest daughter" of the company, adding that it was the only division capable of undercutting Japanese competition.'[125]

Nevertheless the strategic needs of VW took precedence over those of the Czech economy and 'in November 1993, VW decided to share the pain' faced by VW Germany with Skoda. The Czech Prime Minister 'has tried to put a positive spin' on these results by saying that Skoda did benefit from management expertise. But the Economy Minister Dlouhy is 'less sanguine' and states: 'Let's hope that nothing more like this happens in the future.'[126]

The Skoda experience of the negative externalities from inserting lead sectors of a target country's production apparatus into the international strategy of a western TNC is not unique. CKD Praha, the internationally famous heavy engineering group at the heart of Czech industry, produces trams, locomotives, compressors, diesel engines, electrical generators, motors and transformers. It has produced about one third of the world's trams and although it was dealt a devastating blow by the collapse of the Comecon region, 40 per cent of its sales still go to exports and half of these still go to the former Soviet Union. CKD management decided to enter a joint venture between its tram-making subsidiary, CKD Tatra and Daimler-Benz's subsidiary, AEG in 1993. But it has now broken off the co-operation. The CKD spokesperson, Vaclav Brom, explained why to the *Financial Times*: 'Many foreign companies came to the Czech Republic with one aim: to take part in our companies, to control the business, cancel R&D and transfer research work to themselves and use us as cheap labour. We will never agree with such attitudes. We are ready to co-operate with western partners, but under equal conditions.'[127]

Many other examples of such technologically predatory efforts can be found amongst high profile western companies. Thus General Electric, after buying Tungsram in Hungary, closed the latter's production of vacuum equipment, electronic components, floppy disk and magnetic tape products, all of which were considered profitable by Tungsram's management. The Hungarian cement industry was bought by foreign owners who then prevented their Hungarian affiliates from exporting; and an Austrian steel producer bought a major Hungarian steel plant only in order to close it down and capture its ex-Soviet market for the Austrian parent company.[128] Such experiences abound across the region.

5) Small Flow but Large Catch

While the flows of FDI funds into the region have so far been very small, the numbers of state enterprises bought through FDI has been very large. The overwhelming bulk of privatisations of medium and large firms in both Hungary and Poland have gone to foreign buyers[129] and the private investment funds running large and medium firms in the Czech Republic are dominated by western capital. Yet this is not the whole story as far as FDI is concerned. If the FDI flows to the region have been small, the assets they have been able to buy have been very extensive. In the case of Hungary and Poland, in particular, western companies have largely been able to take their pick of the assets they wish to acquire and they have bought very extensively. By the end of 1993, some 55,000 enterprises had been acquired by western companies. In telecoms, power generation equipment, chemicals, glass, cement and pharmaceuticals, the mid-western multinationals have fought each other to gain control of strategic sectors at minimal cost and without short-term plans for significant new investment but with a view to strengthening their global power in the long term.

Average purchase prices have been minimal, as UNCTAD has noticed.[130] In terms of the average amounts of money in invested foreign equity capital, while developed countries averaged $18 million and developing country affiliates averaged $4 million, the Central and East European country average has been only $260,000. Hungary, which attracted most FDI in the early 1990s, gained over $1 million in only 4 per cent of FDI projects.[131] This has been an absolutely predictable result of ST that some warned about at the start of the process. If you plunge the region into the most severe depression known anywhere in peacetime since the Second World War, if you simultaneously bring enterprises to technical bankruptcy through collapsed domestic markets and a fierce credit squeeze, and if you ban governments from restructuring companies before selling them off then you can ensure that western purchasers can buy them for next to nothing.

Globalisation Versus Economic Nationalism?

John Lloyd has sought to defend the ST model and to repudiate the kinds of criticism of FDI as a panacea suggested above by claiming that such criticism is based upon economic nationalism. He goes on to explain that insofar as there is a new world order it derives 'from the death not of communism but of economic nationalism . . .'[132] He thus urges us to forget about nationalism and accept the world of what he calls globalised production. By this he means global companies that produce parts in lots of different countries and assemble them in various places. He then tries to ridicule Jonathan Steele of the *Guardian* because in Steele's important book, *Eternal Russia*, this globalised world 'exists only spectrally, if at all'.

Lloyd is here muddling two very different phenomena: globalised *production*, in the sense of large TNCs producing throughout the world with an integrated internal division of labour spanning many countries,[133] and global *product markets*. *Production* is globally integrated within companies only in a limited sector of the world economy, though an important one. It partially exists in cars and in electronics, though even in South-East

Asia, car production has not been internationalised (while electronics has). Outside these sectors, globalised production is marginal. Further, research on such production suggests that it has not been a growing feature of economic relations. The best indicator of the growth of global production is the growth of intra-firm trade (IFT) since by definition the former requires IFT. Yet the OECD's research on IFT demonstrates that, contrary to Lloyd's ideology of globalisation, IFT does not seem to have grown during the 1980s. The OECD's research on IFT shows that, at least for US and Japanese TNCs, IFT stagnated during the 1980s.[134] And even if it had been growing, Lloyd's case that nationalism was played out would require him to demonstrate monopolisation and nearly insurmountable barriers to entry on a global scale to suggest that nationalist economic ambitions were utopian.

On the other hand, what does exist across most sectors are *increasingly globalised product markets*. Yet to paraphrase Lloyd, 'these exist only spectrally if at all' in his writing, for if he had understood their existence he would have noticed the feverish rise of economic nationalism, most especially in the USA, the EU and Japan, which has become much more intense following the demise of Communism. Every day, the *Financial Times* provides us with new evidence of this. In the context of global product markets, each state seeks to concentrate capital in its main sectors of strength in order to gain sufficient scale and power to fight for global market share. The task of the state is to fight on behalf of its own (domestically monopolistic) players in their ruthless drive to capture markets and/or carve up the globe within their cartels.

In line with this drive, the big western players moving into Eastern Europe have typically tried to require governments there to provide them with monopolistic control of the local market. VW required monopoly-protecting tariffs on Czech car imports before investing in Skoda. Hunslet, the British rolling-stock maker, demanded similar monopoly rights when it bought Ganz in Budapest. General Motors required the right to import its cars duty-free into Poland as a condition for investing in FSO in Warsaw, while requiring high tariffs on non-GM cars.[135] In Hungary, Suzuki has obtained trade protection for its cars and Samsung has done the same for its TVs.[136] For the TNCs, 'globalisation' and national autarchy for their target sector fit perfectly together.

A specific European feature of these developments has been the attempts of the EU Commission to promote its own state-building efforts at an EU level by demonstrating its capacity to defend the base and strengthen the outreach of EU-based multinationals. And in the East European context this has entailed helping them to acquire dominance in their own sectors in the East.

The Interaction of Public and Private Western Operations

There is an uncanny coincidence in the way in which the IMF/WB activities have combined with those of the more predatory TNCs to weaken the capacity of East European states to bargain effectively with, and be able to absorb for national advantage, benefits from FDI while minimising the possible damage. Not only has the WB opposed a national microeconomic strategy involving targeted industrial policy and export promotion. It has sought to weaken the most elementary forms of crisis management industrial policy such as are normal practice in the West in minor recessions, when large swathes of important companies are put into 'intensive care' by the banks. Instead, the WB has urged Draconian bankruptcy laws and an asset-stripping, labour-shedding approach to restructuring. It has taken its lead from the signals of collapsed markets and required action as follows: 'Typically, the restructuring plans will involve closing loss-making production units, carving out non-essential activities, divesting non-productive or under-utilised assets and shedding excess labour.'[137]

Both the IMF and WB have shown not the slightest concern for protecting the educational infrastructures and public R&D budgets as well as other infrastructures for ensuring a future capacity to absorb and diffuse new technologies throughout the economy. Year after year health and education spending in the Visegrad countries has been reduced.[138] In Slovakia, for example, in 1993 education spending was reduced by 30 per cent. In Hungary in the spring of 1995, the IMF required the government to charge fees for higher education as a condition for providing new loans.[139]

Against this background we have seen catastrophic declines in R&D budgets across the region.

Shock Therapy, Democracy and 'Civil Society'

Cardinal goals of ST have been, according to Sachs, the achievement of democracy and freedom. Although Sachs himself has not emphasised the building of 'civil society', this has been a constant theme of ST supporters. Yet these goals have been treated as ends and not means. As ends, they have been discursively very important because they have been used as core justifications of the means of ST.

However the liberal principle that ends should govern means has been operationally rejected within ST in favour of a more 'dialectical' approach: the existing social, legal and political institutions are likely to be resistant to ST, but ST is the only (or best) path to truly democratic, legal and civil institutions, therefore we must negate the existing institutions from above and outside in order to realise the true democracy and civil society.

This has been the substance of much western conditionality diplomacy. It has been applied also in the funding efforts for various pro-western political parties in Eastern Europe, particularly social democratic parties. But it has been at the very heart of the whole operational priorities of ST: to subordinate the will of electorates and parliaments to the overriding priority of rapid systemic transformation to capitalism and the downgrading of constitutional development, social and political consensus-building, and respect for minimal economic and social solidarity.

Insouciance on those issues, as Sachs has more or less acknowledged, led to catastrophe in Yugoslavia. The tensions of ST played a central role in the destruction of Czechoslovakia (whose populations were denied a vote on the issue). But these features of the drive have been most evident in the policy towards Russia and the Former Soviet Union.

The Civil and the Criminal in the New Capitalist Class

The West has urged that those who managed to accumulate money-capital under Communism should form the core of the new domestic capitalist class. These people have been mainly illegal currency speculators and black marketeers as well as corrupt members of state administrations, especially in the import-export sectors. Such people have shown entrepreneurial spirit, albeit of a criminal kind. Lord Howe, appointed adviser to the Ukrainian government in 1991, was quite frank on this point. He urged the need for the development of what he called 'bandit capitalism' in Ukraine and drew a favourable parallel with the great robber barons of American capitalism in the nineteenth century.[140] The governing consideration was to swiftly acquire a capitalist class with strong entrepreneurial and proprietary instincts. In bandit or mafia capitalism there was a solution.

This aspect of western policy has often been overlooked, perhaps because ST supporters have urged action to reduce levels of criminality in the East. Yet the policy has been faithfully reflected in the pages of the *Economist*. It has argued that in the case of Russia, the Communists have had an interest in exaggerating the extent of crime and that in any case the entire Soviet project had been criminal. It has urged that the criminal businessmen 'whose methods of operation hover uneasily between those of Al Capone and those of the early American robber barons . . . need to be encouraged to go legitimate'. To achieve this, it argues, the Russian government has to 'show that it is willing to protect property rights . . . Second, the government has to reduce its interference in the economy . . . The government could be deregulating and liberalising the economy much faster than it is doing.'[141]

The supporters of ST thus turn the idea of building a civil society in the

East into the simple notion of ending state interference, state funding and state control. Society it seems would be civil only if there was no political interference. The respect for popular sovereignty, the building of links between public policy and voter preferences, or responding positively to expressions of public protest or strike action by desperate employees, forms no part of this programme. Strong public protest against forms of privatisation favoured in the West or against increasingly unpopular examples of predatory western buy-outs are to be ignored.

The Polish sociologist Włodzimierz Wesolowski has captured the ST supporters' hostility to democratic will formation when writing of the stance of the new, post-1989 elites in Poland: 'the unvoiced assumption that people had to be demobilised in order to open the way for economic reforms; in parallel, the business of politics should be left to politicians and the emerging class of big capitalists. This was – and still is – the position of leaders of neo-liberal persuasion as well as of many influential journalists.'[142]

With the election in one country after another of governments led by the former Communist parties, hostility towards the effects of democratic politics in the region has become most explicit among some of the American supporters of ST, as expressed in various articles in *Foreign Affairs*. One such piece declared that western efforts to thwart the development of right-wing nationalism in the region were a mistake: 'In Central Europe the greatest danger to democracy and stability does not – and never did – come from the new or old nationalist right. The danger comes from the old left, from remnants of the Communist parties . . . Former Communist parties hold political and economic monopolies which will take years to loosen; until they do, politics will not become "normal" in any western sense in Central Europe or elsewhere . . .'[143]

This sense that electoral verdicts in favour of the post-Communist parties should not be accepted took a more activist form in an extraordinary piece in the same journal by Michael Ignatieff. He declares that 'All the post-Communist regimes are nominally democratic, but in practice the levers of power have usually remained in the hands of the old nomenklatura.' In any case, he explains, 'formal democracy is not enough. Indeed, democracy will degenerate into authoritarian populism' unless new measures are taken by the West. Ignatieff then goes on to spell out how the West must develop what he calls a 'civil society strategy' for the region. This should be a set of programmes administered by the western states within the post-Communist states to fund the mass media, opposition parties, the courts, judiciary and police. The strategy, he says, 'starts with the search for partners outside the state, the leading parties and the bureaucracy'.[144]

Such contempt for the 'formal democracy' of electoral results and such crude proposals for bureaucratic interference in the socio-political life of the region by western states could only further undermine the already strained polities emerging in the region. The post-Communist parties have won support from electorates because, although themselves committed to further privatisation, they are seen as seeking to rebuild the shattered social fabric by maintaining some minimal social commitments and by offering some protection to state enterprises which face political discrimination under World Bank tutelage. These parties have also managed to maintain a communicative interaction with large social groups ignored or abandoned, as Weslowski points out, by the neo-liberal elites.

Constitutionality Versus Shock Therapy in Russia

The most direct and brutal test of the relationship between liberal principle and ST occurred in Russia in 1993. The Yeltsin government derived its authority from parliamentary elections in 1990, during the Gorbachev period. The Russian Parliament elected at that time had then itself elected Yeltsin as Russian president and in the autumn of 1991 it voted him emergency powers for a year in order to give him a free hand with economic transformation. By the autumn of 1992, with real wages down to 40 per cent of their levels as of the start of January 1992, the majority in Parliament began to swing against the Gaidar economic reforms. By the spring of 1993 Yeltsin was on a collision course with the deputies.

Jonathan Steele's important book on the Gorbachev and Yeltsin years has carefully analysed the constitutional and democratic dimensions of these events.[145] Steele reminds us that the decisive shift towards liberal democracy and a legal state took place under Gorbachev, who inaugurated an independent press, the dismantling of the censored press and KGB controls, and free elections. Steele reminds us that the leaders of the Russian Parliament had not started out as opponents of Yeltsin. Rutskoi indeed had been a central figure in Yeltsin's rise, not least in August 1991. The swing of opinion amongst the deputies in the Parliament was all too easily explicable in the context of the catastrophic consequences of Gaidar's ST programme during 1992.

From the spring of 1993 Yeltsin embarked upon a drive to flout the constitution in order to crush his erstwhile supporters within the Russian Parliament. The Parliament's powers were not, in fact, very extensive. Unlike the French parliament the Russian one could not vote on the government's programme or pass a vote of no confidence in the prime minister. And unlike the US Senate, the Parliament could not approve individual ministers. On the other hand, the Russian President did not have the power to dissolve Parliament and the latter did have substantial power in budgetary matters – like the US Congress.

Faced with opposition to his economic programme from the Parliament

Yeltsin decided to flout the Constitution by announcing the dissolution of the Parliament, an act expressly prohibited in the Constitution. When the MPs sought to resist this unconstitutional act by occupying the Parliament building, Yeltsin responded by surrounding and cutting off the building and this led to the ill-judged but constitutionally legitimate effort by the Parliament to strip Yeltsin of power. Yeltsin responded to the march on a radio station with a military assault on the Parliament building, the arrest of Parliament's leaders, and the closing down of Russia's supreme court, which had properly opposed his attempt to violate the Constitution. Yeltsin also imposed censorship and closed down hostile newspapers. MPs who had participated in the occupation of the Parliament building were thrown out of their flats within three days of Yeltsin's victory.

Western governments and ST supporters backed Yeltsin's flouting of the Constitution. The leaders of Parliament were branded by John Lloyd and others as the Old Guard, despite the fact that none had such good credentials for that title as ex-CPSU Politburo member Yeltsin. Lloyd says that 'Yeltsin was faced with the alternative of surrendering to the Old Guard or breaching the Constitution.' This is propagandistic: the Parliament had not been asking Yeltsin to surrender. They had been opposing his ST policy. If Lloyd was more honest he would admit that the choice was between pursuing ST or respecting the Constitution. And that is why Lloyd is, as he says, 'glad that Yeltsin won'.[146]

All this was, in any case, an *ex post facto* rationalisation on the part of Lloyd. At the start of 1993 he had classed as the sole political achievement of 1992 the continued functioning of the parliament-government-president combination. His list of nine dangers for Russia during 1993 made no mention of a threat from the Parliament and one of his list of five hopes for the year ahead was for a 'consolidation of democratic institutions'.[147]

After Yeltsin's autumn 1993 coup the *Economist* declared that one should not be surprised that a Russian like Yeltsin would ignore constitutional proprieties. After all, it explained, 'Russia being Russia' the hope that 'a free market democracy' could be established there by consent was probably 'always absurd'. In short, we in the West should not expect Yeltsin to behave by our standards.[148] The *Economist*'s editor did, however, expect that his readers would have forgotten the *Economist*'s own past editorials. We could thus be relied upon to assume that the flouting of the Constitution was Yeltsin's idea rather than a western one. Yet, a full five months before Yeltsin made his move, at least one influential western voice was urging the path of illegality: the voice was the *Economist* itself. In its 1 May 1993 editorial it raised the question of whether Yeltsin should continue a war of attrition with his opponents in Parliament. It acknowledged that doing so 'has powerful attractions. For one thing, it is legal . . . Yet to continue trench warfare would be a mistake . . . He should abolish parliament, introduce a new constitution, and call elections.' After all, the Constitution had 'become a weapon that Parliament exploits cynically to block reform'.[149] This view was backed by an accompanying article which explained: 'Mr. Yeltsin's dilemma is that, to continue with economic reform, he has got to get rid of the present parliament, which is blocking him at every turn.'[150]

By far the most astonishing aspect of the entire experience of ST over the last five years is the extraordinary resilience of democratic commitment throughout the entire ex-Communist region. The populations of the region have not only suffered atrocious hardships but have elected governments on political platforms that have subsequently been blocked, in Hungary, Poland and Slovakia, by western pressure.

Attempts at ultra-nationalist backlashes by the Christian Nationals in Poland, the Republicans in the Czech Republic, the Slovak Nationalist Party or the Czurka break-away from the MDF have all been repudiated by the electorates of the region. In general, the extreme Right has been far weaker electorally in Eastern Europe during the 1990s than in western Europe. Just as the Far Right has gained far more support in West Germany than in East Germany, the showing for the Far Right has been greater in Austria, Italy, France and Belgium than in the great bulk of Eastern Europe. Instead, voters have turned back to the one political current in the region that has received no support whatever from the West: the ex-Communist socialist parties. These have achieved victories in Poland, Hungary, Bulgaria, Lithuania, Estonia, Ukraine and have become important also in the former GDR.

In this context, East European democrats must wonder why Ignatieffs in the West propose western financial intervention against authoritarian populist currents in Eastern Europe, instead of spending some of that money tackling the anti-statist (civil society?) militias in the US or fascism in western Europe. Similar cynical smiles are being raised in the region about the EU's worried insistence that the East Central European states settle all their ethnic and territorial problems and potential disputes by internationally binding treaty once and for all as a precondition for moving towards possible membership of the EU. Why, they wonder, are western revisionist claims excluded? Why ignore the revisionist claims by the Italian government on Slovenia, claims which led Italy to block an EU Association Agreement with Slovenia being negotiated in 1994? Why ignore German claims on the Czech Republic over the Sudetenland? Why ignore Greek claims in relation to Macedonia? Unlike the East Central European problems which are all potential disputes, these claims by EU members on their eastern neighbours have all been active issues. And this leaves aside the question of double standards for the two halves of Europe: no pressure for urgent treaty resolution is being applied to Britain's Gibraltar dispute with Spain, or its Northern Ireland dispute with Eire.

ST supporters have certainly been both dismayed and embarrassed by the victories of the ex-Communist parties in the region. They have also, rather oddly, been surprised that those declaring themselves Liberals, now inextricably identified with ST, have been on the retreat in most countries.[151]

Yet despite the resilience of the democratic process in Eastern Europe, the message of the electoral victories of the ex-Communist parties provides an important challenge to the West. It is a warning that the electorates of the region reject the drive for ST as implemented by the western powers over the last five years. Voters in the region were initially prepared to trust western policy and its local supporters. But with the possible exception of the Czech Republic, their views have changed. If the West is not prepared to alter its stance towards the region under ex-Communist governments, voters may well turn towards more desperate remedies.

III Conclusions

However it was introduced capitalism was bound to come as a bit of a shock to the peoples of Eastern Europe. Illusions about capitalism were very widespread. Workers did not realise that it would entail a radical drop in their living standards, a great intensification of the work process and chronic insecurity, as well as destitution for a minority. There is a danger of blaming ST for capitalism as such.

There were also widespread illusions about what kind of capitalism was on the market from the West. Many East European intellectuals, long disillusioned with dialectics, wanted Swedish-style social democratic capitalism, not appreciating that if the Communist world abandoned state socialism for post-war social democratic capitalism, that very choice would destroy the possibility of realising it: without Communism it would be taken off the menu. It could also be said that official opinion, at least in the Visegrad states, continued, despite mounting popular opposition in Poland and Hungary, to be resolutely committed to the ST course and that this was not only due to western structural power and pressure.

While this is both true and important, it is also important to see why this commitment by these post-Communist elites has been so strong. In the Visegrad states the idea of rapid, systematic change has been discursively packaged as a quick 'entry into Europe'. In this form it has been the legitimating discourse for the transformation towards capitalism as such. It has been the way for legitimising privatisation, unemployment, social differentiation and the impoverishment of large sections of the population. Those who have questioned this discourse have been marked as opponents of the transition to capitalism as such. Thus to have abandoned the set of western policies and conditions entailed by ST would have required an alternative means of legitimating the social transformation.

Yet at the same time, the claim that this pressure from the governments of the Visegrad region prevented the western powers from pursuing any other policy than ST cannot be taken seriously. The western alliance had at least as much collective capacity to shape the future of Eastern Europe in the early 1990s as the Americans had in Western Europe in the late 1940s. An orientation towards a genuinely pan-European project based upon retaining the regional links of the eastern part of the continent for a long transitional period and moving towards a pan-European confederation bringing the two halves together would have been both viable and far less costly for the peoples of Eastern Europe. It was not collectively advanced by the western powers because it did not serve their economic and political interests.

Evaluating the Outcome of Shock Therapy

The costs of ST have been far in excess of what was, from an economic point of view, necessary. The most damaging cost and at the same time most fundamental feature of ST was the decision to encourage the fragmentation of the Comecon region and to replace it with a hub-and-spoke interaction between isolated, shattered economies and gigantically powerful western forces. From this, all else followed.

ST supporters tend to ignore this governing feature of the policy and invite us to compare domestic national policy cycles of the fragments. On this basis, using growth rates as the key criterion, Poland seems to emerge best and Hungary, amongst the East Central European countries, worst. We are supposed to conclude that ST = Poland = Success.

This is a specious line of argument. It assumes that Hungary didn't follow ST while Poland did. In reality both liberalised prices, reduced wages, freed trade. Both got stuck over privatisation. Yet two very large differences between them stand out: Poland's debt, uniquely, was halved; Hungary's was not even significantly rescheduled; Hungary attracted about half of the entire region's FDI, Poland fared much worse. The only conclusions we can draw are that debt cancellation may be very important from a macroeconomic point of view, while FDI may be irrelevant or worse. As for the vibrancy of the private sector in Poland, this rests uneasily next to the country's export performance, 60 per cent of which was being achieved in 1994 by its much discriminated against state enterprises.

A more relevant and more stark contrast would be between both Hungary, the Czech Republic and Poland on the one side and Romania on the other. The Romanian case may be taken as a paradigm of an alternative, national capitalist strategy of transformation counterposed to the ST cycle of 'opening to globalism'. The Illiescu regime rejected a sweeping liberalisation of prices, avoided bankruptcies and large lay-offs of workers, sought to maintain the big industrial enterprises and directed its privatisation efforts towards management and worker buy-outs, largely excluding foreign capital. The government was also cautious about liberalising its trade regime. As a result of these policies it was largely rebuffed by the IFIs.

Romania initially suffered from acute internal tensions as a result of the form of the transition from the Ceaucescu regime. It also suffered from an acute hard currency shortage. Nevertheless, like Poland, the Romanian economy returned to growth in 1993 with a 1 per cent rise in GDP, grew by 3.4 per cent in 1994 and is projected to grow by more than 4 per cent in 1995.[152] The Japanese Financial Services group, Nomura, made the following comparative judgement on the Romanian economy's 1994 performance: 'Romania, little noticed by the West, delivered last year probably the most impressive performance in Eastern Europe.'[153]

This does not mean that the Romanian experience should be erected as some sort of superior strategy to that of Poland. Since 1989 the Romanian people have probably suffered more than the Poles. It does suggest two possible lines of investigation: first, Romania had no significant foreign debt and this makes it similar to Poland with its debt reductions; and second, the ST opening to global forces is at the very least no panacea if recent growth records are the standard of judgement: Romania has revived far more strongly than wide-open Hungary or the Czech Republic.

Yet attempts to hail this or that country as a success on the basis of current growth tables are a facile way to judge the outcome of ST.[154] The real test is the one proposed by Sachs: will ST provide higher living standards than those which prevailed in 1989, as well as democracy and freedom? We do not, of course, know, yet. But what we can do is work out what would be necessary in order to achieve such higher living standards.

IMF calculations are that even in the most promising country of the region, Poland, living standards will not return to their 1989 levels until the year 2010 at the earliest. Rollo and Stern have calculated that for the region as a whole to return to its 1988 levels of GDP per capita by the year 2000 it would need growth rates of 10 per cent per annum each year between 1994 and 2000. By this measure, on present trends, most of the region will not regain 1988 living standards by 2010. And even with such growth rates Rollo and Stern rule out the possibility that the Visegrad states could return to their 1988 development ranking (their position relative to other states) by the year 2010 as unrealistic: in the best case, it would take more than twenty years. They have calculated the rates of growth that would be needed in order that the CSFR and Hungary reach Spanish levels of GDP per head by 2010 and that Poland reach Greek levels by the same year. This would require catch-up growth of 10 per cent per annum from 1994 to 2000 –

roughly the rate of growth of the Asian NICs and somewhat lower than China's growth rate in the 1980s and 1990s. They then assume 6 per cent growth per annum between 2001 and 2005 and growth rates of 4.5 per cent from 2006 to 2010.[155] These growth targets then provide export growth targets, on the assumption that domestic demand will remain depressed in the Visegrad states during most of the next twenty years. They assume a growth in exports of almost twice the expected 6 per cent annual rate of growth of world trade: in other words, a growth of exports of about 12 per cent per year. Such export growth would have to be in goods sectors with low capital-output ratios – i.e. sectors that do not require large new capital investments. Given the countries' debt problems and likely repayment arrangements, the resulting balance of payments gap that would have to be filled by an inflow of western capital is unrealistically large. This means 'exports will be required to generate even higher volumes of foreign exchange than assumed above. Thus if capital markets plus aid cannot meet the challenge, goods markets will need to be open.'[156]

These are immensely depressing calculations. They imply that even for a country growing like Poland for the foreseeable future, the population will have to wait for the best part of twenty years simply to return to their living standards under a Communist system that had been in a long crisis. And this makes unrealistic assumptions that the West European economies will not enter their next recession in 1997 or 1998, that global casino capitalism will not explode, that shocks of other kinds and business cycles will not hit Poland. This is about as bad as when capitalism was last in Poland, between the wars, and the economy did not grow overall at all between 1913 and 1939. It is a stark contrast with what Sachs likes to call 'the forty ruinous years of Communism', when the living standards of the Polish people were transformed for the better. As for the countries still without growth after five years, like Hungary, not to speak of Bulgaria or countries further East, the prospect is far worse.

Of course, events may turn out very different: these countries may embark upon the kind of growth path that we have seen in China or South Korea. But the entire weight of western pressure has been geared to preventing the region from following the strategies pursued in those countries. As to the fate of democracy and freedom – Sachs's other criteria of successful out-come – it would probably be unwise to speculate, even if we could be pretty certain that if the EU countries were subjected to the sufferings lived through in Eastern Europe, democracy could hardly be expected to survive.

Towards an Analytical Theory of Western Behaviour

Sachs's model displays unexpected asymmetries. He gets most of the economics wrong but is rather strong on the ways of using political power to engineer social change in the East; and his understanding of how to handle East European politics sits alongside a woeful failure of the model to get the behaviour of western actors right.

On the economic side the model produced a slump which Sachs did not predict, a chronic fiscal crisis that Sachs claimed he was there to overcome; an initial export performance that demonstrated competitive potential in state enterprises Sachs believed to be hopeless, an import bonanza that damaged the economies instead of spurring recovery; an investment collapse instead of an investment surge, a domestic consumption-led recovery instead of export-led growth; a trickle of FDI instead of a flood. Yet the Economics Professor's system of constraints and incentives for eastern governments to draw them into ST and to manipulate their policy systems was a remarkable success, at least for the initial stages of the programme. But western actors refused all the roles Sachs assigned them except those involving the imposition of constraints and pressure – with one significant exception which the model gives us no resources to explain: the Polish debt cancellation. Otherwise, debt cancellation was off the menu, macroeconomic grants were off, radical opening of the EU market was off; on the other hand western state subsidies for exports were in, arbitrary protectionist actions were in, subsidies for FDI by their own firms were in. Sachs seems genuinely perplexed and upset by all this. In an article this year he complains that 'not only the Russian economy but also Russian democracy has been put recklessly at risk by western neglect.'[157] He calls US policy towards Russia the greatest foreign policy disaster for decades.

Sachs's diagnosis of this is that the G7 suffer from intellectual problems: they lack vision, or, more cruelly, they are plain stupid. Like a conductor in front of an amateur orchestra, Sachs has been raising his baton repeatedly in front of the G7 yet when he brings it down they continually hit the wrong note. It does not seem to occur to Sachs that they may be playing reasonably well, but to a different score, or a number of different scores.

Trying to read these scores requires an analytical approach which rejects the belief of Sachs or Ignatieff that the western powers are driven by God-like ideals and accepts that they are human, all too human and governed by a will to power. Sachs's ST goal of 'globalised' open door states in Eastern Europe does indeed then serve their interests because it enables their economic operators to penetrate the region effortlessly with their products and their capital, while the macroeconomic consequences of this opening are policed by their IFIs. Democratic polities can also serve these goals since they are more permeable than many other forms of state and can institutionalise values harmonising them with the West. Insofar as the results of pursuing these objectives are prosperity for all, so much the better: but this is a bonus, not the bottom line.

At the same time, these regime goals shared by Sachs and western governments have not been the exclusive goals of western powers in Eastern Europe in the 1990s. Another central preoccupation of the EC governments has been the way in which the international division of labour is to be reorganised in Europe as a whole. The USA has also been preoccupied with these problems from its own angle of interests and in addition it has been trying to reorganise the political balance of power across the entire continent.

It is also fascinating to note the failure of Sachs to understand the roles of the IMF. He accuses its officials of being stupid bureaucrats for failing to disburse adequate funds to target funds flexibly enough, but the IMF can only be as flexible as the leading powers within it allow – and, as the Mexican crisis of the winter of 1994–95 showed, the American government can encourage it to be extraordinary flexible when perceived vital interests are at stake. Further, the task of the IMF is above all that of guarding what integrity there is in the global financial and currency systems, rather than producing sustainable growth in crisis-ridden peripheries. In the immensely strained and unstable international financial conditions of the 1990s, the incentive systems open to the IMF have been overwhelmingly negative ones. For Sachs to expect sweeping debt relief for Eastern Europe when the main western powers are using the debt burdens of scores of states throughout the world as their main instrument for maintaining a semblance of discipline and hierarchy in international affairs is very naive. The very successes of Sach's own project for globalised capitalism could hardly have been achieved in Latin America without those debt burdens acting as powerful negative incentives.

Sachs's plan, as outlined in January 1990, corresponded closely to American thinking on Europe at that time. The Bush administration feared that the collapse of Communism in Eastern Europe could lead to the development of structures across the whole continent in the economic and security fields, embracing both Moscow and the EU and leading to the marginalisation of US power in Europe as NATO withered. This was exactly the vision which President Mitterrand had unveiled to the world in his New Year's Eve address two weeks before Sachs's article was published: a European confederation from the Atlantic to the Urals. Such a scheme would have enabled the French to have kept the East Central Europeans at arm's length while pursuing its plans for strengthening the EU. It would also appeal to Chancellor Kohl, overwhelmingly preoccupied with ensuring a strong relationship with Moscow as he struggled for German unification. The Deutsche Bank president had already outlined an ambitious plan for rebuilding the East as a unified region, a plan which could have brought great synergies between Russian and German economic strength. President Mitterrand had capped this with his own scheme for the process to be planned by a French-led EBRD.

Sachs's plan dovetailed nicely with the politico-economic policy objectives of the Bush administration. These included the following: to break what came to be known as the Visegrad states from Moscow and require a shock transition to capitalism there; to continue to exclude the USSR from a reorganised Europe and to work instead for the absorption of East Central Europe into the western sphere; to pressurise Germany into footing the bill for the rapid transformation of East Central Europe, as Sachs explicitly called for, while an IMF-led restructuring programme would create exporting tigers competing on the basis of cheap labour costs, which would blast a hole in the EU's CAP, would dissolve the EU's trade regime, would lead to a relocation of production from Germany eastwards, would thereby exert pressure to reconstruct the EU's institutional order along American lines as a minimalist safety-net neo-liberal zone. Every single one of these elements was in the Sachs Plan, though more delicately put. It was a plan which also fitted perfectly with thinking in London.

The Bush administration's scheme would make NATO necessary to consolidate the absorption of East Central Europe and thus assure US leadership. The likelihood of EU resistance to the US assault on its CAP and trade regime would make the US the champion of the economic interests of the belt of states between Germany and Russia. In this context, Poland was the geopolitical key and it also had a new elite strongly oriented towards US neo-liberal values and able to draw on a long-standing fund of Polish sentiment sympathetic to America. The cancellation of Polish debt, amongst other things, becomes explicable only in this political context.

The French government was unable to carry the day against Washington because the Bush administration's policy offered adequate scope for German interests. In particular, the anchoring of the Visegrad countries to the German economy was a prime goal of Bonn and once the arrangements with Moscow for German unification were consolidated, the German government ceased to pursue its earlier interest in new pan-European frameworks.

Thus since 1990, the EU has accepted the fragmentation of the Comecon region, but it has not accepted the other parts of the package. Through its rules of origin package it has thrown a ring around the new Associated states, to give a privileged role for capital based within the EU. It has defended the integrity of the CAP and its trade protection regime and has worked to ensure that the new division of labour in the East will be entirely governed by West European economic operators and their interests: the combination of a tough trade policy and strong supports for the export drive and for West European FDI have ensured this. And it has resisted any hostages to fortune in the form of timetabled commitments to the entry of the Visegrad economies.

From the EU's point of view, the policy has been a remarkable success, so far. Poland, the Czech Republic and Hungary are firmly locked into EU ascendancy. The rest of the region still, given Russian weakness, has nowhere else to go. It is true that the Visegrad states are in a weaker condition for entering the EU than they were in 1989 and could have been if their region had not been shattered. But their accession to the EU is not a priority even for Germany: what counts is their being firmly within the sphere of EU dominance.

The task now for the USA is to ensure that the EU's new East Central European sphere is brought firmly under overall US leadership. This goal is to be achieved through NATO's eastward expansion.

Sachs's vision is stuck in a one-sided preoccupation with regime goals, preoccupied with important, but partial, issues like inflation, budget deficits and so forth. It does not occur to him, for example, to ask the question as to what impact billions of dollars-worth of grants for fiscal stabilisation would have on Russia's military capabilities. Russian stabilisation is important, but so too, from an American point of view, is scaling down Russian power.

What remains living within Sachs's plan is its ideological and symbolic role. The idea that economic nationalism is dead and that we live in a cosmopolitan globalised planet is very powerful and even inspiring. And the notion that growth in Poland has been produced by the Poles putting nationalism behind them and going the American way is politically helpful. But it remains an ideology in which the real driving forces in the world are, to paraphrase Lloyd, 'present only spectrally if at all'. To grasp those driving forces we would need to amend Lloyd's remark about the new world order bringing the death of economic nationalism. A better formulation might be that in Eastern Europe, the death of Communism had led the West to try to stamp out economic nationalism in favour of its own national and collective interests in the region. But this does not so much suggest a new era on the globe as something rather old fashioned which, in the days of Communism, used to be called imperialism.

Notes

1. It should be said, however, that Professor Alice Amsden of MIT, together with Jacek Kochanowicz of Warsaw and Lance Taylor of the New School, have provided a damaging challenge to this consensus with their book *The Market Meets its Match* (Harvard University Press, 1994), drawing on East Asian experience to challenge ST orthodoxy.

2. Jeffrey Sachs, *Understanding Shock Therapy* (Social Market Foundation, 1994), p. 25.

3. Ralph Dahrendorf, *Reflection on the Revolution in Europe* (Chatto & Windus, 1990).

4. Jeffrey Sachs, *Poland's Jump to the Market Economy* (MIT Press, 1993), p. 4.

5. American policy in 1990–92 continued to favour the maintenance of a Moscow-centred economic space in the Soviet region except for the Baltic Republics.

6. Jeffrey Sachs, 'What is to be Done?' *Economist*, 13 January 1990.

7. Ibid. p. 25. Sachs noted that the Yugoslav outcome would differ from Poland's for Yugoslavia would maintain, in large measure, its self-management approach to corporate governance.

8. Franco-German proposals to keep the USSR and Eastern Europe linked via a free trade regime were rejected; French ideas for an EBRD which would engage in large public infrastructure projects embracing the USSR and Eastern Europe were emasculated. And the French notion of a pan-European confederation embracing both the EC and the whole of the East was repudiated. Poland, and for a short while Yugoslavia, became the flagships of the alternative approach.

9. Richard Holbrooke, 'America, a European Power', *Foreign Affairs* (March–April 1995), p. 40.

10. A common vulgarisation of ST, much favoured by the *Economist*, involves muddling output and outcome and switching promiscuously between the two as each suits for evaluating ST. This propagandistic vulgarisation is exemplified in its survey of East European economies of 3 December 1994, p. 23.

11. Sachs is printed here as writing 'the developing world' but this must be a misprint: the context shows he means the developed world. See *Understanding Shock Therapy*, p. 15.

12. Ibid., p. 15.

13. Sachs uses the claim that his goal is capitalism as such to claim that he is politically neutral as between all varieties of capitalism, whether Swedish, South Korean or Chilean. Yet his specifics refute such neutrality.

14. Jeffrey Sachs, 'Consolidating Capitalism', *Foreign Policy*, 98 (Spring 1995).

15. Ibid. Though always keeping the number six, Sachs's list differs from the above in his Social Market Foundation pamphlet *Understanding Shock Therapy*. Given the name of the foundation for which he was writing, he astutely adds introducing a social safety net as his sixth core reform, thus dropping the point about meeting the membership criteria of the multilateral institutions. But he nevertheless makes clear the importance of joining these organisations in the pamphlet.

16. Sachs, *Poland's Jump*, p. 3.

17. Sachs, 'What is to be Done?'

18. Speech by Ambassador Donald Blinken at the Collegium Budapest, 16 March 1995 (Mimeo US Embassy, Budapest).

19. John Lloyd, 'How to Make a Market', *London Review of Books*, 10th November 1994.

20. John Lloyd, 'How to Make a Market'.

21. See UNCTAD, *World Investment Report 1994. Transnational Corporations, Employment and the Workplace* (United Nations, 1994), p. 98.

22. OECD, *Integrating Emerging Market Economies into the International Trading System* (OECD, 1994). The actual OECD formulation here is interesting. It puts its statement in the passive voice, saying: 'The contribution of inward foreign direct investment (FDI) is considered crucial to the process of transition to a market economy.' It thus avoids saying who considers it to be crucial, but we are left to infer that the OECD itself believes this to be the case.

23. Ibid. The OECD doesn't explain the force of the must here except to say that foreign companies will be central 'in restructuring the state-owned industries'. This, as we have seen, is because the World Bank in Poland and Hungary would not allow Industry ministries to restructure before privatisation.

24. Sachs, *Poland's Jump*, p. XIII.

25. Ibid., p. 7.

26. Though he curiously downplays them in *Understanding Shock Therapy*. He also eschews public discussion of the tactics of conditionality despite the fact that this must have been part of his daily working diet in his consultancy work in the region.

27. John Lloyd also recognises the power of the G7 states but he rather pompously calls them 'the world' and proceeds to talk about what 'the world' will or will not tolerate. See his 'How to Make a Market'.

28. Sachs, *Poland's Jump*, p. XIII.

29. Stanisław Gomulka has largely subscribed to this view, pointing out that western macroeconomic support or debt reduction would encourage indiscipline among target governments similar to the soft budget constraints enjoyed by state enterprises under Communism.

30. Jeffrey Sachs, 'Beyond Bretton Woods: A New Blueprint', *Economist*, 1 October 1994, p. 28.

31. Sachs, 'What is to be Done?'

32. Sachs, *Poland's Jump*, p. 46.

33. Sachs, *Poland's Jump*, p. 32.

34. He doesn't explain this idea of risk. See 'What is to be Done?', p. 26.

35. Sachs, *Poland's Jump*, p. 83.

36. Sachs, 'What is to be Done?', p. 26.

37. Sachs, *Poland's Jump*, p. 89.

38. 'Big Bang, Big Adventure', *Economist*, 23 December 1989.

39. OECD: *Integrating Emerging Market Economies*.

40. Ibid.

41. Jeffrey Sachs, 'Reply to Jan Adam', *Economics of Planning*, vol. 26 (1993).

42. See Patrick A. Messerlin, 'The Association Agreements Between the EC and Central Europe: Trade Liberalisation vs Constitutional Failure?' in J. Flemming and J. M. C. Rollo (eds.), *Trade, Payments and Adjustment in Central and Eastern Europe* (RIIA & EBRD, 1992).

43. The *Economist* has followed suit, claiming that while 'all the post-Communist economies suffered deep recessions . . . Much of this hardship was, however, the legacy of Communism's failure, not the product of capitalism's arrival.' 3 December 1994, p. 24. No one has, of course, suggested that the slump was caused by 'capitalism's arrival'. Others initially sought to deny the existence of slumps on the grounds that the statistical indicators were wrong.

44. Gomulka, *The Bretton Woods Institutions and the Transition*, p. 23.

45. *Economist*, 15 August 1992, pp. 1–12. A Russian reading such explanations could be forgiven for wondering if the *Economist* was simply driven by hatred of the Russian economy.

46. Ibid.

47. Their study was for the European Commission. See G. Hughes and P. Hare, 'Competitiveness and Industrial Restructuring in Czechoslovakia, Hungary and Poland', in *Commission of the European Communities: European Economy*, Special Edition, no. 2, 1991.

48. My discussion here draws heavily on Holger Schmieding, 'From Plan to Market: The Nature of the Transformation Crisis', in *Weltwirtschaftliches Archiv* (Journal of the Kiel Institute of World Economics), vol. 129 (1993).

49. I have slightly telescoped Schmieding here, avoiding some nuances in his argument that are not relevant to this discussion.

50. *Economist*, 8 August 1992, p. 68.

51. Schmieding, 'From Plan to Market', p. 225.

52. Interview with Timothy Garton Ash, *The Oxford International Review* (Winter Issue 1994), p. 5.

53. C. Randall Henning et al. (eds.), *Reviving the European Union* (Institute for International Economics, April 1994), p. 173.

54. UNICEF, *Economies in Transition Studies, Regional Monitoring Report, 1994. Crisis in Mortality, Health and Nutrition* (1994).

55. Michael Ellman, 'The Increase in Death and Disease under "Katastroika"', *Cambridge Journal of Economics*, no. 18 (1994), p. 349.

56. Ibid.

57. UNICEF, *Economics in Transition Studies*, p. 63.

58. Ellman, 'The Increase in Death and Disease', p. 349.

59. UNICEF, *Economics in Transition Studies*, p. 53.

60. Ibid.

61. Ibid.

62. Alice Amsden et al., *The Market Meets Its Match: Restructuring the Economies of Eastern Europe* (Harvard, 1994), p. 89.

63. Ibid., p. 96.

64. See ibid., pp. 94–95.

65. Sachs, *Poland's Jump*, p. 50.

66. This is one of numerous examples where Sachs's claim to be introducing western institutional models applies only to western ideological models for others rather than to western practice.

67. Giles Merritt, *Eastern Europe and the USSR: The Challenge of Freedom* (Kogan Page, 1991), p. 111.

68. The present writer bought a Philips short-wave radio, costing $75 duty free at Vienna airport for $14 in Kiev!

69. Cited by Giles Merritt, *Eastern Europe*, p. 111.

70. See Amsden, *The Market Meets Its Match*. The OECD supported the establishment of export credit insurance and financing, via Export Credit Agencies (ECAs), provided they would follow the OECD Arrangement on Guidelines for Officially Supported Export Credit. The OECD explained that 'This would put them on an equal footing with OECD countries and therefore not distort trade.' But this is false since various major western countries don't stick to these guidelines. By 1994 various East European countries had set up ECAs but, the OECD explains laconically, they have not been able to work because 'funding has been restricted'. OECD, *Integrating Emerging Market Economies into the International Trading System* (OECD, 1994).

71. Cited by Jan Adam, 'The Transition to a Market Economy in Poland', *Cambridge Journal of Economics*, 18, (1994) p. 613.

72. For a thorough analysis of the European Agreements' trade aspects, see Patrick A. Messerlin, 'The Association Agreements between the EC and Central Europe'.

73. See Messerlin on this, ibid.

74. UN Economic Commission for Europe, *Economic Bulletin for Europe*, vol. 45 (1993), p. 63.

75. In 1993, the year after the Agreement came into force, Hungary's food and agricultural exports to the EC dropped 28 per cent. Poland's dropped 12 per cent. See OECD, *Agricultural Policies, Markets and Trade. Monitoring and Outlook 1994* (OECD, 1994).

76. Ibid, p. 69.

77. C. Mastropasqua and V. Rolli, 'Industrial Countries' Protectionism with Respect to Eastern Europe: the Impact of the Association Agreements Concluded with the EC on the Exports of Poland, Czechoslovakia and Hungary', *The World Economy*, 17: 2 (1994).

78. Stanisław Gomulka, *The Bretton Woods Institutions and the Transition*, p. 11.

79. Sachs, *Understanding Shock Therapy* p. 26.

80. At one point IMF officials publicly raised the case for relief for Hungary, whose debts in per-capita terms have been higher than Poland's. But the G7 has taken no action on this.

81. Though this is nowhere, of course, mentioned as its mission in its charter.

82. Gomulka, *The Bretton Woods Institution*, p. 25.

83. Sachs, *Consolidating Capitalism*, pp. 60–61.

84. See R. Vintrova, 'The General Recession and The Structural Adaptation Crisis', *East European Economics*, 31:3 (Spring 1993).

85. Ibid., p. 83.

86. J. C. Brada, I. Singh and A. Torok, 'Firms Afloat and Firms Adrift: Hungarian Industry and the Economic Transition', *Eastern European Economics*, (January–February, 1994).

87. Vintrova, 'The General Recession'.

88. Brada et al., 'Firms Afloat and Firms Adrift'.

89. Amsden et al., *The Market Meets its Match*, p. 116.

90. Quoted by Alice Amsden, ibid., p. 117. In this case the WB was dealing with Hungary.

91. Quoted ibid., p. 117.

92. Quoted ibid., p. 119.

93. Quoted ibid., p. 121.

94. Virginia Marsh, 'Consolidation and Reform', in Financial Times Survey of Romania, *Financial Times*, 25 May 1995, p. 35.

95. For a useful summary of western governments' stances on these issues, see OECD, *Integrating Emerging Market Economies into the International Trading System* (OECD, 1994).

96. See Virginia Marsh, 'Privatisation: A Complicated Programme' in Financial Times Survey of Romania, *Financial Times*, 25 May 1995, p. 34.

97. For a fuller analysis of both PHARE and TACIS, see Peter Gowan, 'Los Programas de ayuda PHARE y TACIS de la Union Europea' in *Revista de Economia* (Madrid), no. 738, (February 1995).

98. See PHARE Regulation No. 3906/89, *Official Journal* L375, 23 December 1989 and the amending Regulation No. 2698/90, *Official Journal* L257, 21 September 1990.

99. Bulgaria, Czechoslovakia, Yugoslavia and East Germany were included in PHARE in September 1990. East Germany ceased to be a participant after German unification. PHARE aid to Yugoslavia was suspended in 1991 (though humanitarian aid continued to Bosnia-Hercegovina and to Macedonia). Albania and the Baltic states joined the programme at the end of 1991 (see Council Regulation No. 3800/91, *Official Journal* L357, 28 December

1991); Slovenia joined in August 1992 (see Council Regulation No. 2334/92, *Official Journal* L227, 11 August 1992).

100. Article 3, paragraph 2 of the PHARE Regulation.

101. See the Court of Auditors' Report in the *Official Journal of the European Communities*, 15 December 1992, p. 219.

102. Court of Auditors' Annual Report for 1990, *Official Journal*, 13 December 1991, p. 177. PHARE pesticide aid to Albania was declared by the European Parliament in March 1994 to have involved the export of toxic waste. The Parliament called for the aid to be immediately withdrawn and ask the Commission to make a report to it on PHARE aid as a whole and especially on PHARE agricultural assistance. See the proceedings of the European Parliament, 11 March 1994 and the *Bulletin of the European Community*, 3–1994. Parliament also wanted to know whether the Commission had verified whether Albania had needed agrochemicals.

103. Ibid.

104. Court of Auditors' Report on 1991, *Official Journal*, 15 December 1992, p. 216–17.

105. Portes in C. Randall Henning et al. (eds.), *Reviving the European Union* (Institute for International Economics, April 1994).

106. Auditors' Report, *Official Journal* C309, 16 November 1993, p. 191.

107. Court of Auditors' Report on 1992, *Official Journal*, 16 November 1993, p. 185.

108. Ibid.

109. Parliament adopted a resolution on these issues on 18 January 1994. See *Official Journal* C61, 14 February 1994 and the *Bulletin of the European Union*, 1/2–1994.

110. Court of Auditors' Report on 1991, *Official Journal*, 15 December 1992, p. 216.

111. Ibid., p. 218.

112. Projects for less than 1 million ecu can avoid the full clearance procedures and the study had not been asked for by the Czechoslovak authorities. But this study was carried out without a financing agreement with the recipient government, without any prior commitment of funds and without an agreed programme.

113. Ibid., p. 215.

114. A. Mayhew, 'Assessment of the PHARE Programme from the Commission's Point of View' in European Court of Auditors, *Co-operation with the Countries of Central and Eastern Europe – Assessment of Financial Aid* (Commission of the European Communities, 1994), p.148.

115. The US government has also, however, played a role: it emerged that the US was paying a salary of over $70,000 a year to the head of the government agency dealing with privatisation in Hungary, in addition to his regular salary. But this arrangement terminated when it became public and the person concerned lost his job.

116. In 1994 80 per cent of the Polish Privatisation Agency's operating capital was funded by EU grants. See the *Economist*, 17 September 1994.

117. *Economist*, 17 September 1994, p. 47.

118. *Economist*, 8 January 1994, p. 18.

119. On this point for developing countries see: UNCTAD: World Investment Report, 1994 (United Nations, 1994), p. 20.

120. 'The major objective for FDI in Central and Eastern Europe was "markets"'. OECD Working Paper No. 43: Market Access–FDI/Trade Linkages in Eastern Europe (Paris, 1994), p. 5.

121. By the summer of 1992, in retailing, some ninety major Western firms had moved into the region. In Hungary they had by then captured 20 per cent of the retail market. See John Thornhill, 'E. Europe Entices the Bold', *Financial Times*, 19 October 1992, p. 3.

122. Anthony Robinson, 'An Awesome Task', *Financial Times*, 13 January 1992.

123. UNCTAD, *World Investment Report*, 1994, p. 100.

124. This information on Skoda is drawn from Dean Calbreath, 'Together Forever?' *Business Central Europe* (March 1995), pp. 7–10.

125. Ibid.

126. Ibid., p. 8.

127. Kevin Done, 'Shock of the Free Market', *Financial Times*, 2 June 1995, p. IX.

128. See UNCTAD, *World Investment Report*, 1994, p. 106.

129. Of the sixty-five corporations privatised by the Ministry of Privatisation in Poland by 1

June 1993, only nineteen were bought by Polish concerns. See *Privatisation in Poland* (Information Centre at the Ministry of Privatisation, June 1993).

130. UNCTAD, *World Investment Report*, 1994, p. 106.

131. UNCTAD, *World Investment Report*, 1994 (United Nations, 1994), p. 100.

132. Lloyd, 'How to Make a Market'.

133. Ibid.

134. OECD Trade Policy Issues, *Intra-Firm Trade* (OECD, Paris, 1993). The only reliable data on IFT, according to the OECD, apply to the US and Japan.

135. Richard Parker, 'Clintonomics for the East', *Foreign Policy*, no. 94 (Spring 1994) p. 60.

136. United Nations Industrial Development Organisation, *Industry Development Global Report*, 1992/93 (Vienna).

137. World Bank 1993 Enterprise and Financial Sector Adjustment Loan to Poland, quoted in Amsden, *The Market Meets its Match*, p. 124.

138. Except in the Czech Republic, where government health spending rose in 1993 as a result of its decision to privatise health insurance. For an enthusiastic article on the privatisation see the *Economist*, 28 May 1994, p. 48.

139. Prime Minister Horn appealed privately to Chancellors Kohl and Vranitsky to support him in resisting this requirement, but they responded by demanding that he fully implement it.

140. Such concepts were also rationalised by neoclassical welfare economists who argued that bandit capitalism was pareto optimal on the grounds that the politically connected bandit capitalists would gain while nobody else would lose since nobody else owned anything anyway.

141. *Economist*, 9 July 1994, pp. 21–22.

142. W. Wesolowski, 'The Nature of Social Ties and the Future of Postcommunist Society: Poland After Solidarity', in John A. Hall, ed., *Civil Society. Theory, History, Comparison*, (Cambridge University Press, 1995).

143. Anne Applebaum, 'The Fall and Rise of the Communists: Guess Who's Running Central Europe', *Foreign Affairs* 73:6 (November–December 1994), pp. 7–13.

144. Michael Ignatieff, 'On Civil Society', *Foreign Affairs* (March–April 1995).

145. Jonathan Steele, *Eternal Russia* (Faber, 1994).

146. Ibid. The *Economist* was more honest, stating that if Yeltsin had not confronted the Parliament 'little would have remained of his . . . ability to press on with the reforms Russia needs . . .' See the *Economist*, 9 October 1993, p. 15.

147. Lloyd, 'Yeltsin's Year of Living Dangerously', *Financial Times*, 5 January 1993.

148. *Economist*, 9 October 1993, p. 15.

149. *Economist*, 1 May, 1993, p. 14.

150. Ibid., p. 41.

151. The *Economist* had imagined that the Suchocka liberals would win in Poland's 1993 elections (see the *Economist*, June 5 1993, p. 43). It predicted that the opposition in Estonia would not be able to question what it saw as the triumphantly successful policies of its ST government (see the *Economist*, 19 November 1994, p. 54). Yet this government was able to marshal only 5 per cent of the vote in March 1995 elections. It predicted that the Hungarian elections would be a contest between its favourites in the Young Democrats and the Free Democrats. Yet the Young Democrats achieved insignificant results and the Socialists achieved an overall majority.

152. Virginia Marsh and Kevin Done, 'Unexpected Degree of Stability', *Financial Times*, 25 May 1995, p. 33.

153. Quoted ibid.

154. Even more facile are the attempts by the *Economist* to hold up various East European economies as being sounder than western ones on the basis of the size of their budget deficits!

155. J. M. C. Rollo and J. Stern, 'Growth and Trade Prospects for Central and Eastern Europe', *The World Economy* 15: 5 (1992). Their calculations show that 'growth over the whole 1988–2010 period is unlikely, even under the optimistic scenario, to lead to a major improvement in the relative living standards of Eastern Europe'.

156. Ibid.

157. Sachs, 'Consolidating Capitalism', p. 60.

10

Neo-Liberalism and Civil Society

Across East Central Europe in the late 1980s, young intellectuals were sitting down at their desks to write essays on civil society. In 1991 in the Soviet Union, desks were being cleared for the same purpose: to win a Soros scholarship to the West by showing where you stood on civil society. Alumni came for a diet of seminars in places like Oxford to learn about our wonderful institutions (although, naturally, one wouldn't brag). The entire experience was a refreshing one for all concerned. Not least for the teachers. After all, these students seemed to believe in it all, at a time when many of the lecturers were not at all sure what to think, bombarded as they were by the strident assaults on their liberal values, on institutions of civil society like their own liberal universities, the BBC, the higher civil service with its ethic of public service, the local authorities, the serious press, the welfare services, the teachers, the health service, and trade unionism. Government by discussion was ridiculed as the talk shop of the chattering classes. In short the very idea of the liberal democratic state was under assault. And the attack was being waged with all the most sophisticated techniques of mass suggestion, not least by savaging liberalism in the language of liberalism itself. The authoritarian populists were laying into civil society in the colours of so-called neo-liberalism.

Liberals Versus Neo-liberals

For decades western liberals had seen a strong civil society as an integral element within the state acting as a countervailing force to the power of a secretive state executive and to market forces in the determination of public policy. Civil society involved a network of associations and institutions, many of them supported by public funds, which exerted democratic pressures, calling both state executive bodies and big business to account.

And civil society was underpinned by a strong welfare state, providing through its education system, public health systems, public housing and other local services a minimum basis for citizenship. The role of civil society was a political one within the liberal democratic view of the state: to ensure that public policy was governed by wide discussion and public pressure by the citizens through a myriad of civil associations and institutions. *Civil society was integral to the state as a law-governed liberal democracy*, while being always in tension with the state executive and with 'the unacceptable face of capitalism'.

In the 1970s, the attack was rather crude: the cry went up that the state was too weak because of democratic overload. All the pressures from civil society (then called special interests) were making western countries 'ungovernable'. In the 1980s the target and the aim remained the same, but the discursive tactics changed 180 per cent. Neo-liberalism was born and 'the individual' was being crushed by a rapacious state. The crusade was launched against 'the state' to free the individual, the economy and Uncle Tom Cobbley.

Traditional liberal suspicion of the state executive has been replaced by hostility towards the welfare state. The threat now came from the Inland Revenue, behind which stood the sinister forces of local government social services departments, teachers and the fat cats in the Direct Labour Departments or the trade union barons amongst the cleaners in the health service. Liberals were told to stop worrying about civil liberties and rally around to sharpen the sword of the state against the miners. Those who objected were dubbed the chattering classes, the consensus mongers or worse.

The neo-liberals also took up the language of civil society to turn the liberal concept on its head. Instead of being a network of associations and institutions for invigilating state executives and market forces and articulating collective interests and concerns, it was to become a mixture of big business charitable foundations and self-help institutions for the deserving poor on one side; and archipelagos of unaccountable quangos for managing a depoliticised, privatised, publicly passive individual consumer on the other. The institutions of this neo-liberal civil society are above all there to ensure that the population stops prioritising the public welfare, stops looking for collective solutions to society's problems. In the name of freeing society (or the 'individual') from the (welfare) state, the social engineers of neo-liberalism have been attempting to free the state executive from social responsibilities and from accountability to civil society.

Power and policy can be the preserve of a strengthened private network of increasingly incestuous linkages between executive officials and big business people and media barons, to which members of parliament doff their caps in the hope of a 'consultancy' contract.

A Civil Society for Eastern Europe

The Soros scholars and their less fortunate aspirant colleagues in Eastern Europe would have gathered little or nothing of such painful debates from the tranquil prose of one of the most prominent proponents of a civil society for Eastern Europe in the 1980s, Timothy Garton Ash. The clashes between the liberals and the neo-liberal social engineers were surely minor differences when we were faced with a monstrous Communist totalitarianism in the East. Any form of civil society was surely better than that.

In the writings of Garton Ash on East Central Europe in the 1980s, developments in the East were indeed interpreted as being driven by the clash between 'totalitarianism', seeking, in Ash's words, 'to rule over an atomised society' and a civil society which embodied the idea of 'social self-organisation' in the form of networks of autonomous social groups and movements which together would form, as Ash puts it 'a strong civil society, rich in intermediate layers of free and frank association'.[1] These themes were developed by Garton Ash in his earlier book, *The Uses of Adversity*, and were in turn derived from the writings of Adam Michnik. Of course, the paradigm of such social self-organisation was Solidarnosc in Poland, especially its intellectual networks.

But with the disappearance of 'Communist totalitarianism', the discussion about civil society in the East has become altogether more complicated, not to say delicate. And the neo-liberal social engineers have set to work over there. Meanwhile, back in Oxford, Garton Ash's efforts have been strengthened by a new addition at St. Antony's – Michael Ignatieff. We will try to trace how these ideas on civil society have evolved.

Civil Society Mark 1: Infrastructure of Liberal Democracy

In 1990 Ralph Dahrendorf produced a short book on the transformations in Eastern Europe in 1989: *Reflections on the Revolution in Europe*[2] was a fairly classical western liberal statement on what civil society should mean for post-Communist societies. Interestingly, Garton Ash endorsed Dahrendorf's book as a classic.

Dahrendorf sees the civil society as a network of institutions and relationships integral to the liberal state, which he prefers to call, following Karl Popper, the Open Society. He thus endorses the ideas of government by open discussion, incremental policy making in which each step forward is the output of negotiation between executive and civil associations. The right policy is the policy endorsed by the bulk of the pluralistic civil institutions. These collectivities, with their varied and distinctive cultures, outlooks and interests will be strengthened through being included in the open discussion.

His proposals are close to those of Habermas for trying to achieve an undistorted communicative public space. And they restate Charles Lindblom's classic view of best policy as the policy of 'muddling through' via the impact of a host of special groups and outlooks upon initial ideas, altering and even 'distorting' pure concepts to fit these into the particularities of a complex society which are beyond the grasp of a single 'scientific-rational' brain.

Dahrendorf therefore repudiates the temptations offered by the neo-liberal Social Engineers: the planners with their systems. As he puts it: 'The countries of East–Central Europe have not shed their communist system in order to embrace the capitalist system – whatever that is. They have shed a closed system in order to create an open society.' There is no 'correct path', just experiment and trial and error by a large and diverse inter-subjective civil society.

And Dahrendorf is particularly worried that the leaders of the new Eastern Europe will be sold a second-hand western model of how they should engineer their new states. 'The common language we speak today is not the language of the West, now adopted by the East. It is an intrinsically universal language which belongs to nobody in particular and therefore to everybody . . . If any creed has won in the events of last year, it is the idea that we are all embarked on a journey into an uncertain future and have to work by trial and error within institutions which make it possible to bring about change without bloodshed.'

The Neo-Liberal Riposte

Even the busiest of the neo-liberal planners could not let this pass. Despite a gruelling schedule which had involved working over Yugoslavia's federal government in 1989, then sorting out Poland before tackling the biggest heavy engineering job of all in Russia in 1992, Jeffrey Sachs flew in to LSE to reply.

As Sachs puts it: 'I consider Professor Dahrendorf to be mistaken in his view that Eastern Europe did not shed the communist system to adopt capitalism. In my view that is precisely what they have done, and all of their actions are directed towards this purpose . . . If instead the philosophy were one of open experimentation, I doubt that the transformation would be possible at all, at least without costly and dangerous wrong turns.'[3] Sachs was no cynic. He passionately believed in his shock therapy. Nor does Sachs necessarily endorse the full neo-liberal programme for emasculating civil societies in the West – though he is no friend of the welfare state. The point is that Sachs is a professional social engineer and in engineering things must be done methodically – first one thing then another. And the civil society part of the machinery has to be fitted in at the end, not at the beginning: first a capitalist labour market (and unemployment); then with privatisation a bourgeoisie (capitalists); then (with foreign direct investment and an export boom) economic growth; and then, but only then can there be institutional stabilisation – i.e. a stable liberal democracy and civil society. What, you may ask, tides people over in the meantime? Sachs has two answers: first, let us reduce the meantime to an absolute minimum by sweeping aside every obstacle and resistance to getting the capitalist system established. And secondly, put western money in to bolster the supporters of capitalism and buy off opponents or undermine them.

Civil Society Mark 2: Building a Middle Class

In his more recent writing, Timothy Garton Ash has engaged in a conceptual slippage. He wobbles away from Dahrendorf in the direction of Sachs. Ash claims to be against Sachs-style teleology. He says 'we don't know what the transition is to' and he argues that those who pretend to know, 'end up, often quite crudely, awarding place marks in the race to democracy: "The Czechs are in the lead, Poland is lagging slightly, Ukraine is bringing up the rear . . ."'[4]

But there seems to be an evasion here. The neo-liberal teleologists do not make absolute predictions about the future. They know that they face enemies who could derail their plans and turn the objects of their planning in other directions. What the planners do have is criteria of assessment as to the progression or regression in the countries concerned. And so, indeed, do liberals like Dahrendorf: his criteria must be the consolidation of open societies with strong civil networks checking executive power and untrammelled market forces.

And so, it turns out in the same article, does Ash. Or rather Ash gives us two, rather different benchmarks – one vague and one very clear. The first one is not only vague but evasive. He declares that those societies 'in which civil society was developed and there were elements of a middle class and a market economy have made dramatically better progress' while others in the former USSR are bringing up the rear. Yet this is rather opaque: after all, the Czech Republic could scarcely be said to have had elements of a market economy in Ash's sense before 1989. It is also not clear what Sachs is referring to in suggesting that Russia, say, had a smaller middle class – presumably intelligentsia is in some sense referred to – proportionately than, say Poland or Czechoslovakia. And the reference to civil society is unspecified.

Yet, later in the same piece, Ash adopts a different and altogether clearer conception of the criterion for judging success. He states: '. . . the social dimension of transition is a neglected third dimension [between economic and political dimensions], and that is often where the differences between success and failure are to be sought . . .' But now the social dimension is no longer the networks of civil society, but something altogether more solid: a capitalist class, a bourgeoisie. As he puts it: 'There is real truth in the Marxist label for liberal democracy: "bourgeois democracy".'

This is exactly Sachs's point: first we must engineer a bourgeoisie, then the institutional frills of civil society etc. can be added. Ash does not say this. He does not endorse the use of the state executive to forge this bourgeoisie on the anvil of shock therapy. But he endorses Sachs's sequence: first a capitalist class, then the rest.

Civil Society Mark 3: Administered from the West

The delicacy and good taste with which Ash picks his way round these issues contrasts with the tactlessness of Michael Ignatieff, as he tries simultaneously to wrestle with the concept of civil society while locking horns with the new regimes in Eastern Europe.

Ignatieff, writing in *Foreign Affairs*,[5] begins with the conventional idea that, as he had put it in 1989, 'in Hungary, Poland, Romania, East Germany, Czechoslovakia and the Baltics civil society triumphed over the state'. He then takes us through some pages on the theory of civil society before returning to Eastern Europe to discover that everything has changed. 'All of the post-Communist regimes are nominally democratic, but in practice the levers of power have usually remained in the hands of the old nomenklatura.' How the triumph he hails at the start of the article turned out to be illusory we do not learn: there is not a scrap of analysis of the actual fate of civil society in the region between 1989 and 1995.

But Ignatieff proposes the following lines of force as his solution: a strong state executive able to use force to coerce order, and prevent the social beast from escaping its cage. He declares that 'invisible hands are no substitute for the magistrate's sword'. At the same time he reassures us that in Eastern Europe outside Yugoslavia 'state structures remain sufficiently robust to contain ethnic conflict'. Nevertheless danger still looms throughout the societies of the region in the form of authoritarian populism. And the sword of the state executive will not be enough to slay this social monster.

It is at this point that Ignatieff finds a practical use for the concept of civil society. Civil society will be injected into the region as a weapon against authoritarian populism. Together with the sword of the magistrate, civil society will pacify the population. This is what Ignatieff calls his civil society strategy. It means an effort to change the behaviour of populations in the East through bureaucratic engineering by western administrative agencies.

Ignatieff elaborates as follows: 'This means funding independent media; maintaining ties not simply with governments and regimes but with their oppositions; providing aid and assistance to strengthening the key institutions of civil society, the courts, judiciary and police; developing charitable and voluntary associations so that the population ceases to look to the state and begins to look to its own strengths . . .' We must, he says, start 'with the search for partners outside the state, the leading parties, and the bureaucracy'.

Ignatieff's remark here that the population should be encouraged not to look to the state but to its own strengths, may alarm some readers. It could sound like an authoritarian populist call to arms against the magistrate and his sword. But this is to misunderstand Ignatieff's neo-liberal code. It means society should not seek public solutions to their problems through the democratic state: they should solve their problems privately by their own efforts.

His civil society crucially involves 'the refusal to privilege public goals over private ones, [and] the insistence that liberty can only have a negative rather than a positive content'. In other words, Ignatieff's civil society is a strong network for turning the population away from involvement in democratic politics towards finding its own solutions, preferably privately, while interpreting its own freedom as freedom from interference by the democratic state.

The Analytical Vacuum

These bewildering discursive shifts on the theme of civil society evince two striking characteristics. Both Garton Ash and Ignatieff display a jaundiced weariness in their attitudes towards the current situation in Eastern Europe. And secondly, neither of them provides a scrap of analysis of actual civic associations and what has happened to them since their supposed triumph over 'the state' in 1989.

Their posture of civil exasperation with the region contrasts with the bullish satisfaction of Professor Jeffrey Sachs. He is, on the whole, extremely pleased with his efforts at Shock Therapy since 1989. In a recent defence of his record[6] he notes that most of the states in the region have taken his medicine. He does mention that Ukraine was bringing up the rear, but since he wrote his pamphlet, Ukraine too has joined the conveyor-belt. Sachs is pleased because the countries of the region have made strides towards the capitalist market, have created a capitalist labour market with substantial pools of unemployment, have privatised a great deal of industry and have tackled budget deficits (in other words, cut welfare, health and educational spending). Sachs does not waste his time on analysis of the institutional tissues of civil associations in these countries over the last five years. These are tasks for the future.

The Fate of Real Existing Civil Societies

If there is one country where civil society could have been said to have emerged in East Central Europe in the 1980s it was surely in Poland, with the rise of Solidarnosc in 1980–81. We may leave aside in this context whether the events of 1989 in Poland were a triumph for 'civil society' over the state. But without question, the leaders of the new government of Mazowiecki came to power on the basis of their source in Solidarnosc, the bastion of independent civil networks in Poland.

What then happened was governed by Shock Therapy, driven by the conceptions which Jeffrey Sachs has popularised. The IMF and four successive governments claiming allegiance to the Solidarnosc tradition drove this shock treatment home. The networks of societal interests were not consulted and were not drawn into processes of inter-institutional bargaining, consensus-building and compromise. They were railroaded.

The first group to protest were the mainstay of Poland's private sector: the private peasantry. By the summer of 1990 they were already having to take to the streets in a vain attempt to defend their institutions and interests against the drive for Shock Therapy. But the central conflict which has driven Polish politics has been that between the industrial core of Solidarnosc and the neo-liberals in the government, backed by the International Financial Institutions. The syndicalist wing of Solidarnosc wanted to maintain and strengthen the control of state enterprises by their self-management bodies. This was reversed and power was recentralised into the hands of state agencies. The syndicalists wanted privatisation to involve the transfer of enterprises to employees. This was rejected. The government imposed hard wage controls on the state sector and refused to end them. Wage controls were not applied to the private sector. State enterprises faced heavy taxes in order to give private companies tax breaks. These measures driven through by World Bank conditionality were classic efforts at social engineering: to generate demands amongst workers in state enterprises for privatisation on the government's terms.

The efforts to create a demobilised, depoliticised, apathetic society in Poland were to some extent successful. Participation rates in elections dropped dramatically, as they did also in Hungary. Electoral participation in allegedly backward Ukraine was much higher. Yet at the same time political thinking began to evolve within the syndicalist core of Solidarity and within the electorates. In the summer of 1993 in Poland, Solidarity moved against the very government it had spawned and formed an alliance with the ex-Communist Socialist Party and its allied Peasant Party. This alliance brought the government down. The electorate in Poland also moved, with voters turning to the former Communists and Peasant Party allies to give them a majority in Parliament. These parties, portrayed as the totalitarian apparatus that, in Ash's view, aspired to atomise the population, had in fact been the only parties with real social links in terms of significant numbers of active supporters in localities.

This trend has been a widespread one within the region: it has applied in Lithuania, Hungary, Slovenia, Bulgaria, Ukraine and Estonia as well as in Poland. The same trend has been witnessed in Russia. When Gaidar's Shock Therapy was introduced by Yeltsin at the start of 1992, the majority in Parliament had granted Yeltsin special extraordinary powers to try radical economic reform. The consequences of the Shock Therapy turned Parliament against the programme. Instead of recognising that this shift in Parliament's attitude reflected a shift in Russian society that should be respected, the *Economist* (1 May 1993) urged Yeltsin to break with the Constitutional Law governing the country, the legal framework which had enabled Yeltsin himself to be elected leader. Five months later Yeltsin took the *Economist*'s advice, to wide applause from many alleged supporters of civil society and liberal values in the West. (See the admirably dispassionate account of the Russian crisis of 1993 in Jonathan Steele's book, *Eternal Russia*, 1994.) The result was a surge of support not only for the Communist party but also for fascism in the December 1993 elections.

In the fact of these swings back to the former Communist parties in the region, Garton Ash, in *In Europe's Name*, has declared: 'I confess quite frankly that I find it not only distasteful but also puzzling.' A key to this puzzle could perhaps lie in an aspect of these societies in the 1990s that neither Garton Ash nor Ignatieff have deemed significant enough to even mention in their writings on the fate of civil society in the region: the tragedy which everyday life has become for very large parts of these societies.

There has been a catastrophic rise in poverty and malnutrition in many countries. A study in Russia by Goskomstat and the World Bank defined the poverty line as the income needed to maintain food consumption sufficient to maintain a normal body weight at an average level of activity – an austere definition by western standards. The study showed that in 1992, 37 per cent of the Russian population fell below this line, while the figure for children under fifteen was a horrifying 46–47 per cent. A study carried out by CARE and the US Centre for Disease Control in 1992 found that on average Russian pensions were below what the World Bank estimated to be the minimal nutritional support level for a person living alone. Using UNICEF's definition the proportion of Poland's population suffering such malnutrition was negligible in 1989 but had reached 17.9 per cent in 1992. Similar problems, as well as problems of health, housing and life expectancy can be found in other countries of Eastern Europe. It is frankly distasteful to read western discussions about the problems of societies in Eastern Europe which ignore these problems.

Yet it is against this background that we can assess the proposals for the future from Ignatieff. We might expect him to make some suggestions as to how economies shattered by the West's shock therapy policy could be helped. Surely Michael Ignatieff, so moved in the 1980s by the 'power of the powerless' in Eastern Europe might be moved by the plight of the poverty-stricken there now.

The answer seems to be that we just don't know what either his or Garton Ash's reaction might be because if they have noticed the eastern slump, the poverty, and the tattered social tissue left in their wake, they make no reference to it. Instead Ignatieff leaves vague the exact source of the future menace he wishes us to launch a preventive strike against.

Michael Ignatieff's project is for western bureaucracies to disburse funds in support of the values he holds dear, not least the value of 'the refusal to privilege public goals over private ones'. He claims also to value above all negative freedom from state interference, yet with the obvious qualification that such state interference is OK in Eastern Europe provided it comes from western states following his 'civil society strategy'.

Some may be inclined to smile at the crudely bureaucratic forms of thinking displayed here by Ignatieff. The professional social engineers like Sachs do not go in for such old-fashioned administrative methods. They create structured social frameworks into which incentives and sanctions are built in such a way that rational individuals will be more or less bound to behave in the Correct Way. You don't take a state enterprise manager and give him a hand-out; nor do you give him any orders at all. You just change interest rates, impose credit ceilings on banks and alter the tax system to the point where the manager would be mad not to sack some workers. Ignatieff's idea of funding friends in the media is rather crude.

Yet there is an icy remark in his text: that note that 'all the postcommunist states' still being controlled by the nomenklatura. This is rubbish. But what does he mean by the nomenklatura? The term used to mean the permanent officials in the upper layer of ruling Communist Parties. What does he mean by it now? We do not know. But he could mean the officials of the ex-Communist Parties now in government in so many East European countries. And this gives his statement an ugly undertone. For he uses the remark to say that democracy there is only formal. By this he means it doesn't really exist. And that idea can be used to justify western governments flouting minimally civilised standards of behaviour in the region. Is Ignatieff seeking to open a window to covert action against the Socialist Parties in the East? Is his list of targets – the media, the opposition, the courts, the judiciary and police – a signal for exporting to Eastern Europe the manuals on the desks in discreet offices in Latin American capitals accommodating the station chiefs of the CIA? The meaning is unclear. It should have been clarified.

The European Union and the rest of the western alliance is, in fact, taking overt action on these matters: not just by Ignatieff's funding agents, but also through the Pact for Stability. This puts pressure on the states of the region to sign binding international legal treaties renouncing claims to do with ethnic minorities or territorial disputes and granting adequate rights to their minorities. Yet there is a curious oversight in all this. Disputes involving the member states of the EU are excluded from this treaty-making process. Yet if we look more closely, most of the active claims of this sort at present in Europe are claims involving EU members with claims against former Communist countries: Germany has an active claim against the Czech Republic over the Sudeten Germans. Italy has blocked Association Agreement negotiations between the EU and Slovenia because its government in 1994 revived claims against that country. Greece is making claims against Albania and against Macedonia; NATO troops are butchering Kurds in Turkey. There is also, of course, the active dispute between Spain and the UK over Gibraltar, the unresolved dispute involving both territorial claims and minorities between the UK and Ireland etc.

Ignatieff worries about authoritarian populist possibilities in East Central Europe. But what about actualities in Western Europe: the neo-fascists in Italy, the Freedom Party's rise in Austria, the 15 per cent for the FN in France? None of the Visegrad countries nor Ukraine as it allegedly brings up the rear have had anything like these votes for the Far Right. In these matters modesty and attention to facts is surely desirable.

The Passing Moment of Modular Man

Ignatieff points to the fact that we in Western Europe have had a blessed creature whom he calls 'modular man', after Ernest Gellner, individuals with bolted-on attachments of a variety of kinds, many of them transient and driven by profane energies rather than by fundamentalist ideologies. This is surely true. But for how long and why? Ignatieff suggests that this is a defining feature of capitalism or at least western capitalism. He talks about 'the genius of capitalist civil society'. Yet surely in European terms modular man is largely a postwar product. It was hardly a dominant feature of inter-war Europe. It is not a feature of capitalism but of a particular capitalism for a brief period of time. The particularity was the postwar boom, the welfare state and a civil society which did really operate to some degree as Dahrendorf would wish: liberal corporatist negotiations with authoritative civic associations. And there was another factor: the West's upper classes were on their best behaviour and labour benefited in comparison with its past.

Are we, in the West, still in this age of 'modular man' or it is passing? The boom has ended. With the end of the Soviet Bloc, the upper classes no longer have a spur to self-discipline. And the ideological fuel provided for the parties of the Right in anti-Communism needs to be replaced. If Britain's right, the new diesel fuel on which we are to choke is nationalist demagogy. And as for the brand of liberalism which cemented internal peace in the West, the social liberalism of the social democratic state, it seems an expensive luxury of the Cold War, as Pennant Rea, the *Economist*'s editor pointed out: the penal taxation on which it was based, he informed us, was an import from Marxism forced upon the rich by the Cold War.

Ignatieff's proposals have one great merit: by diverting our attention to evil forces that may arise in the East, he makes us feel how lucky we are here in the West. But how long will we be lucky with the neo-liberals and their propagandists like Michael Ignatieff in the ascendant? A world economy largely out of control and a hollowed-out civil society in the West makes the liberal democratic order's future look increasingly fragile. Twice in the last century the western powers have plunged the world into misery. Who will offer us a scholarship competition for a little trip abroad on how to stop it happening a third time round?

Notes

1. Timothy Garton Ash, *In Europe's Name* (Jonathan Cape, 1993) p. 282.
2. Ralph Dahrendorf, *Reflections on the Revolution in Europe* (Chatto & Windus, 1990).
3. Jeffrey Sachs, *Poland's Jump to the Market Economy* (MIT Press, 1993).
4. Interview with Timothy Garton Ash, *Oxford International Review* (Winter 1994).
5. Michael Ignatieff, 'On Civil Society', *Foreign Affairs* (March/April 1995).
6. Jeffrey Sachs, *Understanding Shock Therapy* (Social Market Foundation, 1994).

11

The Post-Communist
Parties in the East

One of the most unexpected features of contemporary European politics is the continued strength of the post-Communist parties. In the five countries of East Central Europe[1] the formerly ruling Communist parties emerged from the elections in 1989–90 as the dominant parties of the Left. In six of these first elections they gained the largest vote of any party. Subsequently, in Poland and Hungary, these parties were to become the most popular national parties. And seven years after the beginning of the transition to capitalism, the ex-Communist parties remain the dominant parties of the Left in all the countries of the region except one (the Czech Republic).[2]

These former ruling Communist parties had swiftly repudiated the political system of the Soviet Bloc: especially the constitutional principle of 'the leading role of the Communist Party', which in practice meant a political monopoly for the Communists and their allies.[3] All changed their names to 'socialist' or 'social democratic' parties except the Czechoslovak Communists, who kept their name, and the Romanian Communists, who organised themselves in a 'National Salvation Front', before rechristening themselves as Social Democrats in 1993. These transformation decisions in some cases led to splits with minorities attempting to maintain the old party or with minorities wishing to go further than the majority and form explicitly pro-capitalist social democratic parties.[4]

Attempts were also made after 1989 to establish new Social Democratic parties hostile to the post-Communists. These parties were initially encouraged by the Socialist International, notably in the case of the Czechoslovak and Hungarian Social Democrats and later in the case of the Polish Union of Labour. Others with some degree of what might be called social liberalism, joined with free market liberals in the centre, notably in the Hungarian Free Democrats and the Polish Democratic Union. Yet with the exception of the Social Democrats in the Czech Republic, all these parties, both Social

260

Table 11.1   The share of the vote in East and Central Europe 1989–96 (post-Communists, independent social democrats and liberal parties, first three elections)

Hungary	March 1990	June 1994
HSP	10.9	33
HSDP	3.6	0.1
HSWP	3.7	3.2
AFD	21.4	19.8

Key: HSP: Hungarian Socialist Party; HSDP: Hungarian Social Democratic Party; HSWP: Hungarian Socialist Workers' Party, later renamed Hungarian Workers' Party; AFD: Alliance of Free Democrats.

Bulgaria	June 1990	October 1991	December 1994
BSP	47.1	33.1	43.5
SDP	0.1	—	—

Key: BSP: Bulgarian Socialist Party; SDP: Social Democratic Party.

Poland	June 1989	October 1991	September 1993
SLD	11.0	12.0	20.4
Dem. Union	—	12.3	10.6
Lab. Solid/UL	—	2.1	7.3

Key: SLD: Democratic Left Alliance, led by the Social Democrats of the Polish Republic (SDPR); Dem. Union: Democratic Union, later called the Freedom Union; Lab. Solid./UL: Labour Solidarity which became the Union of Labour.

Romania	May 1990	September 1992
NSF	67	27.5
SDP	1.1	

Key: NSF: National Salvation Front, later renamed the Party of Social Democrats of Romania; SDP: Social Democratic Party.

Czech Rep	June 1990	June 1992	June 1996
CP	13.5	14.3	10.3
SDP	4.1	7.7	26.4

Key: CP: Communist Party; SDP: Social Democratic Party.

Slovakia	June 1990	June 1992	June 1996
CP/PDL	13.8	14.4	10.4
SDP	1.9	6.1	—
AWS	—	—	7.3

Key: CP/PDL: Communist Party, later renamed the Party of the Democratic Left (PDL) after its fusion with the Social Democratic Party (SDP); AWS: the Association of Workers of Slovakia, a Left split-off from the Communist Party after its fusion with the SDP.

Germany, East	March 1990
PDS	16.3
SPD	21.8

Key: PDS: Party of the Democratic Socialists; SPD: Social Democratic Party of Germany.

Democratic and liberal, are less successful than the parties of the former Communists.

This chapter will attempt to explore the policy dynamics of the transformed Communist parties by examining three topics: first, the possible reasons for the ex-Communists' current strength; then the general environment in which the ex-Communist parties have found themselves in the first half of the 1990s; and finally, the ways in which the party leaderships have sought to respond to this environment with policies which will strengthen – or at least not weaken – their bases of support.

After looking generally at the evolution of the Left throughout the region, we will then attempt to examine more closely the politics of the four main post-Communist socialist parties: the Social Democrats of the Polish Republic (SDPR), which is the main successor party of the Polish 'Communists' (the Polish United Workers Party); the Hungarian Socialist Party (HSP), which is the main successor party of the Hungarian 'Communists' (the Hungarian Socialist Workers' Party); the Bulgarian Socialist Party (BSP), the successor of the Bulgarian Communist Party; and the Party of Social Democracy of Romania (PSDR), the main successor party, via the initial National Salvation Front, to the Romanian Communist Party.

I   Sources of Comparative Strength of the Post-Communist Socialists

There are widely diverging opinions as to why the post-Communist socialists have become so strong. Some hold that these parties, at least in the

Visegrad countries, were more or less wiped out in the so-called Revolutions of 1989 and that their 'resurrection' is the result of protest votes against the painful costs of transition to capitalism combined with moods of nostalgia for the security of the Communist past.[5] The implication of such a view is that the post-Communist protest vote may fade in the future. At the other extreme, some analysts argue that the post-Communists are strong because the basic structures of the old Communist states throughout the region have been changed only superficially.[6] The implication of this view is that unless there is more vigorous western political intervention, authoritarian post-Communist regimes will be consolidated through most of the region.

Both these opposed views share the following widely held assumptions: that the ruling Communist parties had negligible popular support in the last phase of Communism; that the substance of the collapse of 1989 was a revolt by the 'people' or 'civil society' as a more or less homogeneous group against the (Communist) State; and that these societies were not significantly polarised between left-wing and right-wing tendencies.[7] Such assumptions were, of course, a product of the dominant paradigm in the field of Soviet studies: totalitarian theory, viewing Communism as a state-repressive system of managerial control without sociopolitical roots. The initial but ephemeral appearance of anti-Communist coalitions calling themselves civic fronts of various kinds in some countries seemed to give substance to these preconceptions. The collapse of 1989 was thus preconceived as a popular anti-statist revolution and analysis of the politics of the region was then largely assimilated to a supposedly general field of transitions from dictatorship. The initial electoral strength of the post-Communists was viewed as ephemeral and there was an expectation that the political forces that had been linked to the previous regimes would sink without electoral trace as they did in, for example, Southern Europe in the 1970s.

The subsequent electoral evidence of continued ex-Communist strength thus leads those determined to stick to the paradigm towards the view that the 'revolution' of 'civil society' must have been superficial: Communist statism has been able to survive the 'revolution' throughout most of the region. Others have stressed contingent (and thus perhaps temporary) factors behind the revival: backlash protests against the hopefully temporary hardships of Shock Therapy, nostalgic protest votes for the old security, or the initial rightist rejection by voters of the non-Communist Social Democrats after 1989.

But there is a simpler solution to this puzzle produced by the preconceptions of totalitarian theory: it is that the socialist constituency inclined to support the Communists has been fairly strong, though in the Visegrad countries minoritarian, throughout both the 1980s and the 1990s.

The Ignored Socialist Electorate

Opinion surveys during the 1980s in the Visegrad countries and the GDR showed that significant minorities of the population supported the ruling parties. Even in Poland after the imposition of martial law, polls in 1984 showed that 25 per cent supported the Communist Party leadership, 25 per cent were hostile to it and 50 per cent either had no opinions or did not wish to express them.[8] Furthermore, the 25 per cent supporting the party tended to hold socialist social values, particularly egalitarianism and support for nationalised property, while those hostile tended to be anti-egalitarian and in favour of the free market: Polish society was thus politically polarised on a Left–Right basis, with the PUWP supporters occupying the Left. The same poll evidence shows majorities of the population supporting various central aspects of the social principles of state socialism.

Similar evidence is available for neighbouring countries. From 1985, competitive elections were taking place in Hungary, and these demonstrate that as late as 1989, the Hungarian Communists were gaining 30 per cent or more of the vote[9] and such votes were indicative of support for left-wing political and social values.

Polling in the GDR tells a similar story. Polls conducted there between 20 November and 27 November, 1989, showed the SED as having the largest percentage of support of any party – 31 per cent.[10] In Czechoslovakia, polling in December 1989 showed majority support not only for socialised property but for central planning.[11]

A further very important feature of political developments in the late 1980s and early 1990s has been the survival of the official unions of the state socialist period as the dominant trade union confederations during the transition to capitalism.[12] They did so despite concerted efforts on the part of governments of the Right and of western bodies like the ICFTU and the AFL-CIO to weaken them. In Hungary, the main trade union centre, MSZOSZ, retained some 3 million of its 4.5 million 1988 membership in 1991.[13] The Polish official unions, OPZZ, emerged with 4.5 million members in comparison with Solidarity's 2.3 million members. The same pattern emerged in Czechoslovakia where the official federation, CSKOS, predominated.[14] In Bulgaria the official unions faced the most serious challenge with the emergence of an initially strong new union centre, Podkrepa. But this challenge also, later, faded. After rising from about 350,000 at the end of 1990 to over 600,000 at the end of 1991, Podkrepa's membership declined to about 225,000 by the start of 1993. The old official federation's membership also declined, from 3 million at the end of 1990 to 2.5 million at the end of 1991 and only 1.6 million at the end of 1992, but its dominance within the trade union field was maintained. In Romania, the official unions also remained the strongest although they fragmented into competing centres in the early 1990s.

The official unions of the Communist period thus turn out not to have been mere transmission belts for a 'totalitarian' state without a significant social base; there was a substantial trade union constituency remaining in these organisations to be won by parties of the Left if they were prepared to orient towards it.[15]

If, then, there was a core socialist electorate of 25 per cent or more at the time of the regime's collapse, the strong showing of these parties during the first part of the 1990s as the strongest parties on the Left is scarcely surprising. Indeed, the puzzle is why these parties did not do much better in the first post-1989 elections than they did – why their votes were lower in the GDR and the Visegrad zone than polling evidence from the 1980s would have suggested.

One explanation could be that erstwhile Communist supporters were temporarily swept up in the wave of enthusiasm for a transition to capitalism in 1989–90 and switched their support to the parties of the free-market Right. This does seem to have been an important factor in the GDR elections of March 1990. Polling in early 1990 showed over 60 per cent of the GDR electorate holding social democratic or socialist political and social opinions and yet Kohl's campaign promises swung a big majority for the Right precisely in the traditional social democratic Saxon strongholds, leaving the post-Communist PDS with only 16.3 per cent and the SPD with only 21.8 per cent.

On the face of it the same effect seems to have operated elsewhere. In 1990 and 1991, opinion polls showed large majorities in favour of so-called 'market economies' in Poland, Hungary, Czechoslovakia and Bulgaria, with a majority the other way only in Romania. This support had dropped massively by 1994 (except in Romania where there was a reverse trend).[16]

But this evidence of enthusiasm for the market among large parts of the electorate does not explain why the still large minorities hostile to the introduction of the capitalist market did not fully turn out for the post-Communists. The reality is that there were large numbers of abstentions. Indeed, these were so large that many of those who told pollsters they favoured a market economy must have decided not to vote. In the 1989 Polish elections, less than 50 per cent of the electorate voted for Solidarity: the turn-out in this first competitive election was low, with high levels of abstentions. In 1991, when the first full Parliamentary elections in Poland were held, total turn-out was 43 per cent. In the 1993 Parliamentary elections both the turn-out (52 per cent) and the vote for the SDPR went up substantially and detailed analysis has shown that this correlation was central to the SDPR's success.[17] Parties of the centre and right in Hungary also failed to gain support from over 50 per cent of the electorate in a low turn-out and the party calling fairly explicitly for free market capitalism, the Alliance of Free Democrats, gained only 21 per cent of those who voted. In Czechoslovakia, the Civic Forum did not campaign on a free market programme in the 1990 elections.

A more likely explanation is that the post-Communist parties' support went down in 1989–90 because their earlier supporters in large numbers decided not to vote at all. This explanation is reinforced by the fact that the post-Communist parties that gained the smallest percentage of the vote were those of Poland and Hungary – the two countries where electoral participation was lowest. In Hungary, only 58 per cent of the electorate turned out and the figure was roughly the same in Poland – hardly, by the way, a sign of a popular revolution for freedom against 'Totalitarianism'. The high abstention rate in Poland and Hungary suggests another puzzle: why was it that in the only two countries where the ruling Communist Party leaderships took autonomous decisions (in February 1989) to move towards pluralist democratic political systems, and where they had been campaigning for years for 'market reform', did the Communists perform worst of all the Communist parties in the region? If the great issue of these elections was freedom (and the free market) against totalitarianism, why did these two parties perform worse than the two parties that resisted democratic change and the market – the East German and Czechoslovak parties?[18]

This points to the possibility that the poor performance of the Polish and Hungarian parties had nothing to do with freedom versus totalitarianism, but was linked to another feature that distinguished these two parties from the Czechoslovak and East German parties: the fact that their party leaderships had for some years been vigorously promoting policies which tended to contradict the socially egalitarian ideologies of their parties, policies of increasing marketisation and increasing social differentiation, with increasingly negative effects on those sections of the population in whose name they ruled: policies which were not being promoted by the Czechoslovak and East German parties whose economies were more successful under centralised planning.[19]

Evidence from the results gained by smaller parties in the Hungarian elections tends to confirm this view that the HSP's low vote was partly the result of its pro-market orientation. While the HSP gained 10.9 per cent of the vote a further 8.8 per cent of votes went to small parties, mainly further to the Left on the issue of marketisation. The HSWP gained 3.7 per cent, but more significant is the fact that a group of Agricultural Technicians stood on the single issue of opposing the break-up of agricultural co-operatives and gained 3.2 per cent of the vote; finally, some local political leaders from the HSWP days stood separately from the HSP as a network of local leaders and gained 1.9 per cent.

Research on all these issues still needs to be undertaken. What has been offered here is nothing more than a set of hypotheses based upon some empirical pointers. But it would certainly explain the rather general revival of the fortunes of these parties as the 1990s progressed: their levels of support were returning to the trend of the 1980s. And they did so despite strenuous efforts by anti-Communist parties and the media to delegitimise them. It would also suggest another conclusion: that a significant minority of electorates may have held social values to the left of the post-Communist party leaderships and may indeed still do so.

Table 11.2   Communist Party Transformations

Old Name	Date of Change	New Name
Polish United Workers	Feb. 1990	Social Democrats of the Polish Republic
Hungarian Socialist Workers	Sept. 1989	Hungarian Socialist Party
Bulgarian Communist	April 1990	Bulgarian Socialist Party
Yugoslav League of Communists	Feb. 1990 – Party broke up	
Albanian Workers	June 1991	Albanian Socialist Party
Romanian Communist	Jan. 1990	National Salvation Front
National Salvation Front	July 1993	Party of Romanian SD
Socialist Unity (GDR)	Feb. 1990	Party of Democratic Left
Slovak Communist	1990	Party of Democratic Left
Montenegro	1991	Democratic Party of Socialists

Meanwhile in what, in a broad sense, may be called the Balkans, the post-Communists tended to emerge from the first elections as the strongest parties. This occurred in Romania, Bulgaria, Serbia, Montenegro, and later Albania.[20] These initial successes were not momentary: these parties retained strong support even if they were, in Bulgaria and Albania, subsequently to go into opposition.

The Fate of the Non-Communist Social Democratic Parties

Some have suggested that the principal cause of post-Communist strength in the Visegrad zone lay in mistakes on the part of the independent social democrats.[21]

In most of the countries of the region non-Communist socialists created new Social Democratic parties, backed initially by the Socialist International. In Poland after some false starts the main such group emerged from Solidarity and was called the Union of Labour.[22] In Czechoslovakia a Social Democratic Party was re-established. This then divided into a Czech and a Slovak party, respectively the CSSD and the SDSS. In Hungary a similar party, the Hungarian Social Democratic Party, was formed. The Slovene Social

Democratic Party also emerged and similar small parties were created in Bulgaria, Albania and Romania.

All these parties swiftly gained political support from the SI. The German and Austrian parties were particularly active in ensuring financial support for these groups as were the French Socialist.[23] It was not unusual for almost the entire funds of these parties to be supplied from the West.[24]

Yet except in two cases – the Czech Republic and Slovenia – as well, of course, as in unified Germany – these parties failed to compete successfully with the post-Communists for leadership of the Left. They gained between 0.1 and 7.5 per cent of the votes. In most cases they failed miserably. The reason for this is not obvious: standard accounts of popular revolution against Communism would lead us to expect the opposite.

Some have suggested the Social Democrats failed because their names were tainted by their historical and ideological links with Communism.[25] This would explain why they didn't get votes from the right-wing electorate, but it does not explain their failure with the left-wing section of the electorate. Others have suggested an historico-cultural explanation: that social democracy was historically important only in inter-war Czechoslovakia and therefore there was no cultural tradition elsewhere.[26] This may be true of parts of the Balkans but it ignores the dominance of this tradition on the Left in both inter-war Poland and Hungary. It also excludes the possibility that contemporary political activity can play an important role in the contemporary politics of the region.

A more straightforward explanation is that these parties failed because they made no serious appeal to the socialist section of the electorate we identified above. Many of these parties simply stressed the free market programme which the West European Social Democratic parties were arguing for within the region in the early 1990s. The western socialist party leaderships tended, so to speak, to put nation before party in external policy towards the East and to insist upon support for a thoroughgoing free market transformation combined with a strong anti-Communism in East Central Europe. Arguing for policies that entailed first dismantling the egalitarian and welfare arrangements to build capitalism so that one could later construct welfare capitalism seemed disingenuous. These policies wiped out the Social Democrats in the Balkan zone and in Hungary.[27]

In Poland, on the other hand, Labour Solidarity, which later became the Union of Labour (UL), emerged as a left-wing opposition to mainstream Solidarity's neo-liberal Balcerowicz Plan (for Shock Therapy). It raised real issues of concern to working-class people against Solidarity-originating governments. It also broke with the Catholic connections of Solidarity and the Democratic Union, vigorously championing abortion rights in 1993 while the neo-liberals in the Democratic Union sought to appease the Church hierarchy on the issue. As a result of this activity, UL gained a genuine base on the Left in the 1993 elections, polling 7.3 per cent. At the same time, this leftist orientation was combined with anti-Communism. The German Social Democratic leadership supported UL financially in the hope that the organisation could be used to split the Polish ex-Communists. A prominent post-Communist intellectual, Lamentowicz, was drawn over to the party and efforts were made to open a split within the post-Communists between Czymoszewicz and Miller by presenting the latter as an unreconstructed Communist. However, these tactics failed and instead UL itself was split in the 1995 Presidential elections, as Lamentowicz was expelled for supporting post-Communist leader Kwasniewski's candidacy while other leaders of the UL campaigned on behalf of Democratic Union candidate Jacek Kuron. The result was that the UL's own candidate received negligible support.

But non-Communist Social Democrats did succeed in out-distancing the post-Communists in two countries in the region: the Czech Republic and Slovenia. The Slovene dynamics were governed by the break-up of Yugoslavia. While the Yugoslav League of Communists was the biggest party in the April 1990 Slovene elections, its support evaporated in the Slovene drive to secede from Yugoslavia: the Slovene Social Democrats became the dominant Left party on the basis of a strong nationalist appeal.

The really significant exception to the pattern outlined above is the Czech case, and it tends to confirm the explanation offered above for the failures of social democracy elsewhere in the region. In the Czech Republic the Social Democrats initially gained only 4.1 per cent of the vote in June 1990 (against the Communist Party's 13.5 per cent). In the June 1992 elections the Social Democrats' vote rose to 7.7 per cent (while the Communist Party's vote also rose to 14.3 per cent). But in the 1996 elections the Social Democrats decisively established themselves as the dominant party on the Left, gaining 26.44 per cent of the vote against the Czech Communists' 10.33 per cent.

The three crucial factors in this transformation were: the decision of the Communist Party not to seek to occupy the centre-left ground by transforming itself into a socialist party; the decision by the Social Democrats to make a leftist appeal to the electorate; and the capacity of the Social Democrats to establish a serious trade union base. Financial support from the West of course helped: the party was funded from top to bottom from the West. But without the other factors, the money would have been useless.

The decline in support of the Czech Communists was not only the result of their continued adhesion to the Communist tradition: indeed, after 1990 their support actually rose and in local elections they gained almost 18 per cent of the vote – the highest vote of any Communist Party in continental Europe in the early 1990s. But in 1993 the Communist Party was riven by internal conflict, which turned the party inwards and involved both the expulsion of a neo-Stalinist group and the defection of groups on the party's

Right. The majority forces in the party were at the same time unable to develop a coherent strategic identity for the party.[28]

At the same time the Czech Social Democrats were able to present themselves as a serious grouping to the Left of the neo-liberals. In the first place they recruited the economist Komarek, Klaus's boss before the Velvet Revolution, who became a household name throughout the country in 1990 because of his economic reform ideas against the Communists and who then criticised Klaus's neo-liberal economic ideology in a detailed, well-informed way, offering his own alternative economic strategy. This was unique in the region: the best-known non-Communist economic expert, with impeccable political credentials, offering an authoritative alternative to neo-liberalism.

The second important achievement of the Social Democrats was their ability to develop influence with the former official trade union confederation, CSKOS, through a strong Social Democratic representation on its leadership. These links were no doubt strengthened by the assistance given to CSKOS by the German DGB. These advantages were consolidated when Zeman took over the leadership of the party and swung its policy more to the Left.

A further factor in the Czech case, reinforcing all the others, was undoubtedly the country's geopolitical and geoeconomic environment. Wedged between Vienna and Berlin, the Czech Republic has received very strong signals from the German government that it heads the queue for full integration into West European structures. And its highly skilled work force and advanced engineering traditions combine with its geographical location to offer its population the hope of a substantial rise in living standards in the future. All these circumstances combine to give pride of place to a left-wing politics which is pragmatically focused upon specific quantitative problems facing working-class people such as the Social Democrats offer.

But it is also worth noting that the large increase in the vote of the Czech Social Democrats in the 1996 elections was not principally as a result of taking votes from the Czech Communist Party. It was much more the result of winning back from centrist parties that large part of the Czech socialist constituency who had been drawn towards the centrists or who had abstained in the 1990 and 1992 elections.[29]

II   The Environments Confronting the Post-Communist Socialists

The most basic environmental problem for the four parties we will discuss has been the terrible economic slump that hit their economies at the start of the 1990s, connected to the collapse of Comecon trade and payments networks, the break-up of the USSR, the debt burdens and financial crises of the region, and the slump-deepening demands of the International Financial Institutions (IFIs) reflecting the goals of western governments for the region.

The economic crisis has been most severe and protracted in Bulgaria, which had very strong economic links with the USSR and had to default on its very heavy debt repayments. The country remains in a profound depression. The Hungarian economy has been recovering from the slump very slowly and its debt problems are severe. Both the Polish and Romanian economies have been growing since 1993.

Within this general context, the states of the region faced more or less severe resource crises in the form of chronic and acute fiscal problems and debt repayment difficulties and few opportunities for tackling these problems through borrowing on private capital markets at home or abroad. Romania had paid off its foreign debt in the 1980s, but faced acute shortages of hard currency as well as budget difficulties. Poland was uniquely given a large package of debt forgiveness and, combined with economic growth, this has given the parties of the Left in government some room for manoeuvre. But both Bulgaria and Hungary have faced more or less continual financial crisis.[30]

Solutions to many of these problems could have been facilitated if the EU had opened its markets widely for the region's exports, particularly the exports of its more advanced industrial sectors. But the governments of the EU had no economic interest in taking such a step against a background of long-term stagnation and saturated domestic markets within the EU combined with high levels of unemployment. At the same time, the economic and the state financial crises gave the western powers a quite extraordinary degree of leverage over the governments of the region: they could deny governments access to finance and they could deny them a trade substitute for Comecon simply by maintaining the Cold War embargoes used by the EC against the Soviet Bloc.

This leverage was placed in the service of an extremely ambitious western campaign for thoroughgoing social engineering within the region to establish a new social regime: the replacement of regimes of strong social and economic protection in these countries with regimes with less social protection than, say, the UK and with a 'globalised' institutional face to the outside world, in other words an extreme form of open door for products and capital, including hot, short-term money flows. These regime goals were given the label 'market economy' but were in reality geared towards ensuring that these economies occupied subordinate places in the projected new European international division of labour. The guidelines were mainly derived from US tactics since the 1980s for reorganising international economic relations in ways that maximally favoured their own capitals. The Soviet crisis and the collapse of the state socialist regimes enormously enhanced this drive by disorienting and disorganising the Left on a global scale. In such conditions, the USA, backed by the main West European states (though with a partial and half-hearted attempt at resistance by the French government) felt able to attempt to impose this programme on the East Central European states in the midst of their crisis. The campaign initially sharply exacerbated the economic crisis, thus strengthening further western leverage.

It was an agenda that offered very handsome rewards to those within the region with access to capital or with the possibility of partnership with western capital; but it tended to make losers of the majority of the population and to immiserate significant minorities. These latter two groups were, of course, the natural constituencies of the socialist parties. From the point of view of US strategy therefore, the post-Communist parties were bound to be a potential obstacle and vigorous efforts were to be made to weaken them.

But these global regime goals promoted especially by the US and the IFIs were potentially modified by the geopolitical interests of the main West European states. From the start of the transition to capitalism, the Visegrad countries could hope to enjoy some geopolitical advantages over their neighbours to the East and South: their location on Germany's eastern periphery meant that the German government was interested in drawing them firmly under German influence (mainly through EU mechanisms). This offered the hope that for Germany a modicum of stability in these countries would be essential and could override the general regime goals. Slovenia and Croatia also hoped to gain from German foreign policy by separating from Yugoslavia, but for Croatia these gains were postponed by the war. Poland could also exploit its great geopolitical importance for the USA.

As far as Romania and Bulgaria were concerned, they initially lacked much geopolitical interest for the western alliance and during 1990 the latter took an especially tough line towards them. But the development of the Yugoslav war (as well as the resurgence of Greek–Turkish rivalry) has given Bulgaria an increased political salience and the western powers were to soften their stance towards it in what might be called the field of symbolic politics. Romania, on the other hand, has remained to a large degree in international political limbo, despite some efforts by France to sponsor it.

Against these backgrounds, the domestic political agenda was more about 'state refounding' than about what might be called 'normal politics'. The issues were: what kind of social principles for the new state and economy; what kind of institutional structure for both economy and state; what kind of constitution, political system etc. But above all, what kind of class structure and what composition of the new, emergent capitalist class.

In this complicated environment all parties were seeking to find ways of enhancing their own legitimacy and authority, principally through gaining authoritative approval from the West. Here, the most important source of support for parties to the Left-of-centre was the Socialist International, but during the first five years of the transition only the HSP could gain minimal recognition from that quarter by being granted observer status in 1992. On the other hand, the evolution of the PCI in Italy was a powerful indirect source of inspiration for many intellectuals from the ex-Communist parties, as it transformed itself in 1989 into the PDS and sought full integration into the Socialist International.

These environmental conditions were thus extremely difficult for any government in the countries concerned and near-catastrophic for governments of the Left. In a different international environment their behaviour would undoubtedly have been very different and it is not easy to distinguish the endogenous policy impulses within these parties from the exogenous environmental constraints, or indeed positive external diktats, in analysing their behaviour, especially while in government. But we will attempt to do so below.

III The Policy Orientations of the Post-Communists

We will try to examine some aspects of the politics of the post-Communist parties in Poland, Hungary, Romania and Bulgaria. Three of these parties have had a continuity of name and structures since early 1990: the Social Democrats of the Polish Republic (the SDPR), the Hungarian Socialist Party (HSP), and the Bulgarian Socialist Party (BSP). But the Romanian pattern of organisational evolution has been very different.

The Romanian political transition was carried through by a combination of potentially radically opposed forces: popular uprising against the Ceausescu dictatorship and palace coup by Ceausescu's formidable praetorian guard. Political leadership was seized by the pro-Soviet wing of the Communist Party under Iliescu. This group then successfully stabilised a new regime by simultaneously banning the Communist Party and transferring the Communist party's forces into a new National Salvation Front (NSF). In 1992 the NSF split into two separate movements, one led by Iliescu; the other, by his former Prime Minister, Petre Roman.[32] The Iliescu group then, in 1993, formed a Party of Social Democracy of Romania and claimed to support the Socialist International. Meanwhile another group, led by Verdet, established a Socialist Labour Party, claiming allegiance to the traditions of Romanian Communism. The Iliescu group remained the dominant party in all elections up to the autumn of 1996.

Today, in all four countries, the post-Communists claim allegiance to the Socialist International, declare support for the principles of the Council of Europe on human and civil rights, and defend the notion of a 'market economy' and pluralist liberal democratic principles. They all also declare their goal to be eventual membership of the European Union. Yet these declaratory commitments tell us little and obscure the substantial differences between these parties.

Differences on Systemic Change

From an institutional point of view, after the political collapse of the single-party regime, the states of the region could be described as forms of *social* democracy in the strict sense of combining socialised property forms with political democracy. The programmatic goals of these parties thus had a special character: the question was to a great degree the extent to which the parties were prepared to dismantle the existing institutions in the direction of capitalism: how much systemic retreat from socialised property and political direction of economic life.

The decisions on this basic programmatic issue depended very largely upon two judgements: the new international context of their country; and the options open to them in their own societies in the new era.

The Polish and Hungarian leaderships judged that their countries were going to be absorbed into the West European sphere and their parties had to accept the fate of being on the Left within a capitalist and western-oriented country. In the Polish case the outgoing PUWP leader Rakowski clearly spelt out the consequence of this context for the party's future role in a series of speeches in the autumn of 1989: the new party should become the dominant centre-left force in Polish politics, counter-balancing a centre-right party;[33] at the same time, it should accept a new economic system, based upon market forces. In Hungary, acceptance of a transition both to pluralist democracy and to capitalism was universal within the top leadership from the autumn of 1989.[34]

For the Romanian and Bulgarian leaderships, the international conjuncture in 1989–1991 was far less easy to read. There was the possibility still that the Gorbachev effort at socialist renewal in the USSR might succeed; and there was little indication of a strong western drive to integrate their countries into the West European capitalist arrangements. In Romania, President Iliescu therefore initially wagered on the success of Gorbachev, was ready to enter a security pact with the USSR, despite strong western opposition, and laid down the goals of the NSF as being those of Market Socialism: the continuation of a non-capitalist economy, rejecting the regime programme of the West.

But with the Soviet collapse at the end of 1991, this perspective of Romanian development within a Soviet-centred geopolitical and economic space also collapsed. The erstwhile Prime Minister, Roman, responded in 1992 by splitting from the NSF (now called the Democratic NSF) and creating a new NSF ready to embark upon a transition to capitalism and merging with a group calling itself the Democratic Party. The following year, Iliescu also shifted ground with the transformation of his NSF into the Party of Social Democrats of Romania, oriented towards the introduction of capitalism, but of a strongly national capitalist rather than 'globalised' variety. This remained a strong theme in the politics of the Romanian Social Democrats.

The judgement on the international context was most difficult for the Bulgarian Socialist Party leadership. Its international economic links were overwhelmingly with the USSR, but it was, unlike the Romanian government, at the intersection of two potentially explosive crises that the US government has been strongly focused upon and involved with: that in Yugoslavia and the rivalry between Greece and Turkey. So the country's future geoeconomic and political location was obscure. At the same time Bulgaria was facing a desperate debt crisis with western creditors. The BSP leadership sought to maintain some element of ambiguity in its stance on systemic goals, favouring privatisation and 'market reform' in general public statements, but not being enthusiastic in practice. The efforts of the party leaderships generally seem to have been directed towards preserving a powerful state sector and co-operatives in agriculture and towards resisting western pressure to 'globalise' the economy, stressing the importance of maintaining national control over capital assets.

Party Organisational Transformation

The SDPR, the HSP and the BSP were all formed at congresses of the former Communist parties and open debates were held on the new ideological and political parameters of the new parties. New organisational arrangements were also laid down and regular party congresses have subsequently been held, with real debates and evident differences within the parties. But the Romanian pattern was very different.

The formation of the Romanian National Salvation Front (NSF) indicated the profound ambivalence of the new political order emerging out of the combined revolt from below and palace coup from above. The Iliescu leadership group saw its task as to offer a political identity which could somehow be accepted by both these in principle antagonistic forces, hence the formation of the amorphous NSF. The subsequent formation of the PSDR was also not the result of an organic process of political differentiation within the NSF. It was, rather, an initiative from Iliescu's government. The congress that founded the new party did not adopt sharply defined political principles and the new name was decided *after* the congress, from above. As a result, the PSDR has to some extent had the character of a loosely defined group of supporters of President Iliescu himself. While there have been evident divisions within the PSDR these differences are not clearly reflected in open debates at Party congresses. As a result the PSDR resembles what might be called a Leader Party, tending to substitute the leader's will for strongly defined programmatic parameters.

The abandonment of the principle of 'the leading role of the Party' entailed also the sociological separation of the ex-Communist Parties from the large managerial layers of the old regime – both state officials and economic managers. This process of organisational differentiation was massive and swift in both Poland and Hungary in 1989–90 and was underwritten by the SDPR and HSP going into opposition. Their party organisations became western-style parties devoted to electoral political activity.

The process of differentiation differed in the other two countries, where the ex-Communists remained in power after the first elections. As a result, the NSF and the BSP continued to exercise large powers of state patronage and remained a focus for the pursuit of managerial interests. This has subsequently marked the evolution of the BSP, some of whose members have simultaneously been linked to powerful business groups (both state and private). Nevertheless, the BSP's organisational transformation into an autonomous organisation for political communication and deliberation developed more or less along the lines of the parties in the Visegrad countries, especially once it too went into opposition in 1991.

In this field the Romanian case was unique. In some respects the collapse of the party-state complex of the Ceausescu regime left a state elite in place without any real party formation at all and the process of post-Communist party-formation was both slow and led from the state presidency of Iliescu. The highly elitist official ideology put forward by NSF's first ideologist, Brucan, reflected this sociopolitical reality. In the first phase this ruling group sought to maximise its political flexibility by providing the minimum political definition to the NSF, and the PSDR was similarly defined strongly from above by the state presidency. The boundaries between state and party activity were therefore not fully drawn, making the Romanian scene in the early 1990s somewhat similar to the kind of 'party of power' that operated in parts of the CIS after the collapse of the USSR. Even when the 'Social Democratic' party was created, it had little internal life of its own. Thus the party appeared more as an appendage of the elite centre in the state leadership than as a more or less autonomous collective political actor. Nevertheless, as the competitive party system has evolved, the PSDR has had to define its political references and organisational structures more clearly.

Domestic Political Cleavages and Party Policy

The various post-Communist parties have defined themselves through overlapping political polarisations and cleavages at a national level during the

1990s. In three of the four countries the impact of these polarisations on the party system have been to produce divisions on Left–Right lines, but in Romania this spectrum has been blurred by the impact of nationalism.

1) Communism versus anti-Communism

The first great polarisation in all four countries was that between Communism and anti-Communism. At an electoral level, the anti-Communist appeal of the first phase of the transition has largely played itself out in all four countries as it has been overlaid by other polarisations. Nevertheless, this cleavage remains at deeper structural levels a very important one in all four countries because it still divides each country's sociopolitical elites and because of the uncertain futures of these countries.

In all the countries concerned, the parties are identifiable by reference to the origins of these leading members: those from the former Communist establishment and those not. In all the countries also, a basic feature of the last five years has been the construction and legitimation of new capitalist classes and this process has been in large measure a matter of political decisions, connected to privatisations (rather than simply a 'spontaneous' accumulation of private capital within a separate economic sphere). Thus the possibility exists of the party cleavage also reflecting a social cleavage at elite level. If this does emerge as a significant fissure, it may make the emergence of elite consensus on what might be called national strategy beyond party cleavages more difficult.

Allied to this is the problem of constructing an ideological consensus on national and state historical development. In all these countries a vast gulf remains in this sphere: on the Right, amongst anti-Communist parties, the period of state socialism is presented as one of enslavement, while the inter-war years of the Piłsudski regime in Poland, the Horthy regime in Hungary and of monarchism and dictatorship in Romania and Bulgaria are presented as phases of national authenticity. For the post-Communist parties, on the other hand, the period of state socialism had positive, developmental features, not least in ending the legacies of inter-war authoritarianism and fascism.

One bridge across this gulf could have been constructed by strong future-oriented centrist formations of political liberalism, without traditions tied to inter-war regimes or to the state socialist period. This possibility emerged in Hungary with the willingness of the Alliance of Free Democrats to cross the anti-Communist divide and enter a coalition with the HSP. In Poland, on the other hand, the political liberals have so far remained allied with the anti-Communist Right, which draws on the traditions of Catholic and nationalist rejection of all Polish history since 1944. Similar cleavages apply in Bulgaria.

In Romania, on the other hand, both the ex-Communist camp and the anti-Communist camp contain both ideological tendencies. The ultra-nationalist parties which were allied with the PSDR have promoted themes and symbols reminiscent of the Iron Guard and of the Antonescu dictator-ship, while the anti-Communist camp has contained strong monarchist elements. And both liberal and socialist themes are promoted in both camps.

But in general, the future of this cleavage will be decided by the interna-tional and economic future of these countries as much as by endogenous political changes.

2) Neo-liberalism versus social protection

The second great polarisation has been between supporters of neo-liberal 'Economic Reform' and opponents of this platform. This cleavage appeared first in Hungary, and cut across the first cleavage by placing both the MDF on the Right and the HSP in opposition to the Free Democrats and the Young Democrats. In Poland the cleavage opened through the impact of the Balcerowicz plan and as it worked itself through, it both fragmented the anti-Communist front and enabled the SDPR to take the leadership of a broadening coalition of interests and parties. The same basic pattern appeared in Hungary where the supporters of neo-liberalism became minoritarian as its economic and social consequences strengthened the HSP. In Bulgaria the neo-liberal cleavage remained superficial because the UDF did not coherently defend this political stance and in Romania the advocates of neo-liberalism remained weak.

But a much more difficult issue is to define the kind of socioeconomic alternative to neo-liberalism which the post-Communist Socialists are seek-ing to promote. The source of this analytical problem arises largely from the extreme practical constraints upon these parties in power and thence from determining where the boundary lies between external constraint and autonomous political will on the part of these parties.

The SDPR, HSP and BSP all formed strong alliances, while in opposition, with the main trade union confederations. In the Polish case the SDPR formed a Democratic Left Alliance with the OPZZ and as a result some sev-enty OPZZ candidates were elected to parliament in 1993. The HSP placed Sandor Nagy, the head of the trade union confederation, number two on its national party list, below party leader Horn. Similar links were established in Bulgaria. In Romania, dozens of small trade union confederations sprang up in 1990 (according to some, with deliberate encouragement from the government), but shortly after the formation of the PSDR in the spring of 1993, the main successor group from the Ceausescu era merged with other large groups to form a new, dominant trade union confederation. PSDR leaders welcomed this development, which brought some order into industrial relations bargaining.[35]

Therefore, we can speak of a general trend for the post-Communist parties to seek to include the trade union confederations as important partners in national political life with influence on government policy-making.

At the same time, there have been conflicts between the parties in government and the trade unions, especially over wages policies and welfare issues and in no case have the parties been prepared to allow the trade union leadership dominant influence over the matters of concern to labour.

In both Poland and Hungary, the Socialist Parties have felt the need to reassure the International Financial Institutions and the financial markets in the formation of their governments. The HSP did this by forming a coalition with the Free Democrats despite having a majority in the Hungarian Parliament. At the same time, it reserved the Finance Ministry for its own party. In Poland the SDPR appointed a non-party academic, Kołodko, who had been a critic of the Balcerowicz plan but who was an orthodox champion of low inflation and low budget deficits, as Finance Minister.

There have been constant tensions between the finance ministers and other government departments over key aspects of economic and social policy, with the finance ministers generally reflecting the pressures of the International Financial Institutions and the financial markets. The typical pattern has been for the Finance Ministries to win on specific issues, while the President (in Poland) and the Prime Minister (in Hungary) have signalled their dissatisfaction with the general approach of the Finance Ministry.

In Poland a long battle took place between Finance Minister Kołodko and Labour Minister Leszek Miller over an issue of great importance in the country, pensions. Miller fought for pensions increases to be tied to average wages, while Kołodko wanted them indexed to the cost of living. With Miller's removal from the Ministry of Labour, Kołodko won. At the same time, President Kwasniewski criticised his own government for too restrictive an attitude towards public spending and the SDPR reorganised ministries to create a super-ministry of Economics within which finance would be only one component.

The SDPR thus combined defence of the idea of a welfare state with universal benefits, with an orthodox stress on financial stringency. It was able to combine these two elements because of the strong growth in the Polish economy and the earlier debt forgiveness which Poland won under neo-liberal governments. Kołokdo sought to offer, instead of quick improvements in welfare spending, a longer-term perspective of future prosperity for Polish voters by producing a medium-term economic plan with indicative targets for key economic indicators and spending targets over the following years.[37] At the same time it ended the sharp discrimination against state enterprises designed to favour the private sector and sought to strengthen state enterprises through providing them with a more favourable legislative framework. It also committed itself to improving Poland's trade and economic links with countries further East as well as with the West.

The HSP government, on the other hand, was constantly under siege from Hungary's acute financial strains, reflecting both its lack of debt forgiveness and the very sluggish economic recovery from the deep slump of the early 1990s. These problems were effectively used by the IFIs and the main players on the financial markets connected to Hungary to aggressively undermine the HSP's credibility as a defender of a social liberal welfare state. It should, however, be said, that the IFIs had allies within parts of the HSP's leadership.

The crisis began in early 1995 when Prime Minister Horn accepted the resignation of the neo-liberal Finance Minister Bekesi rather than accede to his demands to sell off state hotel chains cheaply to western buyers. The IFIs responded to Bekesi's resignation by making two dramatic demands: first, that Hungary's public utilities be privatised into mainly western hands; and secondly, demanding fee-paying elements be introduced to both health care and education, as well as cuts in old age and disability pensions. This Mexican-style utilities privatisation bonanza was a unique development for the region, offering a large, continuous stream of profits for western investors;[38] and the welfare cuts package was designed in such a way as to break brutally with the values championed by the HSP. Prime Minister Horn made a direct appeal to Chancellors Kohl and Vranitsky (of Austria) for their intervention against the package but was rebuffed.

There followed a series of resignations from the government, combined with a series of supreme court rulings that various aspects of the package were unconstitutional. As large protests and strikes involving employees in education and health continued into November 1995, the Free Democrat Minister of Education felt bound to resign over the changed education policy.

The political dimension of the package was fairly transparent: either the HSP would swing decisively to the Right, losing credibility, or its government would be engulfed by a financial crisis as western (particularly American) funds pulled out of Budapest and the IFIs withdrew support. The expectation in western financial circles and amongst American policy-makers was that one way or the other, the HSP would be structurally weakened, unless it replaced Horn with a neo-liberal as leader. But the party membership continued to support the leadership while being strongly opposed to the policies forced upon it. At the same time, the government sought to rebuild understanding with the trade unions by offering substantial wage increases and by raising the minimum wage.[39]

For different reasons, neither Romania's nor Bulgaria's governments were initially susceptible to the kind of pressure which faced the HSP in

Hungary. In Romania, the absence of a debt burden coupled with the government's tight control over the domestic financial system gave the IFIs and western financial multinationals little market leverage, while the strong domestic nationalist consensus in Romania meant that the ideological linkage with domestic neo-liberalism was very weak. The Romanian government's search for access to western financial markets therefore produced IMF packages focused mainly upon purely financial retrenchment rather than social engineering.[40] The PSDR's privatisation programme was geared towards passing the ownership of the bulk of enterprises into Romanian hands rather than offering large scope for foreign buyers. The party was committed to preserving a welfare state and to building a policy dialogue with the trade unions on wages and social issues.

In Bulgaria, as the economic crisis in the country steadily deepened during the 1990s, crisis management dominated domestic policy-making. The economy is burdened by very heavy debt repayments in conditions of continuing domestic depression. Out of a GDP of just over $10 billion, western creditors were expecting to receive $1.27 billion in 1996 and $1.7 billion in 1997. The IFIs viewed these huge repayments strains as a means of persuading the BSP government to sell the most valuable of the country's enterprises to western buyers, thus producing a short-term injection of hard currency to pay western banks (while incurring long-term dividend obligations to western share-holders). Therefore, when, in 1996, it became clear that Bulgaria would once again be unable to continue to service its debts, the IMF refused to provide assistance until the government had agreed both to selling assets to foreign investors and to closing down non-profitable state enterprises, making at least 40,000 workers redundant. The Bulgarian government's own programme of mass privatisation via domestic voucher sales was no longer enough for the IFIs.[41]

One factor which may have been of concern to western policy-makers was the fact that up to 1996 the Bulgarian private sector was dominated by a few conglomerates, built largely by former officials of the Communist regime, with links to both the main political parties and in many cases also with strong links with powerful Russian business groups.[42] This pattern of power developed in parallel with increasingly close links again being established between Bulgaria and Russia not only in the important energy sector but also in the field of military procurement.

The deadlock between the IMF and the BSP government in early 1996 produced a currency collapse on international money markets and this in turn generated rapid domestic inflation. The BSP government then felt compelled to comply with IMF demands in the summer of 1996. But at this very moment, the IMF toughened its demands, suspending its financial support and demanding Bulgaria impose a Currency Board. The country's financial crisis rapidly mounted, producing terrible social hardship, popular protests and the fall of the BSP government. The most likely explanation of these events lies in US regional strategy: the Dayton Agreement meant that political stability in Bulgaria became less important; meanwhile the Russian government was calling for a security pact with Bulgaria in response to NATO enlargement. These developments made the BSP an unacceptable government for Washington.

3) Nationalism versus Europeanism

Both the SDPR and the HSP have remained strongly identified with an anti-nationalist, Europeanist and internationalist orientation. In Poland, nationalist anti-Europeanism has been overwhelmingly a phenomenon of the Right and it has divided the Solidarity political camp. But the hostility of the SDPR's ally, the PSL, to the European Union's external agricultural policies has turned it towards a more nationalist economic policy. For the SDPR, unlike the Democratic Union, Europeanism has not been linked to support for neo-liberal socioeconomic nostrums but has rather meant a defence of democratic, secular and civil rights against xenophobia and Christian Nationalist authoritarianism. But the SDPR's stance has also involved the priority of integration into western institutions.

Following the SDPR's electoral success in 1993 there were attempts by politicians on the Right to claim that the SDPR was not fully committed to membership of the EU and NATO. Walesa's Foreign Minister Olechowski claimed concerns on that score to be the reason for his resignation in January 1995, but such charges cut little ice either in Poland or abroad.[43] Kwasniewski's election as President, which gave the SDPR full control over foreign policy for the first time, brought no significant shift on these core issues. The priority of western integration commanded all other concerns.

Nevertheless, there have been differences of concern. While Kwasniewski has been as vigorous as Walesa in promoting Polish NATO membership since becoming President, the SDRP and PSL leaderships initially accepted the possible enlargement of NATO without being genuine enthusiasts for it. Both parties would have preferred a greater emphasis upon the development of pan-European collective security structures. And in accepting NATO enlargement they have sought to stress that they are talking about a new, reformed NATO. They, like many others across the continent of varying political persuasion, doubt the wisdom of effectively excluding Russia from the politics of European Security which a NATO enlargement could mean. At the same time the Polish Left will not oppose enlargement if it appears to be the settled will of the main NATO powers.[44]

In relations with the EU, the SDPR continued the stress laid down by former Foreign Minister Skubiszewski in desiring Polish membership of a strongly institutionalised, political EU, rejecting the loose free market concepts of

British provenance.[45] More generally, the leaders of the Polish Left share the widespread cynicism amongst Polish policy makers about the conduct of EU policy towards Poland over the last eight years, but this cynicism does not in the slightest weaken their resolve to make the attainment of full EU membership the country's overriding priority.

In Hungary more than in any other of the four countries, the cleavage between nationalism and Europeanism has been of central policy significance, because of its bearing upon domestic party alignments and also because of its foreign policy importance.

The Hungarian Socialist Party has taken a more or less identical stance on the broad ideological issues as the SDPR and this cleavage between Europeanism and nationalism acquired increasing salience in the run-up to the 1994 elections because of its connection with central aspects of Hungarian foreign policy: the recognition of Hungary's borders and the stance of parties on the rights of Hungarian minorities in neighbouring states. The governing coalition up to 1994 took a strongly nationalist stance on these issues which included an undertone of irredentism while the HSP and the Europeanist camp repudiated this approach. The erstwhile neo-liberal camp of the Free Democrats and Young Democrats increasingly polarised on this issue as the nationalist theme became more prominent in the latter party. The agreement, on this issue, on the other hand, between the Free Democrats and the HSP, was an important element in enabling these parties to work together subsequently, in contrast with Poland where the Democratic Union's anti-Communism and commitment to neo-liberalism led it to make concessions to the particularist Right.

The foreign policy dimensions of this cleavage have been far more pronounced than those in Poland. A triangle of issues has dominated foreign policy debate: integration into western institutions, inter-state relations with Hungary's neighbours and defence of the interests of Hungarian minorities living in neighbouring states. Left and Right have differed on each of these issues and they have also differed on the sequence of priorities in tackling them.[46]

The MDF and its coalition partners, the Smallholders and the Christian Democrats, tended, in office, to present the task of defending Hungarian minorities abroad as an historic mission. Improving relations with neighbouring states – Slovakia, Romania and Serbia – where those minorities live has been made conditional upon those states improving the position of minorities. And Hungarian integration into NATO and the EU has sometimes appeared to be an instrument for furthering the mission towards the minorities.

The HSP has sought to reverse this sequence of priorities: the mission has been integration within the EU. Settling disputes with Hungary's neighbours has been a necessary first task on the road to western integration.

And protecting the rights of Hungarian minorities in those neighbouring states has been viewed as being strengthened rather than weakened by achieving friendly relations with the neighbouring states.[47]

The MDF-led coalition consistently rejected the idea of new treaties being signed with Slovakia and Romania repudiating any change in those countries' borders with Hungary. They cited the existing Helsinki Final Act as sufficient border guarantee, ignoring the fact that the Final Act is not a legally binding international treaty. They also frequently gave the impression of harbouring irredentist hopes, notably through the MDF prime ministers' insistence that they were the leaders of all Hungarians outside as well as inside Hungary's existing borders. The HSP not only accepted the idea of treaty-based border guarantees for neighbouring states, but pledged to seek an historic settlement with these neighbours. The HSP-AFD government moved swiftly to achieve such treaties after coming into office.

The HSP accused the Right of seeking to promote its own ideology within the Hungarian minority movements in Slovakia and Romania, rather than seeking to achieve adequate guarantees of their rights from neighbouring governments. The Right accused the HSP in turn of being ready to put inter-state relations above the interests of the minorities, citing the fact that the HSP pledged only to consult minority organisations over the proposed treaties rather than give them an effective veto over them.

Finally, the HSP criticised the MDF coalition for trying to use its western links for narrow national advantage over neighbouring states. Thus, it suggested that the Right's enthusiasm for swift entry into NATO was governed by the hope that, in the event that Slovakia and Romania were not integrated into NATO, Hungary could use its position within the organisation to strengthen its leverage against these states. By contrast, the HSP has sought to argue that any NATO expansion should be preceded by a longer phase of broad NATO co-operation with all the countries of the region.

On the general issue of NATO enlargement eastward, the Hungarian Socialists, like the Polish Socialists, have not been enthusiasts. There is little doubt that they would have favoured other kinds of security arrangements in East Central Europe, arrangements more inclusive of Russia (and Ukraine). But they have silenced their doubts. The Hungarian Prime Minister Horn did, however, insist upon visiting Moscow to discuss and explain his orientation towards NATO membership and to seek Russian acquiescence. And unlike other parties, the HSP pledged that it will put Hungary's NATO membership (as well as its EU membership) to a referendum.

The HSP leadership has also been far from enthusiastic about the EU's own policies in trade and other fields. But this, of course, only strengthens their determination to enter the walls of the Union. HSP leaders also hope that strengthening links with the EU will enable the country to lessen its vulnerability to the leverage of the International Financial Institutions. And both the SLD and the HSP have some hopes that they may be able to use their links with EU social democratic parties to achieve some leverage of their own in defence of their domestic social goals.

In Bulgaria, the BSP has also increasingly adopted a Europeanist and universalist stance in the general ideological field, after initially being tainted with playing upon anti-Turkish sentiment, and for much of the 1990s it has been allied with the largely Turkish third party. On the other hand, the UDF has become more pronouncedly nationalist, with Far Right elements in its ranks supporting irredentist hopes in relation to Macedonia. But in the field of foreign policy, Bulgarian trends on EU and NATO membership differ from those in the Visegrad countries. While Bulgaria has joined the Partnership for Peace and approves its own inclusion in NATO, for the BSP leadership this support is purely to avoid Bulgarian exclusion in the event of broad NATO enlargement eastwards occurring. And EU membership, along with EU–Bulgarian relations generally, has little actuality for either the BSP or for Bulgarian policy-makers generally in the current context. The West's trade embargo against Yugoslavia hampered the development of EU–Bulgarian trade and Bulgaria remains a long way from being on the threshold of EU membership. There has been a great deal of resentment amongst political elites in the country at the lack of priority given by the EU to Bulgaria since 1989.[48]

Romanian politics has undergone a major mutation in this area. Initially, President Iliescu and the state executive stressed strongly nationalist themes while the opposition held up the banner of Europeanism and universalism. There is evidence that the state executive encouraged the development of ultra-nationalist parties on the Far Right and Iliescu was prepared to form a governing coalition with them (as well as with the nationalist Socialist Labour Party). This domestic dimension was linked to evident irredentist tendencies on the part of the Romanian government in the early 1990s: in particular efforts to re-incorporate Moldova into Romania, and a refusal to accept the legitimacy of North Bukovina's continued incorporation within Ukraine.

But from the spring of 1993, Iliescu's orientation switched in an increasingly Europeanist direction, a first sign of this being the formation of the PSDR itself. Romania's acceptance into the Council of Europe in November 1993 seemed to strengthen this turn.[49] The government gave up its earlier attempts to re-annex Moldova. In October 1995 the PSDR broke its alliance with the extreme Right Greater Romania Party and during a visit to Washington Iliescu called the leader of this party and the leader of another allied Far Right party 'Romania's Zhirinovskies'.[50] Hand in hand with this was Iliescu's positive response to the election of the HSP in Hungary in 1994, expressed in his desire to settle disputes with Hungary over minority and territorial issues, through an 'historic reconciliation' treaty between the two countries.

In the foreign policy field, the turn by Iliescu in 1993 was equally marked. The PSDR government declared membership of the EU and NATO to be its 'strategic goal' and worked vigorously, though in vain, to try to ensure that Romania was allowed to enter NATO at the same time as any Visegrad countries.[51] The government evidently had two serious fears: first, that the first enlargment of NATO might also be the last, with the result that Romania would be left in a security void that Russia would seek to fill and that would in turn pull the country away from being able to join the EU; secondly, the government feared that Romania's exclusion from NATO's first enlargement at the same time as Hungary was included, could generate a new and perhaps serious deterioration of relations with Hungary over Transylvania which could also make Romanian entry into NATO and the EU much more difficult.

4) Secularism versus Church

This cleavage has been especially important in Poland. In predominantly orthodox Romania and Bulgaria, the involvement of the Church in secular and political affairs has not been a major issue of contention between parties, while in Hungary divisions over the role of the Catholic church have generally been subsumed under other cleavages.

But in Poland, Catholicism versus secularism has been a major political issue and the SDPR has, together with the Union of Labour, championed secular rights. The Polish Catholic hierarchy sought to gain support not only from the Right but from the liberal centre in the form of the Democratic Union government of Suchocka for an anti-abortion law in 1993. This was opposed both by the Union of Labour and the Social Democrats, and the new Social Democratic government reversed the law soon after it entered office in 1993. The presidential elections of 1995 brought the issue of secularism to the fore again as the Church hierarchy threw its weight behind Walesa by calling upon Poles to reject the 'neo-pagan' Social Democratic candidate Kwasniewski. The Social Democrats also indicated that the Concordat between Poland and the Vatican, drawn up before they came into office, had made too many concessions to the Church. For important sections of the Polish intelligentsia and urban populations, this defence of secularism and liberal rights is a strong recommendation for the SDPR, given the Church hierarchy's record not only on the issue of anti-Semitism but also in promoting authoritarian values and ultra-conservative views on important aspects of social policy.

5) Domestic ethnic minority rights

In Poland, these issues have not seriously divided the main parties – there has been a broad consensus on the stance towards both the western territories and the German minority. Apart from some remarks by the Primate, Cardinal Glemp, anti-Semitism has been confined to the Far Right fringe in the 1990s.

In Hungary the main issue of minority rights has concerned racism against gypsies and Romanies. Their cause has been taken up seriously only by the parties of the Left, not only the HSP but also the small Marxist Hungarian Socialist Workers' Party.

In Bulgaria the civil rights of the Turkish minority were a major issue in the last phase of the Communist regime as the Bulgarian Communist Party leadership sought to bolster its support by encouraging anti-Turkish sentiment. But despite accusations against the BSP that its leadership was also playing upon such sentiment in 1991, the Turkish minority party has felt more comfortable allying with the BSP than with the UDF on the Right. The plight of the gypsies and Romanies is also very difficult in Bulgaria but it has not been taken up seriously by the main parties. The same problem exists in even more acute form in Romania.

The most politically momentous issue in this field among the four countries is that of Romania's Hungarian minority. This is also an extremely complicated problem over which political partisanship has often entered western treatments and on which non-experts should be very cautious when attempting to make judgements. Antagonism between the two million-strong Hungarian minority in Transylvania and Romanian political movements has deep roots, going back to the days of the Austro-Hungarian Empire when the Hungarian landowners in Transylvania treated the subject Romanian population there more or less like personal chattels. During the war, the German government handed Transylvania back to Horthy's Hungary.

The contemporary leadership of the Hungarian minority is strongly nationalist and contains right-wing irredentist trends within it.

On the other hand, in Romania the NSF and the PSDR have given support and encouragement to Far Right nationalist allies up to 1994, while the latter have taken stridently anti-Hungarian stances reminiscent of fascism.[52]

At the same time the PSDR sought to present itself as a centrist force on the issue, while claiming with some justice, that irredentist political trends within the Hungarian minority were being encouraged by the MDF-led coalition in Budapest. It argued that once the Hungarian government fully guaranteed Romania's existing borders in a binding treaty, tensions between the Hungarian minority and the Romanian state could be quickly resolved. Meanwhile, Iliescu included the extreme nationalist Party of Romanian National Unity led by Gheorghe Fumar, the Mayor of Cluj, in the governing coalition.[53]

One of the main flash-points has been on the issue of educational rights for the Hungarian minority. The main party of the Hungarian minority, the

Hungarian Democratic Federation of Romania (HDFR), has claimed that Hungarian educational rights have been restricted in comparison with the Ceausescu period, especially. In Parliament, despite vigorous lobbying by the HDFR, it was unable to get either most of the liberal opposition or Petre Roman's Social Democrats to support its amendments to the Act and despite promises from Iliescu to look favourably on the amendments only some thirty of his party's deputies supported them. At the same time the OSCE's Commissioner for Minorities' Rights declared that there was nothing wrong with the new law. Other issues, particularly over cultural symbols in the city of Cluj, have brought sharp conflicts with the Hungarian minority.[54]

The main issue raised by the Council of Europe has been the refusal of the Romanian government to grant collective autonomous political rights to the Hungarians. But with the election of the HSP government in Budapest in 1994, substantial progress was made in combining a firm Hungarian guarantee of Romania's border with a satisfactory set of autonomy arrangements for the Hungarian minority. At the same time, the tensions on this issue are too deep-rooted to be expected to disappear even after the ratification of such a treaty and they may be exacerbated by the nationalist right in both countries.

Conclusions

Both the SDRP and the HSP have transformed themselves into western-style social democratic parties and can be seen as bulwarks of the democratic integration of their polities. The PSDR has evolved from authoritarian and oligarchic origins buttressed by a strident nationalism in the direction of a western-style social democratic party. The BSP has also evolved as an authentic socialist party committed to democratic development, though locked into a desperate economic crisis and an unstable political situation in the midst of terrible immiseration of large parts of the population.

Yet in no case is the future of these parties secure. In Poland, a Christian Nationalist Right with deep reserves of anti-Socialist authoritarianism remains a potentially powerful force if it can unite, while the liberal centre is weak and tends to ally with the Catholic Right against the SDPR. A deep elite cleavage thus remains. In Hungary the populist Far Right is today the most dynamic political force and the IFI intervention, utilising the economic crisis inherited by the HSP, has deeply divided the forces of the Left, threatening to destabilise the government. In Bulgaria the prospect of a breakdown of the political order cannot be excluded. Paradoxically, economic growth and the wide base of popular support for a gradual transformation towards a western-oriented national capitalism seems to offer the most secure prospects for the development of a centre Left in a fairly stable political context, now that the

Far Right nationalists are weakened, at least for the moment. But the test of governmental alternance has yet to occur and must be an important one, given the authoritarian origins of the PSDR.

But all these issues will be profoundly influenced by the course of policy on the part of the EU and other western institutions. Much of the instability in the region over the last seven years is a direct consequence of the substance of western policy. If this policy trend continues, the evolution of West European style liberal democracies, which rest very largely on the existence of a strong Left and labour movement, will probably be called into question.

It would appear that an influential group in the American policy debates on the region would prefer it if the post-Communist parties were desta-bilised, viewing them as the main obstacle to the consolidation of what democracy should in their view be about. They regard the authoritarian populist Right in the region as far less threatening to their conception of democracy.[55] The source of these judgements seems to be the new concep-tion of democracy now being promoted within US foreign policy: one that is concerned to promote a kind of polyarchy in which the link between popular opinion and policy formation should be entirely broken and indeed where the whole conception of the state serving collective goals is viewed as a throwback to the age of European collectivism since the French (as well as the Russian) revolution. This conception may be serviceable for consolidating globalised peripheral polyarchies in Mexico but they have nothing to do with overcoming the division of Europe.

Notes

1. By East Central Europe we mean Poland, Hungary, Czechoslovakia, Romania and Bulgaria. With the break-up of Czechoslovakia they, of course, became six.

2. In four of them (Poland, Hungary, Bulgaria and Romania) they have been the leading parties at a national level during the 1990s.

3. This monopolisation of the political arena had, in fact been broken in Hungary since the mid-1980s and had not been total in Poland since the 1950s.

4. The most significant of the Left splits was in Hungary, where a minority maintained the Hungarian Socialist Workers' Party and subsequently gained 4.7 per cent in the first elec-tions; in Poland, a group left by former Gdansk party leader Fiszbach created an indepen-dent group, considering that the new post-Communist majority had not sufficiently trans-formed their party. There were later splits to the Right from the Czech Communists and to the Left from the Slovak Communists when the latter transformed themselves, in 1991, into the Party of the Democratic Left.

5. A sophisticated form of this view is advanced in the useful article by Alison Mahr and John Nagle, 'Resurrection of the Successor Parties and Democratisation in East Central Europe', *Communist and Post-Communist Studies*, 28: 4 (1995).

6. This view is promoted especially in publications of the US Council of Foreign Relations. See the articles by Anne Applebaum and Michael Ignatief in 1996 issues of *Foreign Affairs*. A more sophisticated argument running along similar lines is found in Charles Gati, 'The Mirage of Democracy', *Transition*, 22 March 1996.

7. A good example of this dichotomisation is George Schopflin, 'Obstacles to Liberalism in

Post-Communist Politics', in *East European Politics and Society*, 5: 1 (Winter 1991).

8. Lena Kolarska-Bobinska, 'Myth of the Market, Reality of Reform', in S. Gomulka and A. Polonsky, *Polish Paradoxes* (Routledge, 1991).

9. Bill Lomax, 'Hungary', in Stephen Whitefield (ed.), *The New Institutional Architecture of Eastern Europe* (St. Martin's Press, 1993).

10. Dieter Segert, 'The SPD in the Volkskammer in 1990: A New Party in Search of a Political Profile', in Michael Waller, Bruno Coppieters and Chris Deschouwer (eds.), *Social Democracy in Post-Communist Europe* (Frank Cass, 1994).

11. Sharon Wolchik, *Czechoslovakia in Transition* (Pinter, 1991) and James P. McGregor, 'Value Structures in a Developed Socialist System: the Case of Czechoslovakia', *Comparative Politics*, 23: 2 (1991).

12. See the special issue of the *Journal of Communist Studies*, 'Parties, Trade Unions and Society in East-Central Europe', 9: 4 (December 1993).

13. See Ruth A. Bandzak, 'The Role of Labour in Post-Socialist Hungary', in the *Review of Radical Political Economy*, 28: 2 (June 1994).

14. For a valuable analysis of the Czech trade unions, see Anna Pollert, 'From Acquiescence to Assertion? Trade Unionism in the Czech Republic 1989 to 1995', paper presented to 2nd Conference of the European Sociological Association, Budapest, August 1995.

15. See Michael Waller et al. for discussion of developments in the trade unions.

16. In 1994 the percentages of electorates who said that they had previously supported the market economy but now rejected it were as follows: 21 per cent in Poland; 28 per cent in the Czech Republic; 29 per cent in Slovakia; 32 per cent in Hungary, and 47 per cent in Bulgaria. See European Commission: Eurobarometer Survey, 1994.

17. Wade et al. stress that the higher turn-out 'was perhaps the most important political reason for the strong emergence of the left in 1993'. See Larry L. Wade et al., 'Searching for Voting Patterns in Post-Communist Poland's Sejm Elections', *Communist and Post-Communist Studies*, 28: 4 (1995).

18. The Polish and Hungarian parties did worse than the PDS and the Czechoslovak Communists: respectively 10.9 per cent and 12 per cent as against 16 per cent for the PDS and 14 per cent for the Czechoslovak Communists.

19. A further factor in Poland may have been the fact of the partial character of the June 1989 election: the electorate seemed to have a chance to protest against the PUWP government without facing the possibility of that government being removed.

20. In Macedonia the Communists were the largest party but were not able to form the government.

21. Alison Mahr and John Nagle, 'Resurrection of the Successor Parties'.

22. On the non-Communist Polish Left groups see Nowa Lewica, 'The Ex-Solidarity Left', *Labour Focus on Eastern Europe*, no. 52 (Autumn 1995).

23. See Ulf Lindstrom, 'East European Social Democracy: Reborn to be Rejected', manuscript, University of Bergen, November 1990.

24. The Socialist International itself does not directly supply financial support. The Czechoslovak Social Democrats in exile were already members of the SI. The Hungarians were made members in 1990 but were later demoted to observer status.

25. See, for example, Michael Waller, 'Winners and Losers in the Early Post-Communist Elections in East-Central Europe', in Waller et al., op. cit.

26. See, for example, Lisl Kauer, 'Social Democracy in Eastern Europe', *Labour Focus on Eastern Europe*, no. 50 (Spring 1995).

27. In Hungary the Social Democratic Party's vote declined from 3 per cent in 1990 to just under 1 per cent in 1994 despite being accepted as a member of the Socialist International.

28. See M. A. Vachudova, 'Divisions in the Czech Communist Party', *RFE/RL Research Reports*, 2: 37, September 1993.

29. See Adam Novak, 'Big Boost for Social Democracy', in *International Viewpoint*, no. 280 (September 1996).

30. Discussion of these issues is contained in chapter 9.

31. On the early development of the NSF see Tom Gallagher, 'Romania: The Disputed Election of 1990', *Parliamentary Affairs*, 44: 1 (January 1991) and Mark Almond, 'Romania since the Revolution', *Government and Opposition* (January 1991).

32. Petre Roman's Democratic Party–National Salvation Front has now set up an electoral alliance with the small Social Democratic Party of Romania. The Alliance is called the Social Democratic Union.

33. See, for example, Mieczysław Rakowski, 'Our Actions are Defined by the Wellbeing of Poland', a speech on television, 13 September 1989, reprinted in *Contemporary Poland*, no. 10 (1989).

34. See Ludwik Krasucki, 'On the Horizon – the 11th Party Congress,' *Contemporary Poland*, no. 9, (1989). This article, reporting preparations for the last PUWP Congress, spells out that the PUWP leadership accepted the inevitability of a transition to capitalism.

35. See Dan Ionescu, 'Romania's Trade Unions Unite', *RFE/RL Research Reports*, 2: 28 (July 1993).

36. In Hungary Prime Minister Horn proposed Sandor Nagy as industry minister but this was blocked by the Free Democrats in the government as being financially destabilising.

37. See Mitchell Orenstein, 'The Failures of Neo-Liberal Social Policy in Central Europe', *Transition*, 28 June 1996.

38. See Jeff Freeman, 'Hungarian Utility Privatisation Moves Forward', *Transition*, 3 May 1996.

39. See Zsofia Szilagyi, 'Communication Breakdown Between the Government and the Public', *Transition*, 22 March 1996.

40. The IMF did insist upon the opening of a stock market, but the result was a stock exchange with twelve quoted companies, only one of which was fully private. See Ionescu, 'Romania's Stand-By Agreement', *RFE/RL Research Report*, 3: 18 (6 May 1994).

41. Michael Wyzan, 'Renewed Economic Crisis May End Foot-Dragging Reforms', *Transition*, 23 August 1996.

42. See Kjell Engelbrekt, 'Bulgarian Power Games Give Way to Growing Competition', *Transition*, 26 January 1996.

43. The real origins of Olechowski's resignation seem to have lain in a charge by the SLD that he was acting illegally by combining his post as Foreign Minister with a full salary as the director of a private bank, a charge upheld by the Polish courts just before Olechowski resigned.

44. See Jan B. de Weydenthal, 'Polish Foreign Policy After the Elections', *RFE/RL Research Reports*, 2: 41 (15 October 1993).

45. An important motive here is concerns over Polish-German relations. As indicated in the 1990 Polish-German Treaty, the Polish government will take a more relaxed attitude towards its western territories only after Poland's full integration into a strong EU.

46. See Alfred A. Reisch, 'Hungarian Parties' Foreign-Policy Electoral Platforms', *RFE/RL Research Reports*, 3: 19 (13 May 1994).

47. See Alfred A. Reisch, 'The New Hungarian Government's Foreign Policy', *RFE/RL Research Reports*, 3: 37 (26 August 1994).

48. See Kjell Engelbrekt, 'Southeast European States Seek Equal Treatment', *RFE/RL Research Reports*, 3: 12 (1994).

49. See Dan Ionescu, 'Romania Admitted to the Council of Europe', *RFE/RL Research Reports*, 2: 44 (5 November 1993).

50. On the vituperative dispute which followed these remarks, see Michael Shafir, 'Anatomy of a Pre-Election Political Divorce', *Transition*, 26 January, 1996.

51. See Dan Ionescu, 'Hammering on NATO's Door', *Transition*, 9 August 1996.

52. On the Romanian nationalist parties' background, see Tom Gallagher, 'Electoral Breakthrough for Romanian Nationalists', *RFE/RL Research Reports*, 1: 45 (13 November 1992).

53. After the 1992 parliamentary elections, the NSF lacked a majority in the Parliament and initially sought a grand coalition, but when unable to achieve agreement with the anti-Communist opposition, formed a coalition with ultra-nationalists.

54. See Michael Shafir, 'Ethnic Tension Runs High in Romania', *Radio Free Europe/Radio Liberty Research Reports*, 3: 32 (August 1994).

55. See Michael Ignatieff on the supposedly crippled democracy that results from the continued strength of the post-Communists and Anne Applebaum's argument as to why the populist Right should be looked upon more favourably than the post-Communists.

12

The Enlargement of NATO and the EU

The end of the Cold War is itself now coming to an end as Europe enters a new phase marked by the redivision of the continent. This is the real significance of the NATO enlargement and the likely significance of the next moves of the EU in the long saga of what is called EU eastward enlargement.

This may seem a perverse view of the process that was launched by the NATO Madrid Summit in July 1997 and by the EU Commission's Agenda 2000 documents. After all, the continent has already been divided between those inside the EU and NATO since 1989, and those outside. And are not the decisions of 1997 going to produce a less divided, more inclusive result?

As far as NATO is concerned this will be true only in an arithmetical and not a political sense, because the main political meaning of the NATO enlargement lies not in Poland's inclusion, but above all in Russia's exclusion from a determined effort to consolidate NATO as Europe's main political institution.

In the case of the EU, the break between the hopes of 1989 and the emerging realities has been more gradual, but the result is turning out to be the same: the European political economy is being fragmented once again, in ways that are different in character from those which existed during the Cold War but which, for a number of countries, are likely to be just as deep.

At the same time, the two parallel processes of new divisions – the one involving NATO and the other involving the EU – must each be seen in the context of the other, the impact of each feeding back on the other.

We will attempt, briefly, to analyse the character, causes and consequences of the emergent divisions.

I NATO's Expansion and the Exclusion of Russia

The Liberal Universalist Promise of 1989–91

The populations of the former Soviet Bloc were assured after 1989 that once they became market economies and democracies the division of Europe would be overcome and they would be included in 'the West' and in 'Europe'. NATO officials touring the former USSR and East Central Europe assured audiences that European peace and security were now 'indivisible' and that all Europeans were now 'in the same boat'. Provided all the states became 'market economies' and 'democracies' everybody would be included. With the threat of Communism and of the USSR gone, Europe would, in President Bush's words, become 'whole and free' in a system of collective security without alliances against enemies.

More than rhetoric was involved: the OSCE was strengthened as a pan-European security forum, recognised as a UN regional organisation and given roles in reducing conflict and promoting the peaceful settlement of disputes. A strong, pan-European conventional arms control treaty, the CFE, was approved, limiting force strengths. And the admittedly unsatisfactory NPT was re-endorsed with a supposed commitment on the part of the nuclear powers to move towards deeper disarmament. All these steps were part of a wider framework for what could be described as a liberal vision for building a new kind of security order in Europe, based upon genuine collective security rather than a power politics rivalry such as existed during the Cold War and in the 1930s.

These possibilities seemed all the more realisable because Germany had a political culture very different from the more militarist and nationalist traditions of some other western states (such as France and Britain): strong constituencies in the Federal Republic desired a multilateral civilian model of European development.

NATO's first moves towards the CEECs in the 1990s seemed to confirm this commitment to pan-European security: the North Atlantic Co-operation Council, followed by the Partnership for Peace were, in principle, all-inclusive bodies for Eurasia as a whole.

The seeds of this liberal order were supposed to be contained within the womb of the NATO alliance itself: the NATO powers claimed that their alliance was based not upon power politics but precisely on what contemporary liberal schools of thought about international relations claim: the internal democratic systems and the shared liberal and democratic values of the western states. If this was the case, then there was every reason to hope that the transformation of the former Soviet Bloc into liberal democracies would generate a similar harmony of shared values across the whole of the continent, thus making real collective security based on common observance of shared norms and rules a reality. Such were the declaratory principles of the NATO powers during the 1990s. And, indeed, such are their declared principles today.

Of course, peace and security depend upon more than the design of security and political institutions. They rest on economic and social preconditions: without prosperity and/or economic development, such values and institutions can come under strain, if not collapse. This was the point at which the role of the EU and the other institutions of the West's political economy raised great hopes in Central and Eastern Europe. As in the case of western Europe after the war, the CEECs now hoped that they would be offered a development-oriented insertion in the international division of labour and that the latter would soon be anchored in their accession to the EC/EU. And even if this EU did not stretch as far eastwards as Russia (despite John Major's declared aim of including Russia) a regime of free trade would link the EU to a prosperous CIS. The EU, committed precisely to European unity and having always recognised that Europe included Budapest and Sofia even if it was uncertain about Kiev and Moscow, would adapt to accommodate the CEECs.

Against this background, the CEECs have spent the last decade transforming themselves into market economies and liberal democracies. Today both private capitalism and liberal democracy is the norm – though not universal – across the former Soviet Bloc region. The transformation to capitalism has been extremely costly in economic, social and health terms. But the peoples of the region have largely accepted these privations for one overriding reason: the goal of entering the club of West European-style prosperity, democracy and peace offered to them by the leaders of the western alliance. Of course, neither the capitalism nor the democracy that have emerged are perfect from the standpoint of liberal norms. But that only makes these CEE states similar to their far from perfect counterparts in the West. The main thing is that they have passed the test set for them by the West European states: they have been accepted into the Council of Europe. They are on target.

But now the goalposts are being moved.

NATO Enlargement

In 1994 the US administration indicated it was in favour of NATO's eastward enlargement. It then retreated somewhat, giving no date and promoting the Partnership for Peace as perhaps even an alternative. But in 1996, after the Russian Presidential elections were out of the way, Washington lifted enlargement to the top of NATO's agenda and the process of enlarging NATO began at the Madrid Summit in July 1997 in order to be completed by 1999.

The form of the American campaign for enlargement is interesting because of its complete lack of credibility. We are led to believe that picking suitable entrants to NATO has nothing to do with geopolitics but is rather about which states of the region have achieved high enough standards of democracy and market economy to be worthy. Thus, during Secretary General Solana's tour of the CEECs in 1996: 'The secretary general will be making it clear that no decisions have been taken yet and that each applicant will be judged on individual merit,' a Nato official informed us. 'But it is clear that some countries are more ready to join than others and, obviously, they will be the first to join.' Although Nato has not yet specified formal criteria for admitting members from the former Warsaw Pact, 'it is no secret that countries judged to have made the most progress in democratic and economic reforms will be favoured . . . .'[1]

This is a brave attempt to pretend that NATO is a norm-based collective security body preoccupied above all by democratic concerns, rather than the strategic interests of its main states. But nobody can seriously believe that. In reality everyone knows the main lines of the division which is planned. Only the details on the exact boundaries are in doubt. The American–German-led western alliance will be moving into Poland, the Czech Republic and Hungary through incorporating these countries within NATO. At the same time, the Balkans and the former Soviet Union are to be excluded.

Of course, the exact modalities of Polish membership are not yet clear.[2] But these are essentially insignificant details. They do not touch the main issues: namely that Poland will be integrated into NATO's military capacity and Russia will be left outside.

The first consequence is an inevitable and major political blow to Russia which will tend almost certainly to be as permanent as the old division of Europe was. Russia will be excluded from significant legitimate political influence over the major political issues in the affairs of Central and Western Europe whenever the western powers want it to be excluded. Discussion and decision-making will take place first within NATO and only afterwards will Russia be consulted – or not – as the case may be. This is bound to be as unacceptable to any Russian government as it would be to any British government if the UK was placed in a similar situation by a security alliance stretching from Calais to the Urals. It simply makes a mockery of the notion of respecting Russia's interests as an important European power – never mind a Great Power.

But enlargement into Poland cannot be assumed to be of purely political significance. Even if Poland were not formally integrated into the NATO command and even if there were no permanent stationing of either nuclear weapons or non-Polish NATO troops on Polish territory, the military strategic balance of force profoundly changes for Russia as a result of Polish membership, because NATO acquires the ability to build the infrastructures and co-ordination mechanisms to deploy force on Poland's borders with Ukraine very rapidly in a crisis. As a result, the United States and Germany acquire the ability to use a far more potent form of coercive diplomacy against Russia, in the event that Russian and US interests clash in the zones around Russia's borders. This again is inherent in any expansion of NATO into Poland. Soothing words about strategic partnerships, consultation, etc. between the US/NATO and Russia will not dispose of this fact.

In this connection it is important to recognise the transformation of the balance of military power that has occurred since 1989. Today NATO has three times the military strength of Russia *and the rest of the CIS combined*. With Poland and the other CEECs joining, NATO's factor of predominance will be four to one. This is also important when considering the rhetoric from Warsaw or from the Republican Right in the United States about the continued 'Russian threat': such language as an explanation for NATO expansion is just not credible.

Thus Polish membership of NATO will absolutely inevitably repolarise European politics. Those who say Russia should welcome this enlargement because NATO is purely defensive and threatens nobody are either ignorant of international politics or mendacious, because they ignore the simple fact that Russia will face a mighty nuclear-armed military alliance on its own border (of the Kaliningrad triangle), an alliance whose leading powers are already engaged in a vigorous competition with Russia for influence over its Asian energy-and-minerals underbelly and over Ukraine.

Russia will, therefore, inevitably do what it can under any leadership to undermine this state of affairs. Of course, some argue that Russia will have to come to realise that it must accept the new realities, give up its ambitions to be a Great Power in European politics and accept that what counts now is strength as a capitalist economy. Along this line of argument, NATO expansion actually helps Russia by making her face these facts. But this is itself just the language of *Machtpolitik* and acknowledges that NATO enlargement is a deliberate assertion of power against Russia designed to make its elites sober up and face defeat. It is also a disingenuous argument because the quest for economic strength cannot be divorced from the quest for political influence, above all in Russia's case, where a close relationship with Ukraine and the Caspian and Asian Republics can bring the new Russian capitals very handsome rewards.

Against this background, we can predict an effort by Russian governments to combat NATO's expansion into Poland. This response might take a variety of forms and might develop at a variety of paces over the next decades. Russia could threaten Poland by stuffing Kaliningrad or Belarus with tactical nuclear weapons;[3] it could repudiate the CFE; scrap its START commitments;[4] engage in wrecking tactics in the UN; turn the Baltic states into hostages; turn nasty on the Black Sea Fleet; turn its base on the Dnestr into a threat to Moldova; embark upon a more activist policy to destabilise Ukraine or seek to expand its influence in the Balkans. None of this may seriously threaten the security of Western Europe and it might even strengthen the currently very ragged cohesion of the Atlantic alliance and US leadership in western Europe. But it could cause misery for hundreds of millions of people in Eastern Europe and the former Soviet Union.

Particularly dangerous will be the onset of intense American–Russian rivalry within Ukraine. Russia has powerful levers for pursuing this struggle, not least its economic leverage over the Ukrainian economy, its links within Ukraine's political elites and the crisis of Ukraine's armed forces and state administration (not to speak of its appalling general economic crisis). At the same time, American hopes that it has a strong base of political support in Ukraine may prove unfounded and a deep internal crisis within that country could ensue.

Along the borders between those definitely in and those definitely out, there lies a grey zone of states which may or may not be included. The French government would like Romania in, while other western governments disagree. The German government would favour Slovenia's inclusion; others (notably in Italy) are far less enthusiastic. Slovakia is another grey zone country. The states left out will become a field of political rivalry between Russia and the West and, in the Balkans, between Turkey and Greece. Indeed, there are clear signs that such rivalry is already underway in Bulgaria.

In any case, the results of this expansion can only be to increase insecurity for the excluded states by tilting the local balance of forces against Slovakia, Romania, and Bulgaria. The tendency will be for the excluded to fear a new local assertiveness from the included and to devote more of their extremely meagre resources to military budgets. Thus already overstretched budgets and poverty-stricken populations will be strained even further.

If Romania is left out of NATO while Hungary is included, the potential for conflict between Romania and Hungary over Transylvania will increase, despite the treaty between left-wing governments in both countries regulating their relations on this issue. Both the Romanian and the Hungarian Right are far from reconciled with the treaty in place. The same pattern could occur between Hungary and Slovakia if the latter is excluded from NATO. On the other hand, if Romania is included in NATO, the potential for irredentist projects on the part of a Romanian government towards both Moldova and Ukraine (over North Bukhovina) may create a new zone of tension. A foretaste of such future possible rivalries was given in the late autumn 1996, when Boris Yeltsin suggested that an alliance with Bulgaria might be built: this exacerbated political tensions within that country in ways that could only further deepen the political (and financial) crisis there. The manoeuvres within Bulgaria were directly stimulated by the plans for

NATO enlargement. The whole area of the Southern Balkans may be pushed back into the role of becoming a cockpit for power rivalries as a result of the NATO expansion.

Of course, western policy-makers are fully alert to these dangers. This is why they are trying to insist that NATO's expansion has nothing whatever to do with US power politics and state interests, but is precisely a continuation of the liberal, collective security project: once a state has proved itself to be a consolidated democracy it will be awarded NATO membership irrespective of geopolitics or geostrategy. In other words, those excluded must be persuaded that their exclusion is the result of failings by their governments to come up to western standards of freedom, democracy and liberal rights. Insofar as this message is convincing to the electorates of the excluded countries, the division of Europe will not pose too serious a challenge to European stability and security, at least in the short term. Local voters will blame their own state elites rather than the western powers for their exclusion from the western club of rich states. The politicians who have been demanding sacrifice after sacrifice in order to 'enter Europe' will not be discredited and will be able to call for one more big round of sacrifice to ensure eventual entry into the promised West.

But this public relations exercise carries little weight in a region close to one of NATO's three or four most important states – Turkey – which is currently engaged in a war against the Kurds and systematically uses torture against its own population. They, therefore, like the Russians, ask themselves what is really going on in Washington: what is the real reason – as opposed to the news management absurdities – for the new division of Europe?

The Causes of NATO's Expansion

We can be sure that NATO's expansion has nothing to do with particular current tensions, conflicts or threats in the CEECs today. If potential Russian threats had been the motive, NATO would not be entering Poland, it would be opening its doors to the Baltic states. Yet precisely because Russia would have the capacity to occupy the Baltics, NATO wishes to steer clear of them! At the same time, by entering Poland, NATO actually increases the insecurity of the Baltics.

The conclusion is inescapable, that the first and main basis for the move into Poland is not a Russian threat *but Russia's current extreme weakness.* Because of the catastrophic social and economic collapse inside Russia and the fact that its state has, for the moment, been captured by a clan of gangster capitalists around the West's protegé Boris Yeltsin, the Russian state is in no position at present to resist the enlargement. This Russian weakness will almost certainly be temporary. We must assume the Russian economy and state will revive. It could easily grow ten-fold stronger in resource terms than it is today. NATO is thus exploiting a 'window of opportunity' that will not stay open for very long. It is a case, therefore, of establishing a *fait accompli* against Russia swiftly.

The analogy with Germany's fate after the First World War is all too obvious. The new order then was based upon a temporarily weak Germany and when Germany revived it worked to undermine the Versailles order. After the Second World War, the institutions of Western Europe were built by the US precisely in order to provide a framework for the revival of the strength of the defeated power (or at least of its western part). This time round the defeated power is to be excluded just like the Weimar Republic in the 1920s.

In other words, NATO's expansion into Poland has little or nothing to do with strengthening Europe's peace, security and stability. It is a piece of opportunism, an adventure, gambling with Europe's future security for the sake of something other than security.

The fashionable answer amongst West European diplomats as to what this something-other-than-security actually is tends to be a variant on Disraeli's remark about the causes of the British Empire: it was done in a fit of collective absence of mind on the part of the American administration: Clinton stumbled into it without much thought in his Detroit speech in October;[5] or he was after the Polish vote in the mid-West; or whatever, but the main thing is that once Clinton has publicly committed himself to it, we are lumbered with it and must make the best of it.

These kinds of explanations cannot be taken seriously, not least because they express unwarranted contempt for the American policy-making system. Whatever the weakness of decision-making in the US executive, no American president would be allowed to gamble with Europe's future for the sake of the Chicago vote.

Since the enlargement decision reshapes Europe's future we must assume that the US origins of the policy derive from considerations on an equivalent level: namely, considerations about securing the United States' future as the dominant world power after the Soviet Bloc collapse.

If we approach the search for causes at this level we can engage in 'backward mapping', from the consequences of NATO expansion into Poland for America's power position in Europe, to the likely motives for that decision.

Four main features of an explanation stand out:

1) Norm-based collective security

By asserting NATO power in ways that weaken Russia, the USA is asserting its monocratic dominance in European politics, precisely to defeat decisively European pressures for a norm-based, inclusive collective security order in Europe. To appreciate this, we must distinguish between quite different senses of the notion of norm-based collective security. A genuinely inclusive collective security order involves three core elements:

(a) a collective *decision-making system* on policy and on operations, based upon clear rules.
(b) clear rules on unacceptable state behaviour and on modes of collective action against states which break the rules.
(c) clear mechanisms for joint action to enforce the rules.

Both the Bush and Clinton administrations have consistently opposed such conceptions for the obvious reason that they would undermine its single-power dominance over decisions and operations within NATO. To strengthen the OSCE towards playing these roles would have reduced US power to that of being only *primus inter pares* in European affairs: it would have remained the most influential power because of its military capacity, its military infrastructures in Europe, its leadership of the world economy, the strength of its MNCs and its capacity, assisted by its great media strengths, to dominate the international agenda. But during the Cold War, the US had been more than first among equals: it had dominated and controlled the high politics of Western Europe. A European collective security regime would have required the US to have accepted a loss of direct institutional control, through NATO, of the destiny of Europe.

Worse, under a collective security order, the West European states could have developed their own security identity independently of the USA. The WEU could have replaced NATO as the primary locus of strategic policy-making and as the primary nexus of military forces amongst West European states. NATO could, at best, have become a meeting place only between two centres of strategy and two organisations of force – one American, one West European. And the West Europeans could have insisted that US actions in Europe conform strictly to rules laid down in a strengthened OSCE and in other such collective security fora.

And if Russia had been included, there would have been three power poles within pan-European security – the USA, a unifying western Europe (around France and Germany) and Russia – raising the distinct possibility of the USA finding itself as one against two.

With the expansion of the EU into the Visegrad Countries, this kind of marginalisation could have stared the USA in the face. Key political issues involving Russia, Central Europe and the EU could have been discussed first between EU powers and Russia, since NATO would not be involved with Russia or Central Europe. At the same time, if Russia had been drawn into NATO, the issue of the USA's monocratic power over decision-making and operational command within NATO could not have been avoided.

In such circumstances, given EU expansion into Visegrad, the US faced a potentially very real loss of control-power if NATO stayed as it was without expansion. And by expansion, the USA assures the continuation of its mono-cratic institutional position: no separate West European security policy or operational frameworks.

The USA conceals these issues by using the language of collective security and of a 'West European identity' in quite different senses. By 'collective' it means something arithmetic – a collection of states (under its command); by 'norm-based' it means that *the USA* can be relied upon *to decide* matters on the basis of democratic, liberal, human rights etc. norms; i.e. it will not be *institutionally* bound by any such norms. And as for the 'European identity', this can mean a transatlantic division of labour: the troops will be European and the command will be American (as well as the infrastructures).

2) Germany and Russia

Beyond these matters of current institutional design for Europe's security order, there are deeper questions of geopolitical strategy into the twenty-first century for the USA. As the NSC document leaked in early 1992 made clear, the American government is preoccupied by its long-term position in Eurasia, which in turn governs its capacity to exercise 'world leadership'. The great danger here for the USA is that Germany becomes the hege-monic power in western and Central Europe and then establishes a condominium with Russia over the bulk of the Eurasian landmass. To pre-vent that happening, US political ascendancy in the territory between Germany and Russia becomes pivotal. Via NATO expansion into Poland (as well as via US companies acquiring a strong presence in Poland), US influ-ence in that key country can be secured.

3) *The* Drang Nach Kiev

For American policy planners, Poland is only one part of the necessary geopolitical wedge between Germany and Russia. In many ways, Ukraine is an even more important prize. A combined Polish–Ukrainian corridor under US leadership would decisively split 'Europe' from Russia, exclude Russia also from the Balkans, go a long way towards securing the Black Sea for the USA, link up with America's Turkish bastion, and provide a very important base for the 'Great Game' for the energy and mineral resources of the Caspian and the Asian Republics of the former USSR.

Of course, to move NATO into Ukraine today would cause an explosive confrontation with Moscow. For this reason, US policy towards Ukraine under President Clinton has been marked by considerable subtlety.

Following Bush's notorious 'Chicken Kiev' speech in the Ukrainian capital in 1991, when he attacked 'unrealistic nationalism' at a time when the US was worried about the consequences of Soviet collapse, Clinton joined a partnership with Moscow to ensure that Kiev became non-nuclear. What was not noticed by Russian politicians was that if Ukraine had decided to maintain its nuclear status, it could have done so in the medium term only by means of rebuilding its security relationship with Moscow. Thus, Ukraine's abandonment of nuclear weapons freed it from such future dependence.

With Kiev's agreement to become non-nuclear, the US government has combined a symbolic emphasis on its special relationship with Moscow with an energetic intensification of its relations with Ukraine. Kiev is now the recipient of the third largest amount of US aid. Washington has been vigorously seeking to strengthen Ukraine's mass media integrity and to strengthen military co-operation under the umbrella of the Partnership for Peace, notably through joint exercises and through strengthening military co-operation with Poland. The IMF has been unusually flexible in its approach to Ukraine's socioeconomic problems.

Washington now feels confident that it has a strong policy understanding with the Ukrainian government whereby the latter insists to Moscow on its right to co-operate with the West through the Partnership for Peace (P4P) and on its freedom from any security pact with Moscow. After initially expressing strong reservations about NATO's expansion into Poland and stressing its own 'neutralist' posture, Kiev has evolved towards supporting NATO expansion while saying it has no interest in joining NATO; and at the end of 1996, President Kuchma went further, indicating that in a very distant future Ukraine might itself eventually seek to become a NATO member.

Once NATO enters Poland, it will have the capacity to project its influence across the border into Ukraine in such a way as to ensure that Ukraine could withstand any Russian pressure to enter a security pact with Moscow. In the event of a crisis between Kiev and Moscow, NATO could offer massive assistance to Ukraine. And in the meantime, via P4P, co-operation and assistance can be steadily increased. Without NATO expansion, all this would be much more difficult.

This motive for NATO expansion into Poland, as a means of projecting US influence into Ukraine, was signalled by Polish President Kwasniewski. Speaking in London at the Royal Institute of International Affairs, he said: 'We are confident that Poland's accession to NATO will lead to a projection of stability and security into areas stretching beyond our eastern frontier.' This can only refer to the goal of pulling Ukraine away from a security link with Russia.

In short, NATO's expansion into Poland marks the return of power politics to Europe in place of the project of an inclusive and collective new security order. The relationship between liberal universalism and power politics turns out not be dichotomous: it acquires the complementary of means and ends: liberal universalism is the rhetorical means towards US power politics ends.

4) The new Russian threat

There is an obvious criticism that could be levelled against this analysis of US power-maximisation interests in NATO expansion. This is that it overemphasises what might be called the traditional 'realist' way of looking at international politics: it exaggerates the military-strategic elements of power over the political-economy elements. Along this line of argument, the key way in which the American state assures its global dominance is today less through its military capacity than through its imposition of its global political-economy regime on states. In other words, American ascendancy is assured through reorganising the internal structures of states to allow their penetration by American capitalist companies and through requiring these states to maintain their viability through competition on world markets in which US capital predominates.

All this is true in general: for the US in its relations with most states, military power is a reserve power, not the first means of influence. But it is not possible in the Russian case, because Russia is different: it has such vast energy and raw material resources that even with a gangster capitalist elite on an almost Zairian scale of sybaritic corruption, it has not the slightest difficulty in maintaining a healthy trade surplus and in keeping western capital at bay. And it can do all this without being integrated into the WTO. Moreover, it can offer both energy security and, at least in the medium term, significant credit support to governments looking for alternatives to the IMF. Its big capitals can also already move into other states and establish themselves as influential politicoeconomic rivals to western MNCs, especially in the crucial energy sector.

During the Cold War, this Russian economic capacity did not constitute a serious challenge because of the ideological divide against Communism. But with the Communist collapse, Russia's potential structural power in the energy sector and the expansionist capacities of its capitals constitutes a new kind of threat to US dominance over the international political economy.

Since 1991 the American administration, its MNCs and the IMF have been involved in a complex double operation to influence developments in Russia. On the one hand, there was the real possibility that the Gaidar government would actually open Russia's economic assets to American buyers. If American capital had been able to buy up Russia's oil and gas resources as well as the bulk of Russia's other mineral resources we would not have seen any NATO expansion into Poland excluding Russia. Washington would have adopted a 'Russia first' policy. But the Gaidar–Burbulis drive collapsed, despite the West's successful promotion of the idea of a coup d'état by Yeltsin against the Constitution in August 1993. The US then found itself backing Chernomyrdin-style Russian corporate capitalism against the Communist challenge. In this cleavage, Washington had to back Yeltsin–Chernomyrdin, but the latter was at the same time a potential challenge to the US drive for a 'globalised' capitalism in which all states would have to comply with market institutions designed to favour US MNCs. Thus as soon as Yeltsin had managed to beat off the Communists, the Clinton administration moved forward with a NATO expansion which will have the effect of containing the expansion of Russian capital abroad.

The Rebuilding of US Leadership Through Bosnia

So far we have implied that the US has been able to act more or less as it has pleased in European politics. Yet in reality, despite its assertion of power during the Gulf War of 1991, Washington was in danger of political marginalisation in a Europe that was peaceful and full of enthusiasm for overcoming the confrontation between the blocs in 1990 and 1991. The expansion of NATO today is conceivable only against the background of Washington's successful rebuilding of its authority over the West European states over the last six years. The first step in this US effort was, of course, ensuring that Germany was unified within NATO. The US reconstruction of NATO's ascendancy in Europe then passed through the Bosnian conflict.

With Germany's success in pushing the EC states to recognise Slovenia and Croatia at the end of 1991, the US, which had been against such recognition, found itself threatened with being marginalised on the major political conflict in Europe: that over the crisis of the Yugoslav state. The Bush administration was thus staring in the face the prospect of America's European ascendancy dissolving like a lump of sugar in Chancellor Kohl's coffee cup. In late January 1992, therefore, the Bush administration launched its campaign for an independent Bosnian state. As Susan Woodward explains this US drive for an independent Bosnian state, the US was ' . . . concerned that Germany was "getting out ahead of the US" (according to Deputy Secretary of State Eagleburger) and that it had lost any leverage on the Yugoslav situation after the EC's December decision . . . ' As Woodward adds: 'The re-entry of the United States into the Yugoslav debacle as part of a balance of power dynamic already in play in Europe added yet another element to the particular way in which Yugoslavia would unravel. The United States, though in competition with Germany, remained primarily concerned with maintaining the Atlanticist posture of the Kohl government . . . In place of the confrontation that could have resulted [with

Germany over recognition of Croatia] the United States appeared to move towards a geopolitical division of labour instead, conceding a primary sphere of influence over Croatia to Germany and taking on Bosnia as its responsibility.'[6]

As the West European states pointed out at the time, an attempt to create an independent, unified Bosnian state would lead to war and the war that resulted became the basis for a reassertion of NATO as the primary instrument of force in European politics.

On this basis, the Clinton administration launched the plan for NATO's eastward enlargement into Poland in order to ensure that when the Visegrad countries were pulled under the wing of Germany within the framework of the EU, Germany would not, in Eagleburger's phrase, be 'getting out ahead of the US' in deciding the great political issues of East Central Europe together with Russia, leaving the US marginalised.

II   The Emergent Divisions in Europe's Political Economy

The Hopes of 1989

When Communism collapsed in 1989, the populations of the region were by no means convinced that free market capitalism was the answer to their problems. But opinion rapidly shifted in 1990 as their new elites (except in Romania) argued that by adopting capitalist models their countries could 'enter Europe', in other words both join the European Community and become prosperous.

This remains the official course of the states of Central and Eastern Europe, but the journey has proved appallingly costly for the whole of the region and terrible economic crises are continuing to devastate the lives of hundreds of millions of people in Russia, Ukraine and the Balkans. Even more striking is the fact that the West European states take absolutely no responsibility for the economic fate of these countries: indeed, they go to extraordinary lengths to pin total responsibility for everything that occurs in the region on to the elites of these weak states. Yet a glance at the reality of the region since the start of the 1990s demonstrates that the entire framework for the economic transformation of the region has been imposed by the western powers. It is, of course, true that the social and political elites of the region have, on the whole, accepted this framework and have tried to work within it. Some have been genuinely enthusiastic for it; most have accepted it because they have felt that they have had to.

Secondly, the framework which the western states have imposed has been that of slump-induced transformation towards a particular variant of capitalism, that can best be described as the Baker Plan variant adopted by the US

Treasury in 1985 as the programme for reorganising the Latin American political economies. It is an illuminating fact that despite the large claims made for the power and European leadership capacities of the European Union within Europe, the entire scheme for the transformation of the CEECs has been American designed and American led through the IMF/WB.

Thirdly, despite public relations campaigns to the contrary, the European Union itself has not, as yet, taken even one significant step to adapt its own internal arrangements to accommodate a unification of the continent's political economy. Instead its policy towards the region in the trade field could better be described as one of collective mercantilism.

And finally, as it moves now into a new phase of the long journey towards eastward enlargement, the EU is speaking with two voices: combining an enhancement of its symbolic politics towards enlargement with signs that its main preoccupation is to provide new barriers to membership for most of the ten applicant countries.

The Missed Development Opportunity

In 1989, the United States was in no position to launch a development strategy for the states of CEE because the cupboard was, so to speak, bare in the US Treasury. Grappling with enormous payments and budget deficits and with a very large bill to pick up as a result of the collapse of US housing finance institutions, the United States lacked the financial resources to use positive economic incentives to influence the reorganisation of the East Central European states. When Bush visited Poland in the summer of 1989, he faced ridicule from Lech Walesa when he was able to offer only $200 million – the Polish authorities had been hoping for at least $2 billion. If a Marshall Plan-style development strategy for the region had been adopted, the US government's weakness would have been exposed and Germany and the West Europeans would have taken the lead. As in the field of Europe's high politics, so in the area of Europe's political economy, the immediate aftermath of the collapse of 1989 left the US in danger of marginalisation.

In this context, influential voices were raised in Western Europe, particularly in Germany and France, for a development-oriented framework for the reorganisation and economic integration of the CEECs. One such development strategy for East Central and Eastern Europe was advanced by the German Deutsche Bank President Herrhausen in the autumn of 1989. Herrhausen, who was close to Chancellor Kohl, argued for a major investment effort into the region while allowing it to preserve effective trade protection for its domestic industries. The plan would have allowed the turn towards capitalism in countries like Poland to have proceeded in conditions of economic revival rather than slump, and it would have been carried out in co-operation with the Soviet Union. But Herrhausen was assassinated at the end of November 1989 and his plan was dropped.[7]

A similarly growth-oriented plan was proposed by French President Mitterrand's adviser Jacques Attali. This would have involved a major public development bank with the resources and mandate for large-scale public and private infrastructure investments across the CEECs including the USSR. The plan was championed by the French government and the bank – the EBRD – was actually created, but its role and mandate was emasculated by the Bush administration with the result that it became little more than an adjunct to the operations of the western private sector in the region: it was banned from playing a large role in public infrastructure investment; it was instructed to operate like a private sector bank, on strictly commercial lines, while at the same time it was banned from taking on investment projects which western private sector operators took on. It was, therefore, little wonder that Attali as the Bank's president was hard put to find viable and acceptable projects to invest in during the slump of the early 1990s before he was bounced out of the bank by claims on the part of British and American banking circles that he had been living too lavishly and spending too much money on the Bank's London headquarters.

This was the background to the West's turn towards the Baker Plan approach to the reorganisation and integration of CEE. The US lacked the public credit resources to take the lead itself. Germany, working with the other West European states, would have had ample resources to offer a Marshall Plan-style development project. But the West European states were far too divided amongst themselves to stage such an operation: the Attali plan was in many respects promoted as a rival bid to the Herrhausen scheme and the American administration had little difficulty in manoeuvring to divide the West Europeans and degut the idea of using the EBRD as a real development lever. And once Chancellor Kohl realised that most of his partners within the EC were set upon trying to slow German unification down to a standstill, the final blow was struck against an expansionary approach to the CEECs: Kohl opted for what was in effect an Anschluss and thereby diverted the credit capacities of the Federal Republic (and of much of western Europe during the early 1990s) to its annexed Eastern Länder for the duration of the decade.

Thus did the CEECs end up in the hands of the IMF and World Bank. This was the ideal solution for the United States because it controls the IMF and the World Bank and it could therefore mobilise resources other than its own but under its control. Furthermore the IMF approach requires slumps rather than growth as the favoured context for restructuring since the slump provides powerful pressures on key economic actors and it destroys the social power of labour in economic and political life. And finally, the IMF programme for reorganising political economies is precisely geared to shaping the social, institutional and economic orders of the states concerned in ways that maximise the opportunities for American forms of financial and manufacturing conglomerates.

American Statecraft for a New Division of Labour

Thus, by default, the G7 decision at the Paris summit of 1989 to give the IMF the lead for handling the heavily indebted Polish and Hungarian economies laid the basis for the US approach to completely dominate the integration of the CEECs. This approach was already being tried out on Yugoslavia and at the start of 1990, the US launched its agenda throughout the region by making the Polish Balcerowicz Plan the flagship for its operations through-out the region. The US Secretary of State, James Baker, was able to apply his own Baker Plan, launched with such stunning effect in 1985 upon Latin America's indebted economies, to the former Soviet Bloc.[8]

The huge academic industry on systemic transformation in the CEECs treats Baker Plans as if they have their origins mainly in economic theory or in some autonomous processes in global economic and technological life. In fact, of course, the Baker Plans emerged from the defeat of the containment liberalism of the 1960s, and of figures like Robert McNamara, by the roll-back politics of the Reaganite Right in the 1980s. Reaganite think-tanks like the Heritage Foundation prepared the basis for a great global counter-offensive by the United States to re-establish its dominance after the catastrophes of the late 1960s and 1970s. Rollback applied not only to the Soviet Bloc, labour and Third World revolutions, but also to the Third World states and their development strategies, along with their use of the UN, UNCTAD and other such bodies in pressing for a New International Economic Order. The opportunity to launch the rollback against the countries of the South came with the debt crunch of 1982. By 1985 James Baker, Reagan's Treasury Secretary, was ready to unveil his Baker Plan for the Third World at the Seoul IMF conference that year.

The goal of Baker Plan restructuring has been to transform the states and political economies of the South in two main respects:

1) To replace a national industrial strategy for development through import substitution, and the development of the internal market, with a strategy based upon western MNC direct investment and exports from the target country to the world market.
2) To replace a state-centred financial and industrial system within the country with private financial markets, ownership of economic assets in the hands of private capital, deregulated labour markets and a strong role for western FDI and portfolio investment.

These two goals can be encapsulated in the term 'globalisation'. The result does not, of course, preclude growth. But it makes the local political economy immediately and persistently dependent on 'global' market forces – in other words, on decisions and developments within the core states. The changes have involved a radical restructuring of the social and political structures of non-core states. In some, there have been political breakdowns (notably in Africa), in others the state has survived via gangster capitalism (Colombia, Bolivia), while others have been able to carry through the sociopolitical transition (Chile, Argentina). But these have, nevertheless, faced other menacing consequences: the pauperisation of large parts of the population; a continuing inability to free themselves from debt, requiring constant state intervention from the IMF; and chronic vulnerability to financial crises and breakdowns in domestic banking and financial systems.

As Robert Chote recently explained in the *Financial Times* 'The international financial institutions are now turning their attention increasingly to the state of emerging market banking systems. And with good reason. At least two-thirds of the IMF's 181 member countries have suffered banking crises since 1980. In developing and transition economies, the cost of resolving these crises has approached $250 billion (£160 billion) in total – absorbing between ten and twenty per cent of a year's national income in the cases of Venezuela, Bulgaria, Mexico and Hungary. Banking crises inflict considerable damage on the economies in which they take place. One reason is that bank credit has grown rapidly in many emerging markets, relative to the size of their economies. Often these banks hold considerable stocks of domestic financial assets, operate the payments system and provide liquidity to security markets. So when crises strike they can cripple economic activity, choke off credit and place severe strains on interest rate and budgetary policies.'[9]

With the collapse of state socialism in Central and Eastern Europe, the Baker Plan approach was transferred from Latin America to the eastern part of Europe, with similar results. One state in the region was unable to cope with the transition involved in Baker Plan re-engineering: Yugoslavia.[10] It therefore collapsed. Other states have developed as gangster capitalism – the pattern in Russia and Ukraine. And many states have been struck by catastrophic financial system breakdowns – currently Bulgaria, and earlier Lithuania.

The western powers have required the countries of Central and Eastern Europe to pass through the purgatory of Baker Plan structural transformation as a precondition for applying for membership of the EU. A number of these countries have come through this travail and have returned to growth – notably Poland and the Czech Republic, along with Slovakia and Romania. (Hungary has so far had little real growth following its catastrophic slump in the early 1990s.)

But it remains to be seen whether this growth of the strongest survivors will remain sustainable. The key current bottleneck is a chronic and serious trade deficit. As the *Financial Times* reported at the end of 1996, 'A rising tide of red ink is splashing over the foreign trade accounts of central Europe' and there is 'a looming balance of payments crunch' and this is 'already sparking warnings from central bankers and finance ministers that 1997 will require fiscal and monetary tightening to reduce domestic demand, slow the growth in imports and free resources for export.'[11] By late 1998 this trade weakness had not been reduced. The source of these payments problems is not cyclical, but structural. On the one hand the new propertied classes are sucking in imports of consumption goods, especially from Germany which now exports more to the CEECs than it exports to the USA, according to the Bundesbank. On the other hand, after the destruction or severe weakening of the more advanced industrial sectors in the region during the Baker Plan slumps of the early 1990s, exports from the Czech Republic and Poland are now concentrated in low value-added sub-contracting for West European companies, based on cheap labour costs: 'Many western companies are shifting labour intensive product lines to take advantage of much lower labour costs just over their eastern border. The problem is that the resulting exports often consist of made-up clothes or engineering sub-assemblies made from previously imported cloth or components. This means that higher exports are dependent on previous imports, and labour is the only real net value-added.'[12]

The specific activities of the EU in the trade field have only exacerbated the tendencies towards a general downward restructuring of the CEECs to low value-added, labour-intensive operations through strongly mercantilist trade policies. The consequences of these policies for CEE agriculture have been extremely damaging and the industrial structures of the region have been weakened by the export drives of western companies supported by the subsidies of state export credits (perversely classified by the states concerned as 'aid' to the importing states). The one significant EU programme of aid to the countries of the region, PHARE, seems to have been predominantly geared towards assisting western economic operators to acquire assets and markets within the CEECs, with PHARE funds going less to the 'recipient states' than to western firms.

The EU: From One Dividing Line to Another

The European Union leaders and the political elites of most of the CEECs have been insisting over the last seven years that the IMF-led restructuring has been an essential preparation for the people of these countries to 'join Europe'. The peoples of the region have largely put up with the sufferings of the 1990s because they have believed that the impoverishment, health problems and collapsing infrastructures they have experienced have been an essential precondition for entry into the European Union.

Unfortunately, this is not the case. All the countries of the region, even the richest, are less absorbable now by the EU than they were in the 1980s. To appreciate why this is so requires some consideration of what the key obstacles to EU membership actually are.

In some of the past enlargements of the EU the key problems have been about the readiness of new member states to accept the *acquis communautaire*: in other words, applicants must be ready to accept all the existing policies and laws currently in force within the member states: they cannot seek to negotiate changes in these *acquis*: they must adapt to them and bear the full brunt of the costs of adaptation. But the main problem in the case of the eastward enlargment of the EU is exactly the opposite, namely: is the EU itself prepared to extend the *acquis communautaire* in full to the eastern applicants?

The frank answer to this question is: 'No!' There is no question whatever of the EU extending the current *acquis* as a whole to the Poles or the Hungarians or the Czechs, never mind others further East and South. Instead, there are only two possibilities: either the *acquis* will be changed before some of the Visegrad countries are integrated; or the Visegrad countries will be brought into the EU as second-class periphery states. And the main reason by far for these being the only two choices lies in the relative poverty of the populations of these states, a poverty which has been enormously exacerbated by the Baker Plan 'Economic Reform' which they have suffered in the 1990s.

Table 12.1 shows the transition costs in GDP per capita terms.

Table 12.1 Comparison of GDP Per Capita ($US)

	1989	1992
CFSR	9,048	2,460
Hungary	7,029	3,000
Poland	5,257	1,960
Austria	17,528	23,491
Spain	12,493	14,706

Source: Daniel Gros and Andrej Gonciarz: *A Note on the Trade Potential of Central and Eastern Europe* (J. W. Goethe University, Frankfurt).

The unprecedented destruction of economic assets in the CEE region and the downward restructuring of these economies does not in any way make it difficult for these states to meet the criteria of the *acquis communautaires.* They will be more than happy, for example, to adhere to the Structural Funds, to the CAP, to Free Movement of Labour. These would all greatly benefit them. And since their export industries are increasingly 'globalised' by being inserted into the internal division of labour of MNCs, while their trade protection regimes have already been largely dismantled, they find it fairly easy to change their laws and economic institutions to meet the broad requirements of the Single Market.

But all these pluses for the CEECs in terms of ease of entry are also precisely the reasons why the EU member states are overwhelmingly hostile to extending the *acquis* to the CEECs. To do so would cost the EU very large financial transfers. It would also enable, via the free movement of labour, large numbers of poverty-stricken workers from depressed regions of Poland travelling into Germany in search of work. This problem would be exacerbated by the EU-encouraged efforts of the Polish government to organise a big shake-out of labour in Polish agriculture before accession.

There are, of course, also major problems in restructuring the EU's decision-making institutions for an EU of, say twenty members, but these problems are already acute with or without enlargement: the EU is today scarcely capable of claiming to have a cohesive, democratic decision-making structure with or without the adhesion of the CEECs.

Against this background, the CEECs' governments and political elites are seriously concerned about the real orientation of the EU member states in relation to eastward enlargement. The record so far is far from encouraging.

EU Commitments and Tactics So Far

It was only in the summer of 1993 that the EC gave even a highly qualified commitment, at the Copenhagen Council, to the eventual integration into the European Union of the CEECs. The December 1994 Essen Council did not make the commitment more definite but did initiate a Structured Dialogue between the EU and the CEEC states with Europe Agreements with the EU. It also asked the Commission to produce a White Book indicating the tasks which the CEECs had to accomplish in order to bring their laws and institutions into line with the EU Single Market. The PHARE grant aid programme was also redirected towards assisting the CEECs to prepare for accession. And at the 1995 Dublin Council, the EU decided to instruct the Commission to prepare documents on the issues involved in deciding on eastward enlargement, which appeared in the autumn of 1997. A final aspect of these developments has been the so-called Stability Pact, launched by the Balladur Government in France to ensure that the CEECs sort out all their ethnic and inter-state problems through legally binding treaties, in order to ensure that such problems will not be an obstacle both to European stability and to enlargement.

All aspects of this train of events have been shot through with ambivalence and evasions. By far the biggest evasion lies in the fact that none of the steps taken so far has addressed the central problems of real preparation for enlargement: namely altering the existing *acquis* – in other words reforming the EU in order to make it capable of absorbing the CEECs. All such matters have been postponed until 1999 and instead the impression has been spread that the chief problems of enlargement lie within the CEECs and in their institutional structures and processes in particular.

This suggests an obvious tactical option on the part of the EU: that of delay and division. This option would consist of declaring that unfortunately the CEECs – or at least the bulk of them – are not quite ready for EU membership. The origin of the tactic would be the EU refusal to make the necessary commitments to incorporate the CEECs, or the bulk of them. But this origin would be concealed behind claims that the problems lay with the failures of various CEECs to live up to West European standards of democracy and markets. The real basis would be the clause in the Copenhagen Council decisions: 'The Union's capacity to absorb new members, while maintaining the momentum of European integration, is also an important consideration . . .' But the official basis would be that various CEECs were not quite democratic enough or not quite free market enough. If this is the case, the continent is in for a dispiriting and hypocritical exercise with potentially destabilising consequences.

It will be dispiriting because it could involve us in making invidious and unpleasant comparisons between the two halves of the continent: is the far right stronger in Romania than in Austria or France? Is the Turkish minority more secure in Bulgaria than in Germany? Do the Slovaks have a more secure set of constitutional safeguards than Britain with its unwritten constitution? Have tensions and conflicts involving Transylvania's Hungarian Protestants been handled with greater or lesser respect for the European Convention of Human Rights than conflicts in the UK concerning Irish Catholics? Do the states of the region come off better or worse in the field of public probity or corruption than Italy?

It is also hypocritical in a double sense: first, because such criteria will have next to nothing to do with the real criteria, government EU decisions about EU accession; and secondly, because the degree of democratic stability and economic viability of the CEEC states depends, in reality, as much on what the EU does as on what domestic actors in these countries do.

The real criterion for choosing the countries which will be in the 'fast' track for membership will be neither democratic stability nor economic strength, but the criterion of western geopolitical interests, above all the need to consolidate the incorporation of the states constituting the Eastern flanks of Germany and Austria.

The Double Division of Europe

The divisions accompanying the NATO expansion and those attending the EU's differentiations between applicants will reinforce each other in dangerous ways, mutually reinforcing each other and deepening both splits.

The NATO enlargement takes place before that of the EU. Indeed, contrary to the views of politicians in Poland or Hungary, these countries' entry into NATO will not speed up their entry into the EU, but may more probably actually enable the EU member states to delay it. At the same time, the tendency amongst states excluded from NATO can be to increase insecurities and rivalries, not only in the former Soviet Union but also in the Balkans, thus risking the diversion of budgetary resources to military spending and thus imposing further strains on their crisis-ridden economies. At the same time, the EU signal that some of the associated states can forget accession in the near future will exacerbate internal political strains within them, making them a greater investment risk and raising their costs of borrowing on international financial markets.

Those countries which are offered eventual membership of the EU will probably not join the Union for at least another seven years. And even for them, the prospect of gaining the full current *acquis* can be ruled out. The only question will be whether the systems of transfers will be reformed on the basis of some principle of equity across both new members and old, or whether the arrangements for the new eastern members will be obviously those for a second-class status of membership, as a recent Commission report suggested.

Conclusion: The Need for Shock Therapy

The intellectual key to finding ways to reverse the drift towards a new era of division and conflict in Europe lies in turning current problem definitions on their heads. The current problem-solving agendas in Europe all have one thing in common: all the problems, threats, instabilities and policy disasters are held to reside in the East. Work towards a solution can begin when we recognise that the main sources of the main problems in fact lie in the West. Amongst the latter, two are fundamental and interlinked: the first is an unsustainable model of capitalist growth; the second is an unviable – or, at least, destabilising – model of international political management.

The currently fashionable model for capitalist growth is that of 'globalisation' plus 'shareholder value' – in other words, grabbing market share abroad and putting the interests of rentiers in securities markets first. It is unsustainable because it is economically inefficient on a gigantic scale and it is a systematic breeder of systemic crises. It also ultimately threatens western leadership of the world economy. The fact that it also currently generates enormous fortunes for very small social groups both in the West and in the East only makes it more dangerous because more difficult to change.

Globalisation in the CEECs has been, and is continuing to destroy vast amounts of productive assets, through subordinating economic life to the logics of financial speculation. In 1996, 11 per cent of Bulgaria's GDP was sacrificed on the altar of the preferences of international financial speculation. These kinds of breakdowns are normal and systemic within the globalisation model: to explain them by reference to the activities of a finance minister in a Balkan country is to turn reality on its head.

At present this system is staggering from one local blow-out to another, avoiding a systemic collapse through frantic and ceaseless state intervention by the G7 states via the IMF. This chaotic financial context is linked to deep sources of stagnation in the West's industrial structures. The lack of profitable outlets for productive investment feeds the global speculative bubble. It also threatens fierce industrial wars between the main western states as the semi-monopolies of each state try to grab market shares from their rivals. To prevent such conflicts, the western states seek through globalisation to grab extra market shares for their main companies in the East and the South. They also try to open new regions of capital growth within their own economies via privatisations and attempts to turn welfare systems into zones of capital growth for the private financial markets.

Across all these activities the common theme is pauperising ever-larger groups of the world's population. The weakest regions bear the brunt of the misery.

In these western-centred processes lie the origins of the most serious problems of the CEECs: the groups of gangster capitalists, the corrupt bureaucrats, the social and inter-ethnic tensions, the malnutrition, disease and mounting death-rates in large parts of the region.

This economically and socially regressive growth model is interacting with a system of international governance in the West which is radically dysfunctional. It is also best understood by situating it within inter-capitalist tensions in the West. At the end of the Cold War, the United States faced the possibility that the main West European states could reorganise the political economy of western Eurasia in the interests of their own strategies for international capital accumulation. This could have been managed either in the framework of a pan-European collective security order, or through a co-operative arrangement between a West European WEU and a Moscow-centred Eastern security network, or through some combination of the two. NATO would have declined and withered. For the United States this would have marked a dangerous loss of political and economic influence.

The Clinton administration therefore embarked upon a campaign to ensure its continued 'leadership' over Western Europe's relations with the rest of western Eurasia, first through the Bosnian war and then through the enlargement of NATO into the Visegrad states. US concern for continued control over its West European 'allies' has been the basic rationale for NATO's enlargement. The consequences of this enlargement in the excluded zone and the possible roles of NATO in the East have been secondary details in this entire process.

The West European states were ready to accept this US campaign because their own inter-state system has been gridlocked: only Germany could give a lead but the other main states of the EU devote their energies to preventing German leadership. As a result the only forms of collective action on which the West European states can unite are those where they have a common interest in exporting problems abroad by engaging in collective mercantilism against weaker actors in the international political economy.

Gridlock on international political strategy within the EU forms the basis for the return of American leadership in Western Europe as a supposed *pouvoir neutre* above the petty, provincial squabbles over an essentially trivial agenda within the so-called Common Foreign and Security Policy of the EU and the WEU. The US concept of NATO enlargement met Germany's immediate need of securing Poland as a buffer on its eastern flank, while the French and British had no positive alternative to offer.

The results of these machiavellian power manoeuvres among the Western states is a policy towards the excluded European zone that can best be described as unprincipled ad hocery: the antithesis of a genuinely norm-based, principled approach to security issues. It is entirely unclear what principle, for example, the Western powers stand for in their efforts to re-organise the former Yugoslavia. They are evidently not in favour of ethnic self-determination for the micro-nations of the area. On the other hand, they are also not, it seems, in favour of respecting the territorial integrity of the existing states that have emerged from the Yugoslav collapse. NATO claims the right to launch aggression against a sovereign state – the new Yugoslav state – because it is hostile to the internally repressive policies of that state in Kosovo. But it simultaneously rejects self-determination for the Kosovar Albanians because that would undermine the 'principles' applied to Bosnia at Dayton and the 'principles' applied to Macedonia. At the same time, NATO's American leadership is determined to ensure that it has the right to do as it pleases, unconstrained by UN principles and resolutions. And there is a yawning gap between NATO's attempt to legitimate its power plays in terms of human rights (rather than the rights of states) and its instrument for supposedly enforcing 'human rights' – missile attacks and bombing raids.

There is an overarching strategic concept of sorts in the double enlargement. It is a strategy for Americanising the social structures of Europe within the NATO security perimeter while Centralamericanising the hinterland beyond the perimeter. First, the CEECs have become and will continue to be a significant middle-class market for western multinationals grabbing market share there at will, using the Single Market rules embodied in the Europe Agreements to legitimise their market domination. Second, the CEECs will offer a limitless supply of cheap labour for western multinationals to use for the labour-intensive parts of their production circuits. Thirdly, these attractions will be used by big capital in Western Europe to threaten to exit eastwards unless Western Europe Americanises its labour markets, turns the Welfare States into minimal safety nets and allows British or American-style social inequality, poverty, urban decay and prison populations. Western Europe will be distinguishable from the USA only by the virulence of its internal racist, neo-fascist and xenophobic movements.

And, increasingly, the Europe within the security perimeter will be unified by fear of the ugly arc of poverty and political turbulence stretching from the Kaliningrad triangle to the Balkan mountains. This will be the spontaneous result of the current international political economy regime for the excluded region of South-Eastern and Eastern Europe, and of the current NATO power project's capricious coercive diplomacy. It is simply utopian to imagine that the current trends in Russia, Ukraine and South Eastern Europe can continue much longer without grave and tragic consequences.

But this spontaneous drift will not easily be changed: the globalisation-cum-neo-liberal policy cycle is still on its upward curve in Europe and there is still a rich vein of resources for capital growth to be dug out of western welfare states, CEEC debt and the CEEC privatisations of state enterprises, especially the public utilities. And the political path towards an alternative is firmly blocked by the lack of federal democracy within the EU, the disarray on the European left and the great power interests of the United States in western Eurasia.

It will therefore take more than persuasion to change course in Europe. Therapies will not be applied until an exogenous shock brings home the truth that the West's interlocking structures of accumulation and governance are not acceptable. The best kind of such shock leading to therapy would be a social movement by the peoples of Europe to demand a New Deal. The worst would be a blow-out in the globalised financial system or a full-scale breakdown of order in the big republics of the former Soviet Union.

There is a nevertheless perfectly viable alternative *policy* strategy for the reintegration of Europe on a capitalist basis, but it is one that would require a break with the American-led globalisation–neo-liberal approach in economics and with the American power politics strategy for the European region. Thus the obstacles to an alternative lie not in policy ideas but in political trends.

The alternative strategy is one centred upon market growth within the

Eastern region: a strategy for rapid reindustrialisation in the East through very large infrastructure projects and through a serious pan-European campaign for the desperately needed revival of economic development in the CIS, particularly Russia and Ukraine. The main economic obstacle to such market growth in the East lies in severe payments constraints facing states in the region: heavy indebtedness and current account deficits. With the arrival of the euro, these problems could be overcome through a bold, co-ordinated strategy involving both the European Central Bank and an EU 'economic government'. The currencies in the East could he underwritten, substantial capital transfers for infrastructure investment in the East could be raised through a large public bond issue at EU level, governments in the East could be encouraged to re-impose controls on their capital accounts, they could be given new flexibility in their trade regimes and industrial policies and could be given far more generous access to the EU market. Within such a new strategic framework, Western Europe's economy could revive and incomes could be substantially raised in the East. With rising incomes in the East the new security barriers being erected along NATO's and the EU's borders could be overcome and the European Social Model could be preserved. Such a genuine reconstruction and development effort could be combined with a new, more genuine collective security regime being built across the continent, one that would have the broad authority to mediate and help maintain peace by gaining confidence on the part of both sides in conflicts. And any such new strategy would have to end the dangerous trend towards trying to exclude Russia and Ukraine from European affairs.

There is enormous development potential still in the Eastern region of Europe. Growth rates of 10 per cent per annum in many of these states are not unthinkable if a strong, effective framework for financial, monetary and trade relations was put in place. This strategy might involve a delay in the EU's Eastward enlargement, but it would meet the real goals of people in the CEECs when they seek to join the EU: a strategy for rapid sustained economic development in the East; and a genuine commitment on the part of Western Europe to make the societies of the region genuine equals with Western Europe.

But such a new strategy would require three preconditions that are currently lacking. First, a break with the social projects of globalisation and neo-liberalism. The fate of Oskar Lafontaine shows how far we still are from that. Secondly, it would require a serious international political leadership at the EU level, or at least at the Euroland level. This leadership can come only from Germany and France working together to transform the EU into a genuine political actor capable of acting strategically in the pan-European political economy. It would require a genuinely federal institutional development and the building of a real democratic identity within Europe –

without these, the responses of significant parts of the EU to this strategy would be to oppose it as being, allegedly, too German-centred.

But there is a third great problem with the strategic re-orientation which we have proposed: how to manage the hostility of the Anglo-American state and business elites in Washington and amongst 'Third Way' Labour and its business cronies? This is not necessarily an insuperable problem, but it is one that the social democrats of Western Europe are unlikely, given their past record, to be able to overcome. The line of least resistance is so much easier.

Thus the most likely variant may be back to the future: back to 1920s-style, grossly unequal states in Western Europe with narrow social bases alongside broken down regimes in the East; rising xenophobia and neo-fascist currents in the West, continuing stagnation and mounting social degradation. Only the forms of democratic deficit may be different. We had thought that interwar capitalist society was a thing of the past, a deviation overcome by postwar social progress. But it turns out that the postwar social gains were the deviation and the interwar state and society is again the norm. Postwar social progress was, it seems, a tactical, aberrant form of European capitalism made necessary by the challenge of Communism. We know now the second half of that sentence whose first half, so strongly believed in 1989, stated: 'Western-style welfare capitalism is better than Eastern Communism . . .' The second half went unnoticed ten years ago. It reads: '. . . but Western-style welfare capitalism only existed because of communism'. Europe seems to be drifting towards a divided, turbulent and ugly future.

Notes

1. Adrian Bridge, 'Nato chief tours states fighting to join alliance', *Independent*, 15 April 1996.

2. The December 1996 NATO ministerial meeting informed the Russian government that NATO does not plan to station nuclear weapons on Polish territory.

3. Russian Defence Minister Igor Rodionov has warned that NATO's enlargement might force Russia to target nuclear missiles on countries joining the Atlantic alliance. See the *Independent*, 30 November 1996. Belarus President Lukashenko warned that Belarus might still want to keep the nuclear weapons on its territory if Poland joined NATO. See the *Independent*, 14 November 1996.

4. Lebed, while still Yeltsin's security chief, warned of a change in Russia's attitude towards arms control treaties at his meeting with NATO leaders in Brussels in October. See the *Independent*, 8 October 1996.

5. Clinton's Detroit speech marks the definitive American commitment to rapid NATO expansion.

6. Susan L. Woodward, *Balkan Tragedy, Chaos and Dissolution after the Cold War* (The Brookings Institution, 1995), pp. 196–97.

7. He was assassinated just before he was due to unveil his plan in New York. The assassination was blamed on the Red Army Fraktion but it was an extremely sophisticated hi-tech

bombing that could have been done only by professionals. A senior official in the German Foreign Office was also assassinated at this time. See *Der Spiegel*, no. 49, 4 December 1989.

8. In 1985 Baker had been US Treasury Secretary under Ronald Reagan. The Baker Plan was announced by Baker at the Seoul IMF conference that year.

9. Robert Chote, 'Banking on a Catastrophe: Guidelines May Help Prevent Fresh Disasters in Emerging Markets', *Financial Times*, 21 October 1996.

10. See Woodward, *Balkan Tragedy*, for a pioneering account of this collapse.

11. Anthony Robinson, *Financial Times*, 11 December 1996.

12. Ibid.